Critical Essays on

PETER TAYLOR

CRITICAL ESSAYS
ON
AMERICAN LITERATURE

James Nagel, General Editor
University of Georgia, Athens

Critical Essays on
PETER TAYLOR

edited by

HUBERT H. MCALEXANDER

G. K. Hall & Co. / New York
Maxwell Macmillan Canada / Toronto
Maxwell Macmillan International / New York Oxford Singapore Sydney

G. K. Hall & Company   Maxwell Macmillan Canada, Inc.
Macmillan Publishing Company   1200 Eglinton Avenue East
866 Third Avenue   Suite 200
New York, New York 10022   Don Mills, Ontario M3C 3N1

Macmillan Publishing Company is part of the Maxwell Communication
Group of Companies.

Library of Congress Cataloging-in-Publication Data

Critical essays on Peter Taylor / edited by Hubert H. McAlexander.
       p.   cm.—(Critical essays on American literature)
    Includes bibliographical references and index.
    ISBN 0-8161-7322-2
    1. Taylor, Peter Hillsman, 1917– . —Criticism and interpretation.
I. McAlexander, Hubert Horton.   II. Series.
PS3539.A9633Z62   1993
813′.54—dc20   92-26983
                                                        CIP

The paper used in this publication meets the minimum requirements of
American National Standard for Information Sciences—Permanence of
Paper for Printed Library Materials. ANSI Z3948-1984.♾™

10 9 8 7 6 5 4 3 2 1 (hc)

Printed in the United States of America

For
Edward Stephenson McAlexander

Contents

◆

ESSAYS

General Editor's Note

◆

This series seeks to anthologize the most important criticism on a wide variety of topics and writers in American literature. Our readers will find in various volumes not only a generous selection of reprinted articles and reviews but original essays, bibliographies, manuscript sections, and other materials brought to public attention for the first time. This volume, *Critical Essays on Peter Taylor*, is the most comprehensive collection of essays ever published on this Pulitzer Prize winning author. It contains both a sizable gathering of early reviews and a broad selection of more modern scholarship as well. Among the authors of reprinted articles and reviews are William Peden, Joyce Carol Oates, Robert Penn Warren, Barbara Schuler, Jan Pinkerton, and Marilynne Robinson. In addition to a substantial introduction by Hubert McAlexander, Associate Professor of English at the University of Georgia, there are also four essays commissioned specifically for publication in this volume: Christopher Metress on *A Summons to Memphis*, Ron Balthazor's exploration of the story "In the Miro District," Simone Vauthier on "Venus, Cupid, Folly and Time," and a concluding appreciation of Taylor's artistic mastery by Madison Smartt Bell. We are confident that this book will make a permanent and significant contribution to the study of American literature, and we are delighted to have it as part of the *Critical Essays on American Literature* series.

JAMES NAGEL
University of Georgia

Publisher's Note

◆

Producing a volume that contains both newly commissioned and reprinted material presents the publisher with the challenge of balancing the desire to achieve stylistic consistency with the need to preserve the integrity of works first published elsewhere. In the Critical Essays series, essays commissioned especially for a particular volume are edited to be consistent with G. K. Hall's house style; reprinted essays appear in the style in which they were first published, with only typographical errors corrected. Consequently, shifts in style from one essay to another are the result of our efforts to be faithful to each text as it was originally published.

Introduction

◆

HUBERT H. MCALEXANDER

Throughout his half century as a published author, Peter Taylor has had the respect and admiration of fellow writers. Over this span he has been accorded the praise of three generations of his peers. Robert Penn Warren, in his introduction to Taylor's first volume of short stories in 1948, announced the work of "a very gifted young writer."[1] Twenty-three years later, Joyce Carol Oates acclaimed *The Collected Stories of Peter Taylor* as "one of the major books of our literature."[2] In 1986, a leading member of the emergent literary generation, Madison Smartt Bell, called Taylor "arguably the best American short story writer of all time."[3]

Honors too have come to Peter Taylor from an early period. When he was only twenty-five, "The Fancy Woman" was chosen for the *Best American Short Stories of 1942*. Over the years nine other Taylor stories have been selected for this prestigious annual, the last being "The Old Forest" in 1980. In 1950, Taylor had his first story chosen for the O. Henry Prize collection. Six subsequent stories have been so honored, and "Venus, Cupid, Folly and Time" won the O. Henry first prize in 1959. Despite such recognition, Taylor still felt compelled, when accepting the Gold Medal for the Short Story given by the American Academy and Institute of Arts and Letters in 1978, to respond to the question that had followed him for two decades— "what it is like to be 'really quite a good writer' and have so little reputation."[4] That circumstance did not begin to change until 1985 with the particularly warm critical response to *The Old Forest and Other Stories*. The growing outcry against Taylor's undeserved obscurity was no doubt one factor in his receiving the PEN/Faulkner award for the volume. Taylor's novel *A Summons to Memphis*, published the next year, appeared just at the moment when critical and popular attention to Taylor was building. The sales of the novel were much greater than those of any other Taylor work, and it received both the Ritz-Paris Hemingway Award and the Pulitzer Prize. As a result of the success of the novel, his three most recent collections of short fiction, as well as his earlier novel *A Woman of Means* (1950), are now also back in print. In 1989, Peter Taylor was included in the fourth edition of the *Norton Anthology of American Literature*. Other college anthologies of American literature have followed suit. Finally Taylor appears to have gained canonical status, as well as a larger reading public.

Taylor began his literary career at the age of twenty, when in 1937 he published his first two stories in *River*, a short-lived literary magazine produced in Oxford, Mississippi. These two pieces, which have never been collected, are apprentice efforts. But Taylor's next three stories, which appeared in *Southern Review* in 1940 and 1941, are the accomplished work of a new voice in American short fiction. Military service during World War II interrupted Taylor's writing, but by 1948 he had produced enough additional stories to make up his first collection, *A Long Fourth and Other Stories*.[5]

Taylor criticism could hardly have had a more auspicious beginning than the introduction to *A Long Fourth* written by Robert Penn Warren. Warren, who had won a Pulitzer Prize two years earlier for *All the King's Men*, attracted attention to the book because of his importance as a literary figure and also proved an astute and sympathetic critic. He remarked first Taylor's use of new literary subject matter: "the contemporary, urban, middle-class world of the upper South," and he identified Taylor's particular focus as "the disintegration of families" in a time of changing values. But he was quick to point out the writer's lack of nostalgia and his "skeptical, ironic cast of mind." Warren further noted Taylor's interest in "the smaller collisions and crises of life" and the quality of Taylor's style, "a natural style, one based on conversation and the family tale."[6] Warren's judgments and assessments have been assimilated and echoed by critics over the years. This essay has shaped a great body of the critical response to Taylor.

The reviews of *A Long Fourth* all praised this first volume of a young writer. The brief notice in the *New Yorker* called it "an excellent collection," and the *New Republic* reviewer judged the stories "unusually fine."[7] Coleman Rosenberger, writing in *New York Herald Tribune Books*, found it "a little island of excellence in the flood of books from the South," possessing the "qualities of permanence: a fine craftsmanship, integrity, and the imprint of a subtle and original intelligence."[8] Most critics saw Taylor as a new sort of writer of the South, both in subject matter and attitude. The reviewer of *Commonweal*, short story writer J. F. Powers, distinguished Taylor's subject as not "the people and parts we know already from Faulkner and Caldwell or even from Porter and Welty," and he went on to make sensitive comments on Taylor's method, his refusal "to exploit his material to the limit," because, Powers argued, Taylor "knows that life itself has a very weak story line."[9] The *New York Times* commentator also remarked upon Taylor's originality, his distance from the pattern of Southern literary grotesquerie, and praised the general quality of the stories. But he voiced a criticism that has recurred among some readers—that some stories are too ordinary, "almost quotidian."[10] This judgment is in sharp contrast to Marjorie Brace's assessment in the *Saturday Review*. In what is perhaps the most interesting of all the reviews, she described Taylor as writing "with limpid sobriety, of undramatic incidents." She argued that, while on the surface his material appeared to be not very complex, actually he was experimenting "both technically and psychologically, with very difficult approaches to extremely difficult definitions." She found his method "odd and daring," radical in the strangeness of his associative patterns.[11]

When Taylor's short novel *A Woman of Means* was published in 1950, it was not as enthusiastically received as *A Long Fourth*. The critic of the *Saturday Review* judged it "as slight in effect, in content, and in quality as it is slight in form." She found it lacking "the impact of Peter Taylor's fine stories."[12] The *New Yorker* reviewer called it "a rueful little first novel, faultlessly written," but registered disappointment with the work because Taylor had here "attempted too little rather than too much."[13] Even Coleman Rosenberger of the *Herald Tribune* qualified his praise. He argued that the slightness of the novel was deceptive, that it was a "work of very solid merit." But he added: "It is not, however, the fully realized novel for which a reader of Mr. Taylor's excellent short stories could wish. One suspects that it stands halfway between those short stories and a novel which he will write."[14] A majority of the reviewers found the work's major flaw to be the decline into madness of the title character. They considered it "too feebly foreshadowed," "a glaring weakness," "awkward and superimposed," "ambiguous."[15]

In the midst of such criticism, two reviews stand out as particularly positive and particularly sensitive to Taylor's method. Writing in the *New York Times Book Review*, Robert Penn Warren praised the novel for its "vividness of characterization" and its "sense of the depth and complication of event." He pointed out Taylor's skillful involvement of the reader: "He wants, it seems, to make the reader make his own interpretation, or at least to give the reader the illusion of that freedom and that responsibility."[16] Thomas Wilcox, in the *Sewanee Review*, went a step further than Warren, pursuing the issue of Taylor's irony. "None of these people knows why all this has happened," he wrote, "though none of them is so imperceptive that he cannot find an explanation plausible to him." Then he offered an insight that illuminates many works of the Taylor canon: "What may at first look like simple dramatic irony becomes something different when you begin to explore the tissue of paradoxes Mr. Taylor has contrived. When you try to construe the few events his novel describes you find that no single interpretation will account for everything you have learned and that finally you must credit all the explanations—some of them seemingly contradictory—the characters separately entertain."[17]

By 1950, with a volume of stories and a novel to his credit, Taylor had entered a second phase of his career. These books had begun to establish his reputation among fellow writers and among critics, and for the following two decades he continued to explore themes and techniques first evidenced in this early period. In 1953, Kenneth Clay Cathey published "Peter Taylor: An Evaluation" in *Western Review*—the first essay on Taylor's work in a literary journal. It appeared in a series on "New Writers" that included studies of Roethke, Shapiro, and Bellow. Thus Taylor had been placed alongside some of the most talented members of his generation. But Cathey's evaluation, while flattering in its attention, was patronizing in some of its judgments. Cathey began by calling Taylor "at once the most promising of our newer writers, and the most limited." Though in his conclusion he argued that Taylor had shown "an almost uninterrupted improvement in both technique and content," Cathey criticized the fiction throughout the essay both for narrowness of focus and for what he called a lack of "objectification," that is, a lack of dramatized conflict. This emphasis on the limited range of subject matter indeed forms one strain in Taylor criticism over the following decades, and critics have aligned themselves on different sides as regards the lack of drama. Despite his strictures, Cathey showed particular sensitivity in discussing Taylor's calmness and detachment and in identifying certain aspects of Taylor's development. He saw "A Long Fourth" as a key work. Here, Cathey argued, Taylor had begun the cultural examination— the probing of the situation of women and Negroes in Southern society— that led him to write most of his subsequent nine stories, all published in the *New Yorker*. In Cathey's view, "A Long Fourth also signaled the beginning of Taylor's more complicated structuring of stories.[18]

Taylor's next book, *The Widows of Thornton*, which appeared in 1954, contained a one-act play and eight short stories, all but the last of which, "The Dark Walk," had been discussed in the Cathey essay. The reviewers were far more laudatory than Cathey. Paul Engle of the *Chicago Tribune* praised the collection as another volume "by which Mr. Taylor enriches American fiction." "The stories are remarkable," he wrote, "in being able to reveal insights and human sentiments without sentimentality, in situations which could often be ruined by too much feeling."[19] The *Herald Tribune* critic, Dan Wickenden, found Taylor to be "a first-rate writer," "possibly the most interesting and accomplished new writer to come out of the South in the last ten years." After providing perceptive commentary on the collection, he ended his review with that admonition that has plagued so many American writers of short fiction. He hoped that Taylor could soon "settle down to the major novels he is surely equipped to write."[20] The *Saturday Review* commentator placed the volume in the context of contemporary Southern writing and praised Taylor for creating "a wistful, clinging, but utterly non-depraved image" of the South, as opposed to those of Capote and Tennessee Williams.[21] The basic themes of *The Widows of Thornton*, which were recognized by most of these reviewers, were most economically articulated by Richard Hayes of *Commonweal*. He acclaimed Taylor's achievement as "the portrait of a complex society held in the most fastidious dramatic suspension;

the past impinging upon and molding the present, the present rebelling against the tyranny of the past, the noisy warring of both in the abused heart." While commenting on the Southern cultural context of the fiction, he placed Taylor in a broader literary context. First merely implying parallels with Henry James by describing the stories as "histories of fine consciences," he ended his essay by insisting that Taylor transcended the regional culture that had produced him and of which he often wrote, and Hayes put him in the company of Chekhov.[22] In this brief review, Hayes became the first of many critics over the following decades to suggest comparisons with James and Chekhov in discussing Taylor's art. Frank H. Lyell took a different tack in the *New York Times Book Review*. He saw issues of family, rather than the effect of social change, as being the theme that made *The Widows of Thornton* an "unusually homogeneous" collection, and, as opposed to the many other commentators who had noted Taylor's detachment, he concluded that Taylor had a message: "If the sanctity of the home is preserved, all will be well with mankind."[23]

The emphasis on family was repeated in Andrew Lytle's review of Taylor's 1957 play *Tennessee Day in St. Louis*. The piece began with this oft-quoted opening sentence: "Mr. Taylor is the only American writer, and indeed to my knowledge the only writer in English, whose subject is the dislocation and slow destruction of the family as an institution." Both Lyell and Lytle seemed to be echoing Robert Penn Warren's remarks on the "disintegration of families" as the focus of Taylor's work, but they did not share Warren's sense of the author's irony, skepticism, and lack of nostalgia in treating the theme. In his review Lytle, who was one of the twelve contributors to the 1930 volume *I'll Take My Stand: The South and the Agrarian Tradition*, presented what was very much a hard-line Agrarian approach to *Tennessee Day in St. Louis*, establishing a cultural context for the work by drawing comparisons between North and South, tracing the causes of social change back to the "military defeat of the South," contrasting the situation of "the family on the land" with that in the city, and speaking of the function of the family in a Christian society as opposed to a modern material one. This essay, which introduced the Agrarian line of Taylor criticism and the view of Taylor as Agrarian, was the only significant review of Taylor's first full-length play.[24]

Peter Taylor did acknowledge a preoccupation with the family in the title of his next collection, *Happy Families Are All Alike*, which was published in 1959. But as opposed to *The Widows of Thornton*, Taylor's most unified collection in which most of the stories were meaningfully linked by the characters' ties to the town of Thornton and by the recurring theme of women displaced by cultural change, the ten stories of *Happy Families* were only tenuously connected. The *New Statesman* reviewer, in fact, remarked that the stories were so good individually that it was simply of little value to attempt to explain just how they related to the Tolstoy passage from which Taylor named the volume.[25] It is perhaps significant that Taylor never again provided a collection with a title that suggested thematic unity.

This title, however, gave few reviewers much pause, and the volume was warmly received by critics. Gene Baro, writing in the *New York Herald Tribune*, described Taylor as "one of our best short story writers," one "curiously enough . . . unlike most of his prominent contemporaries." Baro then endeavored to suggest the essence of Taylor's fiction: "One understands Mr. Taylor's characters and their individual situations through understanding the social context of their lives; one sees them through a typical circumstance that is itself the expression of social tension or change."[26] William Du Bois of the *New York Times* made a similar attempt, after pronouncing the volume "a literary event of first importance" and Taylor "a master of the short story form," though known to only "a small but devoted public." "Each of these stories," he remarked, "surveys an experience that is not only accurately reconstructed but also deeply understood. Each centers on a turning point, a moment of controlled crisis that is the hallmark of any effective work of fiction."[27] While Du Bois ended his review by comparing Taylor to Chekhov in his treatment of the effects of cultural change, William Peden, in the *Saturday Review*, made a comparison with James, finding in every story at least one character who becomes, in James's term, "finely aware." After placing Taylor in the James tradition, Peden then attempted a brief but definitive statement of Taylor's method and his concerns: "He examines his characters' lives and assesses their meaning in terms of the conflicts imposed by heredity and environment, by the conflicting values of past and present, by agrarian as opposed to urban values, or by the warfare between intellect and emotion."[28] Commenting in the *Christian Science Monitor*, Ruth Blackman too offered an interesting assessment of Taylor's method, suggesting that he loads "his narrative with detail, like detective stories in which clues and unimportant trivia are given equal mention, and it is up to the reader to pick up the clues." She found rereading rewarding because "so complex are the layers of meaning in Mr. Taylor's stories that what seemed like trivia on the first reading are apt to turn up as clues on the second."[29]

The decade of the sixties saw new stages in both Taylor criticism and the progress of Taylor's career. Literary historians now began to discuss and to classify him as they delineated the development of American fiction after the Second World War. Taylor's work also received the first significant extended analysis when two important literary journals, *Sewanee Review* and *Critique*, devoted parts of issues to him. One also notes in the sixties a change in Taylor's own publishing strategy. The volume that he published in the middle of the decade was his first to gather fiction from previous collections and mix it with his most recent stories. This bringing together of representative work from different parts of his career was an obvious prelude to Taylor's publishing his *Collected Stories* at the end of the decade, when he was only fifty-two.

The first discussion of Taylor in a literary history came in Walter Sullivan's essay "Continuing Renascence: Southern Fiction in the Fifties," which appeared in Louis Rubin's and Robert Jacobs's 1961 volume *South: Modern Southern Literature in Its Cultural Setting*. Sullivan placed Taylor among those writers of the younger generation who "departed most purposefully from the old tradition," and he viewed Taylor along with William Styron as being, "unlike many of their predecessors, . . . more or less at home in the modern world." His final judgment was high praise indeed; he acclaimed Taylor as "the only American of his generation whose work can stand comparison with that of Frank O'Connor and Chekhov and Joyce."[30] In another work of literary history, the 1963 book *Fiction of the Forties*, Chester E. Eisinger saw Taylor as exhibiting the techniques of "the new fiction," but reflecting the conservative bias of older Southern writers like Caroline Gordon and Andrew Lytle.[31] Since two other studies written during this period also considered Taylor fundamentally as a Southern writer, [32] William Peden's approach came as a refreshing change. In his critical survey of 1964, *The American Short Story*, he placed Taylor among a group including John Cheever, Hortense Calisher, John O'Hara, and John Updike, who had "created a contemporary fiction of manners characterized by skill, urbanity, and insight." This group he designated "chroniclers of the non-exceptional."[33]

In the midst of these studies, the *Sewanee Review* recognized Taylor's twenty-fifth year as a published writer by devoting much of the Autumn 1962 number to him. His latest story, "At the Drugstore," led the issue, followed by three critical essays. Considering the fact that this attention appeared to constitute a sort of celebration of Taylor's career, the first two of these essays sounded strangely discordant notes. The title of the Morgan Blum piece, "Peter Taylor: Self Limitation in Fiction," reflected the influence of the Kenneth Clay Cathey view of Taylor articulated in 1953. Although in opening remarks Blum contended that Taylor was one of America's finest writers, Blum's double emphases upon Taylor's "talent" and "its limitations" counteracted each other, and one was left finally with a sense of a writer who had simply compensated wonderfully for all the things he was incapable of achieving. Using a similar strategy in his essay on Taylor's two plays, Brainard Cheney also tended to emphasize failure; in this case, though he found much to praise, he concluded that the plays were "drama best suited for fiction." In contrast to these essays was Ashley Brown's "The Early Fiction of Peter Taylor," an appreciative commentary on *A Long Fourth and Other Stories* and *A Woman of Means*. Brown saw the early stories as exhibiting "a wide range of style and attack," drew suggestive parallels between Taylor's first collection and Joyce's *Dubliners*, and offered insightful analyses of the most significant of the stories and of *A Woman of Means*.[34]

"At the Drugstore," the story opening that issue of the *Sewanee Review* and belying both technically and thematically the view of artistic limitation expressed in the Morgan Blum essay following, was one of the six new stories collected in Taylor's next volume, *Miss Leonora When Last Seen and Other Stories*, published in 1964. But for the first time, Taylor also included work from earlier collections—four stories from *A Long Fourth* and five stories and a play from *The Widows of Thornton*. Reviewers recognized Taylor as "a unique literary personality" and "an important American artist,"[35] and several noted the high quality of his art from the very beginning of his career—calling attention to the "solidity of the work from the earlier volumes" and commending his consistent mastery of form over twenty-five years.[36] In the *New York Times Book Review*, Gene Baro provided an overview of Taylor's fiction, arguing that Taylor was first a writer of place, "for whom place is made up of an infinite number of material and spiritual details," and that his primary theme was time, "how time changes things, changes oneself, the tug of the past, the imprisonment the past is, the duty it imposes." But to put his remarks in perspective, he noted that Taylor's fiction had the "quality of transcending the literal, the limited or the everyday circumstance, even in the act of establishing it."[37] T. A. Hanzo of the *Sewanee Review* addressed the same general point, contending that "too much can be made of Taylor's Southern roots," that in fact other elements were of more interest than the Southern "coloration" of the fiction. He found a frequent ground of these stories to be "a quotidian reality whose chief quality is a kind of emotional deception."[38] Hanzo's commentary, which centered on a discerning analysis of "At the Drugstore," reflected the general tendency of a number of the reviews. More critics of this collection than of any other discovered deeply pessimistic strains in the fiction. Glendy Culligan, writing in *Bookweek*, perceived Taylor's most recurrent theme to be "the failures of intimacy."[39] The *New York Review of Books* critic, John Thompson, provided an elaboration of this idea in what was the darkest reading of Taylor ever presented. In charting the emotional geography of Taylor's fiction, he began with the family: "This warm circle is a desperate one, surrounded by a cold vacuum and surrounding a cold vacuum. There is no outside alternative to this family circle but emptiness, and within it, at its center, is emptiness. The circle itself survives by exclusion, exclusion of two things, thought and feeling."[40]

Three years after the publication of *Miss Leonora When Last Seen and Other Stories*, Taylor was once again the subject of attention by an important literary journal. The third 1967 number of *Critique* focused upon Taylor and Saul Bellow. Leading off the issue was an essay by Barbara Schuler, who in 1964 at Notre Dame had written the first dissertation devoted to Taylor. Seeing the house as "the central, the prismatic symbol" in his work, Schuler offered solid discussions of several stories, most notably "Venus, Cupid, Folly and Time," "Skyline," and "A Walled Garden." Following this was James Penny Smith's study "Narration and Theme in Taylor's *A Woman of Means*," which argued against the charge that the dual focus upon Quint and his stepmother constituted a weakness in the novel. Concluding the Taylor section of the issue was Smith's excellent checklist of Taylor's published work and the criticism responding to it.[41]

In 1969, *The Collected Stories of Peter Taylor* was published, a gathering of sixteen stories drawn from the four earlier collections, along with five new works. The distinction of the collection elicited reviews of very high quality. In the *Chicago Tribune Book World*, R. V. Cassill cited the book as one further piece of evidence that a "Golden Age for the American short story began soon after the Second World War." He judged Taylor's concerns to be "very large," and he argued that in the best of the stories "and certainly in the fascinating configuration of the whole collection, we see how the world spins out from Tennessee and closes its vast circles there"—how the regional forms the universal.[42] That view of Taylor's art was also expressed by Joyce Carol Oates, who called the volume "one of the major books of our literature." She focused on the sense of dream and nightmare beneath the "everyday bustle" of the middle-class world of the fiction, and she carried the motif over into her discussion of form. "Taylor's stories are like dreams," she wrote; "events are brought sharply into focus, magically and dramatically limited, a sequence of sensations and speech passes as if in no important relationship to the rest of the world. And then a mysterious 'point' is reached, a point of surrender or relaxation, and the story is complete, completed."[43] Stephen Goodwin's commentary in *Shenandoah*, one of the most insightful short pieces of criticism ever written on Taylor's fiction, was the first to make the point that the best of Taylor's stories possessed the amplitude of novels—that, in Goodwin's words, "the triumph of his storytelling is that he has managed to enclose so much experience in the confines of the form he has chosen." And Goodwin offered penetrating commentary on Taylor's attempt to render life truly in his fiction. "Taylor never distorts, never diminishes life to secure a resolution for art," he wrote. "The convenient and indulgent fiction of most storytelling—that emotions may be permanent, that revelations may be lasting—is never invoked."[44]

The Oates and Goodwin tributes in literary journals were matched by those of critics in the most widely read newspapers and magazines. Writing in the *New York Times Book Review*, Richard Howard acclaimed Taylor as "one of the very best writers America has ever produced"; Geoffrey Wolff of *Newsweek* called him "an artist of the very first rank" and suggested that Taylor had no living peer among short story writers. Both these reviewers offered thought-provoking commentary on the collection. "The most characteristic parabola of a Taylor story" Wolff saw perceptively as a progress "from contentment through unarticulated worry and confusion, to crisis, to compromise." And Howard noted a significant shift over the course of the career: while the early work had concerned "outsiders, exiles and solitaries," in the later period "not outcasts but intimates take the center of the stage."[45] Naming Taylor "a writer's writer" and placing him "near the top" in a ranking of American writers, John Thompson of *Harper's* offered a refinement of the reading of Taylor's fiction that he had given in his review of *Miss Leonora When Last Seen and Other Stories*. Fixing the background of Taylor's fiction as the "long serenity of our middle class," Thompson pointed out the author's understanding "that all culture, all social contrivance, country club or Army, family or corporation, knife and fork and automobile, all those are only the fragile and necessary contrivances that stand between us and the essential horror of our animal condition."[46]

In the midst of such encomium and insight, however, were heard other voices. It is surprising that there were not more, considering the conventionality of Taylor's fictional world and the social unrest of the time. "The world has passed Taylor by," noted Roger Sale in the *Hudson Review*. For him, Taylor never escaped "seeming precious."[47] The maverick Christopher Ricks, writing in the *New York Review of Books*, described the stories as "slices of life," but noted that "sliced life often has the vapidity of sliced bread" and found that "the anxieties of the liberal conscience steal the show."[48] The most outrageous review, however, found nothing liberal about the collection. Writing in the *New Republic*, Barbara Raskin judged the stories "respectable, careful, craftsmanlike, but ultimately mind-deadening." She then offered this bizarre view: "They are a technical combination of Jamesian precision and symmetry, plus Faulknerian mood and atmosphere. The characters are reminiscent of Williams or Capote." Much of the rest of the essay she devoted to a discussion of Taylor's patronizing portrayal of blacks. A month later the *New Republic* printed a letter from Jonathan Yardley refuting Raskin. Attacking first her "fundamentally untenable premise that all Southern fiction is alike" and her "racing Dixiephobia," Yardley went on to point out just how she had failed to understand the meaning or the value of Taylor's art.[49]

The most significant response to the Raskin piece was Jan Pinkerton's essay-review "The Non-Regionalism of Peter Taylor," which appeared in the Winter 1970 number of the *Georgia Review*. A recurrently debated issue throughout the criticism, Taylor's regionalism here provided the focus for a particularly measured and articulate study of theme and tone, with stimulating readings of several important works. Finally Pinkerton argued that Taylor was heretical: "He is a Southern writer who distrusts the past, a conservative writer who believes in change; those who see him as a stereotyped regionalist are themselves blinded by their cliched responses to setting and style."[50] Another review of *The Collected Stories* marked the appearance of one of the substantial figures in Taylor criticism. The critic for *Commonweal* was Albert J. Griffith, who later in 1970 published the first book-length study of Taylor's work, a volume in the Twayne series. A solid, balanced effort, Griffith's book surveyed Taylor's achievement and provided a helpful introduction, especially for college readers, to the Taylor canon.[51]

In his *Harper's* review, John Thompson predicted of Taylor: "Sooner or later one of his works will hit the best-seller list and he will become as generally celebrated as he is now professionally celebrated."[52] *The Collected Stories* did not enjoy that kind of success, nor bring that sort of recognition. Taylor had unquestionably solidified his position as a writer's writer, but he remained generally unknown. The volume, however, was a watershed in Taylor's career. Even before it had reached the public, Taylor was working in new forms. "I feel that I've done what I want to do as a short story writer," he revealed in a 1973 interview, [53] after having abandoned short fiction for three years and devoted himself instead to the writing of a series of ghost plays and a novel. The novel he finally destroyed, but the plays, which appeared in various literary magazines, he collected in *Presences: Seven Dramatic Pieces*, published in 1973.

The volume, brought out by Houghton Mifflin, was largely ignored by critics. Most of the reviews were simply brief notices, and these were mixed. B. H. Fussell of the *Hudson Review*, for instance, felt that the plays showed "too much artifice," that they were "too schematic and too neatly paradoxical." The *Antioch Review* critic, though concluding rather positively, objected to "Taylor's awkward dependence on contemporaneous themes (drugs, abortion, homosexuality), and the absence of what gives his best stories their density—the restrained suggestion of turbulent drama, painstakingly rendered through social detail."[54] There were only two substantial reviews. Richard Howard's piece in *Shenandoah* was the more qualified in its praise. While commending Taylor for experiment and risk-taking, and pointing to the interesting influence of James's "The Jolly Corner" and "Owen Wingrave," Howard judged the collection "by no means the masterpiece of Taylor's long and still-looming career." Paul Theroux, writing more enthusiastically in the *Washington Post Book World*, praised the plays for "giving voice and shape to what is most private in our mental lives" and insisted that they would establish Taylor as "a playwright of the first rank."[55]

Except for reviews, the early and middle years of the seventies produced no significant Taylor criticism. When Taylor was treated in various literary surveys, the same by now familiar notes were sounded. Alfred Kazin, for instance, in *Bright Book of Life: American Novelists and Storytellers from Hemingway to Mailer*, published in 1973, described Taylor as exploring "the subtle moral disarmaments and dislocations within a seemingly immobile middle class."[56] William Peden's treatment of Taylor's work in *The American Short Story: Continuity and Change, 1940–1975*, was an extension of his remarks in the 1964 edition of this survey, incorporating the insights from his essay-review of *The Collected Stories* published in the *Hollins Critic*. Peden cited Taylor's fiction, as he had before, as a triumph of "moderation, intelligence, and sound craftsmanship."[57] One interesting critical view to emerge during the period came from Walter Sullivan, who was involved at the time in tolling the death knell of Southern literature. In a chapter entitled "The Decline of Southern Fiction" in the 1972 volume *Death by Melancholy: Essays on Modern Southern Fiction*, Sullivan remarked that Taylor "no longer shows us much that is new." Four years later, he elaborated a bit on this rather casually offered judgment in his introduction to *A Requiem for the Renascence*: "It once seemed that Peter Taylor would be the only American of his genera- tion whose work could stand comparison with that of Frank O'Connor and Chekhov and Joyce. But Taylor has remained essentially a writer of short stories, and since the publication of 'Miss Leonora When Last Seen' in 1960 his work has sagged markedly."[58]

The years 1977 and 1978 stand out in bold relief, after the critical aridity of the earlier years of the decade. In this two-year span, Taylor was subject of an entire issue of *Shenandoah*, he brought out a new collection of stories, and two important critical essays on his work appeared. The year's first issue of *Shenandoah*, which was headed "A Garland for Peter Taylor on His Sixtieth Birthday," was a celebration of the life and career. Of greatest value biographically, it was filled with sketches, reminiscences and tributes by people from all phases of Taylor's life: mentors, friends and fellow artists, and students—including Allen Tate, Robert Penn Warren, Robert Lowell, Mary Jarrell, Stephen Goodwin, John Casey, and Robert Wilson. What emerged was a vivid sense of a personality and a sensibility. The critical pieces were brief and some of them slight. Herschel Gower's essay, "The Nashville Stories," treated very much the surface of a part of Taylor's fictional world. Andrew Lytle's rambling reminiscence ended with an interesting reading of "The Captain's Son." Ashley Brown's short essay offered some sensitive remarks on Taylor's 1968 play *A Stand in the Mountains*, his ghost plays, and the verse narratives that Taylor had been recently publishing. The most valuable of the critical essays was Albert J. Griffith's article on *Presences*, which provided the most extended commentary published on that often- ignored volume. The "garland" was closed with a typically idiosyncratic, if complimentary, J. F. Powers review of *In the Miro District and Other Stories*, Taylor's new collection.[59]

In the Miro District was Taylor's first book since 1959 to be composed exclusively of previously uncollected stories, and four of the eight offerings were the new verse narratives that Taylor had recently been experimenting with. Writing in the *New Leader*, Charles Deemer praised Taylor's achieve- ment in both the prose tales and the stories in verse, describing the pleasure of watching "a master craftsman at work." He saw the critical response to the volume, however, as a striking example of divergences in personal taste, citing the reviews in the *New York Times Book Review* and the *Washington Post Book World* as cases in point.[60] Anatole Broyard of the *Times* judged Taylor as, at his best, "a conventional Southern realist" and complained that the most serious effort in the volume, the title story, moved "like a heavily- loaded cotton wagon." Jonathan Yardley of the *Post* began his review with the statement that Taylor was "at the very least a principal contender for the peculiar distinction of being the most thoroughly undiscovered major writer in American literature." Blaming this circumstance primarily on Taylor's choice of the short story form, Yardley defended the genre and pointed to Taylor's particular genius. "No one in our literature has mastered the myriad difficulties of the short story as completely as Taylor has," Yardley wrote, "and this mastery is greatness of a very real kind."[61]

Few of the American reviewers sided with Broyard, and two in particular, Linda Kuehl in the *Saturday Review* and Anne Tyler in the *National Observer*, echoed Yardley in praising Taylor as the master of his form.[62] Critics did disagree on the success of the verse narratives.[63] There was also a range of response among the English reviewers. Harold Beaver of the *Times Literary Supplement*, like Yardley, called attention to Taylor's undeserved obscurity, while the critic for the *New Review*, Edna Longley, argued that Taylor was "not quite the Chekhov of the South that some admirers might wish." She attacked the stories for their dependence on "a simple conflict, dualism or paradox" or upon "predictable irony"; and she found that Taylor's style flattened his narrators into a "rather unvarying and uninteresting persona."[64]

Standing out from all of the other commentary, both English or American, was Stephen Goodwin's piece in the *New Republic*, the most powerful and engaging review and the one most sensitive to Taylor's accomplishment. Goodwin saw the eight stories as "varied and innovative, even rebellious," and the volume as representing a new stage in Taylor's career in subject matter as well as technique: "The menacing forces—of sex, violence, disgrace—which waited just outside the pale of propriety in his earlier stories have here frankly encroached." The effect upon Taylor, he contended, had been liberating. In the two longest stories, which he judged "daring, elating works," he maintained that "we see a master surpass himself."[65]

Later in the year appeared Jan Pinkerton's essay "The Vagaries of Taste and Peter Taylor's 'A Spinster's Tale,' " a rather awkward attempt, and a self-consciously academic one, to fit this early story into various contexts deemed intellectually fashionable.[66] The next year, however, saw two significant critical essays, fresh readings of Taylor inspired by the new collection. In "A View of Peter Taylor's Stories," Jane Barnes Casey maintained that much of Taylor's fiction was a working out of "the great modern problem of how to incorporate the most vital, but also the most anarchic urges into civilized life." She was the first critic to note the shift in Taylor's fictional interest from women to men, and she argued for the pivotal importance of "At the Drugstore," in which Taylor had confronted and explored chaotic, bestial male impulses. She saw the new collection, and most particularly the title story, "In the Miro District," as constituting an "affirmation of masculinity" and representing the furthest point in Taylor's grappling with the basic issue underlying the fiction. "Where Mr. Taylor once seemed to fear chaos," she found, "he now seems to trust the order inherent in experience: an order that does not depend on social restraint for its existence."[67] Alan Williamson's essay "Identity and the Wider Eros: A Reading of Peter Taylor's Stories," while acknowledging the interest of the Casey analysis and other more conventional readings of Taylor's work, offered a different view "intended to supplement not supplant" those perspectives. Seeing Taylor's "subject par excellence" as the "tenuously erotic bonds and imaginative identifications between people," Williamson explored Taylor's varying treatments of the theme and found his most memorable stories to be those "in which some person, or, more commonly, some feeling or human potentiality, is excluded or killed in the dangers ensuing from the wider extensions of love."[68] Though both Casey and Williamson might be charged with misreading some stories, still these pieces possessed an intellectual weight and seriousness lacking in many of the earlier critical essays.

After this burst of critical attention in 1977 and 1978, Taylor received only sporadic notice during the following seven-year span, from 1978 to 1985. Only seven entries from this period are of much import, the first three being English. In 1979, the British writer Paul Binding published *Separate Country: A Literary Journey through the American South*, in which he both drew upon an interview with Taylor and offered often-perceptive remarks upon the fiction. The next item was Walter Allen's *The Short Story in English*, published in 1981. Although Allen concentrated on one type of Taylor story, that in which people are unable to come to terms with the present, he made a fascinating connection between Taylor's stories and the kind of poems approved by his New Critical mentors. The stories succeed, he argued, "in the way such poems succeed, 'in the balance or reconcilement of opposite or discordant qualities: of sameness, with difference; or the general, with the concrete; . . . a more than usual state of emotion, with more than usual order.' " Taylor's art, he concluded, "is an art of paradox." The next year, *The Collected Stories*, published in Britain twelve years after its appearance in the United States, was the subject of a lengthy review in the *Times Literary Supplement*. The critic Zachary Leader placed Taylor intelligently in historical, cultural, and literary contexts, offered judicious readings of a number of stories, and ended by assigning Taylor to "the first rank of living American writers."[69]

The most significant American contribution of the period was the excellent bibliography of Taylor criticism presented in the volume by Victor A. Kramer, Patricia A. Bailey, Carol G. Dana, and Carl H. Griffin entitled *Andrew Lytle, Walker Percy, and Peter Taylor: A Reference Guide*, published by G. K. Hall in 1983. Intelligent critical overviews also appeared, as well as Marilyn Malina's short 1983 essay on "Venus, Cupid, Folly and Time," which sought to explicate the story through parallels with the art works displayed by the Dorsets.[70]

With the publication of *The Old Forest and Other Stories* in 1985, a dramatic turn began in the literary fortunes of Peter Taylor. The signs of change had been becoming slowly apparent. Farrar, Straus and Giroux had issued a paperback edition of *The Collected Stories* in 1979, which was kept in circulation by small printings in 1980 and 1983. Carroll and Graf had brought out *In the Miro District* in paperback in July of 1983. So for the first time in Taylor's publishing history, previous collections were still in print at the time that a new volume was published. Other evidences of a Taylor "revival" were the reissuing of *A Woman of Means* in a deluxe edition by Frederic C. Beil in August of 1984 and the November premiere of a much lauded film of Taylor's 1979 long story "The Old Forest," produced and directed by Steven J. Ross of Memphis State University.

The collection *The Old Forest* contained only two new works, "The Gift of the Prodigal" and the title piece. Gathered with them were a short play and eleven stories (some among Taylor's most powerful) that had not been included in *The Collected Stories*. Like a number of other Taylor collections, then, this 1985 volume offered a survey of the career. But this collection was published at a particularly receptive time. The *Saturday Review* critic reflected the change in the literary climate when he described Taylor's mastery of "the once neglected and now again fashionable short story." Taylor, then, benefited from a new interest in his chosen form generated by minimalists like Raymond Carver and Ann Beattie—even though, as this critic was quick to point out, Taylor was virtually a counter figure to "the new hard-bitten breed of storyteller."[71]

An important note was struck by Anne Tyler in her review in *USA TODAY*, when she counted herself among those younger writers "who have practically memorized all [Taylor] has produced." She acclaimed him "the undisputed master of the short story form."[72] "Like Poe's purloined letter," Walter Clemons wrote in *Newsweek*, "Peter Taylor is hidden in plain sight." Then, restraining himself from scolding the reading public for Taylor's lack of recognition, Clemons simply offered an appreciation of Taylor's career, including some discussion of stories not even included in *The Old Forest* collection.[73] The fullest of the reviews and the most significant in the history of Taylor criticism was the one written by Jonathan Yardley in the *Washington Post Book World*. "By comparison with *The Old Forest*," Yardley commented, "almost everything else published by American writers in recent years seems small, cramped, brittle, inconsequential; among American writers now living, only Eudora Welty has accomplished a body of fiction so rich, durable and accessible as Taylor's." In the course of the review, Yardley provided an overview of the Taylor canon, detailing the central themes and arguing that the late, long stories represented the furthest development of the career. "In the literature of his own country," he concluded, "Taylor can be compared to no one except himself; he is, as every word in this book testifies, an American master."[74]

Robert Towers of the *New York Times Book Review* agreed with Yardley on Taylor's development, finding that the long title story revealed an artist "at the very apex of his powers." And he pointed to Taylor's divergence in these stories from both contemporary practice and received notions regarding the short story form. "His narrative method is to hover over the action,"

Towers remarked, "to digress from it, to explore byways and relationships, to speculate on alternative possibilities—in short, to defy the conventions of brevity and concentration that we usually associate with the genre." In the midst of his praise, Towers did offer one qualification, remarking that Taylor's occasional failure "to endow his situations with adequate energy and tension can result in the tedious analysis of the humdrum."[75]

So very few negative comments of even the mildest sort found their way into the reviews, however, that Adam Mars-Jones's response in the *Times Literary Supplement* represented a dramatic divergence. He began with the charge of "a tendency in Taylor's work to soften the conflicts in the material in a way that restricts his achievement as a literary artist." But as the review progressed, it became apparent that Mars-Jones's dissatisfaction was political and social, rather than artistic. Taylor's loyalty, he insisted, was "to the status quo"; and he concluded with a long quote from "Bad Dreams," which he cited as an example of "Taylor's authorial persona at its least sympathetic, arch, trivially patrician, pretending to a warmth and authority that are outside his range."[76]

At the end of a glowing review of *The Old Forest* in *Time*, Paul Gray repeated the old speculation that a successful novel at some point along the years would probably have brought attention to Taylor's short fiction.[77] Remarkably enough, that novel finally appeared the following year. But even before *A Summons to Memphis* was in press, the growing interest in Taylor generated by *The Old Forest* was having dramatic effects. In February of 1986, Penguin released its paperback edition of *The Collected Stories*. In April, Frederic C. Beil brought out another fine Taylor edition, this time of the 1968 play *A Stand in the Mountains*, and Avon released a paperback run of 25,000 copies of *A Woman of Means*. The size of the Penguin and Avon printings was unprecedented in the publishing history of Taylor books. A month later, Taylor was presented the PEN/Faulkner Award for *The Old Forest*.

This was the propitious atmosphere in which *A Summons to Memphis* was published in October of 1986. "A wise book," the *Publishers Weekly* critic called it, "and despite its deliberate understatement, a profoundly affecting one."[78] The enthusiasm of this response was matched by most of the other reviewers, including those in *Time, Newsweek, USA TODAY,* and the *New York Times*.[79] In the *Washington Post Book World*, Jonathan Yardley, who noted that with the publication of *The Old Forest* the previous year the author had "suddenly found a readership," acclaimed the new book as "quintessential Taylor." He judged it "not merely a novel of immense intelligence, psychological acuity and emotional power, but a work that manages to summarize and embody its author's entire career."[80] In one of the most penetrating analyses of the novel, Ann Hulbert of the *New Republic* remarked Taylor's interest in "distortions of perspective" and cautioned that this novel "demands—and rewards—vigilance." Calling Phillip Carver perhaps the least reliable of Taylor's narrators and "digressive to the extreme," Hulbert argued that as Phillip continues to circle round his tale, increasingly we see "an implicit, and considerably darker, version" beneath.[81]

Robert Towers, writing in the *New York Review of Books*, had less tolerance for Taylor's method in the novel, finding that his "way of circling a subject repeatedly before revealing its fictional core—a technique that contributes much to the distinctiveness of the stories—leads in the novel to prolixity and repetition." He wondered, initially, just how we are to take Phillip, before deciding that the character was, in any case, "an inadequately conceived medium to convey potentially arresting experience." Despite his criticism, Towers concluded that the novel possessed "passages of considerable power, humor, and pathos."[82]

Towers's reservations about *A Summons to Memphis* were mild in comparison with John Updike's, registered in the pages of the *New Yorker*: "After a lifetime of tracing teacup tempests among genteel Tennesseans, Mr. Taylor retains an unslaked appetite for the local nuance," Updike wrote. After damning the preciously provincial nature of Taylor's inquiry in the novel, he suggested the book's Prufrockian cast in his comment that Taylor stirred the familiar Southern waters "with a Jamesian sort of spoon."[83] Interestingly enough, the commentary closest in spirit to Updike's came in Walter Sullivan's essay "The Last Agrarian: Peter Taylor Early and Late," published in the *Sewanee Review*.[84] Whereas Updike took occasional shots at things like the narrator's "leisurely, laggard prose," and the "skimped, even snubbed plot," Sullivan was even harsher. "*A Summons to Memphis*," he maintained, "gives the impression of being at once old and unfinished, as if it were written in the early seventies—when the main action takes place—and resurrected now without revision." Both critics judged *A Woman of Means* the better novel of the two—Updike because it so effectively plunged the reader "into the frightening dark of boyhood," and Sullivan because it presented in its "fullest fruition" Taylor's particular vision of the clash between agrarian and technological values. Underlying their unhappiness with *A Summons to Memphis* was clearly discontent with what they saw as the world of the novel. For Updike, Taylor's vision was such a diminished, secular one, his world "drained of the blood of the sacred." For Sullivan, in *A Summons to Memphis* "the last survivors of the old dispensation are dead or too old to continue the struggle and southern custom endures only in such private confrontations as [these]."

These two essays represent an extreme in their focusing upon the social world of the novel and its moral and religious underpinnings rather than upon the issues of identity and family, of psychological and emotional truth, and of meaning. These issues were the concern of the novelist Marilynne Robinson writing in the *New York Times Book Review*. Arguing for Taylor's "perfect indifference" to the "blandishments" of the Southern agrarian past, she judged him sui generis, and she saw dimensions and implications in the novel clearly unsuspected by its detractors. "*A Summons to Memphis* is not so much a tale of human weakness as of the power of larger patterns, human also, that engulf individual character, a current subsumed in a tide," she wrote. "The moral earnestness of contemporary thought, the eagerness to praise and condemn, almost forbids the utterance of an important fact, which is that most of the time we really do not know just what we are doing or why, or what appearance our actions would have if we could see them from a little distance."[85] The critic for the *Southern Review*, David M. Robinson, also stressed the complexity of the novel, contending that Taylor's "greatest accomplishment" was to "allow us both compassion and judgment." "Taylor deftly balances the novel between a depiction of Phillip's gradual and positive coming to terms with the cause of the 'ruin' of his life and the exposure of the narrator as a weak and passionless phantom, forever chained to a past not of his own creating," Robinson maintained. "On the one hand, the novel is a positive portrayal of the cultivation of an understanding through memory, but on the other, it is an almost merciless exposure of a life of cowardly failure."[86]

By the time the English reviews appeared in the spring of 1987, *A Summons to Memphis* was considered "the success of the season in America."[87] The best of those reviews, that by the novelist Anita Brookner in a May issue of *Spectator*, brought to the book a valuable perspective. Judging the novel a "curiosity," Brookner commented: "On the one hand its oversize subject-matter takes it out of the normal run of contemporary novels, and has one reaching for adjectives like heroic, or, on the other hand, grotesque." "A remarkable achievement," she concluded.[88] A month earlier that judgment had been corroborated in both Europe and America. *A Summons to Memphis* had won both the Ritz-Paris Hemingway Award and the Pulitzer Prize.

In the four years following these awards, four books devoted to Taylor have appeared. In the fall of 1987, Hubert H. McAlexander's collection *Conversations with Peter Taylor* was published as part of the distinguished series of the University Press of Mississippi. The book gathered fourteen interviews given between 1960 and 1987. Two of them were previously unpublished, McAlexander's and that by Barbara Thompson, which appeared almost simultaneously, though in somewhat different form, in the *Paris Review*. The volume, which brought together valuable and revealing material, has been judged "indispensable."[89] Another contribution of great importance was Stuart Wright's definitive *Peter Taylor: A Descriptive Bibliography, 1934–1987*, published by the University Press of Virginia in 1988. In the same year appeared James Curry Robison's *Peter Taylor: A Study of the Short Fiction*, a volume in Twayne's Studies in Short Fiction Series. The book, which is divided into three sections (Robinson's critical analysis of twenty-six Taylor stories, a gathering of biographical sketches and interviews, and a third section containing selections from earlier critical essays), offers a helpful introduction, on several levels, to Taylor and his work. Robinson's own interview with the author is an important addition, and he presents often interesting readings of individual stories, though his overall thesis that Taylor was a "Victorian realist" devoted to the value of decorum pushes a strain of Taylor criticism to an untenable extreme. Completing the group of Taylor books was Albert J. Griffith's revised, updated, and expanded 1990 edition of his Twayne study, first published twenty years earlier.

Periodical contributions to Taylor criticism have also increased since *A Summons to Memphis* was published. The *Journal of the Short Story in English* devoted the Autumn 1987 number to Taylor, the only complete issue of a journal given to the author except for the Winter 1977 number of *Shenandoah*. Editor J. H. E. Paine's interesting interview led the issue, which also included reminiscences, Stuart Wright's useful checklist of Taylor bibliography from 1934 to 1986, Steven John Ross's piece on adapting "The Old Forest" to film, and three critical essays. Of these, the most significant contribution was clearly Simone Vauthier's "Trying to Ride the Tiger: A Reading of 'First Heat.' " The first piece of poststructuralist criticism devoted to Taylor's work, the essay has its faults. Critical terms sometimes obscure and divert rather than advance the inquiry, and other awkwardnesses exist in organization—but Vauthier still manages to deal with psychological and aesthetic dimensions of Taylor's fiction rarely acknowledged before.[90] In retrospect, one sees this clearly as an apprentice effort, because each subsequent Vauthier essay on Taylor has represented a significant development over the last. She has now emerged as one of the two most important Taylor critics of recent years.

The other is David M. Robinson, who also made his debut in Taylor criticism in 1987. The Spring issue of *Southern Review* carried his "Tennessee, Taylor, the Critics and Time," an essay on "Venus, Cupid, Folly and Time."[91] Though providing an often penetrating analysis of the story, the piece suffers somewhat from Robinson's awkward attempt to use this highly artificial construct as an example of Taylor's transforming the regional into the universal. Like Vauthier, however, each succeeding Robinson entry has been superior to the last, as was evidenced shortly by his insightful review of *A Summons to Memphis* published in the very next issue (Summer 1987) of *Southern Review*. Also appearing in 1987 were the Walter Sullivan piece in *Sewanee Review* noted earlier and Lamar York's article in *Mississippi Quarterly* on Taylor's initiation stories.[92]

Though in no year since has the number of critical articles matched the volume of 1987, a small stream of Taylor criticism has continued a steady flow; and among the essays are significant contributions. The only entries for 1988 were two pieces on one of Taylor's earliest and most frequently anthologized stories. The first of the essays, "Determined Failure, Self-Styled Success: Two Views of Betsy in Peter Taylor's 'Spinster's Tale' " by Roland Sodowsky and Gargi Roysircar Sodowsky, offered both Freudian and Adlerian readings to show the "satisfying" ambiguity of the story. The second, Maureen Andrews's "A Psychoanalytic Appreciation of Peter Taylor's 'A Spinster's Tale,' " presented a much more intricate Freudian analysis.[93] Again, in 1989, only two articles appeared. The first was Hubert H. McAlexander's entry on Taylor in the European reference journal *Post-war Literatures in English*, a critical overview of the author's career, supplemented by biographical and bibliographical material. The other essay was Walter Shear's "Peter Taylor's Fiction: The Encounter with the Other," published in *Southern Literary Journal*. While often promising revelations of a new order, the Shear piece lacked final coherence.[94]

Though once again in 1990 only two critical entries appeared, they were among the most important work ever done on Taylor. Not since 1978, when the Jane Barnes Casey and Alan Williamson essays were published, had two critical pieces of such importance appeared at the same time. David M. Robinson's essay on "The Old Forest" in *Southern Literary Journal* displayed an unprecedented grasp of interlocking psychological and social issues in this late masterpiece. A model of lucidity and intelligence, the article by extension cast light on a whole body of Taylor's work. Simone Vauthier's analysis of "Porte Cochere," which appeared in Jefferson Humphries's *Southern Literature and Literary Theory*, was an impressive application of the concepts of recent French theory to this significant work. While offering a full and satisfying reading of the story, it also suggested—as perhaps no previous piece of criticism had—the complex nature of Taylor's imagination.[95]

The first half of 1991 has already seen the first of the requisite two Taylor entries. The essay was David H. Lynn's "Telling Irony: Peter Taylor's Later Stories" in the summer issue of *Virginia Quarterly Review*, an interesting commentary on an important issue.[96]

The last few years suggest that Taylor criticism may continue to replicate the progress of Taylor's own career as an artist, with contributions of quality added from time to time, a slow accumulation of valuable commentary. The four essays commissioned for this volume, however, perhaps reflect some critical tendencies. Certain narrow approaches to Taylor as a regionalist and as a realist have clearly been exhausted, and there is growing interest in distinctive Taylor patterns and structures and in using new critical approaches to reveal Taylor's art. Christopher Metress discovers in *A Summons to Memphis* a significant pattern that finally influences our judgment of the narrator. Ron Balthazor's piece, which is informed by French theory but characterized by the closest scrutiny of the text, deals lucidly and effectively with the complexly intertwined matters of narrative and identity. Simone Vauthier's essay is quite simply a monument in Taylor criticism. It offers a brilliant, definitive analysis of what is perhaps Taylor's most complex and artful construct, one of his most celebrated and least understood stories, "Venus, Cupid, Folly and Time."

It is fitting that this volume should conclude with an essay by an established writer, an appreciation and a thoughtful overview of this writer's writer by one of his peers. In his 1991 article "Time and the Tide in the Southern Short Story," Madison Smartt Bell pointed out Peter Taylor's extraordinary handling of time, a brief discussion that reflected his conviction, first voiced in a 1986 *Harper's* essay, that Taylor was "arguably the best American short story writer of all time."[97] Here, at the end of the present volume, Bell presents his first extended discussion of Peter Taylor's achievement.[98]

Notes

1. Robert Penn Warren, Introduction to *A Long Fourth and Other Stories* (New York: Harcourt, Brace & Co., 1948), vii.

2. Joyce Carol Oates, "Realism of Distance, Realism of Immediacy," *Southern Review* 7 (Winter 1971): 299.

3. Madison Smartt Bell, "Less Is Less: The Dwindling American Short Story," *Harper's* 272 (April 1986): 69.

4. "Acceptance by Peter Taylor," *Proceedings* (American Academy and Institute of Arts and Letters), 2d ser., no. 29 (1979): 31.

5. All statements about Taylor's publishing history are based on information in Stuart Wright, *Peter Taylor: A Descriptive Bibliography, 1934–1987* (Charlottesville: University Press of Virginia, 1988).

6. Warren, Introduction to *A Long Fourth*, viii–x.

7. Anonymous review of *A Long Fourth*, *New Yorker*, 3 March 1948, 124, and John Farrelly, Review of *A Long Fourth*, *New Republic*, 8 March 1948, 26.

8. Coleman Rosenberger, "An Island of Excellence in Short Stories," *New York Herald Tribune Books*, 14 March 1948, 5.

9. J. F. Powers, Review of *A Long Fourth and Other Stories*, *Commonweal*, 25 July 1948, 262.

10. Hubert Creekmore, "Skeletons in the Magnolia-Tree," *New York Times Book Review*, 21 March 1948, 6.

11. Marjorie Brace, "Southern Incidents," *Saturday Review*, 27 March 1948, 17–18.

12. Evelyn Eaton, "Stepmomism," *Saturday Review*, 3 June 1950, 13.

13. Anonymous review of *A Woman of Means*, *New Yorker*, 20 May 1950, 117.

14. Coleman Rosenberger, "Family in Flux," *New York Herald Tribune Books*, 21 May 1950, 10.

15. "As a Boy Grows Older," *Time*, 15 May 1950, 111; James Stern, "The Power of Charm," *New Republic*, 26 June 1950, 20; Robert Kee, "New Novels," *New Statesman and Nation*, 2 December 1950, 566; George Miles, Review of *A Woman of Means*, *Commonweal*, 23 June 1950, 276.

16. Robert Penn Warren, "Father and Son," *New York Times Book Review*, 11 June 1950, 8.

17. Thomas Wilcox, "A Novelist of Means," *Sewanee Review* 59 (Winter 1951): 152.

18. Kenneth Clay Cathey, "Peter Taylor: An Evaluation," *Western Review* 18 (Autumn 1953): 9–19.

19. Paul Engle, "Finely Poised Stories of Southern Family Life," *Chicago Sunday Tribune Magazine of Books*, 30 May 1954, 4.

20. Dan Wickenden, "A Fine Novel of the South," *New York Herald Tribune Books*, 2 May 1954, 4. Note the erroneous heading for a review of a short story collection.

21. Mack Morriss, "South in the Sun," *Saturday Review*, 8 May 1954, 14.

22.   Richard Hayes, "Pain, Knowledge, and Ceremony," *Commonweal*, 17 December 1954, 317–18.
23.   Frank H. Lyell, "The Universal Longings," *New York Times Book Review*, 2 May 1954, 5.
24.   Andrew Lytle, "The Displaced Family," *Sewanee Review* 66 (Winter 1958): 115–20. Albert J. Griffith provides a careful study of the play in *Peter Taylor* (New York: Twayne Publishers, 1970), 97–103, which is reprinted with few changes in his revised edition of 1990.
25.   Jeremy Brooks, "New Short Stories," *New Statesman*, 6 August 1960, 192.
26.   Gene Baro, "A True Short-Story Artist," *New York Herald Tribune Books*, 6 December 1959, 9.
27.   William Du Bois, "Books of The Times," *New York Times*, 12 January 1960, 45.
28.   William Peden, "Assessments of the Finely Aware," *Saturday Review*, 28 November 1959, 33.
29.   Ruth Blackman, "Complex Stories of Family and Community," *Christian Science Monitor*, 24 December 1959, 11.
30.   Walter Sullivan, "The Continuing Renascence: Southern Fiction in the Fifties," *South: Modern Southern Literature in Its Cultural Setting*, ed. Louis D. Rubin, Jr., and Robert D. Jacobs (New York: Doubleday and Co., 1961), 385, 389.
31.   Chester E. Eisinger, *Fiction of the Forties* (Chicago: University of Chicago Press, 1963), 196.
32.   John M. Bradbury, *Renaissance in the South: A Critical History of the Literature, 1920–1960* (Chapel Hill: University of North Carolina Press, 1963), 16, 120; Richard K. Meeker, "The Youngest Generation of Southern Fiction Writers," *Southern Writers, Appraisals in Our Time*, ed. R. C. Simonini, Jr. (Charlottesville: University Press of Virginia, 1964), 173–75.
33.   William Peden, *The American Short Story* (Boston: Houghton Mifflin Company, 1964), 30, 39, 45–46, 61–68. In the 1975 version of this study, Peden presents fundamentally the same treatment of Taylor, though he adds discussions of later stories. See pages 39–44.
34.   Morgan Blum, "Peter Taylor: Self-Limitation in Fiction," 559–78; Brainard Cheney, "Peter Taylor's Plays," 579–87; Ashley Brown, "The Early Fiction of Peter Taylor," 588–602—all in *Sewanee Review* 70 (Autumn 1962).
35.   Glendy Culligan, "Struggling to Swim Clear of the Undertow," *Bookweek*, 8 March 1964, 11; Richard Sullivan, Review of *Miss Leonora When Last Seen, Chicago Sunday Tribune Books Today*, 5 April 1964, 4.
36.   Gene Baro, "How Time Changes Things," *New York Times Book Review*, 29 March 1964, 4; John Thompson, "The Stories of Peter Taylor," *New York Review of Books*, 11 June 1964, 11.
37.   Baro, "How Time Changes Things," 4.
38.   T. A. Hanzo, "The Two Faces of Matt Donelson," *Sewanee Review* 73 (Winter 1965): 106–11.
39.   Culligan, "Struggling to Swim Clear of the Undertow," 11.
40.   Thompson, "The Stories of Peter Taylor," 11.
41.   Barbara Schuler, "The House of Peter Taylor," 6–18; James Penny Smith, "Narration and Theme in Taylor's *A Woman of Means*," 19–30; James Penny Smith, "A Peter Taylor Checklist," 31–36—all in *Critique*, 9, no. 3 (1967).
42.   R. V. Cassill, "The Departure of Proserpine," *Chicago Tribune Book World*, 12 October 1969, 6.
43.   Joyce Carol Oates, "Realism of Distance, Realism of Immediacy," *Southern Review* 7 (Winter 1971): 299–302.
44.   Stephen Goodwin, "Life Studies," *Shenandoah* 21 (Winter 1970): 100–102.

45. Richard Howard, "Twenty-one Holding Actions by a Modest American Master," *New York Times Book Review*, 19 October 1969, 4, 26; Geoffrey Wolff, "Master of Hidden Drama," *Newsweek*, 20 October 1969, 120, 122.

46. John Thompson, Review of *The Collected Stories, Harper's* 239 (November 1969): 130, 134.

47. Roger Sale, Review of *The Collected Stories of Peter Taylor, Hudson Review* 22 (Winter 1969–1970): 710.

48. Christopher Ricks, "The Unignorable Real," *New York Review of Books*, 12 February 1970, 22.

49. Barbara Raskin, "Southern Fried," *New Republic*, 18 October 1969, 29–30; Jonathan Yardley letter in "Correspondence," *New Republic*, 22 November 1969, 27–29.

50. Jan Pinkerton, "The Non-Regionalism of Peter Taylor," *Georgia Review* 24 (Winter 1970): 432–40.

51. Albert J. Griffith, Review of *The Collected Stories of Peter Taylor, Commonweal*, 6 February 1970, 616–18, and *Peter Taylor* (New York: Twayne Publishers, 1970).

52. Thompson, Review of *The Collected Stories*, 130.

53. Stephen Goodwin, "An Interview with Peter Taylor," *Shenandoah* 24 (Winter 1973): 20, reprinted in *Conversations with Peter Taylor*, ed. Hubert H. McAlexander (Jackson: University Press of Mississippi, 1987).

54. B. H. Fussell, "On the Trail of the Lonesome Dramaturge," *Hudson Review* 26 (Winter 1974): 755, and anonymous review of *Presences: Seven Dramatic Pieces, Antioch Review* 32 (November 1973): 700.

55. Richard Howard, "Urgent Need and Unbearable Fear," *Shenandoah* 24 (Winter 1973): 44–47; Paul Theroux, "Old-Family Vapors," *Washington Post Book World*, 25 February 1973, 13.

56. Alfred Kazin, *Bright Book of Life: American Novelists and Storytellers from Hemingway to Mailer* (Boston: Little, Brown & Co., 1973), 38, 46–49.

57. William Peden, *The American Short Story: Continuity and Change, 1940–1975* (Boston: Houghton Mifflin Company, 1975), 30, 39–44, and "A Hard and Admirable Toughness: The Stories of Peter Taylor," *Hollins Critic*, 7 (February 1970), 1–9.

58. Walter Sullivan, *Death by Melancholy: Essays on Modern Southern Fiction* (Baton Rouge: Louisiana State University Press, 1972), 89, and *A Requiem for the Renascence: The State of Fiction in the Modern South* (Athens: University of Georgia Press, 1976), xxii–xxiii.

59. Herschel Gower, "The Nashville Stories," 37–47; Andrew Lytle, "On a Birthday," 11–17; Ashley Brown, "Peter Taylor at Sixty," 48–53; Albert J. Griffith, "Presences, Absences, and Peter Taylor's Plays," 62–71; J. F. Powers, "Peter Taylor's New Book," 84–85—all in *Shenandoah* 28 (Winter 1977).

60. Charles Deemer, "An Old Faithful," *New Leader*, 20 June 1977, 19–20.

61. Anatole Broyard, Review of *In the Miro District and Other Stories, New York Times Book Review*, 3 April 1977, 14; Jonathan Yardley, "Discovering an American Master," *Washington Post Book World*, 10 April 1977, E7–E8.

62. Linda Kuehl, Review of *In the Miro District and Other Stories, Saturday Review*, 14 May 1977, 35–36; Anne Tyler, "Farewell to the Story as Imperiled Species," *National Observer*, 9 May 1977, 23.

63. See, for instance, Keith Cushman, Review of *In the Miro District and Other Stories, Studies in Short Fiction* 14 (Fall 1977): 420–21, and Jay L. Halio, "Persons Placed and Displaced", *Southern Review* 15 (Winter 1979): 252–54.

64. Harold Beaver, "The Shadow of the South," *Times Literary Supplement*, 30 September 1977, 1097; Edna Longley, "Crocheted Castle," *New Review* 4 (October 1977): 59–60.

65. Stephen Goodwin, Review of *In the Miro District, New Republic*, 7 May 1977, 33–34.

66. Jan Pinkerton, "The Vagaries of Taste and Peter Taylor's 'A Spinster's Tale,' " *Kansas Quarterly* 9 (Spring 1977): 81–85.

67. Jane Barnes Casey, "A View of Peter Taylor's Stories," *Virginia Quarterly Review* 54 (Spring 1978): 213–230.

68. Alan Williamson, "Identity and the Wider Eros: A Reading of Peter Taylor's Stories," *Shenandoah* 30 (Fall 1978): 71–84.

69. Paul Binding, *Separate Country; A Literary Journey Through the American South* (New York & London: Paddington Press, 1979), 33, 84, 113–21, 156, 200, 204, 209, 213; Walter Allen, *The Short Story in English* (Oxford: Clarendon Press, 1981), 318–32; Zachary Leader, "Old Times in the New South," *Times Literary Supplement*, 22 January 1982, 75–76.

70. Victor A. Kramer, Patricia A. Bailey, Carol G. Dana, and Carl H. Griffin, *Andrew Lytle, Walker Percy, and Peter Taylor: A Reference Guide* (Boston: G. K. Hall, 1983), 185–243; Thomas Daniel Young, *Tennessee Writers* (Knoxville: University of Tennessee Press, 1981), 77–111; Victor A. Kramer, "Peter Taylor," *Dictionary of Literary Biography Yearbook: 1981*, ed. Karen L. Rood, Jean W. Ross, and Richard Ziegfield (Detroit: Gale Research, 1982), 256–60; Marilyn Malina, "An Analysis of Peter Taylor's 'Venus, Cupid, Folly and Time,' " *Studies in Short Fiction* 20 (Fall 1983): 249–54.

71. J. D. McClatchy, Review of *The Old Forest and Other Stories, Saturday Review*, May/ June 1985, 73–74.

72. Anne Tyler, "Peter Taylor: The Lessons of the Master," *USA TODAY*, 26 January 1985, 3D.

73. Walter Clemons, "Southern Comfort," *Newsweek*, 11 March 1985, 74.

74. Jonathan Yardley, "Peter Taylor: The Quiet Virtuoso," *Washington Post Book World*, 27 January 1985, 3.

75. Robert Towers, "A Master of the Miniature Novel," *New York Times Book Review*, 17 February 1985, F1, F26.

76. Adam Mars-Jones, "After the Trembling of Prestige," *Times Literary Supplement*, 23 August 1985, 923. For a corrective to this view, see Oliver Conant, "Tales from the Veranda," *New Leader*, 25 March 1985, 18–19.

77. Paul Gray, "Codes of Honor," *Time*, 4 February 1985, 74.

78. Review of *A Summons to Memphis, Publishers Weekly*, 1 August 1986, 68.

79. Paul Gray, "Civil War in the Upper South," *Time*, 29 September 1986, 71; Walter Clemons, "You Can't Go Home Again," *Newsweek*, 29 September 1986, 64; Robert Wilson, "Peter Taylor's Perfect Puzzle," *USA TODAY*, 3 October 1986, 4D; Michiko Kakutani, "Books of the Times," *New York Times*, 24 September 1986, 24.

80. Jonathan Yardley, "Peter Taylor's Novel of Fathers and Sons," *Washington Post Book World*, 14 September 1986, 3.

81. Ann Hulbert, "Back to the Future," *New Republic* 24 November 1986, 37–40.

82. Robert Towers, "Ways Down South," *New York Review of Books*, 25 September 1986, 55–57.

83. John Updike, "Summonses, Indictments, Extenuating Circumstances," *New Yorker*, 3 November 1986, 158–65.

84. Walter Sullivan, "The Last Agrarian: Peter Taylor Early and Late," *Sewanee Review* 95 (Spring 1987): 308–17.

85. Marilynne Robinson, "The Family Game Was Revenge," *New York Times Book Review*, 19 October 1987, 1, 52, 53.

86. David M. Robinson, "Summons from the Past," *Southern Review* 23 (Summer 1987): 754–59.

87. Anita Brookner, "Revenge of the Weird Sisters," *Spectator*, 16 May 1987, 34–35.

88. Ibid., 35. See also Michael Wood, "Where the Tentacles Wave From," *Times Literary Supplement*, 1 May 1987, 458.

89. Albert J. Griffith, *Peter Taylor, Revised Edition* (Boston: Twayne Publishers, 1990),

160. See also the review by Joseph R. Millichap, *Modern Fiction Studies* 35 (Summer 1989): 641.

90. Simone Vauthier, "Trying to Ride the Tiger: A Reading of 'First Heat,' " *Journal of the Short Story in English* 9 (Autumn 1987): 73–92.

91. David M. Robinson, "Tennessee, Taylor, the Critics and Time," *Southern Review* 23 (Spring 1987): 281–94.

92. Lamar York, "Peter Taylor's Version of Initiation," *Mississippi Quarterly* 40 (Summer 1987): 309–22.

93. Roland Sodowsky and Gargi Roysircar Sodowsky, "Determined Failure, Self-styled Success: Two Views of Betsy in Peter Taylor's 'Spinster's Tale,' " *Studies in Short Fiction* 25 (Winter 1988): 49–54; Maureen Andrews, "A Psychoanalytic Appreciation of Peter Taylor's 'A Spinster's Tale,' " *Journal of Evolutionary Psychology* 9 (August 1988): 309–16.

94. Hubert H. McAlexander, "Peter Taylor," *Post-war Literatures in English*, March 1989, 1–15; Walter Shear, "Peter Taylor's Fiction: The Encounter with the Other," *Southern Literary Journal* 22 (Spring 1989): 50–63.

95. David M. Robinson, "Engaging the Past: Peter Taylor's 'The Old Forest,' " *Southern Literary Journal* 23 (Spring 1989): 50–63; Simone Vauthier, "Peter Taylor's 'Porte Cochere': The Geometry of Generation," *Southern Literature and Literary Theory*, ed. Jefferson Humphries (Athens: University of Georgia Press, 1990), 318–38.

96. David H. Lynn, "Telling Irony: Peter Taylor's Later Stories," *Virginia Quarterly Review* 67 (Summer 1991): 510–20.

97. Madison Smartt Bell, "Time and the Tide in the Southern Short Story," *Chronicles: A Magazine of American Culture*, March 1991, 28, and "Less Is Less: The Dwindling American Short Story," *Harper's* 272 (April 1986): 69.

98. I wish to express my appreciation here for the intelligence, care, and professionalism of Darren Felty, who served as my graduate assistant as this manuscript was assembled.

REVIEWS

◆

Southern Incidents [Review of *A Long Fourth*]

Marjorie Brace

In an introduction to this collection of stories by a young writer whose work
has appeared in such magazines as *The Kenyon Review, The Southern Review*,
and *The Partisan Review*, Robert Penn Warren says that Peter Taylor has
"a disenchanted mind," but "has succumbed to the last and most fatal
enchantment: the enchantment of veracity. And that is what, in the end,
makes the artist free." Free, that is, to be committed to the artist's never-
ending research into the mysterious nature of reality, to the effort to give it,
not only expression, but order and meaning: essentially, to define it.

Mr. Taylor writes, with limpid sobriety, of undramatic incidents, oc-
curring mostly within middle-class family life in Southern towns. On the
surface, his material is not very complex. In "Sky Line" a boy observes
changes in his suburban neighborhood, new buildings, a vacant lot ravaged
by excavation; over a space of years, there are deaths in his family, and next
door; his father marries again. "Rain in the Heart" describes the night's leave
of a soldier in training-camp: he listens to the gross talk of the men, rides
on buses, has a fugitive conversation on a street corner with a grotesque
cleaning-woman, spends a quiet evening with his bride in their furnished
rooms, watches a rainfall. Even where, as in the title story, the interplay of
events is swift and crowded, with many varieties of consciousness moving
tensely together, the impacts are among experiences of apparent clarity,
presented with directness—a hot weekend, a son's visit home just before he
enters the army, his mother's quarrel with an old Negro servant. And yet,
in these stories, accustomed values are dissolving and shifting fluidly towards
something unknown.

What Mr. Taylor is really doing, with honesty and sureness and beauty,
is to experiment, both technically and psychologically, with very difficult
approaches to extremely difficult definitions. For all its deceptively unstar-
tling appearance, his method is quite as odd and daring as that in any of
Picasso's paintings of double-headed women or seemingly capricious group-
ings of objects.

Mr. Taylor is inquiring into those relations through which things take
on their meaning, and he makes his inquiry, not in unfamiliar language, but

From *Saturday Review*, 27 March 1948, 17–18. Reprinted by permission of Omni International, Ltd.

through connections so unfamiliar that he shakes the reader into emotional insecurity. He deals with states of uncertainty of association, those of a growing boy, a dispersing family, a society where traditions are breaking down, or of people plunged into new experience or seen in troubling lights, and intimates that true realization of life means perceiving the special qualities of old relations, and, through the stress inherent in this, creating new patterns of association.

The form of imagery he employs is peculiarly evocative. It achieves its disturbing significance, not through obscurity of symbol, or any straining for unusual verbal effect, but through the way things are placed together in the narrative itself. The thought of this narrative is not hieroglyphically private, nor does it refer to depths or beatitudes or contorted mazes of emotion, but, rather, extends awareness of ordinary happening and sensation. It suggests, subtly and reverberatingly, a continuous crisis in possible orderings of existence.

The strangeness, and the remarkable effectiveness, of Mr. Taylor's writing comes, never from distortion of reality, but from considered and questioning rearrangement. His is a thoughtfully unpretentious and original talent.

A Novelist of Means
[Review of *A Woman of Means*]

THOMAS WILCOX

It is characteristic of Peter Taylor and of his art that he has been content to write a *short* first novel. *A Woman of Means* is only 160 pages long and there are but five or six important characters. A short first novel may be laudable if only because it indicates that its author has had the good sense not to squander his limited fund of experience and invention on some impossibly ambitious work. In Mr. Taylor's case there are other, more compelling reasons for praise. Clearly the length of his book and the extent of its purview are the results not of a cautious conservation of material but of a sure sense of sufficiency. His novel is precisely as long as it needs to be. And although it is short, it is not small.

Its meaning, the amount of aesthetic activity it affords the reader is great. An image emerges which will bear extensive scrutiny and may be endlessly explored. It is an intricate and animate image of a small complex of lives. And because Mr. Taylor skillfully demonstrates that the course of each of these lives is determined to some extent by the character's social identity, the image becomes a schematization of the structure of a society. Not that his novel can be read as simple allegory; his characters do not wear badges and move in slots. But you are surprised to find when you have finished the book that the pattern they trace as their lives converge, intersect, and diverge is a familiar pattern in American cultural history. Here, as in many of his short stories, he writes of the decay of an urban aristocracy. His scene is St. Louis in the mid-Twenties, and his characters are of three types: those who are working their way up from the South into the world of the beer barons and hardware manufacturers; those who are defending that world but whose insecurity impels them to welcome these newcomers from an older culture; and those who have abandoned that world for the East or for an economic position inferior to their parents'. The narrator, Quint Dudley, is a boy of eleven when he is brought to St. Louis by his father, a Southerner and a successful salesman, who has married "a woman of means." Their life in her mansion begins happily, but it soon becomes apparent that it can

From the *Sewanee Review* 59 (Winter 1951): 151–54. © 1958, 1962, 1986, 1990 by the University of the South. Reprinted by permission of the editor.

remain so only as long as each of Quint's parents retains the active affection of the other's children. His father needs the confidence of his wife's daughters, irresponsible young things who are willing at first to teach him sophistication. His stepmother needs the love of her husband's son, a sensitive boy in whom she finds some of the Southerner's "animal dignity." When the girls desert their stepfather for their Eastern college friends and when Quint leaves his stepmother to become a hero in his prep-school world, their little group disintegrates. The father fails in business and is reduced once again to a simple faith in the infallibility of his superiors. The stepmother goes insane and imagines herself reunited to her first husband, a member of her own class who has left St. Louis for the East. None of these people knows why all this has happened, though none of them is so imperceptive that he cannot find an explanation plausible to him. The reader knows more than any of them; his view is circumambient, theirs is fixed. But what may at first look like simple dramatic irony becomes something different when you begin to explore the tissue of paradoxes Mr. Taylor has contrived. When you try to construe the few events his novel describes you find that no single interpretation will account for everything you have learned and that finally you must credit all the explanations—some of them seemingly contradictory—the characters separately entertain. Thus Mr. Taylor's irony is wonderfully circular: it leads you back into the novel, back into the confusion of motives and the variety of interpretations each of the characters confronts. Why did Quint's parents marry? They themselves offer reasons, and the reader knows that none of them is right. Yet none of them is wholly wrong, and any final reading must comprehend them all. His stepmother suspects that Quint's father has married her for her money, and this is true; but it is also true that fundamental to his nature is a need to believe that "money isn't everything." She herself has more reverence for wealth than he, the kind of reverence only the wealthy can have, and one may infer from several incoherent but revealing remarks she makes at the end (while her daughters plan the wrecking of her house, because "that is the way you can get most money out of these old places") that hers are simply the paranoid hallucinations of a rich woman who sees her wealth and her world under attack. Whatever point of entry you choose, whatever path of explanation you follow, you find yourself involved, as the characters are involved, in a welter of ambiguities. There are no answers to the questions the novel asks; or rather there is one answer, and that is the full statement the novel makes. And it makes its statement by provoking an activity of mind analogous to the activity of life itself.

All this is done by a deft use of very common devices. Mr. Taylor's greatest achievement is his perfect control of tone. His novel is an autobiographical narrative, told by an adult recollecting childhood experiences. It requires the nicest tact to carry this off successfully. He must avoid a self-patronising tone ("I was young then and didn't see what I see now.") and yet he must somehow admit that he *can* relate his experiences only because he is an adult. And Mr. Taylor chooses further to complicate his task by making his narrator, Quint Dudley, his "fine central intelligence," the character who perceives and articulates the meaning of the action. Consequently he must contrive a tone which neither depreciates nor exaggerates his narrator's wisdom as a child. And if he is to preserve the quality I have tried to define above, if he is to provide an inexhaustible supply of meaning, he must make it clear that Quint is implicated in the events he describes and that his perceptions are therefore partial and fallible. The boy must be wiser than his parents, but he cannot be omniscient or he becomes merely a spectator and his interpretation must be assumed to be correct. Mr. Taylor manages to solve all these problems. His tone is carefully modulated to vary the adult narrator's position in relation to the boy and the characters who surround him. And he gives the boy a story of his own which is essential to the meaning of the book.

There are many other evidences of great skill in this novel: a judicious use of authentic detail, a consummate sense of timing, and the kind of simplicity which is the mark of a copious but disciplined imagination. It is a superb book, a book which grows in the mind.

Review of *The Widows of Thornton*

DAN WICKENDEN

On a Memphis-bound train which is carrying an aged aunt back from Washington to spend her last days in the small country town of her birth, Miss Patty Bean encounters Miss Ellen Louise Watkins, whose mother is being taken home for burial. The two spinsters are joined by a mutual acquaintance, Mrs. Jake Werner, just come from her own mother's funeral. Discussing the dying and the dead, commenting on evidences of change and desuetude they observe through the train windows, the three women conjure up much of the past they have in common.

Elegiac, ironic, affectionate—such adjectives occur inevitably—this flawlessly written introductory sketch sets the mood and suggests the theme which unifies *The Widows of Thornton*, a third book by Peter Taylor, who is possibly the most interesting and accomplished new writer to have come out of the South in the last ten years. The mood is sustained, the theme enlarged upon, through six more stories of varying length, and in a one-act play which would be (one guesses) eminently actable if difficult to stage. But it isn't until we have read the novella which ends *The Widows of Thornton* that we understand the title's full significance.

Some of Mr. Taylor's leading characters have stayed in rural Tennessee, and all of them have it for a background. But even those who have gone as far afield as Detroit and Chicago have taken their old life with them. They are haunted by memories of a world dominated and to some extent stultified by the past—a world in which family ties remained powerful, in which there lingered through the '20s that complex, almost symbiotic relationship between whites and Negroes which Northerners can never quite comprehend.

But Sylvia Harrison, the middle-aged heroine of "The Dark Walk," decides that in actual fact the men have already moved out of that world: they know it is moribund. She believes the women have clung to it not of their own choice but because, for obscure reasons, the men have willed them to do so; and that in this way they have been cut off from their husbands, and so from life itself. After she has become actually a widow, Sylvia sets herself free, turns her face toward the future.

Mr. Taylor's comedy is quiet, his drama subtle and generally muted. Passion, violence and the more extreme aberrations are absent from his fiction. Except in the play and in a few of the briefer stories, his narrative method consists more of summary, of distilled reminiscence, than of dialogue and action. And yet he fascinates, entertains and enlightens us as only a first-rate writer could. Immersed in his wonderfully lucid pages, we come to feel that this is not realism, but reality itself. And in the end we are convinced that his is as accurate and penetrating an account of the South—and of the behavior and relationships of human beings anywhere—as we are likely to read.

More substantial than the earlier and notable short novel, *A Woman of Means*, this new book makes us eager for the day when Peter Taylor will settle down to the major novels he is surely equipped to write. Meanwhile, it seems improbable that any American work of fiction more distinguished and enduring than *The Widows of Thornton* will appear this year.

Assessments of the Finely Aware [Review of *Happy Families Are All Alike*]

William Peden

In "Guests," one of Peter Taylor's most moving short stories, a middleaged Tennessee lawyer, contemplating the dead body of his elderly cousin, reflects that "here is such a person as I might have been, and I am such a one as he might have been." Thinking further about the recent curious fusing of his own identity with that of his "country cousin," the lawyer concludes that he had been drawn to the old man because they shared a common heritage.

They came, both of them, from the same "country"—a region that was not merely a geographical place, so and so many miles from Nashville, but a way of life: "the old ways, the old life, where people had real grandfathers and real children, and where love was something that could endure the light of day . . . Our trouble was . . . we were lost without the old realities."

The story is characteristic of most of the selections in "Happy Families Are All Alike." Regardless of their settings—in or around Nashville, or St. Louis, or Paris, or "Chatham" ("not thoroughly Middle Western and not thoroughly Southern either")—Mr. Taylor's leisurely short stories are concerned with moments of revelation, awareness, or insight in the lives of his various characters.

Thus, in "A Friend and Protector," which deals with the interacting relationships and influences between the members of a white family and a Negro servant, the narrator finally realizes that the story of black Jesse's ruined life is also the story of his "aunt's pathetically unruined life, and my uncle's too, and even my own." Indeed, in a moment of tense revelation while the crazy Negro crouches like a mad animal beneath his uncle's desk, the youth concludes that the whites have, in effect, forced Jesse's destruction upon him because they were unknowingly so dissatisfied with the "pale *un*ruin" of their own lives.

Similarly, after months of failing to understand the inner nature of his own adolescent son, the middle-aged father of "Promise of Rain" finally realizes what it means to see the world through another human being's eyes. Only then, he knows, do the experiences of his own life have any meaning; only then does the world "begin to tell you things about yourself."

From *Saturday Review*, 28 November 1959, 33. Reprinted by permission of Omni International, Ltd.

Mr. Taylor works efficiently and perceptively within a literary tradition which has its origins in the stories of Henry James. He examines his characters' lives and assesses their meaning in terms of the conflicts imposed by heredity and environment, by the conflicting values of past and present, by agrarian as opposed to urban values, or by the warfare between intellect and emotion. His stories succeed because his characters and their worlds are real, moving, and convincing. In each story there is always at least one character who becomes "finely aware" (the phrase is Henry James's) of the situations in which they find themselves. It is this fine awareness that gives the "maximum of sense" to what befalls them, which makes these quietly effective stories so meaningful to the reader.

How Time Changes Things [Review of
Miss Leonora When Last Seen]

GENE BARO

Really fine short stories almost always take us in. They don't necessarily depend upon intricate plots or clever surprises—more often the contrary— but they manage to deliver more than we bargained for. They are larger in significance and implication than they appear to be in the course of our first reading. Apparently straightforward, they resonate complexly in the imagination, they continue to give off overtones of meaning. Neatly made, aimed at unity of feeling, the fine short story suggests nothing less than that the world haunts us with the diverse truths of experience.

This quality of transcending the literal, the limited or the everyday circumstance, even in the act of establishing it, is characteristic of Peter Taylor's work. Does it need to be said that he is one of the most accomplished short-story writers of our time? He has published sparingly and has won a number of public recognitions and awards, but his present collection, ten old stories—he began to be known in the late forties—and six newer ones, is itself a recommendation not to be matched by grants or prizes. The solidity of the work from the earlier volumes, *The Widows of Thornton* and *A Long Fourth*, and the vivacity, wit and humanity of the new stories allow us to see him conveniently both in his dominating and in his developing concerns. It seems a pity that nothing should have been given us from his most recent collection, *Happy Families Are All Alike*, which is still in print.

What do we find? Mr. Taylor has been faithful to the Middle South. Most of these stories have their physical location in Tennessee. He is first of all a writer of place, for whom place is made up of an infinite number of material and spiritual details. He can at once, and convincingly, reduce a scene to its meaningful factual or observable elements. For instance, he knows precisely how the small-town drug store has changed, or the railway station. He knows what verbal liberties a Negro servant in a middle-class Nashville home will be allowed, and what liberties the mistress will allow herself. He knows the unspoken assumptions, the invisible idioms of a dozen stations in Southern life.

From the *New York Times Book Review*, 29 March 1964, 4, 30. © 1964 by the New York Times Company. Reprinted by permission.

These are raw materials, building blocks. Mr. Taylor's art is not merely in the coherent rendering of an environment—splendidly as he does it. His excellence is not a matter of social realism. Let's say it—his preoccupation is time, the most poetic and pathetic of human obsessions. The impulse, the search of these stories is for the meaning of time. How time changes things, changes oneself, the tug of the past, the imprisonment the past is, the duty it imposes—these are typical subjects. Sometimes a character looks back through a term of years for the meaning of his existence, as Matt Donelson does in "At the Drugstore"; the past illuminates the present. Sometimes the past circumscribes the present, as in the title story, or in "Allegiance." Sometimes it prefigures the future, as in "Reservations."

Firm detail strengthens this fiction. A sense of the ambiguous nature of social convention, the role-playing element in human life, gives it ironic flexibility. Difficult emotions are made plain here because they are attached to the specific; they are feelings that can be tried against the habits of mind and objective realities of a definable milieu—places in the Middle South at a particular moment in their history. These stories form a kind of dialogue, in time, between feeling and experience.

The condition of Mr. Taylor's art, as I have described it, gives rise to real people meditating actual problems. Time is certainly not the preoccupation of the characters. It operates almost incidentally. Miss Leonora has inherited her uncomfortable position in the town—she is of the family of the founders, and the times have moved finally against them—but Miss Leonora has made the most of her position, according to her lights, and goes on very funnily standing for the things she must stand for. She is a moral force bending but not breaking. In her way, she is rather like the old Negro, Aunt Munsie, in "What You Hear From 'Em?", another fallen out of the march of progress. Thomasville condemns Miss Leonora's property in the name of the future, just as Thornton, facing the disorders of its future, forbids Aunt Munsie to raise pigs within the town limits. The quality of mercy is often strained, as Mr. Taylor sees it.

Another compelling theme has to do with the relations of men and women, as these relations are modified, distorted or frozen by the social roles assigned to each. The most recent stories—all with underlying seriousness— project an irony, whimsicality and comic irreverence which, if not new to Southern fiction, appears for the moment to offer new scope to Mr. Taylor. It is nevertheless the more conventionally realistic stories I prefer; that is, those that seem to be documentary. In such work as "The Fancy Woman," "A Wife of Nashville," "Bad Dreams," "A Strange Story," and "A Spinster's Story," the author has overcome the limits of the particular; emotionally unified, these stories multiply their meanings. They have enduring interest.

Life Studies [Review of *The Collected Stories*]

STEPHEN GOODWIN

While the novel has aspired to the condition of art, the short story has been obliged to overcome that condition. Any college freshman, with the benefit of a single semester of English, can discourse instantly on the form of the short story (that, very likely, is the title of the anthology he's read). This hypothetical freshman might tell us that the short story has acquired a shape as distinct and functional as that of a fiddle; and when we agree, we have to remind him that the fiddle must, after all, be played, and that the story presents itself to our consideration not merely as an object with an admirable symmetry of contour. And should this freshman refer us to Peter Taylor as a master of structure, our reply, to do justice to Taylor, would have to elaborate the material of his stories.

For the triumph of his storytelling is that he has managed to enclose so much experience in the confines of the form he has chosen. The best of Taylor's stories—"A Wife of Nashville" or "What You Hear From 'Em?"—seem as complete as most novels; and a reading of this entire collection—there are 21 stories, 16 reprinted from earlier books—exposes us to life as only the greatest novels do. If questions of art occur to us as we read (they don't always; our first concern is that we are learning something of life), we are usually tempted to defer them; we know perfectly well that the writer is guiding us, as Chekhov or Turgenev guides us, because life never reveals itself to *us* with such clarity, but the revelation is more interesting and more vital than the method.

Taylor never distorts, never diminishes life to secure a resolution for art. The convenient and indulgent fiction of most storytelling—that emotions may be permanent, that revelations may be lasting—is never invoked. His characters are distracted when their sympathy is most required, silenced when they most require sympathy; and the lessons which they learn, or we learn, recede as each story closes, so that their wisdom, our wisdom, is at best a memory we can never be quite certain of. The most urgent cries of the heart are not heard at all, or heard too late. In a Paris movie theatre, an American father hears a child scream, *"Je suis perdu,"* and compliments

Reprinted from *Shenandoah: The Washington and Lee University Review* 21 (Winter 1970): 100–102, with the permission of the Editor and of Stephen Goodwin.

himself on his ability to understand the foreign language. The father doesn't recognize it as his daughter's voice until "rather casually and quite by chance" he glances over his shoulder and discovers that she is no longer behind him. The wife of Nashville, in a temper of respectability, drives from her door the drunken husband of her black maid; only afterward does she realize that she has separated husband and wife forever. She understands finally the words that the maid, as she watched her husband depart, was mumbling: "If I don't see you no more on this earth, Morse, I'll see you in Glory." At moments like these, we realize how scrupulously Peter Taylor avoids melodrama, how he refuses to deal in sudden and easy illuminations. What his characters are up against is circumstance, particularly the terrifying circumstance of their own preoccupations.

But if his characters fail, Taylor never permits us to fail. We must hear the cry, *"Je suis perdu,"* whether or not it is articulated. A characteristic narrative device in Taylor's stories, the use of a confused narrator who wants only to understand his own experience (or perhaps believes, mistakenly, that he does understand it), places squarely upon us the burden of understanding. The troubled citizen who narrates "Miss Leonora When Last Seen" feels but does not fathom his implication in the civic action which drives Miss Leonora from Thomasville. The story is ironic—but this is an especially painful irony because the citizen is pained, and the more we learn of his weakness, the more we feel the heavy price he pays for it. The motive of his storytelling is clear; we hear in every line his desire and need to understand, in every line his failure. Yet this citizen makes claims upon our sympathy that we can't refuse; for he, puzzled as he is, knows enough and cares enough to take upon himself the responsibility for the events which led to Miss Leonora's departure. We who know more can care no less: that is the price we pay.

No revelation is granted to the man in Thomasville, but Matt Donelson, in the story "At the Drugstore," seems to discover meaning and purpose when he visits the city he grew up in. Ugly and unsettling memories overtake him when he enters the drugstore where he used to wait, out of the cold, for the streetcar to school. These recollections of childhood—which provoke in the drugstore behavior of which he is ashamed, conduct which "nobody ever need know about"—culminate in the knowledge of death. "Inadvertently, he had penetrated beyond all the good sense and reasonableness that made life seem worthwhile—or even tolerable. And through the breach, beyond, behind, or beneath all this, he was now confronted by a thing that had a face and a will of its own. It was there threatening not only him and his father but the others too. Its threat was always present really, in him and in every man." Although this recognition produces momentarily an intense love for his family—which, like his earlier shame, he is not able to disclose— Matt Donelson is enough recovered, a few minutes later, to feel "no wonder at the grateful smiles" of his loved ones. Here habit and complacency assert themselves at the very moment when Taylor, if he were a different kind of writer, could put them to rout. The revelation increases self-satisfaction, and the emotion yields to self-esteem.

And so the rhythm of Taylor's stories carries us beyond the fiction of permanence. He demands of us our best emotions and leads us to some of our clearest discoveries—and never encourages our hope that these emotions and discoveries may be lasting. Our consolation is in the tone of his prose; these stories are so full of warmth, of concern and insight, that we must take heart. The resumption of Peter Taylor's voice with each story in this collection demonstrates that even the most radical insight need not cause despair, that expense must be the form of our attempt to overcome the weight of life.

The Departure of Proserpine
[Review of *The Collected Stories*]

R. V. CASSILL

Without hassling too much over the stellar individual achievements or chronological boundaries, I'll take publication of this book as occasion to insist again that a Golden Age for the American short story began soon after the Second World War. Here are several 14-karat contributions to that Age . . . which may still be going on, as Peter Taylor is, along with some other first-class masters of the form who emerged at about the same time. They lit each other's candles, and if there was nothing overtly revolutionary about the long, nuanced, perfectly surfaced, densely structured kind of story they perfected, still they extended its range of expression and inclusion as, say, the development of the piano extended the range of previous keyboard instruments.

Perhaps because so many of them were influenced at first or second hand by the goings-on at Kenyon College inspired by John Crowe Ransom, they brought into prose fiction the hard cunning and resource of poetry without being tempted at all to write with the abominable affectations of "poetic prose." As a matter of fact, one of the stories in this book recounts a holiday trip Taylor took with his Kenyon roommate—surely Robert Lowell, thinly disguised here as "Jim Prewitt"—in 1939. The two young men appear as genuine collegians of that uneasy period, discontented, coltish, and ineptly sophisticated about the "superior" girls they are going to New York to see. They are also artists as young men, natural peers of Stephen Dedalus and nearly as ingenuous as he in their solemnity about the high art they aspire to practice.

In the course of this story the author refers to himself as having become twenty years later "a kind of journeyman writer, a type of whom Trollope might have approved." Except for the modesty of the disclaimer, the characterization is a useful starting point. In Trollopian vein he chronicles the meandering years and cantankerous fortunes of the upper middle class in Memphis, Nashville and environing towns. He catalogues the material details of lives that have become inextricably absorbed in small discriminations of material

Reprinted with the permission of R. V. Cassill from the *Chicago Tribune Book World*, 12 October 1969, 6.

value. Social distinctions that would be invisible to any but the most initiated observer are measured with a meticulousness that might be unwarranted if it were not so just a replay of how his characters measure out their own prides and hopes of salvation. Writing of a Mr. Dorset whose ancient car and mutilated house are offenses to the neighboring property owners, he records that this old crank washes his *own car right out in front* on the street of West Vesey Place, wearing a pair of coveralls for the task: "The skin-tight coveralls, of khaki material but faded almost to flesh color, were still more offensive to the women and young girls than his ways of wearing his sweaters." In another story, a housewife who has been more pleased than not that her well-liked Negro cook worked after hours for an undertaker, discharges her on the spot when she is told the cook has been learning to embalm.

Of such is the kingdom of pathos and drollery. But by themselves accumulations of the droll pathos in small lives might not amount to much more than local color, a superior sort of regionalism. Yet, in some of the best individual stories and certainly in the fascinating configuration of this whole collection, we see how the world spins out from Tennessee and closes its vast circles there—how history itself must be the accumulation of minutiae like those recorded here.

The wife of a man elected governor senses that "politicians no longer had to learn to live like rich people; they had to learn to live like show people." In such enforced discoveries there is the dreadful change which is the author's fundamental preoccupation—those granular shifts by which continents are transformed under the feet, if not before the eyes, of the living. "Dean of Men" is written in the form of a letter to a member of the present activist generation of students. With a patient grandeur that deserves to be called Tolstoyan it exposes the ways in which some fractions of justice emerge from the unjust contentions and evolutions to which men must repeatedly submit as they endure the seasons of this planet. "A Wife of Nashville" probably has more to say about the subjugation of women and Negroes than many fists full of strident pamphlets.

Taylor's concerns are very large. The candid surface of his language is deceptively charged with high voltage wallops, complexities and moral allusions. One of his most potent characters, Miss Leonora Logan, steps from the pages like a figure each of us has known in his home town—quaint, perverse, fair, reasonable and hardy. Someone stern and fond who has watched us grow from boyhood and fail her hopes in us without showing a sign of her dismay. But when, at last, she steps into her antique car and drives away out of mortal ken, she is transfigured by the shaping imagination into a kind of American Proserpine, who lingered with us somewhat longer than her allotted time, so that the winter of her absence, too, will be prolonged and profound. Though Taylor takes her away without melodramatics, the changes that drove her off sound through his varied stories like an infinitely melancholy dirge, sung for us and the times we have known.

Realism of Distance, Realism of Immediacy
[Review of *The Collected Stories*]

JOYCE CAROL OATES

Superficially, Peter Taylor's short stories may seem radically different from Flannery O'Connor's. They are unusually quiet tales of domestic life, the confrontations of common bourgeois Americans of the mid-South with common elements of fate, carefully documented with social observations and oddities of a kind sometimes found in sentimental fiction. But here and there the grotesque shows through: Taylor's restraint sometimes gives way to his sense of tragedy and disorder; the comic and the violent rush together, to give us unforgettable stories. This handsome book, *The Collected Short Stories of Peter Taylor*, is one of the major books of our literature.

Taylor's stories are like dreams: events are brought sharply into focus, magically and dramatically limited, a sequence of sensations and speech passes as if in no important relationship to the rest of the world. And then a mysterious "point" is reached, a point of surrender or relaxation, and the story is complete, completed. Taylor has always been admired by critics to whom the craft of art is extremely important. But he writes stories that are far more than neatly crafted; they are both hallucinatory and articulate, the violence of Taylor's vision being bracketed by, even tamed by, the intelligent and gracious voice of his typical narrators.

The narrator may be Taylor himself, or a spokesman for Taylor; but most of the time it is a man of middle age, gentlemanly and courteous and patient, who means to confess something to us. The confession is amusing but it contains something that will surprise us, upset us. Is it possible, we think, that there are moments of terror in such lives?—the lives of these bourgeois, unneurotic, family-bound human beings? His people tend to be well-off, sometimes even wealthy. They are securely rooted in a region and in history; they own large dark, handsome homes in Nashville or in small towns like Thornton or Thomasville. They are attorneys or businessmen or even politicians; and one excellent story, "The Elect," is about a judge who has just been elected governor of his state. Or they are the wives of such men. They are good people, they are genteel and unalarming.

From *Southern Review* 7 (Winter 1971): 299–302. © The Ontario Review, Inc., 1991. Reprinted by permission.

The stories in this collection manage to tell us nearly everything about these people and their society, everything that is important, everything that is "immediate" and indicates a darker, deeper level of human existence. Beneath the everyday bustle of running a household (and the book is filled with the middle-class problem of the handling of servants!) there are certain dreams, certain nightmares, which must be dealt with. In Taylor the quaintly provincial becomes, suddenly, the universal. The experience is not always a pleasant one, though it begins pleasantly enough. "There" begins with an old gentleman's brusque statement: "Let me tell you something about the Busbys. The Busbys don't wash themselves—not adequately." We read on, fascinated. It is gossip, yes; it is comic. And yet it is much more. The story turns out to be the fateful attraction of people for their home towns, which are a kind of death, the perpetual relentless *there* from which the old man and, hopefully, the narrator himself have been liberated. And "There" is also a romantic love story.

Taylor is obsessed with home towns. And he is obsessed with the convolutions of the past, the burden of old, heavy, expensive furniture, of peripheral, dying relatives, the teasing reassessments we make continually about our performances in the past (were we loved more than we could know? Did we fail to take advantage of that love?)—and the shadowy, alarming selves that appear in our memories, making ghostly claims upon us in the forms of grandfathers or fathers or random cousins. The family is a fierce institution, identifying and imprisoning us. And yet, when someone dies, even a distant cousin, we are deeply and personally involved. The story "Guests" is about such stark facts of life, and about the need to beat the dead back into ordinary, sensible forms—the need to resist their magical power over us, their power to make us somehow into themselves.

Peter Taylor has published six books before this one, and critics have tended to think of him in terms of Chekhov and James. He is certainly "Chekhovian" and "Jamesian"—not so much in style as in the precision of his imagination—and yet he is unmistakably himself, a man who writes with originality about subjects we have taken for granted. In these days much of our literature is apocalyptic and hurried; it is a literature in which the cartoon-like exaggerations of the dream (particularly the American Dream) are given freedom, breaking out from the gentlemanly confines of the well-made work of art. The people who inhabit our literature are not "people" in the old, predictable sense—they do not have "families," they do not have permanent egos—they do not have time, above all, for subtleties of expression. If they participate in their culture it is likely to be negatively, reacting against, destroying . . . and so the stories of Peter Taylor move us deeply, refusing as they do to imitate the formlessness around us (though the disintegration of a way of life is explored seriously by Taylor) by any mimicry of formlessness in art. Taylor's writing is always impeccable: he is a gentleman confiding in another gentleman, certain of his mission and of his talent.

The finest stories in this collection seem to me those which touch lightly upon a kind of fourth dimension, dream-like and haunting and occasionally grotesque. "Venus, Cupid, Folly, and Time," which was awarded the O. Henry Prize for 1959, is an extravagant comedy about an old bachelor and his spinster sister that suggests—but only suggests—their incest, and goes on to make us aware that this "incest" is surely spiritual and not physical, and anyway—as Taylor's slightfuly confused narrator seems to feel—such mysteries cannot be expected to make sense. The chilling "A Spinster's Tale" (the earliest story in the volume, dating back to 1940) quite literally opens the door to a nightmare figure, long dreaded—and then closes it again, permanently. "The Fancy Woman" handles frankly an illicit relationship, based upon the exploitation of a good-hearted alcoholic party girl by a member of the monied "respectable" class. "Cookie" is a Chekhovian master-piece of understatement that reveals the emptiness of a marriage, as husband and wife sit at dinner. "Dean of Men," which although not as dramatically impressive as these stories, shares with them the obsession with the past, the eerie repetition of events, as if we somehow inherited our father's and our grandfather's fates along with our genes. And what subleties of love and hate are everywhere loosed in the intimacy of family life!

No one writes more beautifully than Peter Taylor of the tensions of love—not erotic love, but love of family, love of tradition. *It is all passing*, his people seem to say, lamenting the flow of time and rejoicing in it, sensing themselves increasingly cut off from their sources, from that deepest part of oneself that flows into personal history and is no longer "personal" at all but magical and tribal. And, at the heart of this passage of years, there is the sudden certainty that we are alone. Entirely alone. Our "foolish mysteries" add up to our loneliness, "the loneliness from which everybody, knowingly or unknowingly, suffered" ("A Wife of Nashville," p. 280). It is our human fate not to comprehend the loneliness of others, though we are all equally victims.

Review of *In the Miro District*

STEPHEN GOODWIN

After the publication of his *Collected Stories* in 1969, Peter Taylor told an interviewer that he doubted he would write many more stories. He said that he had a horror of repeating himself, and he wasn't being complacent; the *Collected Stories* is a formidable achievement, one of those unforeseen masterpieces, the sum of smaller masterpieces, in which the design, continuity, and magnitude of a writer's career become clear. Those stories evoke a Tennessee as vivid and intact as any fictional landscape, and Taylor was not inclined to pursue a scorched earth policy.

He did not repeat himself in his next book, *Presences*, a series of ghost plays, nor has he repeated himself in his new collection of stories, *In the Miro District*. He is still the most deft and genial of storytellers, but these eight stories are varied and innovative, even rebellious. Four of them are set as poems—"stoems" Taylor calls these hybrids—in an attempt to break down that rectangle, that black ingot, which prose invariably assumes on the page. Taylor takes risks with his subject matter too, and the menacing forces—of sex, violence, disgrace—which waited just outside the pale of propriety in his earlier stories have here frankly encroached. Taylor's resourceful ironies have given way to a voice which is prepared to take the most significant risk of all: to withold nothing, to disguise nothing, to speak all that it knows. The stories in this collection are not confessions but urgent meditations; in pursuing them, in choosing to be vulnerable, Taylor has found the means of a liberation that he didn't anticipate when he gave that interview. The two longest stories in this collection, "The Captain's Son" and the title story, are daring, elating works in which we can see a master surpass himself.

The Tennessee of these two stories is unmistakably Taylor's Tennessee, not a hillbilly dumping ground but a genteel Tennessee in which, to borrow a line from Walker Percy, everyone but a fool knows what the good life is and everyone but a scoundrel leads it. This Tennessee is removed in time—the stories are set in the first half of the century—and in life style (a word that would not have been in the vocabulary of any of Taylor's characters). These characters occupy comfortable houses—Canton china on the sideboard, oriental rugs on the floor—in the most respectable neighborhoods of Nash-

From the *New Republic*, 7 May 1977, 33–34. © 1977, The New Republic, Inc. Reprinted by permission.

ville or Memphis, and they belong to families which radiate out along the various pikes and lanes, where the high-toned hard-riding "Old South" cousins live, out to the dreary suburbs, "godforsaken, endlessly sprawling purlieus" where alcoholic kinfolk are in exile, out to the "snooty old towns" and upcountry hamlets which are inhabited by stubborn Confererate grandfathers and fundamentalist cousins. This is a social geography, of course, on which latitude and longitude are precisely measured. Where the lines converge at the poles of Nashville and Memphis, the most acute, arcane discriminations are made. These sensible, estimable people "maintained values which only they could understand and that even their children never pretended to understand entirely." In this Tennessee manners are complacent bulwarks which protect against extremity, vulgarity, passion—but they also divide characters from one another, and in particular they divide parents from their children.

Taylor said in that same interview that one of his original motives in writing about this Tennessee, which seems so far-off and long-ago, was to preserve it. With all its fine manners and nice distinctions, this "antediluvian Tennessee," as Taylor himself refers to it, has vanished—and no one knows it better than he does. Critics who have complained that his work is regional and old-fashioned have forgotten James's admonition that writers must be granted their choice of subject matter; worse, they have mistaken subject matter for substance. This Tennessee is Taylor's metaphor for Home, that remote place which his nostalgia tells him is still and serene and lovely. It is none of those things, as his stories discover. His imaginative journey from the diminished present is undertaken to find a solace that is never forthcoming. The narrator of "In the Miro District" says that he wanted to discover what "I was like. Or if, merely as a result of being born when I was and where I was, at the very tail end of something, I was like nothing else at all, incomparably without a character of my own." This is the inflection of the disappointment and need that pervade Taylor's stories, for this character experiences no epiphany, so sudden insight or intuition. His urgent meditation yields nothing but a story, *is* nothing but a story. For Taylor the story is itself a way of knowing, of shaping knowledge; though it cannot restore the past, though it cannot unmake the divisions which existed then, it nevertheless reconciles us to that vanished world and to the present because it is as much as we can know.

Stories have always been a way of mediating between past and present, and we do have a past, or various pasts. It shouldn't be necessary to emphasize that we do, but the story has to justify itself these days. The most resolutely contemporary opinion had renounced not only the form but the very word; short prose works are now called "fictions" or "pieces" or "fables," anything but stories, and a recent anthology goes by the name *Anti-Story*. One of the features of the story which is singled out as anachronistic is its temporality, its obsession with time; the new fiction is atemporal (it was, of course, the work of Borges that inspired the popularity of the term "fiction"; and it was Borges who wrote the sublimely impossible essay, "A New Refutation of Time"). The age, one gathers from the more combative advocates of the new fiction, requires a grimace that is accelerated like ions in an atom smasher, traveling in a dimension that is beyond time.

Peter Taylor's stories wear a more benign expression; unlike much new fiction, they have imaginary countenances which can assume a great many real expressions. Risky, moving unashamed, they are stories, and Peter Taylor knows the difference between the stories of our own and other times. In an astonishing scene, the terrifically drunk 18-year-old boy in "In the Miro District" turns the tables on his grandfather, a dominating old gentleman whose tales of his exploits have become oppressions to the boy. In phrases that he has learned from his grandfather, the boy taunts: " *'Tell me what it was like to lie in your bed in that shackly, one-story, backwoods hotel and have it come over you that it was no dream . . . that there really was at every unglazed window of your room the raw rim of a shotgun barrel.'"* This language, rehearsed and melodramatic, is interrupted by Taylor in his own tongue. *"I hear myself going on and on that Sunday night. As I babbled away, it was not just that night but every night that I had ever been alone in the house with him. I had the sensation of retching or of actually vomiting, not the whisky I had in my stomach but all the words about the nightriders I had ever had from him and had not known how to digest—words I had not ever wanted to hear."*

This reversal shows us that the stories we know by heart, the stories we inherit, may like manners divide us, generation from generation. Yet they have to be told one last time, for this telling, Taylor's narrator tells us, "was the beginning of my freedom."

Peter Taylor: The Quiet Virtuoso
[Review of *The Old Forest*]

JONATHAN YARDLEY

This new collection by Peter Taylor contains one novella, one short play and a dozen stories. The 14 pieces were originally published over four decades, from 1941 to the present, and they display Taylor in his full range of themes, settings and moods. This is to say that they provide a generous, incomparably rewarding introduction to the work of the American writer who, more than any other, has achieved utter mastery in short fiction. By comparison with *The Old Forest*, almost everything else published by American writers in recent years seems small, cramped, brittle, inconsequential; among American writers now living, only Eudora Welty has accomplished a body of fiction so rich, durable and accessible as Taylor's.

The pity (not to mention the oddity) of it is that he has done this almost entirely unnoticed by the larger world of serious readers, who simply have no idea what a treat they have missed. Taylor has won his share of honors, to be sure, and many of his fellow writers understandably hold him in awe. But not one of his eight previous books—a novella, six story collections and a volume of plays—has had a genuinely significant sale, and the mention of his name too often draws blank stares even from knowledgeable readers. In some measure, perhaps, this can be explained by his refusal to follow literary fashion; nowhere in his work is to be found the language of the gutter, his treatment of sexual business is subtle and reticent, his references to academic life are more often mocking than reverential, and he has not once in all these years corrupted a piece of fiction in order to advance his political opinions.

Rather, in all these years Taylor has quietly—though not, I believe, without deep frustration at the neglect to which he is subjected—gone about the business of transforming the small world he knows best into a place that has the look of a universe. This world is centered about the two Tennessee cities of Memphis and Nashville, with occasional forays to St. Louis and beyond. Its principal residents are white people of the middle and upper classes, though this being the South there are also many black people who, in the self-centered and wildly mistaken view of whites, are "completely

Reprinted by permission from the *Washington Post Book World*, 27 January 1985, 3. © 1985 the *Washington Post*.

irresponsible and totally dependent upon us." This world's central preoccupation, as stated by the narrator of the title novella of the collection, is with "the binding and molding effect upon people of the circumstances in which they are born."

Perhaps more than any other it is this theme that gives Taylor's fiction its universality; no matter what world a person may be born into, his stories say, that is the world that shapes him, and this we all have in common. Read superficially, Taylor seems to be a chronicler and defender of the old Southern order, a society that suppresses women and oppresses blacks. Yet as the stories in *The Old Forest* make abundantly clear, from the outset his strongest sympathies have been with the powerless, and his abiding interest has been in discovering what strategies they devise for acquiring such power as may be available to them. He depicts the world as it exists rather than the world as we wish it might be, so some of the social settings and personal relationships in these stories may seem unfortunate to today's enlightened reader; but the truth is that his portrait of the white middle-class South, though drawn with sympathy and affection, is as withering as any we have.

All the tales in this book can be used to prove the point, but the paradigmatic example is "The Old Forest," which I do not hesitate to call an American masterpiece. It was originally published in the late 1970s; it is one of four stories published over the past decade, the others being "The Captain's Son," "In the Miro District" and "The Gift of the Prodigal," that are arguably the finest Taylor has written. As is true of much of Taylor's recent fiction, it is narrated by a gentleman of moderately advanced years who is looking back into his own past with a mixture of nostalgia and puzzlement, attempting through the exercise of memory to understand an event that, however trivial on its face, had lasting repercussions in his life.

In this case the event is an auto accident that occurs in Memphis on a snowy day in the winter of 1937. Nat Ramsey is at the time 23 years old, "a young man who had just the previous year entered his father's cotton-brokerage firm, a young man who was still learning how to operate under the pecking order of Memphis's male establishment." He is a week away from his wedding to Caroline Braxley, like himself a child of Memphis society. But the person in the car with him when the accident takes place is not his fiancée; she is Lee Ann Deehart, a girl of "a different sort," a member of a loose confederation of young women who eschew society, dabble in literature and the arts, and are "liberated" by the standards of the day, though her relationship with Nat is not sexual.

The accident is "a calamitous thing to have happen—not the accident itself, which caused no serious injury to anyone, but the accident plus the presence of that girl." Lee Ann leaps from the car and disappears into "the old forest of Overton Park," an "immemorial grove of snow-laden oaks and yellow poplars and hickory trees." It is a place that has deep meaning in the history and character of the city:

It is a grove, I believe, that men in Memphis have feared and wanted to destroy for a long time and whose destruction they are still working at even in this latter day. It has only recently been saved by a very narrow margin from a great highway that men wished to put through there—saved by groups of women determined to save this last bit of the old forest from the axes of modern men. Perhaps in old pioneer days, before the plantation and the neoclassic towns were made, the great forests seemed woman's last refuge from the brute she lived alone with in the wilderness. Perhaps all men in Memphis who had any sense of their past felt this, though they felt more keenly (or perhaps it amounts to the same feeling) that the forest was woman's greatest danger. Men remembered mad pioneer women, driven mad by their loneliness and isolation, who ran off into the forest, never to be seen again, or incautious women who allowed themselves to be captured by Indians and returned at last so mutilated that they were unrecognizable to their husbands or who at their own wish lived out their lives among their savage captors.

No such fate awaits Lee Ann Deehart. We know from the outset that in four days she emerges from hiding and that her presence in the car does not cause Caroline to break her engagement to Nat. The suspense of this story, as is always true of Taylor's work, lies not in the unfolding of its plot but in the disclosure of the circumstances, both actual and psychological, of its characters' lives. These discoveries will not be revealed here. Suffice it to say that they have to do with "a world where women were absolutely subjected and under the absolute protection of men," a world in which women must "protect and use whatever strength [they] have." They also have to do with themes to which Taylor has devoted his entire career: the fragile bonds of kinship, the injustice of arbitrary power, the infinite complexity and ambiguity of the human community, the sense of irretrievable loss that is an inescapable aspect of adult life.

"The Old Forest" is the best of the stories in this collection, and the most characteristic in that it so comprehensively summarizes Taylor's work: not merely his settings and themes, but the marvelous subtlety and ingenuity of his leisurely, humorous storytelling method. But it is the best of an exemplary group. Mention certainly must be made of "The Gift of the Prodigal" and "A Friend and Protector," both of which examine the vicarious life; of "Promise of Rain" and "The Little Cousins," stories about children and their parents; of "A Long Fourth" and "Two Ladies in Retirement," which have much to do with matters of race; and of the short play, "The Death of a Kinsman," which in its exploration of "family happiness" and "how well we know our roles and how clearly defined are our spheres of authority" is another paradigmatic example of Taylor's art.

Gathered together as they now are, all of these tales serve admirably as a supplement to Taylor's *Collected Stories*, first published in 1969 and now available in paperback. Like that earlier volume, *The Old Forest* is both a thorough sample of Taylor's work in all its diversity and consistency, and clear evidence of his steady maturation over these four decades. Unlike most American authors, he is a better writer at 65 than he was at 45, for further confirmation of which see his previous collection, *In the Miro District*, also available in paperback. It is significant that the two finest stories here, "The Old Forest" and "The Gift of the Prodigal," are also the two most recent; midway through his seventh decade, Taylor is still expanding his world and his understanding of it.

Taylor has been compared, by Randall Jarrell and others, to Anton Chekhov; certainly both are virtuosos of the short story and of human psychology. But in the literature of his own country, Taylor can be compared to no one except himself; he is, as every word in this book testifies, an American master.

Summons from the Past
[Review of *A Summons to Memphis*]

DAVID M. ROBINSON

A Summons to Memphis is a book of memory, as are the best of Peter Taylor's stories. If the South is a culture of memory, Taylor is surely one of its central prophets. His reminiscing narrator in this case is Phillip Carver, a Manhattan publisher and rare book collector, who feels "a surge of happiness that I had got away [from Memphis] so long ago." Nevertheless, he cannot put his Memphis past behind him, as his narrative reveals. The summons of the title is ostensibly the call Phillip receives from his sisters to return to Memphis and help them prevent his elderly father's remarriage. But the operative summons of the book, we gradually discover, was his father's original decision to leave Nashville for Memphis during Phillip's youth. This was an act which, in Phillip's view, broke the lives of his sisters and mother, and withered his own as well. It is the first of a series of expressions of parental authority against which he cannot quite bring himself to rebel, though his resentment of them festers painfully in his arid midlife. The move from Nashville to Memphis obsesses his memory as the symbol of this crippling authority. Taylor deftly balances the novel between a depiction of Phillip's gradual and positive coming to terms with the causes of the "ruin" of his life and the exposure of the narrator as a weak and passionless phantom, forever chained to a past not of his own creating. On the one hand, the novel is a positive portrayal of the cultivation of an understanding through memory, but on the other, it is an almost merciless exposure of a life of cowardly failure. Do we finally sympathize with him through watching his battle to accept his father—and himself as his father's son? Or do we find the very process of his own self-analysis the means by which we come to distance ourselves from him as a character whose only remaining passion is an aborted vengefulness? Taylor will have it both ways, and his greatest accomplishment in this novel, so typical of his fiction, is to allow us both compassion and judgment.

Compassion, I think, is the more difficult achievement, because Phillip Carver is not a wholly likable man. The novel could with some justice be described as one long, brooding pout, except that somehow Taylor shows us

From *Southern Review* 23 (Summer 1987): 754–59. Reprinted with the permission of David M. Robinson.

that Phillip's complaint matters, and matters to others as well as to himself. If a wounded man, he is capable of feeling his pain and determined to locate its source in the past, particularly in his relation with his father. If a passionless man, it is because the great love of his youth was thwarted by his family's interference. Taylor's retrospective narration thus recovers that pain and passion and asks us to mold them as best we can into the voice we meet in the novel.

A Summons to Memphis is thus another in a series of works which confirms Taylor's most effective narrative strategy. As in "Venus, Cupid, Folly and Time," and "The Old Forest," Taylor establishes a narrative line through memory and complicates it with a narrator conscious that his telling of the story must also be an act of interpretation and of self-comprehension. Phillip Carver is telling us of his painful trips home, and of their basis in his troubled past, but he is also trying to understand his pain in that depiction. It is the struggle toward self-understanding in Taylor's narratives that gives them their principal resonance, even when that struggle is unsuccessful. Though deeply rooted in the psyche, Taylor's stories generally escape confessional solipsism through their depiction of the close relation between psyche and manners. Taylor's characters search for self-understanding in a context in which their selves have been heavily determined by a dense and formal social culture. Self-comprehension thus takes the form of social analysis. Taylor follows Henry James in this endeavor, but closer to home, he also shares it with Eudora Welty. In that passion for cultural self-understanding that burst forth in the Southern Renaissance and spilled into a following generation, Welty and Taylor will, after Faulkner, prove the most durable voices.

In A Summons to Memphis, Taylor has written a novel whose present is abstract and bodiless, while its past is richly realized. That fact is chiefly indicative of the narrator's mind. We never get any feeling of his life in Manhattan, except for some opaque details of his relation with Holly Kaplan, a companion (one hesitates to use the word lover, given the emotional distance between them) remarkably like him in her own battle with her past. It is a relationship that arouses our curiosity and inevitably leads us to take Phillip's reticence as a sign of his emotional aridity. In Phillip's mind, Manhattan's most valuable characteristic is that it is not Memphis; he uses it as the symbol of his asserted escape from his Tennessee past. Manhattan life does not seem to engage him deeply; it is as if his entire emotional energy is devoted to guarding himself against a past which continues to haunt him. But Phillip's haunting past is Taylor's richest literary property. When Phillip turns to the past for analysis or explanation, Taylor deftly brings that Tennessee past to life.

One of the novel's most vivid scenes is the recounting of the arrival of the Carver family in Nashville at a time when it seemed that it would be their permanent home. Phillip's father, George Carver, has come to Nashville to take a position as an attorney in Merriwether Lewis Shackleford's growing business empire. Shackleford is more than an employer, however. His business relationship with Carver is based on admiration and solid friendship, the depth of which is suggested by Phillip's memory of his family's arrival in the Shacklefords' driveway deep in the night. Taylor is able to communicate the family's shared feeling of elation as they arrive, and the excited bustle of the Shacklefords in response. Their welcome is profuse and endearing—"the servants already had the beds 'turned back,' " they are assured. As Phillip's mother observes, "we were like travellers in the Tennessee wilderness a hundred years back being welcomed at the isolated cabin of a pioneer family." As it happens, Nashville becomes a modern business wilderness for their father. Shackleford betrays Carver, involving him against his knowledge in questionable practices when his businesses are threatened during the Great Depression. After living in Nashville six years, Carver leaves, with his family, in a profound rage.

Phillip is able to impress us with the trauma of that removal. To go from Nashville to Memphis is to move from the upper South to the deep South (as always, Taylor's regional discriminations are very finely tuned), and there is a corresponding displacement of manners and social milieu. The displacement especially upsets Phillip's marriageable sisters, on the verge of their entry into Nashville society. Although he has dragged his unwilling family to Memphis, George Carver is one of the first to criticize what he finds there. His daughters' new suitors "seemed countrier to him—more Mississippian it was, of course." As Phillip explains, the roughly two hundred twenty miles between Nashville and Memphis were long ones. In Nashville, one was "two hundred twenty miles nearer to Richmond, to Charleston, to Savannah." These two hundred and twenty miles have in recent years become Peter Taylor's Yoknapatawpha. His stories of Nashville and Memphis, and the small towns like Thornton near them, seen during the period between the wars, have formed a memorable and compelling portrait of a region and time. Taylor's territory is southern, but it is a region aware of its tenuous hold on that southern identity, and ambivalent about clinging to it. Small town origins are often visible in the background of his urban or suburban settings, but there is a similar ambivalence about that past as well. He portrays a time and region bristling with social gradations based on a socioeconomic structure that, while never very stable, was undergoing even more rapid change. It is, as Taylor has been able to convince us, compelling territory for fiction because its social complexities have pronounced psychological costs. Thus the Carvers make, for the reader of Taylor, a move across significant country, and their sense of displacement is important. The move eventuates, one is led to believe, in Phillip's mother's invalidism and the spinsterhood of his two sisters. It also rearranges the crucial relationship between the children and their father, making a patriarch into something of a tyrant.

The clearest evidence of such tyranny is that George Carver manages later to sabotage Phillip's intended marriage to Clara Price, a woman whom he adores. As Phillip tells it, after their first sexual encounter, "we were truly lovers and imagined ourselves bound to each other for life." Phillip remembers his six-month affair with her as "a grand and glorious reality that I came upon out of the drabness of my life both before and afterward." No good reason for his father's opposition to the marriage is ever given, and we can surmise none other than a stubborn refusal to let his family go. He had similarly destroyed the engagement of one of Phillip's sisters, and Phillip also sees this pattern of willful possession in his father's decision to move the family to Memphis after his break with Shackleford.

Things have a biblical way of repeating themselves among Taylor's fictional generations, but Phillip Carver's opportunity to repeat the sin of his father comes quickly. After the death of his mother, Phillip begins to receive reports from his sisters concerning his elderly father's nightlife and courtship of a number of women. Presented to him humorously at first, the adventures eventually cause alarm in Phillip's sisters when things begin to get serious—that is, when the possibility of his father's remarriage surfaces. Phillip finds it difficult to take the reports to heart and is inclined not to interfere, but his sisters make it difficult for him to shirk family duty, and he answers their summons. But he returns to Memphis very undecided about how to carry out his role. Will he prevent the marriage and become his father's keeper, reversing their lifelong relationship?

Phillip's indecisiveness in this, as in many things, is characteristic. He is caught between the pressure of his sisters and what he knows will be his father's iron will. But his decision is made for him when he sees his father waiting on the landing strip at Memphis to meet his flight from New York. Phillip's description of his emotions when he first sees his father contains the psychological core of the book. After he first discovers, with surprise, that his father is waiting for him ("He was a man who never ran any such domestic errands"), the full force of his own situation strikes him. He has been asked to defy this man, when he has never been able to do more than attempt to escape him. His original move to New York had been arranged by his sisters so that Phillip could entirely avoid any direct confrontation with his father. Nor had they confronted each other directly about his love affair with Clara Price. This lifetime of avoidance rushes into Phillip's consciousness as he sees his waiting father. The details of his father's immaculate dress remind Phillip of his father's mastery of the world and capability of control, and the clothes themselves trigger Phillip's memory of the wardrobe closets that his father moved to Memphis. Their heavy identity with his father's ability to possess symbolizes Phillip's growing feeling of psychological enclosure. As he approaches his waiting father, "it was as though someone had thrown open the double doors to one of those wardrobes of his, and, figuratively speaking, I was inhaling the familiar aroma of his whole life and being. Only it wasn't like an aroma exactly. For one moment it seemed I was about to be suffocated." It is as if his entire adult life has been erased, "as if I had never left Memphis."

But this fear, even revulsion, should not be misunderstood. It is part of a complex of emotions in Phillip which seems to invert itself as quickly as he understands and communicates it. Phillip discovers that his father has come to take him to serve as best man at his wedding. His father's warm greeting, his absolute assurance that Phillip would gladly so serve, the way "he smiled at me and pressed my hand made him seem irresistible." Phillip is indeed a child again, but now a happy one, his father's son. Suffocation has mysteriously slipped over into belonging. Few recent writers have been able to equal Welty and Taylor in their portrayal of the passionate problematics of the relations between parents and children. Phillip demonstrates for us Welty's dictum "that all the opposites on earth were close together, love close to hate." But though we see it through Phillip, how far does he understand this of himself? Our judgment of Phillip ultimately rests on our sense of the degree of his self-comprehension. On this point, Taylor is masterfully ambiguous.

George Carver's planned remarriage does not, in fact, occur. Phillip's sisters have interfered sufficiently in the situation to assure that. But Phillip learns that in this instance, at least, he either lacked the will to defy his father or found the compassion to accept his father's choice. A far more ambiguous decision, or lack of one, marks a later return to Memphis, when his father has, to the chagrin of his children, decided to renew his friendship with Lewis Shackleford. Again, Phillip is asked by his sisters to prevent his father from leaving to pay an extended visit to Shackleford. In this case, Phillip goes further to fulfill their wish, although his motive is open to question. The circumstance of Shackleford's death intervenes to spare Phillip from a final decision about blocking his father's plans, and the issue of his assuming final control over his father is left unresolved. This stands as one of the more important, and also more difficult, moments of the novel to assess. We are left to wonder, finally, whether spite has not become a dominant motivating force among all George Carver's children.

In both of these decisions, Taylor depicts for us a character in the painful process of growth, a man whose own self-possession is vitally connected to his relationship with his father. At one point in the novel, Phillip refers to his sisters as "perpetually injured adolescents." There is some evidence to back that observation, but much more to suggest that it applies to Phillip himself. He struggles to understand this about himself, and to address it in his life, and we are impressed with the range of feeling and the discrimination of mood and motive that he brings us. That is one of the great joys of Taylor's writing. But we also see that despite his progress toward self-possession and maturity, he continues to lack something vital. At the novel's end he refers to Holly Kaplan (he seldom calls her Holly) and himself as "two . . . serenely free spirits." The reader must take this ironically, but whether the irony is intended by Phillip is a vexing question. We suspect that he is not "serenely free" because he never accepted his Memphis fate, his fate as a son, his past. When he described his long dialogues with Holly Kaplan, Phillip told us that two competing theories of the past emerged there, theories which help explain his own predicament. She came to feel that one must accept the past, as embodied in one's parents, with forgiveness. He argued instead that one must simply forget the past—act as if it never happened. That insistence on trying to forget the inescapable past is Phillip's most salient characteristic, and his most grievous flaw. The novel is a long testimony to our absolute inability to forget, and Phillip Carver, far from serenely free, is the chief rememberer.

The Family Game Was Revenge
[Review of *A Summons to Memphis*]

MARILYNNE ROBINSON

Peter Taylor is a novelist and short-story writer who for almost half a century has produced fictions about a distinctive world of Southern inland cities, and about a characteristic stratum of society whose members are both provincial and urbane, descended from plantation-owning stock but very comfortably ensconced in the finest neighborhoods of Nashville and Memphis. They marry their own kind and honor the leisurely rituals of their caste, careful stewards of their own good fortune. These are not the tormented souls we are accustomed to finding in literature of the South. The motive force in most of these lives is complacency, the genial expectation that the young will succeed to the quiet privileges that their parents, in enjoying them, have preserved.

Let us call this Peter Taylor's donnée. His work is compared with the fiction of Henry James, and the comparison has value, even though, in terms of style, the two writers are very different indeed. Both are conscious of having as their subject what is called manners, small fields of nuanced and estheticized behavior that, as Flannery O'Connor observed, should never be thought of apart from mystery. Henry James as American in England, Peter Taylor as Southerner in America, write about societies whose bounds and particularities they are intensely aware of, and whose manners they can see as an interplay of stylized gestures, spontaneous or inevitable as they may seem to those who enact them. James, like a Whitman scanning an especially elegant stream of the human throng for glimpses of transcendency, taking esthetics as a holy mystery and a most mannered class as a sort of priestly caste, described a world for whose meaning he imagined no limit, however narrow a world it might be. Thoreau did not bring loftier expectations to his bean patch.

Peter Taylor approaches the mystery of manners another way. He reminds us that people, like spiders, impose geometries on thin air, which are fragile but will be replicated, which are ingenious and also involuntary; that given an angle, we will colonize void and disorder, putting a tiny Euclidean

From the *New York Times Book Review*, 19 October 1986, 1, 52–53. Reprinted by permission of Marilynne Robinson. © 1986 by Marilynne Robinson.

patch on exploding reality. The sense of limit in Mr. Taylor's work alludes to the littleness and frailty and also the resilience and inevitability of the webs we deploy to make experience habitable. While James finds his limited world inexhaustible, Peter Taylor finds the limitedness of his world inexhaustibly suggestive.

Mr. Taylor's gentry behave well at the rate and to the degree that convention is a worthy guide to the conduct of life. They are seldom distinguished for good or evil. Their "manners" are the terms in which their lives are understood, terms that, in Mr. Taylor's world, differ bewilderingly even as between Memphis and Nashville. In his beautifully ironic new novel, *A Summons to Memphis*—his only previous novel, *A Woman of Means*, appeared 36 years ago—he describes, with scarcely a smile, how a family is destroyed by a betrayal, rarely mentioned even among themselves, that took place more than 40 years before. Phillip Carver, the 49-year-old son of the family, is called back to Memphis by his two older sisters to prevent their widowed father from remarrying. In narrating the story of his return, he recalls how the treachery of their father's business partner caused the family to remove from Nashville and a life blessed with meaning to Memphis and gathering despair. The change is only the more insidious for being almost undetectable.

It is usual to say that a Southern writer is chronicling the passing of a society doomed and overwhelmed. Such statements sidestep the vexed question of the relationship of any fiction to any reality. They seem particularly misleading in the case of Peter Taylor, for on the one hand his stories do not really present themselves as the social anatomy of Tennessee, and on the other hand one recognizes in them an authentic old regime, less regional than provincial, whose decline is neither greatly to be regretted nor likely to happen soon. In describing the disruptions and erosions that beset it, Mr. Taylor is innocent of a common error. He knows it is *because* these social structures are unstable that they will not change. His stories and novels are variations on a theme. He returns again and again to one question: what is stasis? And how is it achieved?

He does not make the odd though familiar assumption that the stability of a society is any proof of its goodness, nor is he interested in reviling people who, despite houseboys and fox hunts, are dead ordinary. It is rather as though he wishes to describe the pressures that toughen structure, as gravity thickens bone. Imagine a sort of adversary, to borrow a word from Job—a pressure, ubiquitous and protean, that has made every creature the fossil of a harrowing history, the porcupine a war machine, the skunk an avenger, the turtle a walking state of siege. In *A Summons to Memphis*, as in all Peter Taylor's fiction, stasis is defended, not voluntarily or even consciously, by means honorable or pernicious as the circumstance requires, not because it is goodness or value or virtue but because it is stasis—as it would not be if it had not found strategies of persistence in this Heraclitean world. Subversion and erosion take dozens of forms, every one of them more or less like fishing moonlight from the sea in a net, or stifling it in a cloud, or drowning it in a flood.

Among the satisfying ironies in Mr. Taylor's work is a sort of patterning or recurrence of the threat of betrayal that makes of disruption and continuity in one thing. In *A Summons to Memphis* the three middle-aged children betray their old father in a way we are told to consider characteristic of Memphis. The novel demonstrates the gradual naturalization of the Nashville family to the norms of a less humane civilization, one, interestingly enough, more dominated by landowning. These wealthy and childless heirs to an old man's fortune, when they learn that he plans to marry, resort almost reflexively to cruelty and coercion to prevent him. The very familiarity of the tale of the mistreatment of an old parent is a great part of the point—none of us would do such a thing, and yet such things get done, and so commonly that when Shakespeare wrote *King Lear* he thought best to begin it in the manner of a folk tale, the story being as plain and ancient as its historical provenance.

Speaking of their father's business partner, the narrator of *A Summons to Memphis* says: "I cannot resist this opportunity to point out how the evil which men like Lewis Shackleford do, men who have come to power either through the use of military force or through preaching the Word of God or through the manipulation of municipal bonds, as was Mr. Shackleford's case, how the evil they do . . . has its effect . . . at last upon myriads of persons in all the millennia to come." This comparing of great things with small is amused, yet the novel proposes a complex reading of the world in which almost impalpable forces work as imperviously as fate, making whole cloth of what is done and what is suffered.

The father, in making his dignified retreat from Nashville, the scene of his betrayal, shocks his family profoundly. His wife takes to her bed and his children remain unmarried, the two daughters still dressing like girls in corpulent middle age, a sort of taunting allusion to the time when the rituals that would have supported their passage through life were disrupted. The shock of their father's being betrayed is transmitted as his betrayal of them. The narrator, too, who has long since moved to Manhattan and established a life there with a Jewish woman from Cleveland, attempting to naturalize himself to the part of the world that is not Tennessee, blames his father for disrupting his only chance at marriage, when he was a young man. So the family is frozen in one moment, the offspring oxymoronically "middle-aged children" far too engrossed with their father. A recoil is built into the situation. The children do as they feel they have been done by. They betray.

In *A Summons to Memphis*, as in tragedy—I take the title to invite such comparisons—what these people do for reasons that are personal and unique to them, and wholly sufficient to account for their actions, coincides neatly with larger patterns that exist outside them. Oedipus went to Thebes imagining himself a stranger. These people have considered themselves strangers in Memphis. Yet, as the narrator makes clear from the beginning, anticipating events as precisely as any oracle, they re-enact a situation he sees as "some kind of symbol . . . of Memphis"—in the typical pattern he observes in that city, "a rich old widower" is "denounced and persecuted by his own middle-aged children" when he decides to remarry. While the energy of malice in the Carver children comes from their being obliged to move to this alien place, its last expression takes a form that makes it clear they are assimilated to Memphis altogether.

The children are not villains or connivers. They are the beneficiaries of the fact that their pettiness has so many precedents as almost to perform itself. Their actions, if they are thought of as freely chosen, are abetted by the recurrence around them of like actions, which make them seem determined. So two apparently contrary models of human motivation are not only affirmed at the same time but shown to be mutually reinforcing. That is a neat piece of work. While the narrator declares people of his sort now to have only an attenuated existence, their past and milieu hold them so powerfully that if attenuation exists at all among them its only effect is to make them, paradoxically, less resistant to such influences—just as, having lost Nashville, the family falls completely under the sway of Memphis. Behavior, like matter, will have one form or another.

A mistral blows through Peter Taylor's world. Although it is manifested often in betrayal of friend by friend, father by son, son by father, most vulnerable of all are the blacks. In many of his stories, they are drawn into near-familial relationships, and then at the same time subject to being scolded or dismissed at any time, at any age, embarrassed for any imagined offense. They have made, as a magnanimous response to intractable necessity, lives for themselves out of interest in the lives of uningratiating people and affection for children not their own, but have enlisted nothing of the duty or loyalty or identification that sometimes shelters the feelings of family. These stories are very painful to read, as they should be. The problems of race in Mr. Taylor's writing are not historical or political so much as they are the extreme expression of the strange energy loose in his world, an injuriousness like Poe's gratuitously destructive "perverse."

Black characters are not prominent in *A Summons to Memphis*. All of them are servants, they move over the same terrain as the Carver family, standing by the road during the departure from Nashville to gaze wistfully in the direction of the small country town they and the Carvers have come from. To one who has read Mr. Taylor's stories, the presence of the black characters in this novel is a reminder of the potent shocks that can run along the lines of loyalty and family.

Southern writing often seems to me cloyed with the fusty apologetics of 19th-century reaction, to be indebted a little too deeply to Walter Scott and such inventors of the mystique of past and place, the moral opiate inevitably in demand while Scots were being routed from their lands and driven into wretched industrial cities and death from famine and cholera, and while blacks were being carried from their own lands and put to the uses of an industrialized agriculture, treated as articles of commerce, with no acknowledgment of their ties to any place or community or family. This subordination of human beings to sheep on one side of the Atlantic and to cotton on the other is smuggled into our consciousness disguised as an old order, and the noble depopulators and the aristocratic slaveholders as the few, fading survivors of a more human world. History holds few examples of such chutzpah.

Even the best Southern writing nevertheless subscribes too willingly to the idea that there is a past that some people have and others lack, and that this past is dignifying and full of a sort of plenary grace upon which the present can still draw. So intimate was the connection between the American South and 19th-century industrialism that during the Civil War cotton workers in Manchester, England, died in the streets. The past is an industrial byproduct.

All this is by way of giving emphasis to my admiration for Peter Taylor's perfect indifference to the blandishments of this tradition, an indifference more remarkable because he sets his stories in wide temporal expanses and gives great play to social and generational influences. The present resonates with the past, but history is not a sort of monosodium glutamate, an instant, all-purpose intensifier of experience.

Peter Taylor's fiction is full of rewards. It is hard for a reviewer to do justice to the pleasures of understatement. Mr. Taylor's tact in preserving narrative surface, allowing fictional "meaning" to remain immersed in its element and preventing the degeneration of question into statement, leaves him open to being seen as another interpreter of an important tradition, when in fact he is as sui generis as middle Tennessee.

A *Summons to Memphis* is not so much a tale of human weakness as of the power of larger patterns, human also, that engulf individual character, a current subsumed in a tide. The moral earnestness of contemporary thought, the eagerness to praise and condemn, almost forbids the utterance of an important fact, which is that most of the time we really do not know just what we are doing or why, or what appearances our actions would have if we could see them from a little distance. I think the real accomplishment of Peter Taylor may be to have conjured the great slow shapes of epic and tragedy, so they can be glimpsed in the little segment of an ordinary life, restoring to our myths their most unsettling implications.

Back to the Future
[Review of *A Summons to Memphis*]

ANN HULBERT

Peter Taylor is routinely and rightly praised for the glasslike lucidity of his prose, yet he is interested above all in distortions of perspective. For more than 40 years, he has written about well-born families in the upper South who have lost much of their assurance about what to look up to and whom to look down on. His Tennessee, as Robert Penn Warren wrote in 1948 in his introduction to Taylor's first collection of stories, *A Long Fourth*, "is a world vastly uncertain of itself and the ground of its values, caught in a tangle of modern commercialism and traditions and conventions gone to seed, confused among pieties and pretensions." That world was still a contemporary one then. It no longer is—the old rules of order between the generations, the sexes, and the races are history. Yet they are important history, and Taylor has continued to scrutinize the place and epoch of their passing in fiction that seems old-fashioned—at least on the surface.

Taylor's new novel (his second, if you count the short *A Woman of Means*) looks like another contribution to that absorbing enterprise. In a sense it is. *A Summons to Memphis* is largely a gathering of Phillip Carver's memories of growing up happily in Nashville and then unhappily in Memphis in the 1930s and '40s. But Phillip's "very irregular notebooks," which he writes in New York miles and years away from his family past, are also an occasion for Taylor to explore an even more uncertain world than that densely textured South. Scribbling in a gloomy Manhattan apartment in the 1970s, Phillip is suffering from a very contemporary anomie. With his deracinated narrator, Taylor has brought to the surface the psychological theme that has always been at the heart of his social portraiture: how resilient, or else resistant, human character can be in the face of disorder and change.

It is a familiar Southern preoccupation, but Taylor's "under-style," as Warren termed it, and his quiet emphasis on the mysteries of character (he's often compared to Chekhov) set him apart from the gothic regionalism of much Southern writing. He is neither pious about the past nor much impressed by the present, and his ruminations about human motives and actions

From the *New Republic*, 24 November 1985, 37–40. © 1985, The New Republic, Inc. Reprinted by permission.

have always had a deliberately inconclusive quality. Above all, they have never been simple. Certainly they aren't in *A Summons to Memphis*, which might best be described as a dramatic monologue—a virtuosic example of the often disconcerting genre. Taylor lets Phillip do all the talking, but that doesn't mean he trusts Phillip's account of self-discovery or intends us to. Phillip may well rate as Taylor's least reliable narrator, and this book demands—and rewards—vigilance. Phillip's reckoning with his own history, Taylor ironically implies throughout his character's monologue, is hollower than it appears. This dispassionate narrator is strangely bloodless, and in the end he has lost his bearings.

A Summons to Memphis has the outline of a familiar Taylor story: a man is unexpectedly jolted into a confrontation with an oppressive, puzzling past and then has a brief revelation—Taylor's characteristically inconclusive kind of epiphany. A reclusive New York editor and rare-book collector of middle age, Phillip Carver receives calls one evening from his older spinster sisters in Memphis, who announce that their aging father, recently widowed, plans to remarry, and that they want Phillip to help them stop him. Phillip is prompted to dip back into his past to explain the family resentments that motivate Betsy and Josephine and to examine his own feelings. He unearths memories of a father who was shamefully domineering but also admirably adaptable in a way Phillip himself will never be, and he manages to forgive him. While his sisters sabotage the remarriage (and also their father's reconciliation with the best friend who once betrayed him), Phillip stands aside.

Yet the way Phillip tells the story lends support to an implicit, and considerably darker, version. The prose is as limpid as ever ("like a glass-bottom boat," said Randall Jarrell), but Phillip's method is digressive in the extreme: he veers unpredictably between past and present, circles around obviously important memories, repeats himself again and again. His long-winded, hairsplitting manner results in some quite comical passages—to Taylor's obvious delight. But Phillip's own detachment is strangely awkward, not witty. Despite all the minute observations he offers, he is emotionally impassive as he pauses to describe the woman with whom he has lived for years or his best friend from Memphis days, or surveys his family—or assesses himself: "I think I felt totally indifferent," says this man from whom sentiments flee. Each page seems to hold out the promise that Phillip is about to frame a memory in a way that might free him from his aloofness. Yet the happy ending that Taylor stages in the last, frigidly lyrical paragraph of these notebooks is heavily ironic—as his apparently comic conclusions so often are. This narrator is numbly suspended between the past and the future, between the power to will and the power to feel.

Throughout Phillip's monologue, Taylor nudges us toward this deeper reading: here is a man whose ostensible resilience is finally only a sign of abiding passivity. For such an evasive soul, Taylor suggests, a confrontation with his family past can do little to instill, or strengthen, a sense of generous self-possession. Instead it becomes an occasion to avoid responsibility for having become the remote person he is. The convoluted tour Phillip makes of his youthful ordeals reveals a vulnerable man bent on blaming others for his own self-centered vulnerability. He starts out by claiming that the source of his sisters' (and his own) resentment against their father lies in the move George Carver forced on the family some 40 years earlier, in 1931. Betrayed in Nashville by his best friend and principal legal client, Lewis Shackleford, George Carver picked up and established a new and successful career in the more commercial, less custom-bound city of Memphis. But for his wife and children, according to Phillip, the uprooting was a disaster George selfishly ignored. Phillip's mother lapsed into "thirty years of real or imagined invalidism," his sisters started down the road of brittle spinsterhood, and 13-year-old Phillip suffered "a trauma he would in some way never recover from."

Phillip himself half-admits that it sounds preposterous to assign such importance to the shift between the two cities, "with their almost imperceptible difference—laughably alike they would seem to an outsider." What he doesn't seem fully to appreciate is that he has undermined his own credibility, which casts his succeeding accusations in a more questionable light. Is this narrator either the former helpless victim or the current clear-eyed judge he makes himself out to be? The actual disaster, he eventually claims, was that the imperious George Carver meddled in his children's romantic lives, denying them independence when they needed it most. He openly rejected Betsy's suitor and Josephine's beaux, and the once beautiful girls turned into eccentric characters. With Phillip he was sneakier but no less assertive: behind his son's back George Carver saw to it that Phillip's sweetheart was dispatched to South America. Phillip in turn secretly absconded to New York, where he claims he's been enjoying placid independence ever since with a woman whose greatest virtue is apparently her detachment.

Phillip has sketched a grim caricature of the provincial past that often looms in Taylor's stories. The changing local Tennessee customs that unbalance so many of his characters seem to have disoriented Phillip in a radical—almost surreal—way. For him, the familiar overbearing power of family traditions and expectations has turned tyrannical. Not that he's presented it so starkly. Shifting constantly among scenes and times, Phillip makes a show of groping for a clearer perspective on a past he's brooded over but never before brought to the surface—yet he's more successful in raising further questions about his own failures to act and react.

Toward the end of his notebooks, Phillip is given what appears to be the reprieve Taylor sometimes offers his protagonists: the chance to put his past, if only provisionally, in more realistic proportion. Yet Taylor implies that Phillip may be as misled about his mature liberation as he was about his youthful enslavement. His supposed act of imaginative sympathy with forceful George Carver serves in the end as another way for Phillip to assuage his uneasiness about his own wan existence—to convince himself that from now on he is choosing it freely. Taylor grants him a few moments of empathy: there is a vivid scene in which Phillip is swept up and out of himself by the old man as the two ride in a car to the wedding his sisters have secretly canceled.

But by the close of the book, Phillip has drifted into dry speculations instead. Sitting in his Manhattan apartment with Holly Kaplan, the woman with whom he's lived peacefully and passionlessly for years, he sips a watery drink and talks endlessly about principles of family reconciliation—about forgiving versus forgetting—rather than about real people. He says he can now see and admire his father as an energetically adaptable man, completely different from himself: "It was his very oppositeness from me that I could admire without reservation, like a character in a book." Contemplating an unchanged, utterly quiet life ahead, he announces in his last line that he and Holly have emerged "serenely free spirits."

Yet "serenity" and "orderliness" and "reasonableness," the supreme values in Phillip's limited existence, are hardly Taylor's high standards. Conceiving of the past as the realm of determinism, Phillip seizes upon the future as the province of choice—and is left with no true human choices to make. The static, unencumbered fate that Phillip and his companion look forward to with self-satisfaction is sterile—a vision of the weightless contemporary world eerier than any Taylor has presented before. Shut up in his dim apartment with Holly, surrounded by manuscripts rather than children, Phillip may see his notebooks as evidence of the birth of understanding, but in fact they are the testimony of a disoriented soul.

"Peter Taylor has a disenchanted mind," Robert Penn Warren wrote 40 years ago, "but a mind that nevertheless understands and values enchantment"—"the enchantment of veracity," he hastened to say, not of fantasy. The trauma of maturity, Taylor's fiction has always proposed, involves more than seeing through the oppressive pieties and pretensions of the past. But he has rarely so starkly dramatized the real, and more daunting, challenge: to find some humane way of living with precisely the terrifying truth that those family and social customs are meant to camouflage—the chasms between selves. Some of his characters are lucky enough to "see the world through another man's eyes," as the narrator of the story "The Promise of Rain" puts it, and thus have a chance of truly seeing into their own heads, and above all their own hearts: "It is only then that the world, as you have seen it through your own eyes, will begin to tell you things about yourself."

For the less fortunate in Taylor's fiction, the price of myopia is high. Some turn into tyrants at home. Some become victims out in the world. In *A Summons to Memphis* Taylor has suggested an even more alienating possibility in Phillip, who has no real home and rarely ventures into the world: the danger of turning into a "free spirit" trapped within the bounds of the self.

ESSAYS

♦

Introduction to
A Long Fourth and Other Stories

ROBERT PENN WARREN

In 1936 Allen Tate sent two stories by a boy in Memphis, Tennessee, to the office of *The Southern Review*. They were obviously the work of a very gifted young writer who had a flavor and a way of his own. The editors of *The Southern Review* recognized those virtues, but decided to wait for the next showing by Peter Taylor. He was very young, just starting college, and there seemed to be plenty of time. There was not enough time, however, to allow *The Southern Review* the privilege of introducing Peter Taylor's work to print. The next year at least one of the editors felt ruefully compelled, when he saw the stories in the little magazine *River*, to admit that he had made a mistake. But the young writer allowed the editors of *The Southern Review* to redeem themselves. Three of the stories in the present collection did appear in that magazine—"A Spinster's Tale," "Sky Line," and "The Fancy Woman." They are the earliest of the pieces here presented, having been written in 1938, 1939, and 1940.

Peter Taylor was born in Trenton, Tennessee, into a big Southern political family, or rather into two of them, for his mother's family was as political-minded as his father's. He grew up in an atmosphere of arguments about politics and reminiscences of old campaigns. When a very young man, an uncle had run up the steps of the Capitol at Nashville to tell Governor Andrew Johnson that he had been elected Vice President, but fainted the moment he got into the Governor's presence. The same uncle, Alf Taylor, had campaigned against his brother for Governor in the famous race of 1886, and had run again in 1922.

Peter Taylor was raised in a country town and in Southern cities like Nashville, St. Louis, and Memphis. He went to college at Vanderbilt University and at Kenyon College, where he had followed Professor John Crowe Ransom and where he was an academic contemporary and friend of the poets Randall Jarrell and Robert Lowell. After Kenyon he went to Louisiana State University for graduate work, but he quickly decided that that was not for

From *A Long Fourth and Other Stories* by Peter Taylor (New York: Harcourt, Brace and Company, 1948). Introduction by Robert Penn Warren, vii–x, copyright 1948 by Harcourt Brace Jovanovich, Inc. and renewed 1976 by Robert Penn Warren, reprinted by permission of the publisher.

him. He dropped his courses and spent the year reading and writing fiction.
He was a fiction writer and he knew it. Then the war came and four years
in the Army, with a period overseas. Stories had to wait.

Neither the experiences of the war nor the tales of politics have provided
the material for Peter Taylor's stories. Nor does the small-town and rural
life of Trenton appear in them. But those things are important as background
for the stories. The war does provide the remote occasion for "Allegiance"
and "Rain in the Heart," and sets them in a certain perspective of feeling.
The atmosphere of family tale-telling, the echo of the spoken word, modifies
both the temper and style of stories like "The Scoutmaster" and "A Long
Fourth." And in the last two stories, as in "The Fancy Woman," there is
the hint of the rural life lying not far away in space or time from the life of
the Southern city. It is an element that still colors the manners and attitudes
of cities like Nashville and Memphis even if those cities have forgotten the
fact.

Peter Taylor's stories are officially about the contemporary, urban, middle-class world of the upper South, and he is the only writer who has taken
this as his province. This world which he delineates so precisely provides a
special set of tensions and complications. For instance, the old-fashioned
structure of family life still persists, disintegrating slowly under the pressures
of modernity. Six of the stories in this volume—all except "Rain in the
Heart"—are stories involving families, and all six are pictures of the disintegration of families. Lost simplicities and loyalties, the role of woman, the
place of the Negro—these are topics which properly appear in the drama of
this urban world. It is a world vastly uncertain of itself and the ground of
its values, caught in a tangle of modern commercialism and traditions and
conventions gone to seed, confused among pieties and pretensions. "The
Scoutmaster," "The Fancy Woman," "A Spinster's Tale," and especially "A
Long Fourth" are rich fables of this situation.

So much for the material of these stories. But what of the level at which
the storyteller takes the material and the cast of mind with which he views
it? We have here not two questions, but one, for the cast of mind determines
the level of interest. If Peter Taylor is concerned with the attrition of old
loyalties, the breakdown of old patterns, and the collapse of old values, he
regards the process without too much distress to his personal piety. The
world he is treating, with its mixture of confusion and pretension, would
appeal readily to a satiric eye. The older world from which it sprang more
nearly knew, for better or worse, what it wanted, and was willing to pay the
price; it was not confused in the same way, and if it had pretensions they
were pretensions based on its own efforts and not on the true or false memory
of the achievements of others. Because it was a human world it was subject
to satire, but satire could scarcely strike it in its vitals. It could be damned
more easily than it could be satirized. The new world invites satire, and

there is often a satiric component in Peter Taylor's treatment of it. In the whole effect, however, he stops somewhere short of satire. Rather, he presents an irony blended of comedy and sympathetic understanding. Uncle Jake of "The Scoutmaster" and Harriet of "A Long Fourth" are comic creations, but comedy does not exhaust them. We find an awareness of character beyond what explicitly appears. Peter Taylor has a disenchanted mind, but a mind that nevertheless understands and values enchantment. The family affections and loyalties are real, and the memories compelling. It is sad that they cannot exist without being entangled with shoddiness, stupidity, and even cruelty.

The skeptical, ironic cast of mind prompts a peculiar respect for the material it treats. Such a mind hesitates to impose itself on the material and to organize a story like a theorem. It can be satisfied only with a deeper strategy than is common, a strategy that will lure the reader on to his confusion. The reader who can accept the challenge of such a writer may pass through confusion to revelation. He will have reached the revelation, however, with a fuller sense of the complexities of things and of the shadowy, unsaid, unreconciled meanings that must haunt every story worth writing or reading. For such a writer, or reader, fiction is experience, not a footnote. And Peter Taylor's stories are not footnotes.

This skeptical, ironic mind finds its appropriate level in the smaller collisions and crises of life. Only one story, "The Fancy Woman," deals with violence, and even here the violent situation is refracted through the woman. In the end, it is the movement and temper of her being, and the ambivalence that this gives the story, that engage our interest. And in "Sky Line" and "Rain in the Heart," which lack the positive ironies of the other stories, we find the characteristic qualities of poised reserve. Perhaps the level at which Peter Taylor takes his drama accounts for the fact that his most successful and fully rendered characters are women—the fancy woman, the spinster, and Harriet of "A Long Fourth." The small observation, the casual word, the prized sentiment give the stuff that he works with and makes significant. The things that the menfolks live by are here too, but these things are, by and large, brought down to the scale of the household.

The style of these stories is one appropriate to the level of interest. With the exception of "Allegiance" it is a natural style, one based on conversation and the family tale, with the echo of the spoken word, with the texture of some narrator's mind. The narrator may be identified, as in "The Spinster's Tale," or he may have no formal existence, as in "The Fancy Woman" or "Rain in the Heart." But even in the last two stories we are fully aware of how Josie or the soldier would have told the story. This is what often makes the style of these stories seem neutral. The style is secreted from the inwardness of the material and is an extension of the material. It has no substance of its own and offers nothing to come between us and the story. This is not to say that such a style is the end of virtue, that there is no place for the style that dominates and, as it were, interprets the material. It is to say, simply, that such an "under-style" can have a virtue of its own and that the virtue here is organic and right.

The stories of *A Long Fourth* are by a very young man. To recur to this fact is not to apologize for the performance here. Instead, it is to congratulate ourselves that we can look forward to many more stories from Peter Taylor. In the fullness of time he will write many more stories, stories probably deeper, fuller, richer, and wiser than these. But it is not probable that those unwritten stories will be any truer than these. I have said that Peter Taylor has a disenchanted mind. In terms of his very disenchantment, however, he has succumbed to the last and most fatal enchantment: the enchantment of veracity. And that is what, in the end, makes the artist free.

The Early Fiction of Peter Taylor

Ashley Brown

Mr. Taylor has been publishing stories for twenty-five years now—his first two appeared in the little magazine *River* in 1937—and one is surprised that he is still sometimes referred to, despite his comparative youth, as a "young writer." In fact he was unusually gifted and assured even as an apprentice, and when *A Long Fourth and Other Stories* was published in 1948 he was already a leading member of his literary generation. Following Miss Welty's *A Curtain of Green* (1941) and J. F. Powers' *The Prince of Darkness and Other Stories* (1947), *A Long Fourth* was one of the best collections of short fiction which appeared during the forties. Meanwhile Mr. Taylor has quietly produced a small but impressive body of work which demands a critical presentation; he can no longer simply be put down as one of the young Southerners.

A Long Fourth was introduced by Robert Penn Warren, who described its subject as ". . . the contemporary, urban, middle-class world of the upper South. . . . It is a world vastly uncertain of itself and the ground of its values, caught in a tangle of modern commercialism and traditions and conventions gone to seed, confused among pieties and pretensions." Now Mr. Warren is correct but perhaps misleading about this. Is Mr. Taylor really picturing the urban middle-class South? Is he concerned primarily with the cultural milieu? Certainly many of the forms and manners of this society are "done" in the most precise detail even as they are dissolving; the future social historian will find a good source here. But Mr. Taylor is not directly interested (as writer) in the public institutions of church and state which have absorbed so much of the South's energy. He does not take us, for example, to the political rally or the adult Bible class. A Southerner is frequently reminded of these things. (In my state university a faculty group was recently informed by several of its members that Wednesday night is for prayer meetings and is therefore unsuitable for official university business.) Indeed one is struck by the lack of "public" life in Mr. Taylor's stories. Almost nobody goes to church or votes. Religion and politics are intended mainly for other people, like old Senator Caswell in the play *Tennessee Day in St. Louis*, who is considered quite absurd by the younger members of his

From the *Sewanee Review* 70 (Fall 1962): 588–602. © 1958, 1962, 1986, 1990 by the University of the South. Reprinted by permission of the editor.

family. (People *are* increasingly suspicious of politics: A friend of mine, who bears the name of one of the historic political families of the lower South, shocked his parents by successfully running for a minor office in New Haven, Connecticut.)

Yet Mr. Taylor is entirely true to a leading feature of Southern society. Mr. Warren pointed out that six of the seven stories in *A Long Fourth* involve the disintegration of family life. Here we arrive at the definition of Mr. Taylor's subject: it is precisely the family, its slow decline and its occasional survival, that he is concerned with. When he departs from this subject or works on its periphery, his fictional convention usually becomes reminiscence, as in "1939," which is a charming memoir of Kenyon College in its little golden age of a generation ago, but to what purpose? Mr. Lytle (in *The Sewanee Review*, 1958) has described the family in *Tennessee Day in St. Louis* as the archetypal institution of Southern society; and he might have followed Aristotle in describing it as the basic equilibrium of *any* society. It is Mr. Taylor's special achievement, then, to have presented his characters almost entirely within this one institutional setting. Even "Rain in the Heart" (which Mr. Warren stated is outside the general subject) is about the bride and groom—implicitly the family—precariously surviving the war and its attendant social disruption. Mr. Lytle of course means the family in the largest sense: a configuration of humanity in which the several generations with their "connections" are a microcosm of the community. (Mr. Lytle would say that the family *is* the community.) Now it may be that the family in this sense is reaching the point of its disappearance. A young playwright and politician, Gore Vidal, who is close to the First Family itself, emphatically stated so last year, and certainly many issues in our national life are based on this (largely unarticulated) premise. In that case I should think that Mr. Taylor's stories would document for us an important phase of our recent history, and not only the history of the South.

We are concerned, however, with Mr. Taylor as an artist. The first thing to say about his early stories is that they exhibit a wide range of style and attack. There is no one style that the reader can point to and identify as Mr. Taylor's. Back of his work one can sense here and there his reading of Chekhov, the Joyce of *Dubliners*, occasionally James, and perhaps Miss Porter. These modern masters have long been read in many quarters, and Mr. Taylor must have absorbed his "sources" even before he started writing. But *A Long Fourth and Other Stories* does have some of the thematic unity of *Dubliners*: childhood, youth, marriage, and maturity: these are the headings which Joyce once gave to his fifteen stories. Similarly the stories in *A Long Fourth* chart the life of the family from childhood to old age. Again—to extend the comparison—Joyce's "The Dead," the culmination of his book, gathers up many of the situations in the earlier stories and dramatizes them at another level. And that is precisely what Mr. Taylor's title story does at the end of *his* book. These seven stories, as the author has grouped them, move through a series of rhetorical shifts which accurately control the various narrative contexts, and this is where the comparison with Joyce is most valid.

As an example of the skill with which Mr. Taylor manages his resources at an early stage of his career, we may take "Sky Line," which dates from 1939. This is a story of loss, and it registers the deterioration of a family by way of a boy who lives in the vivid present and who would seem incapable of viewing his plight in any perspective outside his own. Mr. Taylor, that is, has deliberately scaled down the action to the sensory impressions which are so strongly felt by this adolescent, and, to intensify the case, he has rendered the story in the present tense. He has not even permitted himself the kind of free-association with which Faulkner brings together past and present as a continuum in the first three parts of *The Sound and the Fury*. What is the justification of this method? The boy lives in an anonymous suburb (outside Memphis perhaps?) where history does not make itself felt and where time is measured by the space that is gradually filled:

The new Catholic church is hardly finished in August when the new school building is started in the next block. The church is of yellow brick with a great round window above the main doorway. And for the new school the workmen are digging in the ground all through August. The lot they work in has always been covered with waist-high yellow grass, and every day the boy looks at the grass which the workmen have trampled down until it lies flat like the hair on a boy's head. He has never played in that lot with its high grass as he once used to do in the church lot, and has felt that it looked like "the central plains of Africa." But the workmen dig deep, and now the heaps of red dirt look like the "forbidding Caucasian mountains."

In this setting, during the Depression thirties, the boy Jim (whose family name is never stated) gropingly perceives the destruction of feeling and behavior. The very intensity of his perception, moment by moment, which at first seems to preclude any significance, in the end allows him to come to terms with his defeat. I suppose if Joyce or Faulkner were using this familiar situation, the boy would be "initiated" into his manhood through some ritualistic survival, but Mr. Taylor has excluded any appeal to history, and there is no one here who can properly direct the boy's instincts.

At the end of the story there is an ugly scene in which Jim, disillusioned with his father (who has finally married the mistress installed in his dead wife's place), is thwarted in an attempted sexual encounter with his new step-sister. (Jim, that is, wants to repeat his father's action.) The harsh images which invest the scene (the yellow "bilious" light, the "puffy" gray clouds, the girl's red cosmetics) prepare for her sarcastic laughter in "the room which once was his own." But this failure does not break him. For the first time his sensations converge into some kind of meaning, and the scene resolves as the storm erupts around them:

He doesn't know how long the laughter lasts. The rain falls outside the open window, and now and again a raindrop splashes through the screen onto his face. At last it is almost night when the rain stops, and if there is any unnatural hue in the light, it is green. His heart has stopped pounding now, and all the heat has gone from his face. He has heard the hanging baskets beat against the house and felt the silence after their removal. He has heard the baseball smacking in the wet gloves of the men and seen the furniture auctioned on the lawn. The end of his grandmother, the death of his mother, the despair of his father, and the resignation of his new step-mother are all in his mind. The remarkable thing in the changed view from the window which had once been his lies in the tall apartment houses which punctuate the horizon and in the boxlike, flat-roofed ones in his own neighborhood. Through this window the girl too, he knows, must have beheld changes. He takes his hand from the sill and massages his taut face on which the raindrops have dried.

When he faces her again, he says that they must prepare some sort of welcome, that they must get busy.

What I have tried to establish is that Mr. Taylor's method in this case has paid off handsomely. These characters *are* trapped in the present moment. The family must have come from somewhere and have some communal memories and inherited forms, but these things have dwindled away in this anonymous place. J. F. Powers in "Blue Island," a recent and more sardonic story of suburbia, has used a larger social reference than Mr. Taylor, but the effect of chaos is no more powerful.

Following "Sky Line" in *A Long Fourth* is "A Spinster's Tale," which was written even earlier. Here the dissolution of the family is more gradual and more subtle in its revelation. The narrator, Elizabeth, a motherless child, is misplaced in a masculine household. Her gentle father and her amiably drunken brother and her uncles cannot replace the balance lost by the death of her mother. The equilibrium of this family, where old-fashioned courtly manners still prevail (it is Nashville in the first decade of the century), is deceptive, simply because the masculine courtesy has no true challenge from the other sex, and Elizabeth, being young, is discouraged by this masculine indirection:

> It was, I thought, their indifferent shifting from topic to topic that most discouraged me. Then I decided that it was the tremendous gaps that there seemed to be between the subjects that was bewildering to me. Still again I thought that it was the equal interest which they displayed for each subject that was dismaying. All things in the world were equally at home in their arguments. They exhibited equal indifference to the horrors that each topic might suggest; and I wondered whether or not their imperturbability was a thing that they had achieved.

The "ladylike" style of this story is beautifully sustained by Mr. Taylor. In a way it is a period style, where echoes of the old finishing-school and its

Latinate education provide a kind of linguistic convention: "But I had learned not to concern myself with so general and so unreal a problem until I had cleared up more particular and real ones." The young lady in this story, that is, would appear to have a sensibility which is less perceptive than that of the boy in "Sky Line." But her prim response to events is nevertheless devastating in its results.

Through the center of the story moves Mr. Speed, a fallen gentleman of the community whose drunken pathos has long been tolerated with good humor by the men in Elizabeth's family, but who is a fearful affront to her. She is outside a closed circle in which the men, who live by a code of indirection, refuse to acknowledge the breakdown of civilized behavior which Mr. Speed represents. And of course there is no matriarch to provide the example of authority on the feminine side. Thus Mr. Speed becomes to Elizabeth the symbol of brutality and indifference which she finds in *all* men. The innocent social rituals of her father and uncles, from which she is excluded, are to her the source of depravity: "As their voices grew louder and merrier, my courage slackened. It was then I first put into words the thought that in my brother and father I saw something of Mr. Speed. And I knew it was more than a taste for whisky they had in common." At the climax of the story Mr. Speed, during a heavy rain, beats on the door and is admitted by the servant. Elizabeth, reacting to his helpless rage with an "innocent" violence of her own, calls the police and has him humiliated—something her father would never do. The final paragraph brings to a focus everything which has gone wrong; the even tone of the speaker (a willed rage to order, as it were) conveys the horror that lurks below:

> I never discussed the events of that day with my father, and I never saw Mr. Speed again. But, despite the surge of pity I felt for the old man on our porch that afternoon, my hatred and fear of what he had stood for in my eyes has never left me. And since the day that I watched myself say "away" in the mirror, not a week has passed but that he has been brought to my mind by one thing or another. It was only the other night that I dreamed I was a little girl on Church Street again and that there was a drunk horse in our yard.

In "The Fancy Woman" (1940) the violence is real and the social dissolution is far more advanced. Here we are almost in John O'Hara's world, where the family exists merely as a convenient arrangement for "the best people"; it is not an institution in the old sense at all. But the attachments between the members of the family, being the expression of self-love, are passionate and indeed excessive, since there is no longer the configuration of humanity to balance the affections. The action in this case turns on the vanity of a rich Memphis business man who, having separated from his wife, brings a prostitute to his house and forces her to be the respectable hostess to his guests and his adolescent sons; but things do not work out so easily. (The wife, who has now taken a lover of her own, sends the boys to their father.) The situation of "Sky Line" is compounded; the brutality of feeling is almost total. The author approaches the subject by having the prostitute, Josie Carlson, near the post of observation, and he thus complicates the focus of the story in an unexpected manner. This girl is from the countryside and she retains in her own way a crude natural perception and even a sense of propriety which are lacking in the "refined" guests in her lover's house. But eventually she is the victim of her feelings; she cannot force herself to leave her equivocal rôle; and she will be broken:

> She locked her door and threw the big key across the room. She knocked the bottle of toilet water and the amber brush off the dressing table as she made room for the victrola. When she had started "Louisville Lady" playing she sat on the stool and began to wonder. "The kid's head was like a ball of gold, but I'm not gonna think about him ever once I get back to Memphis," she told herself. "No, by damn, but I wonder just what George'll do to me." She broke the blue seal of the whisky with her fingernail, and it didn't seem like more than twenty minutes or half an hour before George was beating and kicking on the door, and she was sitting on the stool and listening and just waiting for him to break the door, and wondering what he'd do to her.

Mr. Taylor has quite successfully conveyed the "feel" of this suburban milieu and this calculating family as they appear to Josie Carlson; but he has not sentimentalized her, that is, given in to her point of view; the language is finally the author's. Her judgment of the family is a partial one at best; and, as Mr. Warren says, "In the end, it is the movement and temper of her being, and the ambivalence that this gives the story, that engage our interest."

These early stories all end in incidental violence, but it is not the violence of tragedy. There is no hero anywhere in sight, and suffering is private and ironic as the social situation dwindles behind the individuals who emerge in the foreground. In the case of "Sky Line" especially I have stated that history no longer operates effectively; the characters do not have the dignity of a myth, of an historic rôle, however imperfect, behind them. (My political friend in New Haven once said, "It's rather nice to have a social myth in the background, even if no one lives up to it.") Sometimes they try to summon up a feeling for the heroic. For instance the young soldier in "Rain in the Heart" reads Civil War history while he is in service in Tennessee (fairly obviously, Chattanooga) during World War II. The foreign battlefield he may fight on seems "distant and almost abstract," and he tries to find a meaning in this Southern landscape:

> The sergeant's eyes had now grown so accustomed to the darkness inside and outside that he could look down between the trees on the slope of the ridge.

He imagined there the line after line of Union soldiers that had once been thrown into the battle to take this ridge at all cost. The Confederate general's headquarters were not more than two blocks away. If he and she had been living in those days he would have seen ever so clearly the Cause for that fighting. And *this* battlefield would not be abstract. He would have stood here holding back the enemy from the very land which was his own, from the house in which she awaited him.

But like the protagonist in Mr. Tate's Ode, he must dismiss the heroic age as illusory. Some of these characters, however, live a kind of double existence; their memories of "the old times" (a very recurrent phrase) keep them from being altogether committed to the world around them. Mr. Taylor's later and more characteristic work, in fact, is essentially social comedy in which the incongruities of past and present offer an inexhaustible source of materials.

Such a work is "A Long Fourth," the culmination of Mr. Taylor's first book. In this story Harriet Wilson, the good Nashville matriarch, is faced with a series of crises within her family which even her sympathetic husband "Sweetheart" cannot solve. Naturally affectionate, she does not understand why her children should wish to be otherwise. Her daughters, who are very tall, do not attract many beaux, and Harriet reflects that "In her own day there had been more tall men, and tall women were then considered graceful." The daughters not only refuse to be conventional Southern belles; they are frequently coarse in their behavior. Son, the family's only heir, is likewise unconventional: a brilliant student at the university, he has gone to New York, where he is said to have "radical" ideas which get into the "disturbing" articles he is writing with such success. Now he is returning home for the long Fourth of July week end with his "friend" Miss Prewitt, who edits a birth-control magazine. The Wilsons, given this younger generation, would seem to have a dubious future. But Harriet is very proud of her son, and on the eve of his induction into the Army during World War II, she anticipates his home-coming with delight and apprehension. Mr. Taylor has a double-plot here. Harriet's beloved servant, Auntie Mattie, the Negro matriarch, has *her* troubles with her nephew BT, who is to Harriet a "sullen, stinking, thieving, fornicating" scoundrel; and like Son he is about to be inducted into the Service. When Auntie Mattie draws a comparison between Son's departure and BT's, Harriet is affronted and she withdraws in irrational anger:

. . . she felt it her bounden duty to in some way make that black woman feel the grossness of her wrong and ultimately to drive her off the premises. And it was in this vein, this very declamatory language, this elevated tone with which Harriet expressed herself in the solitude of her room. She was unconsciously trying to use the language and the rhetoric of her mother and of the only books with which she had ever had much acquaintance. Between the moments when she even pictured Mattie's being tied and flogged or thought

of Mama's uncle who shot all of his niggers before he would free them and of
the Negro governor of North Carolina and the Negro senate rolling whisky
barrels up the capitol steps, of the rape and uprisings in Memphis and the
riots in Chicago, between these thoughts she would actually consider the
virtue of her own wrath. And recalling her Greek classes at Miss Hood's school
she thought without a flicker of humor of Achilles' indignation.

Her rage subsides, however, and, as the week end proceeds, it is increasingly difficult for her to make her moral discriminations according to received
convention. Her ungainly daughters, for instance, present themselves in a
more attractive way in her moment of crisis. Miss Prewitt, the "terrible
woman of the future" (as Henry James would say), finally assumes the
traditional rôle of romantic passion which Harriet would covet for her daughters. Son, the perfect gentleman, becomes the cold, indifferent observer
of other people's weaknesses. And Mattie, out of her own confusions and
sentiments, forces Harriet to a strange humility which brings no rewards:

> Mattie raised her eyes to her mistress, and there was neither forgiveness nor
> resentment in them. In her protruding lower lip and in her wide nostrils there
> was a defiance, but it was a defiance of the general nature of this world where
> she must pass her days, not of Harriet in particular. In her eyes there was grief
> and there was something beyond grief. After a moment she did speak, and
> she told Harriet that she was going to sit here all night and that they had all
> better go on to bed in the house. Later when Harriet tried to recall the exact
> tone and words Mattie had used—as her acute ear would normally have allowed
> her to do—she could not reconstruct the speech at all. It seemed as though
> Mattie had used a special language common to both of them but one they had
> never before discovered and could now never recover. Afterward they faced
> each other in incommunicative silence for an indefinite time. Finally Harriet
> moved to the door again, but she looked back once more and she saw that
> besides the grief and hostility in Mattie's eyes there was an unspeakable
> loneliness for which she could offer no consolation.

This last scene in "A Long Fourth" is comparable to that last scene in "The
Dead" where Gabriel Conroy is confronted with *his* vanities and illusions.
The family social occasion, in each case, has ironically provided the setting
for the revelation, but Mr. Taylor's situation contains a further irony: his
Harriet Wilson in a sense *is* the family, whereas Joyce's Gabriel Conroy is
mostly peripheral to the social situation—his ideas about other people's
actions are ineffective and private.

"A Long Fourth" thus carries forward the situations of the earlier stories,
and there is a new assurance about the author's practice which can be seen
in his treatment of Harriet Wilson. As matriarch, she embodies many of the
representative features of the Southern family, and her part in society is
decisive. It is Mr. Taylor's contention that after the Civil War the men of

the South, as they pursued money as an end in itself, largely abandoned their privileges as arbiters of civilization and left them to their wives and daughters. One of his later books, *The Widows of Thornton*, explores the results of this historic shift. But already in "A Long Fourth" one sees how the two matriarchs—white and black—control the ethos of the family, and the final scene is absolutely central to the subject. Harriet and Mattie, in fact, are the only persons who actually *suffer* the revelation of the family's failure.

In *A Woman of Means* (1950), a short novel, Mr. Taylor has extended the subject by way of the St. Louis matriarch, Anna Lauterbach, who is not Southern at all but who perhaps envies the Southern code which makes possible the importance of a woman like herself. She is deceived. She is very rich as the result of the money left to her by her father and her first husband, but she chooses to marry Gerald Dudley, the young business man from Tennessee, partly because she fancies that he represents something old-fashioned and substantial that she has lacked in her own money society, partly because she wants a son; and Gerald Dudley's son by *his* first marriage thus becomes an asset. But Anna cannot play the rôle of matriarch effectively—not under these conditions. She wants to be loved for herself; when she was a girl her father stressed her importance as a private person by naming his house Casa Anna; and this virtual cult of individual fulfillment does havoc to the social relationship. As for Gerald Dudley, his rejection of his Tennessee background is a matter of "hard-headed" principle. If his attempt to live by "business ethics" in the St. Louis of the twenties is not altogether successful, that is not because he refuses to play the game. Since he is the husband of a rich woman, his position in her house and with her daughters is always equivocal, and this is symbolized by the billiard room, the only room in the house where he "seemed to have taken possession." His young son figures his career in this single image: "My father was a picture of youthful virtue justly rewarded. The half-forgotten times when I had seen him in boarding house parlors, in small hotel rooms, on day coaches, returned to me for a minute now and made me aware of the complete elegance of this room. Then the thought that this wasn't anything but a poolroom, no matter how elaborately fitted out with red draperies and green plush couches, strengthened my first impression. And suddenly Father was saying, 'You like it here, don't you, son?'

'Yes, sir,' I said. 'Yes, sir.' "

It is the boy, Quintus Cincinnatus Lovell Dudley, who occupies the fictional center. He respects his father and loves his stepmother and up to a point he has a charmed life. He is, as it were, a pawn in a game played by Gerald Dudley and his new wife. His "Southern-ness," which at first seems to exclude him from his class-mates at the Country Day School, presently becomes his advantage. (Like other Southerners in exile, he finds that the sentimental Northern image of the South can be turned to good account.) But the game eventually breaks down. Gerald Dudley fails in business through the treachery of his associates, and deprived of his "manhood" he acts irrationally towards his wife. She, always at the mercy of the men in her family (her indulgent father, then her erratic first husband), gives way under the strain and goes mad. These disasters are observed and indeed participated in by the boy. More than his father, he feels the pull of "the old times" in Tennessee from which he was wrenched, but which he too knows cannot sustain his father in his present predicament. At the end of the novel Mr. Taylor has the boy obsessively reading the newspaper stories about Charles Lindbergh, the hero of a "high-flying" decade, who says, as he is lifted from *The Spirit of St. Louis*, "Well, I made it." The successful modern Daedalus thus contrasts with the fallen Gerald Dudley, about whom one of the step-daughters delivers this comment: " 'Poor, Father,' she said, half in exaspera-tion, half in sympathy. 'Poor *man*.' Then she turned, facing him again, and I could hear her heels scrape on the tile floor of the conservatory. Neither of them spoke for a time. At last she said, 'Of course, nobody's really to blame. It's only the circumstances, and this dreadful life here in St. Louis.' " This family, brought together for a time under very precarious circumstances, will not even survive as a convenient arrangement; each of its members elects to make his own way in an uncertain social order.

One might call *A Woman of Means* the farthest extension of Mr. Taylor's subject; the dissolution of the family could hardly proceed beyond this point. But the subject is far from exhausted here, and Mr. Taylor has demonstrated in his later work that he can use it effectively at various levels at different moments in the historic decline. I should mention as examples of his versatil-ity "Bad Dreams" in *The Widows of Thornton* (perhaps his most powerful story), "Heads of Houses" and "Guests" in *Happy Families Are All Alike*, and *Tennessee Day in St. Louis*. Sometimes one senses (as in his recent story in *Encounter*) that he has drawn the subject thin and dulled his perceptions, as though he wished to confer dignity on a family which has in fact already lost its equilibrium. Sometimes he falls into a nostalgia which is unwarranted; the phrase "the old times" occurs too often to be convincing, because Mr. Taylor is essentially ironic about history, and many of his characters have accepted the world as it is. Indeed there is scarcely any Southern writer who depends less on the great myth of the South as it has been raised by Faulkner and his generation, and perhaps in forfeiting this advantage Mr. Taylor has lost something. But I should think that he has gained something, too, because he has a special insight into the way our society presents itself at this moment, and his subject should continue to produce a rich yield.

The House of Peter Taylor

BARBARA SCHULER

In the summer of 1939, when Peter Taylor was a senior at Kenyon College, one of his poems was published in the *Kenyon Review*. Its title was "The Furnishings of a House," and one of the lines read: "My house, though comprehensive, is unready."[1] What Mr. Taylor said then is as true now as it was in 1939, at least in one sense. In many other senses, however, he has gone on from this early poem to construct a body of work which is both comprehensive and complete: four volumes of short stories, two plays and a short novel.[2]

Although a comparatively young writer, Peter Taylor must certainly be considered a member of the Southern Renascence group. Allen Tate was his first mentor and John Crowe Ransom his second—the latter at Vanderbilt and then at Kenyon; Randall Jarrell was a close friend; and Taylor himself is a native of Tennessee, presently residing in North Carolina. Unlike the work of many of his fellow Southern writers, Taylor's is neither grotesque nor violent. Thematically, however, he shares much with them, dealing, as they all do, with the encroachment of modernity and the changing structure of the South. His subject matter is almost always the significance of this change; he shows the family and the individual adjusting to both loss and debatable gain. His characters are "normal" members of the middleclass, vulnerable before the ethically deteriorating influences of urbanization, industrialization and shifting social pressures which have destroyed a way of life and given no satisfactory substitute. The land has been left, and more and more his people find that they have no roots in place, in family, or in self. While the action takes place in the present-day city, the memories are in the land, in a structured society, in personal and cherished possessions, in tradition and family history. Always his characters have broken with the past, but the sleepy small town remains in their memory and, in the midst of their involvement in city life, in the midst of its competitiveness and dehumanization, the dream of one day returning comforts them. Taylor has caught in his fiction the decay of order, the search for a new order, and the sometimes-compromise, or acceptance of counterfeit values.

From *Critique* 9, no. 3 (9167): 6–18. Reprinted with permission of the Helen Dwight Reid Educational Foundation. Published by Heldref Publications, 4000 Albemarle St., N.W., Washington, D.C. 20016. © 1967.

Since his major theme is the disintegration of the family in the New South, it is not surprising that his stories are most often set in homes. The house is, indeed, the central, the prismatic symbol; central—because in most instances the action concerns it, or occurs within it; prismatic—because in each case it casts a different light and color, and reveals new facets and new meanings. It has both limits and universality; it is a symbol and, in every sense, a planned structure.

At times, as in "Their Losses," the house represents a dying past to which a character clings in spite of the intrusion of modernity: "What she saw was only a deserted-looking cotton shed and, far beyond it, past winter fields of cotton stalks and dead grass, a two-story clapboard house with a sagging double gallery. The depot and the town were on the other side of the train, but Miss Patty knew this scene and she gave a sigh of relief" (4). The view is familiar, and to the character whose roots are in the past, the old country house is security and home, even though seen only over the broken stalks and the dead grass of a more ordered life. In any case, it is preferable to the town and the depot, perhaps present too, through the years, but now symbols of growth and restlessness.

In "What You Hear From 'Em?," one of Taylor's best known stories, the narrator speaks of the houses in Thornton, the little fictional country town: "The heirs who had gone off somewhere making money could never be got to part with 'the home place.' The story was that Thad Tolliver nearly went crazy when he heard their old house had burned, and wanted to sue the town. . . . Yet Thad had hardly put foot in the town since the day his daddy died" (31–32). Although the younger generation has left the land, has become alienated in many respects from the past, they still want to know that the family home exists. They will not live in it, except in memory.

The story in which Taylor makes perhaps his most obvious use of the family home as symbol is "Venus, Cupid, Folly and Time," certainly his most grotesque picture of the decadent Southern family. The general impression is one of perversion and decay. The house is the family in ruins, destroying itself by inversion and a sick substitution of values: "They lived in a dilapidated and curiously mutilated house. . . . In order to reduce taxes the Dorsets had had the third story of the house torn away, leaving an ugly, flat-topped effect without any trim or ornamentation. Also they had had the South wing pulled down and had sealed the scars not with matching brick but with a speckled stucco that looked raw and naked" (74). The impression given is that of the disintegration of a human body, "curiously mutilated," with "scars," and looking "naked." The "flat-topped effect" is functional in that it meets the demands of modern taxation; but, it also leaves the house without any ornamentation, just as life in a competitive society leaves no room for leisure and gracious living. Certainly it is relevant that it is the "South wing" which has been destroyed.

The theme of incest and decay in a dying Southern family is extended in Taylor's description of the Dorsets' hobbies, and other aspects of the house. He speaks of Mr. Alfred's concern for his (bi-sexual) fig trees: "The bushes were very productive, but the figs they produced were dried up little things without much taste" (75), and he mentions, too, Miss Louisa's tireless creation of paper flowers. Both fruit and flowers, to further the analogy, are sold by the Dorsets. The sterility is emphasized in the seductively lighted "plaster replica of Rodin's *The Kiss*," the "antique plaque of Leda and the Swan," and the "tiny color print of Bronzino's *Venus, Cupid, Folly and Time*" (79)—all artificial, all "reproductions." Later in the story the author refers to "a queer sort of bathroom in which the plumbing had been disconnected, and even the fixtures removed" (94). The house has been emasculated and crippled, a signal picture of the family.

While it is most often the house itself which represents the family structure or the enclosure of the individual, the use of the term may be expanded, I believe, to include some mention of "A Walled Garden." In the story so-named Taylor uses the enclosed garden as the objective correlative of the imprisoning love of a mother. While the setting is Southern, the psychological aberration is certainly not peculiar to that section of the country. Here it would seem that Taylor is dealing with a personal maladjustment, but he is also concerned with the destruction of those who will not or cannot expand their horizons. Again he conveys his thought symbolically, using the garden as the equivalent of the "house":

> We've walled ourselves in here with these evergreens and box and jas-
> mine. . . . I created it [the garden] out of a virtual chaos of a backyard—
> Franny's playground, I might say. For three years I nursed that little mag-
> nolia there, for one whole summer did nothing but water the ivy on the
> east wall of the house; if only you could have seen the scrubby hedge
> and the unsightly servants' quarters of our neighbors that are beyond
> my serpentine wall (I suppose, at least, they're still there). (142–43)
> . . . . She deliberately climbed into her swing
> that hung from the dirty old poplar that was here formerly (I have had it cut
> down and the roots dug up) and she began to swing . . . and stared . . .
> through her long hair—which, you may be sure, young man, I had cut the
> very next day at my own beautician's and curled into a hundred ringlets. (147)

The character of the mother is clearly delineated through the description of the garden. Not only has she walled her daughter and herself into this unnatural island of beauty, but she has destroyed the girl's playground in doing so. She has nursed the plants faithfully, but ignored the needs of the people around her, even shutting them from her sight by means of the symbolically serpentine wall. The mother has played God, creating her own Garden of Eden, symbolically petrifying the serpent of insubordination, and even marshalling the flowers into their respective plots, and her daughter's long hair into short "permanently" controlled ringlets. Frances Ann "has finally made her life with me in this little garden plot" (143), subdued by the sheer weight of her mother's will, and overcome by the threat behind her repeated and insidious command: "You must make your own life, my child, as you would have it . . ." (144). "But now she does see it my way, you understand" (143).

Taylor is primarily concerned with the change in the structure of Southern society, with the decadence of those who cling to the non-existent past, with the loss suffered by those who live only in the present, and he adapts his symbolism to his major theme. The "house," as he has used it, has broken up, sometimes literally. The modern Southerner has felt the call to the city and moved into the world of anonymity where the home itself is of less importance and where he suffers a consequent weakening of the bonds to family and to land. This is, in fact, the theme of the very first story he published where he writes of the anguish of a young husband, a farmer, whose wife has a yearning for the gaiety of city life which has temporarily intruded itself into their farm-haven.[3] He includes it also, more subtly, in "Cookie," where the husband, unfaithful to his wife, maintains all the forms at home, and expresses great solicitude and courtesy toward his wife while he is in the "house." Taylor concludes the story: "He went out, closing the door softly behind him, and as he crossed the porch, he could still hear their voices inside—the righteousness and disillusion of Cookie's, the pride and discipline of his wife's. He passed down the flight of wooden steps and stepped from the brick wall onto the lawn. He hesitated a moment; he could still hear their voices indistinctly—their senseless voices. He began walking with light, sure steps over the grass—their ugly, old voices. In the driveway, his car, bright and new and luxurious, was waiting for him" (398). As he passes from the warmth of the family structure, the husband passes too, from the "pride and discipline" which keeps up appearances and holds things together. He steps over the brick wall of formality and artificially imposed order which surrounds the house, and onto the spreading lawn of freedom. His car, "bright and new and luxurious," will carry him to a different and easy "love," in a large and anonymous world.

The anonymity of modern life, of city life, is developed to a much greater extent in "Skyline." In this case everyone and everything are nameless, even the streets and the city itself. People are designated only by their function or their relationship. Taylor projects, in this way, the complete break of the family with its past; the characters have no history beyond the story itself. They are the rootless products of a newly urbanized South. The story is written in the present tense—the center of consciousness a young boy whose impressions are strongly sentient. Thus, there is a powerful sense of immediacy as if the action occurs in a timeless but deeply felt present. Permanence exists neither in the literally local tradition, nor in the family relationships which crumble before Jim's eyes. His growth is uncertainly defined in the midst of flux and meaninglessness; the individual is threatened with loss of identity in a disordered world. Jim's sense of the historical is neither developed nor acute. He does not question the changes he sees, though they do reflect further displacement: "Things have changed in the suburb; repeatedly he has told the new children how things once were, he is that conscious of it; but something forever keeps him from trying to observe too closely just how the new buildings go up" (87). At the end, "the remarkable thing in the changed view from the window which had once been his lies in the tall apartment houses which punctuate the horizon and in the boxlike, flatroofed ones in his own neighborhood" (103). An increase in ugliness and in the numbers of unknown people surrounding him, is the only change he can observe or look forward to. The apartment building, with all its anonymity, is the "house" of the present.

In the same story, however, Taylor uses the family structure as he has in others—as a symbol of protection, of possible order—even though, in this instance, it stands in a nameless city, on a nameless street, and is full of nameless people. Here the boy experiences proximity to death at first only as he sees from his window the coming of the neighbors to pay their respects. He is exposed to knowledge vicariously, to impressions and ideas, through windows: "He wonders, sitting in the glare of the many-windowed school-room" (94)—he is inside, looking out. When his father and a neighbor are caught up in a deep rivalry and antagonism while playing ball in the pouring rain, Jim "feels only an occasional drop, for he is under the eaves of the house" (85), protected by the family structure (such as it is) from dangerous experience. He is also prevented premature involvement: the girl "scans the windows of the house, but she cannot make out his figure through the black wire screen" (88). Later, however, when they are both older, when he is outside (mature), he can discern "the figure of the girl at the window of her bedroom. . . . The electric light burns in the girl's room, and he can see her in the window through the black screen" (101).

As in the beginning Mr. Taylor concentrated on the disintegration of the Southern family, so now, in his later work, still similarly concerned, he is more inclined to leave the house as setting, and to show his characters in the restless movement which has subtly invaded the South in the wake of urbanization and industrialization. More and more, in place of the "house," he chooses as setting a place other than the home—a park, a means of public conveyence, a car, a hotel. This is, after all, appropriate, for the house has lost its significance as the historical dwelling of the family, and man today is alone, and in motion.

In "Two Pilgrims" (published in September, 1963), the country from Memphis to northern Alabama is seen through the eyes of a seventeen year old (the new generation), and his two older companions whom he is chauffering: "From the time we left the outskirts of Memphis, the two men talked . . . of almost nothing but bird dogs and field trials, interrupting themselves only when we passed through some little town or settlement to speak of the fine people they knew who had once lived there. . . . At La Grange, my uncle pointed out a house with a neoclassic portico and said he had once had a breakfast there that lasted three hours" (328–29). The older men see the country as a backdrop for the gracious living and comfortable life of the past; they see it in relation to its people, to an established social structure and to romantic history. The boy's comment is: "Under a bright, limitless sky the trees and the broad fields of grayish cotton stalks, looking almost lavender in places, gave a kind of faded-tapestry effect" (329)— tapestry, a man-made, indoor, artificial decoration; a static picture, perhaps pastoral, faded with age; no longer alive, no longer vitally significant; framed by the windshield of the swiftly moving car. This is what the countryside is to the eyes of the young Southerner.

Again, toward the close of the story, the boy-narrator refers to the area they had passed. " 'That godforsaken-looking stretch back there. . . . It's just ugly, that's all' " (341). He is answered by the indignant and defensive older men: " 'Every countryside has its own kind of beauty. It's up to you to learn to see it, that's all. . . . How could you judge, flying along the highway at fifty miles an hour. . . . You would have to have seen that country thirty years ago to understand. . . . It had the prettiest stand of timber on the continent' " (341–42). The boy's practical reply is: " 'But what's that got to do with it? . . . It's how the country looks now I'm talking about' " (342).

While the theme here is the same which runs through all of Mr. Taylor's stories, the younger generation is portrayed as being impatient with its nostalgic elders. The older men are passengers in the car; they "go along" with progress, looking with nostalgia at the passing past. The boy is in the driver's seat.

In "Nerves," a so-far uncollected story which appeared in the *New Yorker*, in the September 16 issue of 1961, Taylor treats more specifically of modern transportation to indicate the cultural changes which have occurred: "Those big smelly buses sneak through traffic with no bells to clang, no rights of their own, no dignity of any kind. The passengers all sit looking out of the windows as if none of them knew anybody else was on board, never speaking a word to each other" (40). Things have taken on a life of their own. The new is impersonal, without dignity of any kind, and man, a non-entity, is reduced to being a passive passenger.

No single setting used by Taylor, however, is a more perfect objective correlative of modernization and the new mobile society than the train station in "At the Drugstore." Though rather long, the section is, I believe, worth quoting in its entirety. The change is observed by Matt Donelson who, with his own family, is returning once again to visit his parents in the city of his youth. The first part describes the depot as it had appeared on previous visits; the second, as it is in the present:

With whoever came to meet the train—father or brother—Matt and Janie and the boys would walk the length of the great Depot lobby, between the rows of straight-back benches on one of which a pathetic family would be huddled together and on another a disreputable looking old bum would be stretched out, asleep with his head on his bundle and with his hat over his eyes. And when the party came directly under the vast dome that rose above the lobby, Matt's father or brother would tell the boys to look up and see the bats whoozing around up there or see the absurd pigeon that had got himself trapped in the dome and was flapping about from one side to the other.

It had been a very different scene last night, however. The dimly lit lobby of old had been transformed. A false ceiling had been installed no more than ten or twelve feet above the floor. And a new, circular wall, with display windows for advertisers and with bright posters declaring how many people still rode the trains, altered the very shape of the room, hiding the rough stone columns around which the children had used to play hide and seek. As for the wooden benches, they were replaced by plastic, bucket-bottomed chairs on which huddling together would have been difficult and stretching out alone quite impossible. And the lighting, though indirect, was brilliant; there were no dark corners anywhere. (55)

The physical alteration of the station is a startlingly vivid projection of the corresponding change in the social structure.

Earlier, the members of a family—though perhaps in misery—were, at least, able to derive some comfort and mutual support, huddling together on the benches. There was room, too, for the man who had cut himself off from society to enjoy his own individuality. Perhaps the bench and the bundle were not the softest of beds, but he had the additional freedom of eliminating even their hard reality with his tilted hat, and sleep. In former days there had been room too, for those idiosyncratic individuals who occasionally achieved grotesque extremes and were, like the bats and the pigeons, trapped in the height of their absurdities. All were accommodated in the ancient structure.

The transformation is, however, complete. The false ceiling immediately sets an absolute limit for all. The circular wall hides the shape of life itself; it makes everything public, and allows for neither differences nor advance. While the stone columns had been rough, they were also an obvious source of support—and, incidentally, of intrigue of the children who played in their shadows. They, like the pillars of the family, are perhaps not gone, but obscured by a philosophy which belittles the value of tradition and encourages impersonal display. The new plastic, bucket-bottom chairs make it impossible for the family to huddle together, or for any individual to have complete freedom of position. Each person is separate, but identical with all the others, without the possibility of either warming contact or individual differences. It is ironic that the chairs which have been made for the individual, styled for his greatest comfort, fitted and molded to the human shape, deprive him, simultaneously, of his greatest need. Furniture, in being "humanized," has deprived man of his humanity. And there is a parallel irony in the fact that the railroads, which have made things so completely impersonal in the station, have themselves become selfconscious, sensitive to the number of people they can attract. Finally, the mystery and softness of life are erased in the brilliant light of anonymity and depersonalization—"there were no dark corners anywhere."

In two of his most recent stories Mr. Taylor has come to grips in a more complete way with the destruction of the family and of the "house." In both cases the destruction is absolutely literal: the old family homes are to be destroyed to make place for modern "necessities." In "The Throughway,"[4] Harry and Irene represent the town dwellers: "They were a couple who had lived always in the same house since they had first married—not one they owned but one they had been able to rent all through the years" (559). To an extent they are already displaced persons, having no real home of their own, although "the house was in an old section of the city, the very part of town in which they had both grown up" (559).

As is the case in so many of Taylor's stories, the husband wishes to cling to the house itself, the house which is, in this case, to be demolished to make place for one "leg of a new throughway system, connecting all the outlying sections of the growing city . . ." (560). His wife, more practical, knows that it is not the physical structure of the house which is of such great importance, but rather it is their possessions, the things which they have shared and cherished as a family. " 'But this isn't *our* house—or *your* house. It's a house we've *rented*. Our furniture's our real home, Harry. And we're taking that with us, Harry' " (564). In the lives of these already rootless people urbanization has been pushing, forcing them to take their places in the ranks of an almost completely mobile society: " 'They've widened this street every ten years since we've been living here, Irene. The trees went, the grass went next—now the people' " (567). At the conclusion, Harry and Irene are forced, as is inevitable, to move to an apartment and so to submerge themselves in an even more nameless and fluid world.

In "Miss Leonora When Last Seen" Taylor reveals the final and predictable conclusion. Through all of his stories as they have appeared from 1937 the movement of his characters has been away from the family home. His work has portrayed the ever-increasing inroads of industrial expansion: the exposure to the attractions of city life, the movement of families to the city, the ambition of the young husbands to establish themselves among the well-to-do, the dilapidation of the old homes, and the gradual destruction of the ties binding his characters to the past and to their families; he has dealt with the consequences of the move: division between husband and wife, divorce, frustration, rootlessness and anonymity. In "Miss Leonora When Last Seen" Taylor reaches the apex, what could be a final statement—loss of identity and complete mobility in an ever-changing society, where man has no destination.

The incident which evokes the action of the story is the fact that Miss Leonora's family home had been chosen as the site of the county's new consolidated high school, and condemnation proceedings had been begun and completed in spite of Miss Leonora's objections. She, herself, had taught for twenty-five years in the old high school, and had been a strong influence on the young people of the little town of Thomasville which had been founded by her ancestors. She had seen the decline of her family and the past in the drowning of her young kinswoman, in the burning of the old schoolhouse. Now she sees the approaching destruction of her home, seemingly an expression of the thoughtlessness and ingratitude of the townspeople to whom she has given so much of her life. In all of these things she perceives, too, the end of her usefulness, the end of her unique identity and, almost literally, she kicks the traces. Through the years she had maintained a strictly modest and decorous appearance. Her only outlet was in excursions through the country where she adopted a pose she thought suited to the occasion, fostering along the way the belief that the old families still existed, with their pride, their idiosyncrasies and their traditions, even though they had fallen on hard times. But now Taylor indicates her capitulation to "progress" through her sudden change into modern attire:

> She had done an awful thing to her hair. Her splendid white mane, with its faded yellow streaks and its look of being kept up on her head only by the two tortoise-shell combs at the back, was no more. She had cut it off, thinned it, and set it in little waves close to her head, and, worse still, she must have washed it in a solution of indigo bluing. . . . For a minute I couldn't remember where it was I had seen this very woman before. Then it came to me. All that was lacking was a pair of pixie glasses with rhinestone rims, and a half dozen bracelets on her wrists. She was one of those old women who come out here from Memphis looking for antiques and country hams and who tell you how delighted they are to find a southern town that is truly unchanged. (274–75)

Already Miss Leonora Logan has begun to "look too much like a thousand others . . ." (278).

Finally, Miss Leonora is seen all through the story in motion: "orbiting," "driving," "setting out on similar excursions," "killing time until night falls and she can take to the road again" (247–52, passim). Taylor states at the beginning: "Unofficially, in the minds of the townspeople, she is a missing person" (246), and he ends the story: "She says nothing about when we can expect her to come home" (279). Miss Leonora is, of course, a "missing person"—she has lost her connection with the past, her identity, and she no longer has a home to which to return. She has been absorbed by the tentacles of conformity and will forever remain in motion in a fluid society.

* * *

The place of Peter Taylor in modern short fiction is secure. In the years since his first publication as an undergraduate in 1937, he has built for himself a fine body of work, his own house of fiction. And as his skill has become more natural, more self-assured, he has struck more deeply into his subject matter, revealing with ever greater clarity the shifting and complex motives which drive his characters—and all men.

It may seem strange that although he has published six volumes, and some of his stories have received national recognition and praise, he has received comparatively little critical attention. His books have, of course, been favorably reviewed in the major papers and periodicals; his work has been mentioned in studies of the short story and of Southern literature, and there have been a few articles analyzing his fiction. In general, however, his work seems to have caused no real critical excitement, perhaps because, as Gene Baro puts it, he "writes so simply and powerfully he seems scarcely to be exercising his craft."[5] The very qualities which are so distinctive in his writing militate against him in this respect. His "acceptable" subject matter, his quiet style, his indirection and understatement are profoundly unlike the sensationalism, contortion and richly suggestive language of some of his fellow Southerners. His people are not grotesque, his action is not violent, his language is not flamboyant. Mr. Taylor's strongest impact comes through the quiet revelation of the unconscious complexity of human motivation, and his knowledge of the limited vision which determines our simplest actions.

His major theme—the disintegration of the Southern way of life as embodied in the house and family—connects him with his fellow Southern writers, for this is their concern too. But even in this Taylor differs from most of them, for he is one of the few to show the modern Southerner living *in* the city, with his memories and problems. Andrew Lytle has aptly said of the earlier stories that they may best be described by the phrase *"exiled at home."*[6] In Taylor's more recent work, however, the movement is farther and farther away from the home and reflects the restless movement which has invaded the South. Now his characters would appear to be merely "exiled."

Peter Taylor gives no answers. He presents a situation, and demonstrates its ramifications, its extensions in life. As Jeremy Brooks says, Taylor is "after the reality that lies behind the seeming reality of any situation; and because he is a true artist he makes no pretense of having once for all apprehended it."[7] His house of fiction is Southern, but the "voices in the rooms" belong to all men. As the South itself is divided so, too, the modern family, the individual, in the face of the advance of civilization. Tensions such as these operate within the house of Peter Taylor, but they are universal tensions which rise above the local and the particular to include all those who live in society. They will never be resolved, and, in that sense the "house" will forever be unready. Yet, Taylor's work itself, the "house" of his fiction is supported by fine craftsmanship and universality and certainly, in this sense, he can no longer say: "My house, though comprehensive, is unready."

Notes

1. *Kenyon Review*, I (Summer 1939), 308.
2. Collections of short stories: *A Long Fourth and Other Stories* (New York, 1948), *The Widows of Thornton* (New York, 1950), *Happy Families Are All Alike* (New York, 1959), *Miss Leonora When Last Seen* (New York, 1963); plays: *Tennessee Day in St. Louis* (New York, 1957), *The Death of a Kinsman*, *Sewanee Review*, LVII (Winter 1949), 86–119; novel: *A Woman of Means* (New York, 1950). The volumes include the stories mentioned in this article as follows: "Their Losses," and "What You Hear From 'Em?" in *The Widows of Thornton*; "Venus, Cupid, Folly and Time," and "A Walled Garden" in *Happy Families Are All Alike*; "Cookie," "Skyline," "Two Pilgrims," "At the Drugstore," and "Miss Leonora When Last Seen" in *Miss Leonora When Last Seen*.
3. "The Party," *River*, I (March 1937), 4–8.
4. *Sewanee Review*, LXXII (1964), 559–68.
5. "A True Short-Story Artist," *New York Herald Tribune Book Review*, Dec. 6, 1959, 9.
6. "The Displaced Family," *Sewanee Review*, LXVI (Winter 1958), 116.
7. "New Short Stories," *New Statesman*, Aug. 6, 1960, 192.

Narration and Theme in Taylor's
A Woman of Means

JAMES PENNY SMITH

Almost any critical survey of American fiction of the last three decades mentions Peter Taylor, but his fiction has received little attention beyond the most damning polite respect. In 1962 *The Sewanee Review* devoted a good many pages to three articles on Taylor's achievement (in celebrating his twenty-fifth year as a published writer); even there emphasis was given to his self-imposed limitations. But if his stories have been neglected badly, his one novel, *A Woman of Means*,[1] is really unknown. The usual comment denies that *A Woman of Means* is a novel at all and demands that Taylor stick to writing short stories. Such critics fail to see what the novel achieves, for although its scale is not large, the novel has, as Robert Penn Warren has said, "such a vividness of characterization and such a sense of depth and complication of event that the effect is one of full-bodied narration."[2] By looking more closely at the narration and theme in *A Woman of Means*, we can more properly see its virtues and its own success as a "full-bodied narration."

The plot of the novel describes the brief marriage of Quint Dudley's father, Gerald, to Anna Lauterbach, whose first marriage ended in divorce. Quint's mother died at his birth and left her salesman husband to raise the boy in a series of boarding-houses. The only "permanent" home for Quint comes to be his grandmother Lovell's farm, Belgrove, in Tennessee. Gerald feels that he must make money and provide a settled life for Quint, preferably in St. Louis. He becomes the president of a hardware company and marries Anna who already has two older daughters. She eagerly accepts Quint as a son while Gerald tries to establish himself as the girls' father. He fails, but Anna comes to be all important to Quint. Through the treachery of his business associates, Gerald loses his position and again becomes a salesman, insisting that the family live on his salary rather than the enormous wealth of his wife. Anna suddenly becomes insane and the family dissolves.

Such an account hardly suggests the interests of the story or the several

From *Critique* 9, no. 3 (1967): 19–30. Reprinted with permission of the Helen Dwight Reid Educational Foundation. Published by Heldref Publications, 4000 Albemarle St., N.W., Washington, D.C. 20016. © 1967.

novelistic problems that Taylor solves primarily through the manipulation of point of view. Most of all, such an account cannot deal with the subtly indicated relationship between Quint and Anna which embodies the central issue of the novel. Several questions must be answered by the reader of *A Woman of Means*. Is the novel correctly titled? Is the book about Quint, its narrator, or about Anna? What attitude is defined toward the conflict between country and city life, a continuing concern in Taylor's stories and plays? How useful and how successful is the symbolism in defining the central concerns? And, finally, what responsibility individually have Quint, Anna, and Gerald Dudley for the collapse of the marriage and the family? A number of answers derived from technical considerations are possible.

In the terms suggested by Wayne Booth, Quintus Cincinnatus Lovell Dudley may be described as a first person dramatized narrator-agent whose usually reliable narration is given support or correction through the opinions of the adults among whom he lived, but from whom he is separated by age and, therefore, by moral and intellectual differences. Quint is also separated from the events he describes by an unspecified time and views his story from a position closer to the reader than either that of his boyhood self or the adults in his story. A further limitation is imposed by the fact that most of his story is narrated through scene rather than summary, thus depriving him of the opportunity to comment directly, a technical limitation which becomes a part of his characterization of himself and integral to the novel.

Dominating the story of the family's disintegration is the account of the growing understanding by Quint of himself and his relationship to his family and its past. Just as Joyce uses the name Stephen Dedalus to indicate the nature of his protagonist, so Taylor uses the name of his narrator. Indeed, in one passage *A Woman of Means* seems clearly to echo the scene on the beach in *A Portrait of the Artist as a Young Man* where the boys call Stephen "Bous Stephanoumenos! Bous Stephaneforos!" Quint, like Stephen, has been sent to a school which he dislikes where the other students tease him about his odd name Quintus Cincinnatus Lovell Dudley and shout after him as he runs to catch his trolley, "Quintuscincinottus . . . Quintoscincinottusquintocinci . . . Notasquintocinci . . ." (71). Quint, too, is bothered by his name; one of his fellow students asks, "Don't you like your own name, Cincinnatus?" (70). Other boys call him Cinci-nottus, Cincy, or Old Nat, distortions of his real name. Even his usually affectionate step-sisters call him Cincinnatus or Lovell and mock his Tennessee drawl. The mockery of the boys reminds him of similar taunts from his country playmates on the night his father came to tell him and his Grandmother Lovell of the plans to remarry: "I felt that I was nobody and nothing and that I did not exist and that all the decisions that the rich widow and her daughters and my father might make could not affect me. And then, as I lay there, I recalled a picture of a Chinese city in my geography book and the caption under it: *What Happens in China Affects YOU*. We were going to St. Louis that night;

we were taking the Midnight; we would be there in the morning if the switchman in Evansville made no mistake" (79). Ironically, at this moment when he feels so lost, the children are calling him "Quintus," the fifth son, a name indicative of a secure place in a family succession.

In the scene following the one in which his schoolmates call his name, Quint arrives late at the Country Day School. The masters decide to make him attend Saturday Session as a punishment, but the headmaster, whose sister had gone to school with Quint's stepmother, identifies Quint as "Anna Lauterbach's boy" (81), an identification which helps the boy to "adjust" to his new school life.

Indeed he adjusts so well that he wins the Dartmouth Cup, a prize given for the best-all-around-boy in the middle school. But it is a prize he wins through a subtle form of cheating and by deliberately catering, in a self-burlesque of his Southern qualities, to the other students' tastes, sacrificing his true identity. In still other ways, Quint forgets who he is: as a part of his campaign to win the Cup, he accepts a "prominent (feminine) role" in the senior musical comedy. Later, he helps to start the Tom Swift Club "whose main purpose was the exchange of Art magazines among its members" (115). Each member carries a different volume of the Tom Swift series "with the pages glued together and a hole cut in the center for carrying cigarettes." The boys are called according to the volume they carry; Quint who carries *Tom Swift and His Motorcycle* is known as "Motorcycle." But as he lies awake after his days of campaigning, Quint does not entirely forget who he is or might be: "I thought of the boy I might have been in the place where I was born, and it seemed that that was the boy I should have been. It seems ridiculous now, but the notion that I should have loved my grandmother as I actually loved my stepmother, and the whole idea of my own failure and guilt, and above all, the fantastic notions of the strong character I might have developed so disturbed and depressed me that I resolutely shut off memory and persuaded myself that I was quite sleepy" (113–114).

The full name Quintus Cincinnatus Lovell Dudley tells us even more about who this boy is or should be. The names "Dudley" and "Quintus" establish him in a family with a sense of past and place, both of which the boy is in danger of forgetting. Significantly, the gift from his grandmother on his twelfth birthday is his grandfather's watch which had been promised him for his twenty-first birthday. Quint is proud of the watch, but when the other children at his party laugh at it, he comes to see it as a piece of junk. His other names, too, suggest his proper identity. "Cincinnatus" immediately reminds us of "traditional" rural values and "Lovell" surely suggests "Love," the emotion Anna and Gerald sadly find lacking in their marriage. Quint, too, must learn what real love is and who his real mother was.

Although Taylor dwells at some length on his narrator's full name, the boy is nearly always called "Quint," another name suggestive of a more complex view of the boy's nature. Critics have noted that *A Woman of Means* is Jamesian, but no one has mentioned the suggestion of James's Peter Quint in the name of Taylor's protagonist. The association is perhaps a surprising one, but the older Quint, the narrator of *A Woman of Means*, implicitly sees himself as "villainous" and partly "responsible" for the failure of his family. The responsibility of James's Peter Quint is never clearly defined, only suggested; the same is true of Quintus Cincinnatus Lovell Dudley.

Gerald Dudley, more clearly than any other character in the novel, states the problem of identification, although he too has difficulty in defining his own dilemma. Like Quint, Gerald would probably have been truer to himself had he not left his rural past so far behind. But Taylor is careful never to allow Quint or his father to state the difficulty in such over-simplified terms. Dudley, like Willy Loman and many other characters in American literature, pursues the wrong goals, yet in pursuing them achieves some sort of dignity. While moving about the country and living in boarding houses with Quint, Dudley promises, "If I ever get to be anybody . . . we'll live in St. Louis all the time" (22). After they move to St. Louis, Dudley and Quint begin to spend much of their time with Miss Moore, a young woman who almost became Quint's fifth grade teacher. One evening, going to a concert, Gerald appears in a tuxedo wearing brown business shoes, an error which Miss Moore points out. He and Quint rush back into their boarding house and the boy borrows a pair of black shoes for his father from the janitor. To Quint, Gerald says, "This won't happen again . . . I can promise you that. But you remember it. Don't *ever* forget tonight, son. You and I must learn these things" (29). Thus Gerald commits a kind of *hubris* and Quint realizes that he and his father are both involved: "I realized . . . that I had always hated what they called my father's 'business drive,' and simultaneously I realized that I was myself the very center and core of it, that the decisions Father sometimes had to make at this very table were, for all practical purposes, decisions about me" (32).

Through his father, Quint himself comes to understand something of the conflict between the two ways of life, symbolized by his Grandmother Lovell's farm, Belgrove, and his stepmother's house, Casa Anna. Pleading with Gerald, Mrs. Lovell says: " 'I've raised my own children differently— the way your own mother must have done hers, Gerald. It seems second nature. And children *learn* things on a farm, real things—even about the animals. . . . Give him to me, Gerald. It's better to grow up in the country. It's what people need. . . . He needs a mother!' " (46). To these arguments, Gerald says: " 'Quint needs other things. . . . He needs a mother who has never seen a farm. He needs to go to city schools where they teach you something, and he needs money' " (46).

No one cause is sufficient to explain the woes that come to the Dudleys. It is not just that Gerald leaves Tennessee nor just that he pursues money; Gerald makes errors and tries to face them, but he fails to notice his worst mistake. Gerald's announcement of his intention to marry Mrs. Lauterbach is given to the boy as a dream described to Quint in his father's conference room, father and son sitting at opposite ends of the table. Gerald says:

> I had a dream last night. I dreamed that . . . *that you, that I, rather,* [italics mine] had gotten married to a woman—the very nicest sort of woman—and that you liked her just as much as I did and were very glad I was married and that we were living in a house I had bought and were about as happy as we could be—with somebody to look after us, you know. . . . Quint, it seemed like this woman was kind of young—much younger than your grandma, for instance, and was a person more like yourself who had always lived here in St. Louis : . . and known people. (31–32)

The error of self-deception (the dream story, the house he has paid for, the younger woman) is evident. Gerald does not face reality about himself or his world; he dreams. The happiness of the marriage ("someone to look after us") doesn't last. Anna is forty-two, five to ten years older than Gerald; her house was paid for by her father; and although she is "the nicest sort of woman" and "a woman of means" as Gerald describes her to Quint's grandmother, Anna too fails to find her proper identity and fails in her relations with her family (especially with Quint and his father) and eventually becomes mad.

Gerald deceives himself about his marriage but at moments sees himself clearly. He tells Quint the story of how he tried at some expense to get a job with a man in Chattanooga shortly before marrying Quint's mother. He did not get the job, yet says that the sales manager who would not hire him was "a peach of a fellow. . . . That fellow was dead right, though, about my experience. I had only worked country towns with hardware then" (24–25). Still later, after he has returned to his job as a traveling-salesman, Gerald speaks of other salesmen who criticize the company's executives and say that he should be running the firm. "If I were the good executive Mr. Reese or Mr. Beerman or Mr. Waymeyer is, I'd still be in an executive position" (141). Ironically, he says to his son, "The truth is, Quint, your mother sets great store by money—in a sense that you and I may not understand" (123). Later Anna, talking to Quint, suggests that Gerald married her for her money "but doesn't remember it now" (127), an opinion Gerald himself shares. But Anna fails to remember whether or not she married Gerald to get Quint. In the last scene of the novel, Gerald says to Bess, one of his stepdaughters, "if I'm to be blamed, I would like to know it" (159). He will accept his responsibility, but the girl says, "Of course, nobody's really to blame. It's only the circumstances, and this dreadful life here in St. Louis," perhaps suggesting indirectly a very real source, modern city life, for the blame. But when Gerald answers that he cannot see how "the quiet, easy life" Anna has lived could have caused her illness, Bess shouts that Gerald as well as Anna's father and most particularly Quint are to blame.

Clearly, then, Gerald Dudley (perhaps the name *Dudley* is significant) helps Quint define his importance and his identity. Through Gerald's questions about blame, we are guided toward a proper judgment of the events Quint only presents to us without comment.

Although the novel is "about" Quint's growing awareness of himself and his relation to his world, the theme of faulty identification of one's self and the resultant problems is most fully dramatized through Anna's story. The novel *is* quite properly named for her, for she represents the embodiment of Gerald Dudley's dream and her subsequent insanity demonstrates its falsity. All the reasons suggested at the end of the novel for her insanity are plausible and are developed throughout the book. But only Quint understands her dilemma and at the end weeps for her. Even he can only describe her illness and its causes by telling his complicated story, making the novel in a sense what he has learned from Anna.

Like Quint, Anna lost her mother before coming to maturity and says: " 'Papa really built the house for me so that I wouldn't have to go back to the old house in Vanderventer Place where I had seen Mama suffering, so long; she died of cancer, and her suffering was horrible, Quint' " (19). After her mother's death and their trip to Italy, Anna's father built her an "Italian palace out here in St. Louis, Missouri," and guided her through her debut, only to die a year after the house was finished. Already, within the story of the building of the house we can see the seeds of the problems which eventually destroy Anna, both the suggestion of "things that happened in her childhood" (most specifically, too much dependence on her father), and the suggestion of escapism and lack of roots in the turning away from the city and the house of her mother's death. Anna suggests that her father died from the strain of directing the building of her palace, but the whole novel implies that he died from lack of the kind of life embodied in Quint's grandmother. Escapism is certainly indicated by the Italian palace in the mid-West, by the trip to Europe, and by the turning away from human suffering and death. Even the name of the house, Casa Anna, is an indication of the selfishness of the family which builds it. The father's retreat from reality is also shown in his insistence on gas lights as well as electricity in every room. At Anna's debut ball, "The gas lights had burned that night as a concession to her papa, who liked the soft light and the shadows and who said you could not have a *really* formal party under the glare of electricity" (20). Appropriately, Anna remembers that she used to tell her father that "he looked like the English archaeologists we saw in Egypt" (19).

In still another way the source of Anna's later difficulties is suggested by her memories of the past. Much against her will, when she was only thirteen, her parents sent her to Switzerland to school where she was called "the American millionairess." Here she was cut off from her proper setting and forced to become suspicious of other children who she supposed liked her only for her money. Not too surprisingly, she sympathizes with Quint when he has difficulties adjusting to Country Day School and children of another class. Nor should we be surprised at Anna's accusations that Gerald married her for her money.

She hints that her marriage to Lauterbach was ended by his adultery and describes the divorce as a terrific storm, a description she immediately withdraws as a romantic exaggeration. In describing to Quint the collapse of her first marriage, Anna says that they were both very rich and looked upon a large family as "merely another of the luxuries that we knew we could afford." (65). Lauterbach, as she says, "continued to be 'dashing' " and did not want to get old. "And in a sense I did not want to." After the second daughter was born, Anna began treating her as a boy, revealing more about herself through this desire for a son than through any other aspect of her character.

The need for Quint, Gerald says, made Anna marry him, but of course Quint can never be her real son, a fact which Anna instinctively realizes, for the first serious manifestation of her madness is a false-pregnancy. In her insanity she says: " 'The nurse says it will be a boy. . . . If it's a boy, Quint, I'm going to name him for you, though of course his surname must be Lauterbach' " (151).

Throughout the book, the idea of Quint as her lover is carefully suggested. As we have seen, Gerald Dudley makes such identification in describing his dream; "that you, that I, rather, had gotten married." Too, Quint likes being fondled by his stepmother: "At first I had thought that maybe it was only the pleasant roundness of her arms and the soft wave of her hair that attracted me to her. But soon I knew that it was more even than the feel of her cheek on my forehead when she would hug me to herself saying, 'I always wanted a boy, and now I have one of my very own.' From the outset I sensed that she wanted me as I wanted her" (38). During the Thanksgiving holiday he thinks: "Could anything in the world make my stepmother stop loving my father or me? *Me*? If so, I wished I could get sick and die, and be dead when it happened. How could I want to live, what would be the point, what sense would anything make?" (94). Later in the arguments between Gerald and Anna about whether or not to keep the house after Gerald's dismissal as president, Quint takes his stepmother's side, believing her "completely misunderstood by my father" (126). Anna realizes some of his difficulty and says, "Suddenly, Quint, you seem a grown man to me. . . . We're making you old before your time" (128). But she grows more possessive of the boy and says: " 'I often think that you're closer to me than most boys are to their mothers.'

'You bet I am,' I would say with a wink. But she did not respond to my gaiety nowadays.

'I like to hear you say that. When you're older, you'll understand how it is' " (143). Quint himself grows to feel jealous of his father: "I found myself becoming painfully conscious of the significance of their sharing a room together, of their private relationship which excluded the whole world, and I became most perplexingly aware of my own ignorance and of my real incredulity concerning the act of love between husband and wife" (147). Clearly, the notion of naming her baby for Quint shows that the mad Anna in some ways imagines him as one of her lovers, although she suggests he is angry with her for having two husbands and a baby (152). Bess, in her denunciation of the Dudleys at the end of the novel, explicitly says that father, husband, and son are all one in blame for Anna's insanity.

One should always remember that the information about the other characters and himself comes from Quint, himself an agent in his own story. As I have suggested, his norms as narrator are close to those of the reader's, but particularly at the end he cannot quite state for himself the meaning of what has happened. He rarely comments directly on his story and never gives his present interpretation of what he has experienced. As a boy he cannot "understand"; as an adult narrator he can present actions and push the reader toward the meanings. Significantly, the novel ends, ". . . standing in the center of the room, without even putting my hands to my face, I wept bitterly, aloud" (160).

But what about Quint's own responsibility for what has happened to Anna and his father? At first glance, he seems an innocent child caught in an adult situation which he can scarcely comprehend or control. In part such a view is correct, yet he, too, has an awareness as his account of winning the Dartmouth Cup indicates. Since he wins the Cup by cheating in basketball and by presenting himself as a parody of the Southerner, his sense of guilt is revealed in his description of the presentation of the Cup. As he begins to work toward the award, he tries to avoid thinking about the meaning of what he is doing but finally lies awake worrying. When he is given the Cup, he thinks he should present it to Anna who sits in the audience, "but when I looked into her face with its eager, earnest expression, again I felt that she was an intruder, that she was demanding the Cup, and that it was not of my own will that I was about to give it to her" (116). He walks past her and hides until time for classes; he becomes miserable and terribly tired and falls asleep on the special trolley home, but suddenly he wakes and feels "that I had never been so happy, that my happiness belonged to me alone and was not connected with anything else that had ever happened to me" (116–117). He does not identify his happiness, but clearly it comes from the sense of belonging to his school, an identification achieved by his own efforts, however devious. He thinks he has proved himself to himself, but he has forgotten his name and all the virtues it symbolizes.

The narration is developed through a number of symbolic elements, such as the watch or the Dartmouth Cup, used with considerable relevance to the developing theme. One element, however, is particularly crucial. Lindbergh's arrival in Paris on May 21, 1927, is introduced in a scene in which Quint is consciously trying to avoid his step-mother because she has become noticeably possessive and protective toward him as his father's difficulties have increased. Quint tries to hide from her when she calls at the school for him in her chauffered car, but he is caught by the driver Gus: "As we walked up the path toward the parking lot, I tried to make conversation about the Cardinals and the Browns and about Charles A. Lindbergh, who was planning to fly the Atlantic in his plane called *The Spirit of St. Louis*" (142–143). Here Lindbergh, like Daedalus for Joyce's Stephen, personifies escape and achievement.

Near the end of the novel, following his final interview with Anna, Quint reads a newspaper account of the aviator's safe arrival. As he reads, his mind keeps moving to his future with his father in boarding-houses, summer jobs, and public school. He even thinks of returning to his grandmother but rejects the idea. "Instead, I suddenly had a clear image of myself as an independent stranger pushing through vast throngs of people" (157). When Gus hands him the paper, Quint says, "I knew he would make it" (156), just as Lindbergh is reported to have said on his arrival, "Well, I made it." The newspaper further describes the greeting Lindbergh received: "Twenty hands reaching for him and lifted him out as if he were a baby. One thousand Frenchmen were waiting to take him to their hearts" (158). After learning of this reception, Quint turns to the scene between Bess and his father, an argument which ends with Quint's view of his father:

> At that moment I was struck by the thought that he was still a very young-looking man, that there were still no gray hairs in his head of thick black hair, that he was the same man who had come for me in a taxi long ago at my grandmother's farm. I went back into the library, and seeing the morning paper which had fallen to the floor, I read the headlines again. And when I read the headlines I was overcome with grief for my step-mother; standing in the center of the room, without putting my hands to my face, I wept, bitterly, aloud. (160)

Clearly, Quint identifies himself with Lindbergh; like his idol who has flown through darkness, he, too, symbolically "makes it." That he comes through and once more sees himself as his father's son, with a sense of guilt and sorrow, is a recognition of himself and, therefore, of his own chance to fly alone.

Notes

1. Peter Taylor, *A Woman of Means* (New York, 1950). All references are to this edition.

2. Robert Penn Warren, "Father and Son." *New York Times Book Review*, June 11, 1950, p. 8.

The Non-Regionalism of Peter Taylor

JAN PINKERTON

I

Under the title "Southern-Fried," a writer in a national weekly recently reviewed *The Collected Stories of Peter Taylor** and proclaimed that we have had "enough of eccentric or incestuous families tending their faded houses and lives, enough social events which the teen-aged children of 'good' families attend in now-decadent mansions, enough about the humiliating behavior of not-so-nice relatives and 'fancy ladies' who drink too much"**. The reviewer concludes, in fact, that "Taylor's return to the same insipid, if not insidious, situations, events, remembrances and nostalgia finally implicates and indicts the author as much as his work." And Taylor's final error: "He does take these people seriously."** The author is indicted, in other words, by his continuing to deal with—and to take seriously—the characters he draws from a presumably out-of-fashion regional setting.

It must be said, of course, that much of this pique is directed not at the region itself but at the social hierarchy associated with that region. The reviewer is attacking the depiction of what is supposedly a quaint form of snobbery. Yet, we might ask, how different are the class distinctions in Taylor's milieu from those in any other part of the country? Do they differ, in basic ways, from all the other forms of social stratification currently alive and flourishing in America? Certainly one of the stories scornfully referred to, "The Fancy Woman," explores subtleties of social ambition that would be considered trenchant and incisive if the setting were not Memphis, Tennessee—or if the stereotypes evoked by that setting did not immediately click into readers' minds. In fact, the story documents, mainly by negative example, the criteria for determining a person's place within a social hierarchy—a matter which is as subtle and yet as all-prevailing today as it has ever been, and which finds distinct incarnations in such varied locales as the university campus, Harlem, or exurban Connecticut.

Yet perhaps this story has not been as well understood as it might be. Perhaps many of Taylor's stories, in fact, have been read in terms of stereotypes—and of consequent value judgments, both favorable and unfa-

From *The Georgia Review* 24 (Winter 1970): 432–40. © 1970 by The University of Georgia. Reprinted by permission of *The Georgia Review*.

vorable—that a closer examination would demonstrate to be inaccurate. The current collection, although containing only about half the author's published stories, nevertheless provides an opportunity for discovering some of the special qualities that take him far beyond the generalizations usually offered to explain lesser-known Southern writers. Taylor draws upon a specific milieu, to be sure, but he frequently entertains ideas that contradict the dogmas popularly believed to be the point of all Southern literature. In terms of regional stereotypes, then, his stories should be seen, not as chronicles of more of the same "situations, events, remembrances and nostalgia," but as treatments of these matters that are controversial and even heretical. We have already suggested that certain "Southern" themes—of which Taylor makes considerable use—are not exclusively regional at all; we must now explain the specific heresies that Taylor propounds when he deals with these themes.

II

Another "regional" matter, then—beyond that of social stratification—is the presumed Southern attitude toward the past. The reviewer we have quoted implies that Taylor also, like all Southerners, is in love with the past; like the elderly Aunt Munsie, "the author too seems to believe that those really were the good ole days." That Taylor is nostalgic for the past is, to be sure, a standard critical statement made by even the most favorable readers; he has long been pronounced a writer of jeremiads lamenting the breakdown of traditional modes of life. But what the reviewer and most critics have failed to see is the distinction that must be made between Aunt Munsie and many of the other characters, on the one hand, and Taylor, the author, on the other. The character who mourns the past is usually shown by the author, through a variety of narrative techniques, to be limited in perception, to be ignoring obvious truths of the past, to be fantasizing an ideal age that never existed. We might add, of course, that such unrealistic thinking is not peculiar to one region. Yet it has, like the concept of a social hierarchy, been associated with the South—and has thereupon been judged harshly, along with the region itself. Taylor, however, is the analyzer of this phenomenon, not its true believer; he views the nostalgic stances of his characters with often-critical detachment, although ultimately he bestows the sympathy he always gives his imperfect human beings.

"Southern" themes of class-consciousness and of nostalgia, then, can be quickly spotted in Taylor's work but must not necessarily be identified with the author's own views. Many of his stories, in fact, are far more deeply involved in other matters—in personal power plays, in the battle of the sexes, in the human compulsion to play roles, in frigidity, in the loneliness of women. These are issues that transcend region and make it difficult to pin-point any particular ideological formula on the part of the author, beyond the broad and generous outlook that he so clearly holds. There is, moreover, one further cliché from which he should be rescued: he is not the mourner of the decline of the family, that institution traditionally considered the stabilizer of a society. He often records the discontinuities of contemporary family life, but he does not imply that families of the past were superior or preferable; there were always conflicts and neuroses, he makes clear, and even a seemingly stable family façade has always been blighted by the basic and constant flaws in human nature.

Most of Taylor's stories, then, have a Southern setting; most include characters who express a nostalgia for older times; most take place within a disordered family situation. Yet, as we have indicated, the chief substance of the stories is not these more obvious characteristics. The earliest piece in the collection, "A Spinster's Tale" (1940), is the study of a girl's psychological warping, set within a family context, to be sure, but most logically because the topic depends on such a setting. The family is disordered, but in this instance it is by the death of the mother; the causes of disruption are medical, not sociological, and the tale is in no way inextricable from the region or paradigmatic of social breakdown. The story itself is of a girl's fears of masculinity and of her development into a formidable woman capable of dealing authoritatively and harshly with the masculine world. It is a tale of frigidity and of the inevitability of spinsterhood, a subject, incidentally, that has been more frequently associated with New England than with the South. Region, in other words, is secondary here, and any clichés, if they exist, are Freudian rather than Southern.

This early story is in many ways complementary to the latest story of the collection, "Dean of Men" (1969), the narrative of a man who is determined to succeed in a world of masculinity, to live among men—and not to follow the example of his father and grandfather, who had suffered defeats in business and politics and had retreated to a woman's world of family and household. "A man must somehow go on living among men," he tells his son, whose own ability to play a masculine role the narrator seems to doubt. As he tells tales from the life of both his father and grandfather, he makes clear that the family was at no time an ideal institution, despite the myth to the contrary; it might have served as a refuge, but it always had negative qualities: "People in my grandfather's day disliked admitting they did wretched things to each other at home or that there *were* family scenes in their families." We can conclude, then, that if there is a physical breakdown of the family in modern times, it is only an outward enactment of the disharmonies that have always existed. There is nothing in this story to convince the reader, in other words, that older times were better times. If Taylor is a "conservative" writer, as he has been called, it is not because he looks to the past but because his view of human nature is pessimistic, because he sees a constancy in human nature, the chief characteristic of which is its imperfectability.

III

So the narrator of "Dean of Men" worries about his role as a man, and the narrator of "A Spinster's Tale" worries about how she, as a woman, will deal with men. We can identify, then, a basic theme in Taylor: a concern with role-playing and with personal identity. It is easy to say that this concern ties in, after all, with the breakdown of a stable society and of its chief institution, the family; in more stable times, one could say, role and identity were well governed and understood. But Taylor himself never gives support to such conclusions. Role-playing, a constant and universal human action, is the individual's carrying out of a particular mode of behavior offered by his society; excessive, or even pathological, role-playing can take place within a "stable" society as well as within one that is chaotic. The identity confusions that Taylor portrays, moreover, occur within contexts both of social rigidity and of social laxness. Regional or ideological formulae simply do not apply when a writer is drawing upon a broadly knowledgeable view of human nature.

Yet the claims of region still persist in Taylor's work; it is as inaccurate to deny them completely as it is to insist on their being the ultimate key to the interpretation of his stories. A valid connection with a Southern tradition, for instance, can be found in the manners of the region—the emphasis on forms of etiquette and protocol that persist more wholeheartedly in the South than in other parts of the country. Here is a connection with "role" that can account for Taylor's persistent use of the theme. When an individual participates in formal social codes, he is limiting his range of possible behavior and expression; perhaps a long-time participant develops a special sense of prescriptive role-playing—or perhaps he is merely more conscious of the procedures of living with others. For whatever reason, Taylor is constantly depicting the social formalities that seem to evolve easily into well-defined roles, and (as in "Guests," "Heads of Houses," or "Cookie") these formalities do not necessarily contribute to human happiness. They provide a measure of communication on one level, but they deny it on a deeper level. In a society with divisions between class, race, and sex, a social code can achieve a formal rapport between these divisions, but yet—as Taylor demonstrates with frequency and poignancy—it can exclude a more intimate rapport among those for whom such communion would relieve the loneliness and misunderstanding that bring misery to so many of Taylor's characters.

The ultimate statement on role-playing is to be found in "Miss Leonora When Last Seen," the story of an eccentric small-town spinster given to taking automobile trips in which she assumes various identities: the "great lady" in the lace choker, the farmer's wife in dungarees, or, finally, the Memphis lady in stylish clothes looking for antiques or country hams. It is easy to say, of course, that Miss Leonora has lost her own identity because there is no longer a place for her in modern life or in a family that has dispersed. Yet her "real" self has always been problematic; no one has ever known her well, and the narrator admits that it is "hard for any two people to agree on what she is really like." Even in the past she had often been seen in terms of her external garments; she had at one time been identified by the uniform of a teacher at the Female Institute, and later by "what amounts to a uniform for our high-school teachers—the drab kind of street dresses that can be got through the mail-order catalogues." Nor does she herself see others except in terms of a generalized role; the narrator, formerly a student of hers, finds her seeming awareness of him to be flattering, "until presently you realized it was merely of you as an individual in her scheme of things for Thomasville. She was still looking at me as though I were one of the village children that she would like so much to make something of." When people are seen solely in terms of their roles—when human interaction is reduced to merely a kind of protocol—the result is loneliness and isolation. Miss Leonora, herself an abstraction and seeing others as abstractions, has always denied, and been denied, the benefits of human intimacy. The transition, then, from her earliest role as a member of the town's leading family to her latest role, that of a modern tourist, is not necessarily a change for the worse. The narrator of this story laments the change ("She will look too much like a thousand others") but he is shown to be an unremarkable man still committed to the small town; and it is the small town in which Miss Leonora has always been a "character"—but, as such, a public figure and not someone to whom others could relate on an individual or intimate basis. Perhaps her new facelessness, then, is essentially no different from the old; perhaps her new fluidity is even preferable to the stagnation of her previous life. We will return to what seems to be Taylor's heretical espousal of transience, of motion, even of uprootedness.

But there are other stories about the stifling dominance of role over individual personality. There is the example of Miss Patty Bean, for instance, in the story "Their Losses." She is one of three women, each with her own sense of loss, who meet on a train outside of Memphis. The loss that Miss Patty articulates is for a past order, although obviously there are other deficiencies in her life as well. Taylor, moreover, clearly not sharing her nostalgia for the past, makes her the most grotesque of the three women. She is bringing home from Washington a dying aunt, whom she sees as a symbol of past superiority; her people, she makes clear, were "not of *this* world but of *a* world that we have seen disappear. In mourning my family, I mourn that world's disappearance." Yet she feels no obligation to express love for these people as individuals; they are mourned solely for their roles in a larger abstraction: "How I regarded the members of my family as individuals is neither here nor there." It is obvious, in fact, that love was singularly lacking in Miss Patty's relations with others. Moreover, there are final revelations in the story: first, that the aunt has turned Roman Catholic; second, that she is a mental patient who does not remember the members of the family at all. Everything that Miss Patty has made her a symbol of is, ironically, not only dying, but also, like the aunt, alien and demented. Miss Patty's reverence for her family's role leads us to question the soundness of the role—and the soundness and credibility of the world of the past as well.

Indeed the most grotesque of all the Taylor characters in this collection are also those most attached to an idealized past: the old Dorset brother and sister of "Venus, Cupid, Folly and Time." They, too, play roles ("We are all young, we all love one another") and, like Miss Leonora, they cast the young people of the town into collective roles. At their parties for the socially acceptable young people, they make no individual distinctions among them: they "made no effort to distinguish which of their guests was which. . . . The way they had gazed *at* the little face instead of into it had revealed their lack of interest in the individual child." It is, of course, the Dorsets' lack of individual distinctions that makes it possible for the children to add the extra guest, a procedure which itself involves role-playing among the young people and which brings the Dorsets' party-giving to its bizarre end. Thus the old people are defeated by being totally lost in abstraction, an abstract sense of their own lives, an abstract sense of the lives around them.

IV

We cannot say, therefore, that Miss Leonora, Miss Patty, or the Dorsets are the way they are because the modern world has betrayed their mode of life. Taylor lays no blame on the times, on modernization, on industrialism, on a new commercial economy. In a number of stories he explains what did go wrong: it was the failure of these people either to initiate change or to respond to change. The Dorsets talk about proper breeding and they scorn the idea of money, but yet at the end of the story we learn how their own family had been established in Chatham: "They were an obscure mercantile family who came to invest in a new Western city. Within two generations the business— no, the industry!—which they established made them rich beyond any dreams they could have had in the beginning. For half a century they were looked upon, if any family ever was, as our first family." So it was money after all that made the Dorsets what they were. But most of the family moved on to other successful ventures, leaving behind only the old brother and sister who now claimed disgust at money and commercialism. If it is easy to speak of the breakdown of the stable Southern family and the loss of old virtues, Taylor clearly countermands such facile conclusions in this story. Instead of lamenting decaying families, he introduces the question, *Why* is this family decaying? And the answer is that this old brother and sister are the ones who have *not* picked up stakes and moved on elsewhere. It is for this reason that they are now sterile and decadent. The other members of the family, says the narrator, "knew that what they had in Chatham they could buy more of in other places. For them Chatham was an investment that had paid off." And so they moved on to Santa Barbara and Long Beach, Newport, or Long Island. It was commercialism that made this family in the first place; its decline, as embodied by the old bachelor and spinster, is *from* commercialism to gentility, not the other way around. In fact, admits the narrator, the spirit of the early Dorsets was really close to that of the rest of the people in Chatham: "The obvious difference was that we had to stay on here and pretend that our life had a meaning which it did not." That is precisely what the brother and sister had done. They were those without the vigor for further ventures, and so they settled down into make-believe, pretending that their way of life was the old way, the meaningful way. This, too, was role-playing. And the conclusion is unmistakable: all the "meaning" of the old order is pretense, an elaborate defensiveness on the part of those who are non-enterprising and defeatist.

The beginnings of this pretense, indeed, can be seen in the fact that some of these families, while spending their time elsewhere making money, nevertheless tried to block "progress" in their own home towns. Miss Leonora's family was guilty of this maneuver, and so was Mrs. Billingsby's family in "Mrs. Billingsby's Wine." The latter family tried to prevent street lights and sidewalks in the small town of Blackwell; yet "they went off long ago to Memphis and St. Louis and even Detroit and made or married stacks of money." One old-timer used to say, "Ever time they seen a dollar they taken after it and they never stopped a-running till they cotched it." Yet Mrs. Billingsby, one of those who left Blackwell, is gracious, personally kind. Money, obviously, does not harm one, the preaching of the Dorsets notwithstanding. Nor, apparently, does urban life. Mrs. Billingsby has left the small town, has lived in Memphis for forty years; and she has none of the eccentricity of the less-affluent Miss Leonora, who stayed behind. Their families pursued similar paths, seeking money and seeking urbanization, although both families tried to keep the new from the town of their origin; but Mrs. Billingsby, while less of a "character" than Miss Leonora, is surely more gracious than the spinster who indulges in ludicrous role-playing and sees the townspeople only as abstract role-players as well. Mrs. Billingsby, in fact—and this is one of the points of the story—remembers in individual terms the young woman from Blackwell who calls on her. And she is, of course, far removed from the bizarre Dorsets, who also stayed in the small town, speaking vehemently against money and commerce.

What is the moral of these stories? It seems to be: keep moving, be open to new experiences. The alternative is to stagnate. Yet is this a "Southern" theme or a Yankee theme? It sounds like the essence of the putative American experience, the official American code of conduct. The Southerners Taylor writes about, in other words, are those who stagnated because they did not move on, who fell into worship of an unreal past because they did not keep themselves refreshed by new ideas. This is Taylor's message, his heresy. He is a Southern writer who distrusts the past, a conservative writer who believes in change; those who see him as a stereotyped regionalist are themselves blinded by their clichéd responses to setting and style.

Notes

    The Collected Stories of Peter Taylor. New York: Farrar, Straus and Giroux, 1969. 535 pp. $10.00.
    **Barbara Raskin, *The New Republic*. CLXI (Oct. 18, 1969), 29–30. An excellent rebuttal by Jonathan Yardley appears in the November 22 issue.

Presences, Absences, and Peter Taylor's Plays

ALBERT J. GRIFFITH

"I suspect you have sensed it," the writer in Peter Taylor's "Missing Person" says, ". . . that this is the time in my life when reassessment may be in order."

If Peter Taylor's sixtieth birthday is to be taken as just such a time for reassessment of his achievement, then his most recent major publication, *Presences: Seven Dramatic Pieces* (Boston: Houghton Mifflin, 1973), may well be chosen as the focal point for the reassessment. Since *Presences* is the only volume of totally new material Taylor has published since 1959, it should merit considerable critical interest on that score alone; since it also marks Taylor's most significant departure to date from the short story form, the genre in which he has always done his most distinguished work, it provides further good reason for close critical scrutiny. In addition, *Presences* offers some intriguing new variations on some of Taylor's oldest and most enduring themes—variations which may reveal more succinctly than anything else what the essence of Taylor's work has been.

The seven one-act plays (or "dramatic pieces") in *Presences* are not, of course, Taylor's first excursion into the theatrical medium. He has previously published one short play, "The Death of a Kinsman" (1949), and two full-length ones, "Tennessee Day in St. Louis" (1956) and "A Stand in the Mountains" (1968). Like these earlier works, the plays in *Presences* seem in many ways more like "closet dramas" than like fully-realized theatrical experiences. The publisher's blurb quotes Taylor's own rationale for the choice of medium:

> The plays are full of ghosts and fantasies. I believe we all live with ghosts and fantasies whether or not we acknowledge them. It seems to me that I live with them more every year that passes. Before putting pen to paper, I give considerable thought to how I might best present such experience and have it believed in and felt. I came to the conclusion that ghosts as well as the fantasies that we invent about living people require too much artifice when presented in fiction . . . Whereas in a play, the ghost simply walks upon the stage. We do not question his presence. He is as real to us as any natural character in a

Reprinted from *Shenandoah: The Washington and Lee University Review* 28 (Winter 1977): 62–71, with permission of the Editor.

play; he seems as real to us in the audience as he does to the other character or characters who, out of their urgent need or unbearable fear, have created his presence through their imagination.

Taylor, then, has selected the ghost play as the genre which will best permit him to objectify some of the prevailing influences he senses in his characters' lives. In reading these dramas, however, with full awareness of Taylor's prior accomplishments, we note two other kinds of "presences" emerge as well: the first, as palpable as any characters on the stage, are those remembered Taylor traits of theme and technique which are again embodied in these very plays; the second, like apparitions hovering in a background mist, are those traits so dominant in Taylor's fiction which have no counterpart in drama and must be banished from the stage, yet linger as after-images, felt absences whose loss or deprivation is itself a kind of presence. We will attempt to analyze all three types of "presences."

The ghosts who materialize as characters in the seven plays derive their identities from the memories, fantasies, and projected roles of the flesh and blood people they appear to. "I'm coming," an old lady in one of the plays responds to a knock on the door as she hides the ghosts in her room, ". . . But I have certain encumbrances." And that essentially is what the ghosts in all the plays are: encumbrances the characters must struggle under or against. Taylor has often attempted to represent the same sort of encumbrances in his fiction; perhaps the most obvious example is in "The Dark Walk," where a recently widowed Southern matron finally realizes that the furniture she had carried with her from city to city throughout all the moves of her married life had been the sign of her bondage to all that was "old and useless and inherited." The characters in *Presences* are no freer than that widow, though their psychological and spiritual encumbrances are here represented as spectral visions rather than as a van full of furniture.

The first play, "Two Images," introduces us to a thirty-five-year-old much-divorced woman, Meg, and her younger brother, Nicky, as they summon opposing apparitions of their deceased father. To Nicky, who remembers his father as a philanderer, hypocrite, and bully, the ghost of a silent, overweight, disheveled, middle-aged man appears; the ghost submits to Nicky's lectures, orders, and verbal abuse just the way Nicky once had to submit to his father. To Meg, who has idealized her father as a man who dedicated his life to his children, a slender, straight, correctly dressed, and highly dignified ghost approaches her seductively; at curtain close, she succumbs to his lover's embrace. Nicky's ghost had come to him many times before, but Meg's ghost could materialize only after Nicky's reminiscences of the father's sexual promiscuity made Meg let herself see him. The ghost specifically tells Meg, "I am just as I always was, am I not Meg?" In short, the point the play makes somewhat too explicitly is that Meg's erotic attachment to her father had always been present—throughout her four loveless marriages—but could not be faced for what it was until her idealized image of the father was transformed and released by Nicky's iconoclastic countervision.

The second play, "A Father and a Son," also is built on the device of two images of a dead person, although in this instance the images are remarkably similar, albeit equally imperceptive. The single subject of the images is the daughter of old Nathan and the mother of young Jack; she regularly visits both her father and her son as a ghostly minister, attending to their emotional needs. But they—her father and her son—have no real understanding of her or of her unselfish passion for her husband, whom both Nathan and Jack jealously resented and despised. "Poor darlings," she says of them to her husband who has lately joined her in death. "If only they could understand what it is to love someone." The father and the son know she comes to them because they need her; they cannot seem to realize, however, that her ne'er-do-well husband needed her even more and so her commitment to him was even more engrossing and enduring. "It's your *presence* that *is* everything," Nathan once tells his daughter's ghost, cherishing her memory when, if he had been more willing to share, he might have been enjoying her reality.

The ghost in the third play, "Missing Person," is not a memory of another person but a character's projection of himself into "what might have been." On a lecture trip to his old hometown, Virgil Minor, a successful novelist, spends an evening with his old sweetheart, Flo Abbot, now a widow and the mother of three children. As the evening wears on, they recall another side of Virgil that would have been content in the hometown the way Flo has been. As Virgil admits: "There *was* another side to me once. When we are young we all have more sides than one. When we are young we have lots of possibilities. Lots of potentiality. It seems almost impossible that those other aspects of one's self besides the one you finally concentrate upon, don't go on developing somewhere. I've kept thinking all day today about that other side of me you refer to. Was he around somewhere? Would I see him? Ever since I stepped off the plane I've found myself watching for him." Later, as the lights blink on and off in a storm, the "missing person" appears and Virgil sees himself as he might have been as Flo's bourgeois husband. This alter ego confesses, "I've had to do things you couldn't have brought yourself to do," but he is unable to tell Virgil whether these things were "worth it." Flo perceives that Virgil has seen this "missing person" and confides that he is "always here" in her house, where he, not the actual real-life Virgil, has been the object of her love and yearning. Flo and Virgil then part, lamenting the terrible "narrowness" which has doomed them to be only one aspect of themselves.

"Whistler," the fourth play, also involves projections of the "might have been." In this instance, Emma and Harry Patterson recall their fears for their son Tom, who is now "missing in action." Harry had feared that Tom would be a long-haired hippy conscientious objector; Emma had feared he would become an animal-like killer; both had failed to realize his life and death were not theirs to determine. Now Tom's ghost appears separately to each as the actualization of their worst fears. Each parent welcomes the son just as he is, glad of his presence and oblivious to the role he enacts. Tom's message to each before he disappears is to tell the other parent he is alive. But the play ends with the two grieving parents acknowledging together the death they can no longer deny.

The projection of fears is carried still further in the fifth play, entitled "Arson." Rob, a student, returns to his mother's apartment with a young black radical, Leo, with whom he has been involved in the burning of a college building in a campus protest. The mother, Liz, implants in Rob's mind the idea that Leo is homosexually attached to him, and Leo in turn suggests that Liz is incestuously possessive. Rob then fantasizes each of them approaching him in their hitherto unperceived roles. It seems to him a nightmare he is having, but a nightmare he must "finish out" by stripping off his clothes and building a ritual holocaust in the center of the apartment. Leo and Liz reappear in their ordinary guises, and Rob declares: "It was only a dream—or a wish I had. It was not your real selves I saw. It was my own. It is myself, isn't it, I have exposed, revealed, disrobed, unmasked tonight. You two are only—always—what I wish for you to seem. And now I have wished you back the way you were. It's no good the other way. So we'll have another fire." As he lights the pyre at curtain close, he proclaims, "Fire also is only a wish—a dream of escape."

In some ways the most complex of all the plays is the next to last, "A Voice Through the Door." Here, Maisie, a septuagenarian maiden aunt, shares her suite in her niece's house with the ghosts of all her deceased relatives, who sit before her sewing, knitting, whispering, even chewing and spitting tobacco. All her life, her family has "protected" her from various things, including an ill-advised romance in her youth; now her still living family is protecting her from a visit by her grand nephew Bobby, who has shocked one and all by coming home from college with long hair and beard. Maisie hears a voice through the door and, despite veiled insinuations by her spectral companions, lets Bobby in. Maisie learns of Bobby's plans to live his life as he pleases and to go off on his own against his family's will; she asks him to express his feelings so she can share them vicariously. Bobby, in turn, confesses he returned home only because of Maisie, because he needed to see once more how she had done what he could never do, "always managing to go along with them," the domineering family. Eventually, the spirits of the kinfolk about her force Maisie to recognize that Bobby is another ghost: the spirit of her long ago lover projected into the image of her grandnephew. Meantime, the real Bobby has succumbed to family pressure and shaved his offending beard and promised to return to college. Maisie then forgets once more her long lost lover, and the spirits of her kin promise to be with her till the end.

The seventh and final play, "The Sweethearts," makes the theater audience a kind of ghostly presence, judging the propriety and decorum of the characters. At center stage, as it were, are Janet and Louis, a middle-aged couple who still enact the roles of sweethearts. "We are entitled to a life of our own, to being our *selves*—not always somebody's child or somebody's parent," Janet says defensively when they agree they were right to put Janet's senile mother in a "Home." Grandmom, a feisty old lady who appears to owe not a little to Edward Albee's Grandma in *The American Dream*, doesn't want to return to the Home, however, and she recognizes the "married sweethearts" as a dangerous enemy to everybody in the family, since "sweethearts *have* to be alone." Carol, the daughter of Janet and Louis, realizes the same thing when she tells her parents that she and her husband are planning an abortion and her parents turn away from her problem and back into their own self-absorption as lovers. In near hysteria, Carol cries: "What a way to forget you're somebody's parent or somebody's child, or somebody's husband or wife even! What a way of shutting out the world! What a way of forgetting about the life . . . or the child you don't ever have!" As both Grandmom and Carol have made clear in earlier comments, the role of sweethearts is enacted before other people, represented by the theater audience, who "manage to carry on" through other types of "play-pretend."

Just as the ghosts and spirits in the seven plays are concepts or fantasies which make themselves immanent in the lives of the other characters, so there are typical themes and techniques of Taylor which hover as literary presences throughout the entire dramatic sequence. And just as the characters in the plays often have clarifying visions of their ghosts, so the readers of the plays can gain unusual insights into Taylor's art from some of the devices which, while obscured from ready view in his other works, become transparently obvious in these plays. Perhaps the chief literary revelation which the plays force upon us has to do with Taylor's characterization: we discover how often his characters represent abstractions manipulated in mathematical arrangements, like factors in a formula. Taylor uses ghosts openly in *Presences*, but this use calls attention to the abstract presences his artifice has deliberately concealed in his fiction. Frank Moore Colby in *Imaginary Obligations* (New York: Dodd, Mead, 1904) once made fun of Henry James for the intellectual phantoms he passed off as characters and the demonstrations of theorems which he passed off as plot. Good Jamesian that he is, Taylor may have more wraiths and bogies in his work than he has been given credit for. His characters, all the way from *A Long Fourth* (1948) to *Collected Stories* (1969), are all too frequently arranged as opposing sets of values, operating as spectral encumbrances on each other. The characters seldom engage in overtly dramatic actions; what they do is regroup and realign themselves in new postures and juxtapositions. A denouement is almost never a murder or an adultery or a joining of the French Foreign Legion; it is more frequently a heightened awareness of some difference of value or change of tradition represented by one or more of the other characters. This is particularly true of the stories about Southern families (and that would be the majority of his stories) in which the assorted uncles and aunts and cousins and grandparents and in-laws and servants function as controlling presences which limit freedom and individuality.

These recent plays also indicate how consistent and enduring are Taylor's themes. From the beginning, his works have emphasized the individual in conflict over social roles: "The Scoutmaster" (1945), "A Wife of Nashville," (1949), "Two Ladies in Retirement" (1951), "Heads of Houses" (1959), and "Miss Leonora When Last Seen" (1960) are just a few of the more obvious examples. In *Presences*, inherited sex roles, the generation gap, and societal expectations again trap individuals into various kinds of compromise between sheer rebellion and abject capitulation. Unlike the more romantic characters of some other writers, the typical Taylor character reaches some kind of accommodation with his social context. As Virgil puts it in "Missing Person": "But there comes a time when . . . you know that what you need from life is not stimulation but rather the tranquillity and the quiet satisfaction of life that will allow you to work."

Another all pervasive theme throughout Taylor's career has been the complex intricacies and tensions of family relationships. Every single play in *Presences* deals with families, just as have the great majority of all Taylor's other works. Again, families appear as manipulative, dominating forces which often stifle individuality as the price for "protection" from unnamed external ills. "A Father and a Son" depicts the living relatives speaking of the freedom their mutual kinswoman has gained in death; yet her servile attendance on them as a ghost suggests there is no freedom from the bondage of family love even after death. "A Voice Through the Door" only carries Taylor's favorite family theme to its logical conclusion in the other direction, as it represents the living still in thrall to the deceased kin who remain ever present. "But one thing I'm sure of," old Maisie says in this play, "the living cannot protect us from our dead, just as the dead cannot protect us from our living."

It is Maisie also in "A Voice Through the Door" who gives one of the most explicit revelations yet of Taylor's notion of the love-hate paradox which inextricably binds families together. "It's tempting to follow certain inclinations one has, to be self-indulgent, but the love of one's family is like a different kind of yearning, hunger—one that must be satisfied as well as any other," Maisie says. "One can't entirely live without it if ever one has tasted family life, family love. And one should not try." Maisie then indulges in an explanation which the materialized presence of her deceased relatives drives home: "The family body is as real, as organic as the individual body.

The fact that its various members can walk away, if they will, doesn't necessarily mean it is not as real and organic as a person. We hear of the individual's rights in society, but nothing of the family's rights. The family must live, too, and sometimes one of its members must yield—." From the spirit of her long ago lover, Maisie finally learns how sometimes the individual can assert his or her freedom from the family: "You don't do it against their love, or against their will. And you do not love them less. What you do, what you have to do, is make them not exist so much. You make yourself exist more. You must make yourself exist in someone else or something else that you are going toward." This is almost precisely the revelation that Taylor had provided for Sylvia Harrison in "The Dark Walk" written nearly twenty years before: "She knew, at least, that in the future she would regard the people she loved very differently from the way she had in the past. And it wasn't that she would love them less; it was that she would in some sense or other learn to love herself more."

Presences, then, reveals some of the pervading strengths of Peter Taylor's literary art, strengths which were present in his prior works and which persist in these seven plays. Yet probably few readers would find these plays as esthetically satisfying as the best of Taylor's short stories. The plays, as clever and craftsmanlike as they are, seem to lack some of the attributes which made stories like "Rain in the Heart," "What You Hear From 'Em?", "1939," "*Je Suis Perdu*," "Two Pilgrims," "There," and "End of Play" so impressive. There are felt "absences" as well as felt "presences" in these plays, and these absences are those fictional devices that have served Taylor so well and true in his short stories but which are here ruled out by the nature of the dramatic medium. One of these is the use of a central consciousness point of view—either a narrator's or a character's—to give unity and integrity to the perceptions of the story. Another is the digressive-progressive narrative technique, which permits a leisurely meandering back and forth in time and space, savoring experience until its essence is distilled. The relatively straightforward objective thrust of the plays has its artistic effectiveness, too, but it is better for hammering home abstract messages than for proceeding delicately from nuance to nuance of barely discovered meaning.

And finally and most importantly, the plays in general lack the richness of texture of Taylor's stories, the plethora of realistic and homely detail, the ambience of place, the tints and tones and moods that make up cultural context. The first three plays have St. Louis specified as setting, but there is none of the delineation of locale that is found in A *Woman of Means* or "Two Ladies in Retirement." Several of the plays could be set almost anywhere, with only an unusual exaggeration in their codes of manners to suggest the South a little more than other regions; only "A Voice Through the Door" has much realistic detail. The characters in most of the plays are given few individuating traits; they tend to function first as abstract symbols and only secondarily as persons, which is the exact opposite of the characters in such richly textured stories as "A Long Fourth," "The Other Times," or "Miss Leonora When Last Seen." Even their speech patterns lack the cultural resonance of the distinctive characters in "The Scoutmaster," "Guests," "Porte-Cochere," and "A Friend and Protector." Perhaps because of the condensation inherent in the one-act format, we learn little about their likes, dislikes, tastes, attitudes, education, religion, hobbies, interests, ambitions, or frustrations—except those few which bear directly on the dramatic conflict. But the creation of authentic milieu has always been Taylor's forte— witness the marvelous, long, almost extraneous description of an old-fashioned Colorado summer resort at the opening of "The Dark Walk" or the painfully nostalgic recreation of a railway depot in "At the Drugstore"—and this gives credence to his characters. "Location is the ground-conductor of all the currents of emotion and belief and moral conviction that charge out from the story in its course," Eudora Welty has observed in *Three Papers on Fiction* (Northampton, Mass.: Smith College, 1962). "These charges need the warm hard earth underfoot, the light and lift of air, the stir and play of mood, the softening bath of atmosphere that gives the likeness-to-life that life needs." Taylor's stories have this; these most recent plays do not.

Taylor has stated he chose the theatrical medium for *Presences* because he wanted to escape the artifice his ideas would have required in fiction. There is little question that he has made the dramatic genre work for him successfully in the presentation of his abstract themes. If he has lost something we have come to prize in his fiction, there is no reason to think it has not been a conscious sacrifice for the purpose of the experiment. Peter Taylor as a playwright is a significant artist. It's just that Peter Taylor as a fiction writer is an even better one.

A View of Peter Taylor's Stories

JANE BARNES CASEY

As an author, Peter Taylor is more often praised than understood. The respect his work inspires frequently seems taken in by appearances, by the fact that in a formal sense, his material *seems* fixed. His stories usually take place in Tennessee—in Memphis or Nashville or Chatham; the characters are drawn from the upper middle class or from the Negro servant class; people are seen in terms of the family, rarely as isolated individuals or divorced ones or even single ones; the stories occur before 1960, and some take place around the turn of the century, while others are governed by the events and history of the 19th century, particularly, of course, the Civil War.

Yet the limitations Mr. Taylor sets on his work barely contain the shifting, probing attitude he constantly turns on his material. He is a great craftsman, but of a foxy sort, intent on working as much complexity as possible into the world behind his simple surfaces. In his best stories, his masterpieces, every detail is present in all its vital controversy; every part hums with its own inner fullness, as well as in its relation to every other part. He is a master of contradiction, though we have only to mention this quality when Mr. Taylor's singlemindedness must be accounted for. His work has always been concerned with the conflict between affectionate, civil society and chaos, regardless of whether the disorder is sexual, drunken, or natural. From "A Spinster's Tale" when this chaos appears in the form of Mr. Speed, who's compared to a "loose horse," through "There" when the theme is recast as all that's mortally, tragically unattainable, through "In the Miro District" with its extraordinary descriptions of the 1811 earthquake, Mr. Taylor has never been far from his preoccupation with the social world and the forces which threaten it.

The purpose of this essay is to discuss the way Mr. Taylor's handling of his recurrent themes has changed and evolved toward his newest collection of stories, *In the Miro District*. The book invites us to look back. Tonally, particularly in the experimental prose poems, the book evokes the author's earliest stories when he wrote out of oneness with the domestic context he so lovingly described. Reading "The Hand of Emmagene" with its casual,

Reprinted by permission from *Virginia Quarterly Review* 54 (Spring 1978): 213–30.

unforced pace, its love of furniture and china and cooking, it is impossible not to think of "A Long Fourth," one of Mr. Taylor's most lusciously written first stories, full of sympathetic descriptions of the characters, family routines, and relationships. Both "The Hand of Emmagene" and "A Long Fourth" have marriage at their moral center, but the difference between the marriages is enormous. In "A Long Fourth," Harriet and Sweetheart's happy union is what creates the fullness of tone. Their freshness and purity and unexamined goodness is the measure by which we know the problems in the story. As Harriet's hysteria testifies, it is, in many ways, an inadequate measure. But much as Harriet wants to deny the connection between Son and BT, the black cook's nephew, they are equivalents. BT is bestial and incompetent when compared to his aunt, just as Son is unfruitful in comparison to his parents. The South in which Harriet and Sweetheart bloomed has somehow been reduced to rampant carnality, on the one hand, and sterile respectability or sterile radicalism, on the other. We end by feeling both the sadness and confusion that Harriet and Sweetheart feel about the tragic problem of race and the inability of the younger generation to proceed. But just because the emotions we feel are in the old-fashioned style of Harriet and Sweetheart, we also feel Mr. Taylor's oneness with them: his sense of the modern world as acid, biting into the soft medium he loves.

By contrast, in "The Hand of Emmagene," the narrator's marriage is stable and happy, but the narrator and his wife differ from Sweetheart and Harriet in having real knowledge of the world. Whereas Harriet has a romantic hope for Son and her daughters, one which skirts the issue of sex, in the prose poem, the narrator and his wife are good people, but they are not innocent. Though the poet is moved by horror, as well as sympathy for Emmagene, these are the wholesome emotions of someone who trusts reason, who sees extremism from the perspective of normal affection and sexuality. Between "A Long Fourth" and "The Hand of Emmagene," marriage has grown tough enough to bear the stresses of the modern world, though the question of whether society can pass happy marriage from one generation to the next seems to have withered away. Emmagene is certainly a failure in this regard, but she is a freak too. In fact, she is all that is freakish and uncompromising in human experience, as opposed to what is unsuitable say, or unacceptable.

Originally, Mr. Taylor seemed to give himself to Southern society, even though it was doomed, but his loyalty has undergone a transformation. While he continues to regard marriage as central, the conditions for its survival are more mythic than regional. What is interesting is that what appears to have made the reaffirmation of marriage possible is an avowal of sex as part of love; more importantly, this avowal is synonymous with an affirmation of masculinity.

In The Miro District is basically about men. In two of the stories, the central characters are young men involved in rites of passage. Until this collection, Mr. Taylor has written more from the female point of view, using it as a screen through which he has observed disorder. Almost without exception, disorder has been associated with men trampling the social restraints enforced or represented by women. In his earliest stories, in "A Spinster's Tale" and "The Fancy Woman," through Betsy's frailty and Josie's vulnerability, we see the destructiveness, the cruelty, the violence of the male. And in later stories, such as "At the Drugstore," Matt Donelson subdues what is brutal and anti-social in himself out of a sense of duty to women.

"At the Drugstore" is nonetheless a melancholy story, written in a dry, analytical, even agonized style. In it strong moral impulses run neck and neck with disillusion, and the unresolved tension between the two gives the story its dominant quality—a haunting, straw fragrance like that of pressed flowers. It's a story which shows what Mr. Taylor has gone through to arrive at the consonance of *In The Miro District*, and like "A Long Fourth," it also takes place around a homecoming. Unlike Son, Matt Donelson has successfully gone on to have a family of his own, one which he thinks he is proud of. To his surprise, on his first day home, he finds himself on the way to the drugstore in a kind of numbed, neurotic fog. Once there, his apparent purpose—the purchase of shaving lotion—turns out to be an excuse for a deeper confrontation. On one level, his attention is caught by the relation of the pharmacist and his son; on another level, Matt is preoccupied with recollections of school days and the curiosity he felt about Mr. Conway and his female assistants. Matt identifies with the son's difficulties with his father, but he is also jealous of him for being so at home in what is expected of him.

Matt's disaffection with his family emerges in his awareness, while the causes of his alienation arise in his memory. He relives his terror and fascination as he recalls how a school mate once wrote "Mr. Conway sleeps with his mother" in full view on the mirror behind the counter. It's not too much to say that Matt seems to raise up and resolve his Oedipal dilemma in the course of his visit to the drugstore. When he goes home, he brings with him an awareness of all the forbidden sexuality which underlies family life and conflicts with domesticity. At the same time, he assumes authority in and for himself, having come to terms with his father. Matt now views his life and his choices with his own eyes, without the aid or illusion of tradition, and though he conceives of his choice as bleak, lying as it does between a brutal, selfish self and a resigned one, he commits himself to continuity, society, and civil discipline.

BT's carnality and Son's radical ideas meet with a positive outcome in Matt's dilemma. He becomes more suited to his life by realizing his nature, though this is one of Mr. Taylor's most mercurial stories, and the closer we come to explaining it, the more mysterious it remains at the core. The question is: has the hero in fact realized his nature? Isn't there a way in which he treats his carnal self to the same morality he finds so eroded in family life?

He construes his inner outlaw as guilty of wanting to sleep with his mother, of wanting to despoil the relationship which is the basis for honor and purity and love in all other relationships. Yet to conceive of sexuality in terms of this kind of Freudian original guilt is to punish himself by a code he has come to doubt. The story goes to great lengths to suggest that marriage, for Matt's class anyway, is a form being emptied of real emotional content. The contemporary world is seen as defined by change, by the exact undoing of the family though it represents "all the good sense and reasonableness that made life worthwhile—or even tolerable."

What makes this story bleak is not that Matt has to choose between the lesser of two evils. That bleakness is present, but there is a deeper bleakness stemming from a sense that bourgeois morality is insufficient—it cannot embrace the whole complexity; nonetheless, it is all there is to see us through the chaos between birth and death. There is a flaw in this reasoning—perhaps snarl is a better word because Mr. Taylor has gone on to untangle it in his new book. The snarl, as I see it, is in the contradiction between the potential Matt discovers in himself and his impulse to label it critically. The story suggests that Matt is torn between two equally powerful parts of himself, one anti-social, the other not, and yet in fact, these impulses are not treated equally, or not experienced equally. Matt looks beyond taboo, but he suppresses what he sees. The story is structured in terms of a Freudian analysis of Matt's experience, committing him from the start to a responsible, social resolution. The content of the story is not quite what it purports to be: Matt's self-discovery is prejudged. It's been found guilty of being savage before the narrative begins.

II

In "A Long Fourth," Mr. Taylor wrote out of identification with the large-hearted goodness of Harriet and Sweetheart; they were emblems of a coherent social world in which the younger generation had gone astray. In "At the Drugstore," the author writes from the point of view of the younger generation, struggling to find a morality which will enable them to do as much good for others as Harriet and Sweetheart were able to do. *In The Miro District* shows Mr. Taylor as having arrived at the goal he set for Matt Donelson. The interior conflicts have once more been realigned and subtly expanded beyond the scope of the narrow Freudian arguments, though at the same time, *In The Miro District* seems specifically organized to recapitulate Mr. Taylor's career, while demonstrating step by step his move from narrowest possible vision to the broadest, most humane one.

The first story in the collection, "The Captain's Son," appears to be a deliberate caricature of all the elements normally associated with "Southern" fiction: complex family ties, historical skeletons in the closet, dark sexual problems. Not only does it seem to be a deliberate caricature of a genre, but it also seems to be a wholly negative one. In an author who once treated the same society so sympathetically, it is hard not to feel that "The Captain's Son" is literally a regional critique. The villain—though Tolliver proclaims it and Lila's family deny it—is in everybody's breast. The villain is snobbery in one form or another, though the guilt is equally divided between Tolliver, who wants to retreat by marrying, and his father-in-law, who allows him, even compels Tolliver to marry into the household.

Each man believes he represents good breeding; both act out of noblesse oblige, though they emphasize different aspects of it. Tolliver's Deep South Planter background celebrates class differences and glories in its own privileges. His father-in-law, as a good liberal democrat, wants to mask inequalities in class and wealth. This doesn't stop him from honoring them in his heart—so much so that he takes control of his daughter's marriage lest Tolliver "turn out to be a high liver and a big spender and so, during times when nearly everybody was hard up, be a source of embarrassment to us all."

Both Tolliver and his father-in-law want to preserve a way of life, but they are willing to do it at the expense of life itself: Tolliver, after all, is impotent. Not coincidentally, Tolliver will not or cannot find employment. His impotence and joblessness are reflections of each other, and the connection of the two is the most powerful expression so far in Mr. Taylor's work of male despair in the modern world. Yet this despair is entirely associated with the rigid enforcement of Southernness—the deference of men to the social necessities of marriage. In "The Captain's Son," however, marriage is no perpetuation but a sacrifice of the couple who marry.

Looking back from this collection, it's as if Southern chivalry toward women had been strained until it snapped, until what is Jamesian in Mr. Taylor's sensibility had been revolutionized by a Laurentian awareness. For as long as women hold the moral reins in his stories, men suffer from emasculation. As opposed to the castrating women in much American fiction, the women in Mr. Taylor's earlier stories do not undermine their men personally. There are, in fact, many real heroines, among them Miss Lenore and the amazing Aunt Munsie in "What You Hear From 'Em." The problem is an historical or cultural one for men. Women's lives are more meaningful because they remain morally potent in the domestic sphere; meanwhile the possibility of moral potency in the political sphere has been lost for men in a world where they have no real effectiveness. It is a world described in "Dean of Men," in which the political power of the hero's grandfather has shrunk to the paltry gray arena of college administration.

Women are not blamed for the demoralization of men, but there is a coincidence between strong women and unhappy men, at least until *In The Miro District*. To some extent, this condition prevailed as long as Mr. Taylor preserved the notion that the woman's domain was the house and family, while man's was the exterior one of commerce and politics. More precisely, this condition prevailed as long as Mr. Taylor accepted women as the carriers of the social conscience. The honor of Southern womanhood and her purity were once part of a successful ethical arrangement in which men let women have charge of the spiritual accounts. "A Long Fourth" is a portrait of that world in its final phase. But the trade off, the swapping of covert for overt power, ceases to be that; increasingly, as men's crucial energy is no longer invested in the affairs of the world, the restraint exercised by and for women is entirely negative.

In "At The Drugstore," the man's problem is what to do about this energy. It is a source of potency and vitality, but in its disengagement from meaningful work, it is also lawlessly sexual. As a Southerner, Mr. Taylor seems to have been concerned with the question of how a man can go on being a man in the modern world without undermining the moral basis of society—without, in other words, rebelling against the woman's role as it has been traditionally defined. Though the sexes are assigned roles in this dilemma, the problem is deeper than sex. It is the great modern problem of how to incorporate the most vital, but also the most anarchic urges into civilized life. Is it possible for the individual to be completely alive without adding to the existing chaos and suffering?

Tolliver's failure as a man seems to be laid at the doorstep of a Southern conspiracy to perpetuate the most trivial, most murderous aspects of itself. The next story, "Daphne's Lover," returns to the theme of "At the Drug-store," but treats it without bias. "Daphne's Lover" is about sexuality and contrasts Frank Lacy's life of affairs and marriages with the narrator's devoted monogamy. Having admitted the power of male desire or passion, the next question is whether any sort of reasonably decent social order can survive it. Once the restraint of custom has given way, is there anything to stem the flood of erotic selfishness?

In "A Long Fourth," the choice was between unleashed sensuality and arid abstraction; "At the Drugstore" brought the beast and the intellect together, but with a sense that both were aspects of the fallen nature of man—guilty and picayune—all there was in the absence of immutable truths and, simultaneously, not enough. "Daphne's Lover" transcends these painful limitations, having at its core the image of Daphne eternally pursued by Apollo. Though *Ode on a Grecian Urn* is neither quoted nor alluded to, the story is haunted by its cultural ghost, by our inevitable association between figures frozen in the chase and Keats's lines:

> More happy love! more happy, happy love!
> For ever warm and still to be enjoy'd;
> For ever panting and for ever young;
> All breathing human passion far above . . .

Mr. Taylor's story lifts carnality into the realm of the imagination, into the timeless ideal which can only remain perfect in art. But as Daphne only escaped Apollo by becoming a tree, so Mr. Taylor suggests there is no escape from desire as long as we are human and for just as long, our experience of it will be incomplete. We are born with built-in restrictions on what we are capable of doing. Willy-nilly, we are types.

This given is what replaces the restraints of Southern gallantry and good manners. It governs us more strictly that any psychoanalytic theory. Whether, like Frank Lacy, we give our urges their full expression or, like the narrator of "Daphne's Lover," we marry once and happily, we are only going to know one half of all there is to know of love. The whole is in our imaginations. We may find it rendered whole in art or we may try to complete our limited experience through friendship, as the narrator does with Frank; but we are born subject to the laws of our own natures which will rule us whether we want them to or not. For this reason "a healthy imagination is like a healthy appetite. If you do not feed it the lives of your friends, I maintain, then you are apt to feed it your own life, to live in your own imagination rather than upon it."

But there is another dimension to "Daphne's Lover," one it is necessary to mention as it helps pave the way to the final story, "In the Miro District." Frank Lacy, the rake figure in "Daphne's Lover," is also the most sympathetic. While the narrator is outraged by the little girl who dresses up and blows kisses out the window, Frank seems to understand and tolerate her wildness. When she writes her flirtatious graffti on his back fence, Frank simply paints it over, unruffled by her teasing but moved to protect her from people who might misunderstand her (such as the narrator who calls her a "whore"). Frank is also friends with Janet Turner, another high-spirited girl of whom Mr. Taylor observes (in a line that contains a world of variation on decorum and goodness), "Alone with a boy she was a model of propriety, but in public she was difficult."

As a character, Janet harks back to Josie of "The Fancy Woman," a high-spirited, sexually unconventional girl who sleeps with a married man. Her problem is that she accepts the conventional male estimate of a girl who does what she's doing. She sees herself as a slut, though the author sees her as a social victim who is unfairly made to think too little of herself. Though her lover's son appreciates her romantic qualities (and is himself too young to understand why she does not), the society as a whole does not tolerate unmarried or extramarital sex.

In "Daphne's Lover," Janet is a freer agent than Josie, unafraid to be herself, though she also dies young: she remains an outsider. Unlike Josie, she is not a romantic figure. She is utterly independent, but in a way which makes her sexually unattractive (or threatening) to the men in the story. For the author, the question seems to be whether or not a romantic attitude toward women could survive without the system. Though Mr. Taylor had pictured the morality invested in women as more and more of a dead weight, still that stone shores up illusion. If family life and civilization might fall apart without the woman as its conscience, so would sweetness and imagination and fun.

III

But when the girl spends the weekend with the young narrator in "In the Miro District," the event is both romantic and natural. It involves not the slightest social embarrassment for either the girl or the boy; being in love is enough to justify sleeping together (their embarrassment is only over being caught). Mr. Taylor writes as simply and directly of their weekend as if there had never been anything in his work to suggest that such an occurrence was ever forbidden. It's as if the book's progress were towards a full airing of things as they really were, beginning with a cry from the heart on behalf of the male, moving through a recognition of masculine passion and then, necessarily to the admission that women are passionate too. If Southern chivalry has snapped, it's because in some way it was false or reduced to empty appearances. The easy atmosphere of the narrator's love-making suggests that sleeping with respectable girls was something people did when they were in love, though society felt it was important not to admit what really went on. Yet Mr. Taylor himself seems to have waited to tell the truth and has only been released by finding a moral framework large enough to hold the broken pieces of the old order.

"In the Miro District" provides this in its profound and economic use of the narrator's relation to his grandfather's frequently repeated stories. These stories are the crux of Mr. Taylor's story. They are unvarnished tales of "the eternal chaos we live in," and the grandfather insists on telling them instead of the Civil War stories he is expected to tell. His account of seeing his law partner shot and his own surrealistic escape into the swamps, his recounting of the hallucinations which made him imagine he was living through the New Madrid Earthquake (described to him by his own father), these stories are his witness to the mysterious violence in which human history pathetically, fraily unfolds. The grandfather's association with the earthquake links him with a time before his own, and through that time to the early American South when French and Spanish settlers were swept away "like so many Adams and Eves before the wrath of their Maker." In this final image, his experience is associated with the human condition since the beginning of time. What he knows about it is terrifying, but he won't suppress that truth. He refuses to submit to the stylized, domesticated version of chaos entertained by Southern society in its endless retelling of the Civil War. He lays no claim to his privileges as a Civil War veteran; he will not allow himself to be promoted in their artificial military ranks, and he will not let his real experience be altered so that it can adorn his daughter's living room.

When the narrator drunkenly begs his grandfather to tell about Reelfoot Lake, he then goes on to mock the old man's stories by telling them himself. But as he does, the boy—without realizing it—actually imagining the opposite—is acting out the moral of his grandfather's tales. He is himself behaving crazily; but in this, as an outlaw, he also demonstrates his resemblance to the old man. The boy sees the beginning of his independence in the moment when he flings back what he's listened to all the times the strange pair has been forced together. And yet it is precisely his defiance that shows him to be his grandfather's equivalent. It is what sets them both apart from the generation between them—a generation living by a modified version of the code the grandfather still strictly observes.

By his code, an absolute distinction is made between public and private life. The grandfather, for instance, never drinks in public as his daughter and son-in-law do. To him, there is never any excuse for liquor, though he might indulge in it out of weakness. If he does, it does not make liquor any better. Between his generation and the boy's, drinking has become socially acceptable in a way the grandfather finds appalling. And his grandson matches the old man's absolute morality—by taking his parents' liberalism to its natural conclusion—by doing whatever he feels like doing in public, to whatever extreme. The boy is willing to admit openly and completely what they will only half admit.

The grandfather and grandson clash on three occasions: when the old man arrives and finds him drunk, when he arrives and discovers the boy and a bunch of friends in bed with girls who aren't so nice, when he arrives and interrupts the narrator and his best (nice) girl while they are making love in the grandfather's bed. On the first two occasions, the grandfather is firm but sympathetic. When he finds the boy drunk, he tries to calm him down and sober him up. When he finds the girls in his daughter's house, he sends them packing, but he treats them in an understanding fashion and even helps his grandson clean up. When he finds the respectable girl naked in his wardrobe, he leaves and is not seen again until he's put on the social costume his family has wanted him to adopt all along.

The fact that he chooses to draw the line at the respectable girl creates an interesting ambiguity. Does the boy go too far when he denigrates Southern womanhood (as opposed to Southern tarthood)? Or does it finally become clear to the old man that the boy will continue to break the fraying rules until he finds moral zero? Will he try murder next to see if that's rock bottom? It is not entirely clear whether the grandfather is disturbed by what the boy has done or of what he might do. Until then the grandfather has refused to stand for conventional wisdom, but now he moves into his daughter's house and allows himself to be trotted out at dinner parties as a Civil War relic.

Given the drift of the whole collection, the grandfather's resignation is probably meant as his acknowledgement that traditional moral authority, based on the Southern woman's honor, is dead in his grandson's generation. For him, the woman's importance has been so deep he will not even speak of his wife by her first name. The absolute privacy of their relationship, its mysterious and sacred quality has been the balance to God's mysterious and terrifying relation to man. In the old Christian world, at home and in nature, the male was ruled by powers higher than himself. The grandfather's faith lay in a sense that the outer chaos was governed by a retributive God, and that the society which successfully brought his kidnappers to trial was one whose laws bore some real relation to what was just.

But just as woman's honor is dead, so is God in the grandson's generation. From the grandfather's point of view, there is no stopping anyone from doing anything. When he sees his own code dismissed by his grandson, the old man assumes the entire world of spirit has collapsed. There are no beliefs, but there is nothing to inspire them either. At that point, the grandfather lays his authority at the service of the liberal society he regards as hypocritical. It is his way of demonstrating to his grandson that conventions, though they are only rules (not principles, not absolutes) are still better than nothing.

And yet this is not entirely a story of defeat. When Aunt Munsie in "What You Hear From 'Em" puts on a bandana and "took to talking old-nigger foolishness," when Miss Leonora puts on all but the rhinestone glasses of the silly old lady tourist, one feels they have really been broken in the tug-of-war between the old moral order and uprooted contemporary society. "In the Miro District" revolves around the same conflict, but the outcome is different: if one world has clearly passed away, another has come in its place. It has always been part of Mr. Taylor's complexity that he saw how the new order brought new possibilities too. In "Mrs. Billingsby's Wine," his heroine profits from the inexorable democracy that undermines social order and high principles by making no one person or ideal better than any other. In part, the appeal of "Mrs. Billingsby's Wine" is that it blithely contradicts two of the author's most powerful stories—"What You Hear From 'Em" and "Miss Leonora When Last Seen." But it is also appealing because of what seems to be a mischievous reversal of what has come to be the obligatory progress of the modern short story. Instead of getting sadder and sadder as things move along, the heroine of "Mrs. Billingsby's Wine" gets happier and happier and ends by realizing that she'd had what she wants all along.

Still, this very element of mischief makes the happy ending seem possible because anything is possible and not because the new world is run according to a coherent design. The method Mr. Taylor uses in "Mrs. Billingsby's Wine" is the same one he employs elsewhere to point up a more demoralized truth. In "Mrs. Billingsby's Wine," he carefully shows how the young woman and the older one are humanly equal—alike in their vitality and goodness and in their being at ease in the experience of their different generations. The story—like so many of Mr. Taylor's stories—is a tissue in which the parts of the subject become so enmeshed that we finally feel there is no difference between things that seemed opposite at the start. It is not that opposites become indistinguishable but rather that they become equivalents. Son and BT are an example, Tolliver and his father-in-law are another.

In "A Long Fourth," the likeness of BT and Son suggests that it doesn't matter which alternative one picks: they are equally bad. In "The Captain's Son," the opposing parties are equally to blame. The sources of tension in these stories are slowly transformed in a way which often emphasizes the futility of their having been distinguished in the first place. Mr. Taylor repeatedly raises moral dilemmas only to show they can't be solved because there are no black and white moral categories. Yet when we come to "In the Miro District," the equivalence of grandfather and grandson is ultimately what makes the story one of renewal.

The boy imagines that the greatest difference between him and his grandfather lies in their attitude toward love. "He might know everything else in the world, including every other noble feeling which I would never be able to experience. He might be morally correct about everything else in the world, but he was not morally correct about love between a man and woman." Just as the boy wrongly imagines he is freeing himself by spewing back his grandfather's stories, he errs when he congratulates himself on knowing more about women than the old man. In fact, for both of them, love is central, though the grandfather refuses to speak of it while the boy insists on being frank. The grandfather's romantic silence about sex and his grandson's open acceptance of it are mirror opposites, but this means the boy's view is just as good as the old man's and more: "In the Miro District" shows the boy to be as deeply and inescapably part of a universal order as his grandfather.

For the boy, this order is one that has developed through the collection—it is the one that governs Frank Lacy and the narrator of "The Hand of Emmagene." It is an order in which the disruptive side of human nature is subject to the laws of human reason. The author's willingness to trust fallible human reason seems to arise from a sinewy faith in the survival of an order larger than man and one which resembles the Christian universe, though the Christian vocabulary has been washed away.

Mr. Taylor insinuates this impression by having the boy as his narrator. He slowly circles through his grandfather's stories, telling them again and again, each time with different emphasis, in a spare, almost heartlessly serene language that the reader unconsciously identifies with the old man's voice. This, of course, contributes to the interchangeableness of the two characters, but even more remarkable is the way the device confuses our sense of the universes in which the two men dwell. The boy's imagery stresses the Christianity of his grandfather's world but in the broadest possible terms. It is not the Christianity of Christ's Resurrection or compassion. It is actually only Christian in the sense that a God oversees the universe—that there is a Maker of an Adam and Eve. If we articulate all that's implied in the boy's tone, the Maker is a thoroughly disinterested One who tended to be identified with Christian terms in the grandfather's day, but who always was and always will be a Force beyond our control. The hard edge of the boy's voice seems to imply there has never been a hope of salvation, though there has always been a God. Beneath his boastful recounting of his youthful escapades, the boy speaks with an ancient sense of the helplessness of man, seeing it stretch backward to the beginning, feeling it there, undermining the present.

"Men, women and children, during the first bad shock, hung on to trees like squirrels. In one case a tree infested with people was seen to fall across a newly made ravine, and the poor wretches hung there for hours until there was a remission in the earth's undulation. Whole families were seen to disappear into round holes twenty feet wide, and the roaring of the upheaval was so loud their screams could not be heard." The horror of the scene is timeless. The soundless agony of the Earthquake's victims is made to seem like the lost agony of all the victims in history, all those who've perished inexplicably and horribly from the first Flood through the holocausts of our own time. They die in the darkness that runs alongside the bright, lit, fragile world of unwitting survivors.

Human social life has always seemed precarious to Mr. Taylor, but at first its greatest threat was human violence. Gradually, his allegiance to a specific social order has yielded to his growing insight into the total insecurity in which custom must survive. In his most recent story, "In the Miro District," custom itself is questioned as a stable vessel, or rather our need for it to be fixed is questioned. "In the Miro District" is about the revolution in custom between the grandfather's day and his grandson's. Both live according to entirely different conventions, but the difference is one of detail. For both men, custom has not changed in its essential reference to love. The woman who once had all value vested in her honor still represents all that's important. Once her importance was expressed by not acknowledging her passionateness, now the opposite is true.

But there has been no loss of hope or of fulfillment. The ease attending the young lovers in "In the Miro District" derives from the eternal nature of love. Where Mr. Taylor once seemed to fear chaos, he now seems to trust the order inherent in experience: an order that does not depend on social restraint for its existence. Through his career, he has altered and refined his questions, viewing the problem of order and disorder from different, even opposing, perspectives, testing the sanity of reason and the vitality of the irrational, mixing them until his questions have given way—not so much to answers as to moral sureness.

Identity and the Wider Eros:
A Reading of Peter Taylor's Stories

ALAN WILLIAMSON

Eros, says the later Freud, is a force of social cohesion. Its effort "to combine organic substances into ever larger unities" (*Beyond the Pleasure Principle*, Chapter V) tends naturally, and not perversely, to move beyond the single sexual relationship, and include more and more people in more and more complex structures of affection. Yet this impulse, however natural, is challenged at almost every point by equally deep-rooted sources of division. Jealousies intervene; the taboos against incest and homosexuality set up strong and, in their metaphorical ramifications of uneasiness, quite extensive barriers. Affection between men cannot ignore the other relations between men to which society gives primary emphasis—competition, money, politics; love between men and women encounters equally age-old grounds of hostility. Modes of handling affectionate feelings can be, simultaneously, modes of aggression; the person who makes the entire worth of his or her life depend on another person is exercising a kind of power, as is the person who greets admitted love with manipulativeness or indifference. In the best of circumstances, the notion of blending, of loss of boundaries, challenges crucial ideals of individuality and self-reliance, and may involve the acceptance of an undesirable weak image of the self. It is, finally, almost as difficult and frightening for human beings to manifest the breadth and depth of their loves, as to control their aggressions and hatreds.

Comedy is the literary form traditionally most concerned with the larger communities of Eros, and the obstacles to them. The circle of fellowship, satisfaction, forgiveness at the end of—to choose a particularly salient example—*Twelfth Night*, from which the clown steps forth to give his fusing, archetypal summary of human fate, is built on the overcoming of just such dangers as I have enumerated: the narcissism of love-no-matter-what (Orsino); the narcissism of indifference (Olivia), the possibility of homosexuality (the relationship between Orsino and the supposed Cesario); and the suspicion of betrayal, mercenary or sexual, in nearly every relationship in the play. But, of course, all are not reconciled; the—for this reason—famous Malvolio

Reprinted from *Shenandoah: The Washington and Lee University Review* 30 (Fall 1978): 71–84, with permission of the Editor.

is there, swearing revenge, a living emblem that the ring is never closed, that the self-exposure, and exposure to deception, one courts in love may lead to an ostracism, or a madness (depending on one's point of view), from which there is no return.

As a comic or tragicomic writer, Peter Taylor has had much to say about the triumphs of the wider Eros; and about the problems and dangers it poses for the individual identity. Tenuously erotic bonds and imaginative identifications between people are in some sense his subject *par excellence*. Yet he is more often discussed as a writer concerned with community in the literal sense—with the family, class, changing *mores* and codes—and Freudian mainly in a dark, conservative awareness of the chaos of the id ceaselessly lurking outside institutional bulwarks. (Jane Barnes Casey's recent essay in *The Virginia Quarterly Review* sees this latter point of view transcended, but only in the very latest stories.) These perspectives are not wrong; but they need the slight corrective the more anarchic, potentially far more affirmative, comic themes provide, if we are to see how subtle and unique a writer Peter Taylor really is. (The great recent story "In the Miro District" might be seen as Mr. Taylor's own unresolved debate between a traditionalist point of view, in which the battle lies between institutions and chaos, and a late-civilized one, in which imposed rules and divisions are rendered superfluous by the free community of love.)

Some of Mr. Taylor's stories can be classified as pure comedies, in which the barriers to unity are gradually, almost ritually, and completely purged.[1] The delightful story "Reservations" (though it deals with a single couple, and not, therefore, with a communal Eros) is a case in point. Given the opportunity to dramatize, and to project onto alter egos, their "reservations" about each other—jealousy, fear of ulterior motives, and also deeper fantasy-images of sexual coarseness and degradation—the newlyweds of the story merge into an archetypal couple. And the style reflects this, withdrawing at the end into the consciously naive, universalizing tone ("And Franny was equally stunned by Miles's manly beauty as he stood before her in his blue silk pajamas"—p. 79) of the clown's song in *Twelfth Night*.

A subtler instance of the pattern is "1939," a story unfortunately read more for the *à clef* appearance of subsequently famous literary figures than for its independent value as a study of adolescent identity, and of the brush-off, even cruel, quality of college friendships. The literary boys of Douglass House at Kenyon College, growing up in the stern heyday of the New Criticism, value only "objectivity," and the "mature experience" they believe will magically turn them into writers. Though they are seen as a very close-knit group by the rest of the college, they refuse to seem one to themselves:

> There were times when each of us talked of leaving Kenyon and going back to the college or university from which he had come. . . . It was a moderately polite way each of us had of telling the others that *they* were a bunch of Kenyon

boys but that *he* knew something of a less cloistered existence and was not to be confused with their kind. We were so jealous of every aspect of our independence and individuality that one time, I remember, Bruce Gordon nearly fought with Bill Anderson because Bill, for some strange reason, had managed to tune in, with his radio, on a Hindemith sonata that Bruce was playing on the electric phonograph in his own room. (p. 329)

On the preceding page, the narrator remarks, "Such students. . . . don't really know what kind of impression they want to make; they only know that there are certain kinds they *don't* want to make." That is to say, having little to include in their identities, they create them by continuous exclusions. Though they see fraternity School Spirit as tantamount to proclaiming oneself a child, they also suspect those of their number who have had adult literary successes of having "sold out" (p. 332). And the reason for their love of privacy, and animosity toward each other, seems disarmingly simple: they recognize their common indefiniteness and immaturity in each other, fear being swallowed up by it, and try to distinguish themselves by the very act of harsh perception, of "objectivity." On the train back to Kenyon, after being jilted by his fiancée, the poet Jim Prewitt consoles himself by writing a poem "For the Schoolboys of Douglass House," telling them how to grow up. On the same train ride, Jim and the narrator, who has suffered a similar misfortune, get into a fight which, fierce as it is, perfectly epitomizes the desire for non-contact which lies behind the hostility. Driven by "a mutual abhorrence and revulsion toward any kind of physical contact between us," the narrator hits Jim—and Jim hits him back—"not with my fists, or even my open hands, but with my shoulder, as though I was blocking in a game of football." The goal of the fight is, quite simply, to get the other out of the smoking compartment, "out of sight behind the green curtain" (p. 356).

The fight seems purgative, for Jim and the narrator spend the rest of the trip in "uninhibited and even confidential talk about ourselves" (p. 357). On their return, they find that the other boys have invaded their room, and are now "sprawled about . . . in various stages of undress," and cooking a meal on the narrator's hot plate. This triple violation of taboos—property, privacy, nakedness—"on top of what had happened in New York seemed for a moment more than flesh and blood could bear" (p. 358). But instead of getting angry, Jim and the narrator laugh, and ask for food. And suddenly the narrator identifies the group with the permanently immature figures he has pitied but perhaps, less consciously, envied, the hoboes on the railroad tracks outside Kenyon. An atmosphere of community and communion pervades the story. In the tolerance for a weak image of oneself which permits the sharing of experience to be comforting rather than frightening, the boys are likely to strike the reader, for the first time, as mature.

This, then, is the purely comic pattern. But a larger number of Mr. Taylor's stories—the most troubling, the subtlest psychologically, and therefore probably the most memorable—belong to a second type, in which there is Malvolio: in which some person, or, more commonly, some feeling or human potentiality, is excluded or killed in the dangers ensuing from the wider extensions of love. Since these stories tend also to be the most intricate, in their plots and in the judgments they require of the reader, it will be necessary to limit ourselves to two of the best, "Dean of Men" and "Venus, Cupid, Folly and Time," and consider them in some detail.

In "Dean of Men," a father is attempting to write a sympathetic but homiletic letter to a '60's-generation son whom he does not know very well, having gotten divorced when the boy was quite small. But by the third sentence, we come to this: "From the way you wear your hair and from the way you dress I do find it difficult to decide whether you or that young girl you say you are about to marry is going to play the male role in your marriage—or the female role" (p. 3). The narrator goes on to say, "I am not trying to make crude jokes at your expense." But that is just what he has done; and why he must do it—why, of all cultural changes, the blurring of sexual roles upsets him so much that he becomes boorish where he intends to be sympathetic—is really the central question of the story.

The narrator explains his feelings—but, given Mr. Taylor's consummate irony, explains much better than he knows—by telling of an incident that has recurred, in almost identical form, in three generations of his family. Each time, the father has lashed out savagely at a female member of the family, in order to cover his own shame over a professional defeat, a failure as provider—a failure, furthermore, always involving a betrayal by a beloved male friend or group of friends. In all three generations, the outbursts seem mysteriously final, unforgivable, in their effects. When the grandfather, in anger at the grandmother, flings a silver dollar into the sugar bowl, the grandmother has the bowl put aside, silver dollar and all, to eternal disuse, a revengeful relic. The father's taunt seemingly prevents his daughter from marrying the rich man she sincerely loves. And though the narrator's own explosion has no concrete ill effects, at about the same time he has a mysterious—and, as it turns out, self-fulfilling—intuition that his marriage will not last.

It is noteworthy that of all the unhappiness in the story—and there is much—only the betrayals by men are relived with the minuteness of traumatic repetition. Early in the story, we endure every second of the father's wait at the train station for his dishonest partner, Lewis Barksdale, to return and explain. The narrator's own experience of betrayal is especially painful because it follows what can, reasonably, be called a seduction. The narrator, a professor, is persuaded by a group of young colleagues to use his friendship with a trustee to prevent the college's Dean of Men (a former coach) from becoming President. He accedes not only because he agrees with his colleagues; or because he is flattered by their deference; but because their physical presence gives him a sense of shared and enhanced identity: "How well I can see them on my front porch, in the bright porch light I had switched on. They were a very attractive and intelligent-looking bunch of men. With their bright, intelligent eyes, with their pipes and tweed jackets, and with a neatly trimmed mustache or two among them, they gave one a feeling that here were men one would gladly and proudly be associated with, the feeling that one had found the right niche in life, that one had made the right choice of career" (p. 27). The plan succeeds; but when the narrator is made the sole object of the Dean's singularly petty revenge, the other men desert him. He waits—in an excruciating replay of the Barksdale sequence—through a long faculty meeting for his case to be broached, and is then told it would have been "strategically . . . a very bad move" (p. 35). At this point, rather than compromise his pride, he resigns from the college.

Traumatic as the betrayals are, they are met, in all three generations, with a curious refusal to retaliate or show anger; and they lead to peculiar mutations of character. The grandfather withdraws from the world, and, pretending to be the family man he is not, becomes a petty domestic tyrant. The father—who really is a family man—becomes more so, but unhappily, as the narrator perceives it. In his old age, he mysteriously resumes his friendship with Barksdale, and their telephone conversations—again, as the narrator sees it—"made him seem livelier than anything else did during those last years" (p. 23). The narrator's own defeat leads first to apparent uxoriousness, then to divorce—a divorce immediately occasioned by his decision to accept a position as Dean of Men, procured for him by the trustee who has passively permitted his betrayal.

The moral the narrator draws from all this is astonishingly simple. He has avoided the mistakes of his ancestors, by remaining in the masculine world, even sacrificing his family to it, rather than withdrawing into the family. The male community, however unjust or opposed to one's ideals, is so necessary to self-respect that it must be accepted on its own terms; and this lesson is, the last paragraph of the story implies, a sufficient refutation of the idealisms of the 1960's.

But the story, of course, leads one to some rather different morals. Where the narrator sees himself as having broken a family pattern, he has in fact repeated part of it in a more grotesque form. His father simply forgave Lewis Barksdale; the narrator feels compelled to please one of his betrayors by remaking himself in the image of his triumphant adversary, the Dean of Men. Bested by the male community, he reenters it with the self-abasing homage of chimpanzees turning their backsides; and renounces many of his claims to individual uniqueness in the process, giving up the scholarly endeavors that may lead to a form of immortality for the cooperative ones that lead to anonymity.

The narrator's either/or judgments do not hold up much better in the marital area. His divorce may, indeed, be inevitable, but if so there is little that is sudden or mysterious about the inevitability. Here, too, the issue is shared identity, but it is now feared rather than desired. The wife, Marie, is a large-spirited ambitious woman, and the narrator has displayed, over years, and almost pathological fear of having her strength in any way act upon his life—not only influencing her to give up her career, but refusing to discuss his professional life with her, since "it was understandably difficult for her to refrain from advising and criticizing me in matters she considered she knew as much about as I did" (p. 25). What he cannot stomach is, in fact, the change in this arrangement that must result from the defeat and their common plight. When he returns from the faculty meeting, he will not embrace her; she embraces him, and at that very moment he has his premonition of divorce. "I *wouldn't* be consoled," he admits, "though I consistently made an effort to seem so" (p. 36). When they begin to lead a life of greater sharing, he carries it to an extreme ("Before the first semester was over, Marie was helping me grade my papers"—p. 36) that suggests resentment, self-punishment, or despair, rather than gratitude. Perhaps his need to resist, and ridicule, any inter-identity between men and women comes from an identification of femininity with the weakness, the tendency to let events take the lead, he has good reason to fear in himself. Certainly the extent of the identification with weakness, and its quick connection to woman-hatred, are made clear by one of those bits of sudden, revealing craziness so characteristic of Peter Taylor: " 'And I spent hours in the park with you, Jack. I don't suppose you remember the little boy there who kept purposely interfering with your play on the jungle gym until one day I caught him and spanked him. His mother threatened to call the police. I'll never forget the satisfaction I took in laughing in her face and threatening to give her the same spanking I had given her little boy' " (p. 36). The only way to avoid being turned into a baby, it would seem, is to turn someone else (suitably weaker) into one first. This incident is the nadir of the narrator's moral possibilities, from which he never recovers enough to love, or be, someone his own previous size. He responds to Marie's really quite tentative threat of divorce with what can only be called relief; and they both remarry "people who shared none of our professional interests" (p. 38).

It is a complicated story, and I am sure one's own views on generational and sexual changes affect one's sense of how complete the narrator's moral faiiure is. But what I hope is clear is that the tragic tensions lie between the roles of marriage and of male comradeship, and the possibilities for a more intense blending of selfhoods those relationships hold. "Venus, Cupid, Folly and Time" also deals with a tension between conventional limits and an intimation of greater closeness—though here we have to do not with mild homoerotic overtones, but with a primordial threat, incest.

To the upper-class community of West Vesey Place, the brother-and-sister couple the Dorsets are at once sacred cows (because of their particularly blue-blooded ancestry) and untouchables. The distaste they inspire is of an obscurely, but fairly obviously, sexual nature; we are repeatedly told that Mr.

Dorset's behavior is peculiarly offensive to female neighbors, Miss Dorset's to male ones. The offense lies, it would seem, in the public revelation of customarily private aspects of life: the Dorsets go shopping with "the cuff of a pajama top or the hem of a hitched-up nightgown showing from underneath their ordinary daytime clothes" (p. 291); Miss Dorset cleans house in her bathrobe or, on one occasion, stark naked. But sometimes the revelation takes place mainly in the eye of the beholder: Mr. Dorset's habit of tucking in his sweater makes the women neighbors "feel as though [he] had just come from the bathroom and had got his sweater inside his trousers by mistake" (p. 292). Finally—as remarks like "even husbands and wives . . . had got so they didn't like to joke about it with each other" (p. 291), or "To us whose wives and mothers did not even come downstairs in their negligees, this was very unsettling" (p. 293), accumulate—we come to feel that the Dorsets' impropriety is a kind of demonic antithesis summoned up by the community's own extreme standards of intra-family privacy.

The Dorsets have no social contact with their adult neighbors, but they exercise their role as "social arbiters" by giving an annual party for the children of the most select families. The children are invited only once, at thirteen or fourteen—when they are old enough to have awakened to their own sexual being, but not to have acted on it. And the party is intentionally a kind of initiation (or perhaps, as it turns out, anti-initiation) rite, in which the children are led to half-see—as if out of their own depths of fantasy—sexual secrets:

> The source of the light was usually hidden and its purpose was never obvious at once. . . . A shaft of lavender light would catch a young visitor's eye and lead it, seemingly without purpose, in among the flowers. Then just beyond the point where the strength of the light would begin to diminish, the eye would discover something. In a small aperture in the mass of flowers, or sometimes in a larger grotto-like opening, there would be a piece of sculpture—in the hall a plaster replica of Rodin's "The Kiss," in the library an antique plaque of Leda and the Swan. (pp. 298–99)

(The hint of polymorphous perversity, with Leda, is confirmed by the title Bronzino, a picture which suggests to many views an unnatural relation between Venus and her son.)

The Dorsets proceed, in the course of the party, to retell their life story to the children. The message they wish to convey is in part a snobbish one: by rejecting the "nobodies" who courted them, and the relatives who wished them to marry beneath them, they have known the integrity of "living with your own kind" (p. 306). But as their recital rises to a religious-sounding antiphon—the same every year—a further message insists itself: they are inducting the children into a kingdom where "we all love one another," and where, by holding sexuality back from exclusive, exogamous choice, they have remained "young forever" (pp. 308–09). One is easily reminded of the history of other utopian religious communities—how they have always veered between total chastity and pansexuality in the attempt to give a body to undifferentiated love.

One year, the normal course of the party is disrupted. Two of the children, Ned and Emily Meriwether, conspire to present a plebeian inter-loper, disguised as Ned, while the real Ned sneaks in unobserved. The false Ned then begins to embrace and kiss his "sister" whenever the Dorsets' backs are turned. The Dorsets observe this and are pleased; though the narrator, by saying that they "understood, or thought they understood" (p. 313), leaves us uncertain whether they specifically approve of the incest, or merely of what they call a "silly flirtation." But, in an unplanned *dénouement*, the real Ned expresses his growing disquiet and jealousy—and, probably, projects his horror at its implications about himself—by screaming, "They're *brother* and *sister*!" (p. 314). The Dorsets evidently take this as an intended exposure of their own guilty secret; a melodramatic chase ensues, the parents are sum-moned, and the tradition of the children's party comes to an ignominious end.

But the real Malvolio of the story is the "childhood intimacy" between Ned and Emily. Having glimpsed the possibility, or tincture, of incest in its depths, they revert to, and exaggerate, the community's standard of reserve, becoming "indifferent to each other's existence," almost enemies (p. 322). And, while Ned marries conspicuously exogamously, his wife's preoccupation—at the end of the story—with the history of the Dorsets tell us, very subtly, that his affections have remained in some more general way constricted.

And yet, the story leaves us with one curiously radiant image: that of Emily withdrawing contemplatively, during the chase, into the niche where she and the interloper have previously substituted themselves for Rodin's "The Kiss." For one person, it would seem, the Dorsets' contrivance have succeeded, as a genuine myth of the half-narcissistic, unfocussed beauty of the moment of sexual awakening. The image foreshadows a later group of stories, in which, though there is loss and limitation enough, there is no psychic maiming, but rather a peculiar imaginative acceptance and transcen-dence. To resume our Shakespearean analogy, if "1939" is a comedy, and "Venus, Cupid, Folly and Time" a kind of problem play, stories like "Daphne's Lover" and "Three Heroines" are romances. (This is not to imply a rigid chronological sequence.)

The opening theme of "Daphne's Lover" is one which Peter Taylor has often (in "The Captain's Son," "The Hand of Emmagene," and—in an inverse form—in "There") given a tragic line of development: an attachment formed not to an individual but, more impossibly and dangerously, to a family, an ambiance, a way of life. The narrator of "Daphne's Lover" says, of his boyhood friends in Memphis, "It is almost as though I have lived the lives of these friends as well as my own life" (IMD, p. 112). His best friend, Frank Lacy, if he does not articulate the feeling, acts it out, at times, with surprising literalness: "More than once I came home from an afternoon spent with other friends and found his magazines scattered on the floor of my room and Frank sprawled on my bed, taking a nap" (IMD, p. 106). What draws the two boys together is really more their differences than their similarities. For Frank, the narrator's close-knit family—where the children's comings and goings are noted and regulated, but where all clearly enjoy each other's company—is the opposite of his own freer but colder upbringing. The narrator, for his part, is fascinated by Frank's precocious successes with women. Frank, who, unlike the narrator, has no sisters, but has a mother accused of infidelity, has a deep sympathetic understanding of women's ways of gaining sexual attention—whether subtle, brazen, or downright disruptive. Though this understanding is undoubtedly the key to his conquests, it would be less accurate to say that he exploits it than that he complies, with a sad, fatalistic protectiveness ("Poor girl is not responsible"). Above all, he cannot endure to see such behavior criticized by other men. The narrator is, naturally, most often the critic: angry, jealous; sexist by current standards; and yet in a sense healthier, in so far as he presupposes a possibility of moral contact Frank has implicitly given up on. "I still wanted to make that little redhead change her ways. And that was what Frank didn't seem to understand or like about me" (IMD, p. 115). The *reductio ad absurdum* of Frank's attitude is his response to the mad girl who asks him to cut her throat: "You bet your life I will if that's what you want" (IMD, p. 108). And yet—and notwithstanding the fact that he later reproaches the narrator for taking women "for granted"—one feels that ease and loyalty between the sexes, as well as the generations, are part of the desirable, alien experience Frank craves from the narrator's family.

There are dark possibilities in this symbiosis; what is remarkable is how little they actually materialize, and how the symbiosis grows if anything stronger, at least for the narrator, as adult identity solidifies:

> But from the time of my meeting with Mary my interest in Frank's romances seemed greater than ever, somehow. It was as if once I knew what my own life was to be, I needed to participate more wholeheartedly in the lives of others. It was as if I could only sustain my own kind of life and find satisfaction in it by allowing myself that participation. . . . I tell myself that a healthy imagination is like a healthy appetite and must be fed. If you do not feed it the lives of your friends, I maintain, then you are apt to feed it your own life, to live in your imagination rather than upon it. (IMD, p. 130)

The critic John Leonard has described this passage as "edgy," in its undertone of abiding self-dissatisfaction. It is; yet the story goes a long way toward persuading us that such dissatisfaction must be universal. Jane Barnes Casey has stated this beautifully: "Whether, like Frank Lacy, we give our urges their full expression, or, like the narrator of "Daphne's Lover," we marry once and happily, we are only going to know one half of all there is to know of love. The whole is in our imaginations." The symbol for this insight is, of course, the myth of Apollo and Daphne. Both—insight and myth—are acted out in the one moment of real grief in the story, when Frank allows the narrator's girl to trap him into kissing her, appropriately enough, during a game of fly-ball. As the narrator watches, with agonized fascination, "Her left arm moved gently about his neck, and I won't ever forget how her free right arm fell loosely behind her as she bent backward and how relaxed and beautiful and almost marble-like the arm seemed to me" (IMD, p. 129).

That petrified arm is, I think, intended to remind us of the fronds sprouting from Daphne's body. More cruelly than foliage, it demarcates that aspect of the girl's will that the narrator's character is not so constituted as to touch. And yet, it is also something that Frank Lacy will never see; being an aspect of will, it lies, metaphorically as well as literally, outside his involved, compliant perspective. In that sense, this Daphne eludes both her Apollos.

Still, it is the narrator who suffers the erotic wound, and makes it bearable by converting it into an aesthetic acquisition. And I think where the story speaks of its resolution as "imagination" we may also, justifiably, read the impulse to art—the one human activity in which we do appropriate other lives without harming them or paying their penalties. Art and sublimation are, after all, immemorially part of the Daphne story, as Marvell reminds us in "The Garden":

> Apollo hunted Daphne so,
> Only that She might Laurel grow.
> And Pan did after Syrinx speed,
> Not as a Nymph, but for a Reed.

Our real claim to what we have experienced merely imaginatively is asserted still more positively in the poem-story (Mr. Taylor's own term for a genre he has invented, organized in lines for pacing and emphasis, but without the necessity of even a free-verse cadence) "Three Heroines." The story concerns the narrator's dying mother's insistence on going to one last formal party—a feat of self-mastery and noblesse oblige prompted, in part, by her identification with her grandmother, who lived through the Civil War with a similar stoic frivolity, though divided in her loyalties between a Union husband and a Confederate brother. The narrator's attitude toward the excursion changes gradually from a queasy distaste, which he shares with the mother's doctor, to loving admiration; until during the car ride home, as the mother retells the grandmother's story one more time, he feels he does not know "whether / It is my mother I am with / Or my Great-grandmother

Haynes" (IMD, pp. 153–54). (That this theme of transcending generational boundaries has an Oedipal variation, in the son's position as his still "beautiful" mother's "escort," is everywhere evident and nowhere stressed. It is mentioned that the mother has—like the grandmother—remained loyal to both sides in the battle between respectable husband and literary son.) At the end, the narrator has a kind of revelation: that the mother's self-affirming energy, as it has put aside—not denied—the fact of dying, has also put aside, in its sense of adequacy, the accidental limitations of any single human life. If she is not a "heroine" like her grandmother,

> She has been always ready
> And would have been up to whatever
> Might have come. And all this she knows!
> She *knows!*
> Yet she is not jaded or disappointed
> At not having had her chance to show.
> And that, what is that?
> Why, that is better than having shown.
> It is something more than life.
> Death doesn't exist for it, Beloved Doctor.
>   (IMD, p. 155)

Aimez qui vous aima du berceau dans la bière, the mad poet Gérard de Nerval advised; Mr. Taylor goes further and suggests that—in a kind of boundary-realm between life and death, like the realm of art—we, if we have realized our natures, not only love but are all the same archetypal person. (At this point, the problem of incest becomes insignificant, as the problem of betrayal became unreal in the art-world of "Daphne's Lover.") In the beautiful, as yet uncollected, poem-story "Knowing" (*Agenda*, Vol. 13 No. 4—Vol. 14 No. 1), the narrator realizes that his fantasy of his future life, at a moment when he thought he was going to die, equalled, in all important respects, the life he was actually to live. There is the same sense of a shared, primordial sufficiency in being itself, to which experience—and even the uniqueness of being human—can add nothing.

> We know nothing and everything from the
>   beginning.
> The day we are born
> It's all there.
> We are finches and fieldmice
> We are beavers and barn owls
> We are the cat curled, purring at my feet,
> Knowing, knowing, knowing.

In gathering together stories which either emphasize the problem of identity and inter-identity, or else adumbrate mystical oneness or transcendent love, I have intended to supplement, not supplant, the more usual views of Peter Taylor's writing. Many stories are more saliently about the realities of class, locality, and changing customs; or about a vision in which the psychic underlife is primitive and genuinely frightening. But I think the reader will find that the tincture of themes of identification and symbiosis extends more widely than their actual dominance. It helps some of the stories about race ("What You Hear from 'Ems?" "A Friend and Protector") to acknowledge both damage and closeness in ways not available to more conservative or more radical writers. Its catalytic presence allows stories about generational conflict ("Promise of Rain"), or proper and improper sexuality ("The Other Times"), to become, also, stories about the generosity that breaks down such distinctions. It accounts for much of the glee and happiness in the stories, and, perhaps, for their peculiarly hollow, depleted ring when (as in "The Captain's Son," or "Guests," or "At the Drugstore") human contact goes wrong, is unfulfilling. To my own taste, it is the element of idiosyncrasy and universality, beyond the concerns and merits common to much good Southern writing, that makes Peter Taylor a writer who matters on any scale whatsoever.

Notes

1.   All references, unless otherwise noted, are to *The Collected Stories of Peter Taylor* (New York: Farrar, Straus, and Giroux, 1969). References to *In the Miro District* (New York: Alfred A. Knopf, 1977) are indicated by the initials IMD.

Determined Failure, Self-Styled Success: Two Views of Betsy in Peter Taylor's "Spinster's Tale"

ROLAND SODOWSKY AND GARGI ROYSIRCAR SODOWSKY

Several critics have noted the depth and richness of the characters in Peter Taylor's work,[1] a complexity which makes his stories particularly apt for psychological interpretation. An especially good example is "A Spinster's Tale,"[2] in which the protagonist, Betsy, may be seen from a Freudian point of view as being trapped by the forces of parent-child relationships and sexual fears or from an Adlerian point of view as choosing and controlling the unsocial direction of her life.

Set in an upper-class home in Nashville around 1900, "Spinster's Tale" is narrated by an unmarried woman named Elizabeth who recalls events beginning with her mother's death and ending about a year later, shortly after her fourteenth birthday. Her mother has died a few days after bearing a stillborn child. Elizabeth, called Betsy by her eighteen-year-old brother, lives with her father, brother, and several servants. During a moment of grief one afternoon about six months after her mother's death, the girl observes an old man passing the house, red-faced, drunk, stumbling and cursing. Seeing this man, Mr. Speed, causes her to become "dry-eyed in my fright" (486) and to remember vividly the burial of the stillborn infant and a few minutes spent with her mother just before her death. Betsy recognizes Mr. Speed as a "permanent and formidable figure in my life which I would be called upon to deal with" (489), and thereafter she observes him from the parlor window each time he passes, even though the sight of him makes her teeth chatter. Much of the rest of the story consists of variations of this basic pattern in which the terrified girl watches the old man, anticipating the day when he will come to her door.

In one variation, Betsy stands at the door of her bedroom late at night while her drunken brother, whom she intuits as a less menacing version of Mr. Speed, climbs the stairs. With apparent incestuous intent, she entices him into her bedroom. Thinking about the encounter later, she wishes she had made him aware of "some unmentionable trouble" (493) they have in

Reprinted from *Studies in Short Fiction* 25 (Winter 1988): 49–54, by permission.

common. In another variation, she learns the unwelcome lesson that her brother and Mr. Speed are more alike than she had thought. In another, just after the girl's father and uncles jokingly accuse her of flirting with a boy, Mr. Speed appears outside and she becomes hysterical.

In the final variation, Mr. Speed, caught in a rainstorm, actually enters the house, frightening both Betsy and Lucy, a maid. After letting him in, the maid flees up the stairs, but Betsy calls the police. The old man tries to leave but falls from the porch and is knocked unconscious. The police find him thus a few minutes later and take him away.

"Spinster's Tale" is replete with objects and actions for which, in his discussion of dream symbols in *The Interpretation of Dreams*, [3] Sigmund Freud assigns various sexual meanings. A study of Betsy's reactions to these symbols suggests that despite the lonely girl's desperate attempts to deal with the phenomena these symbols represent, she cannot adjust to them. Instead, she projects her unacceptable, frightening sexual impulses to external dangers. Thus she fears maleness and male sexuality and thereby copes projectively and unconsciously with her fears, although in a deviant manner.

Except for a flashback to the burial of the stillborn infant, the girl is never seen outside the house, which she repeatedly describes as "shadowy," the dream-like setting thus making an interpretation in Freudian terms especially appropriate. Although her father, brother, and the servants also occupy the house, she persistently calls it "my house," "my door," to which Mr. Speed will eventually come, reminding one of Freud's symbolization of persons as male organs, of the house as body, doors as apertures, and rooms as female; churches too are equated with the vagina, and Betsy's house is on Church Street. Mr. Speed carries a top coat, a later version of the cloak, one of Freud's phallic symbols, and a heavy walking cane, also phallic, with which he beats the trees or pokes at the "soft sod along the sidewalk." [4] When the March wind blows off his hat, another male genital symbol, [5] it rolls across the lawn toward the house. And when he finally does come to the door, he raps on it with his cane. Once inside, however, he throws the cane on the floor in an apparent gesture of defeat.

Betsy unconsciously defends herself, displacing her guilty, fearful at-traction for Mr. Speed upon her brother, a safer target. She remembers her brother in terms of phallic images. He shows her "a box of cigarettes which a girl had given him" (488); he chases after and returns Mr. Speed's hat, thus identifying himself more closely in Betsy's eyes with the old man; in her white nightgown, symbolizing chastity, she watches her brother from her bedroom doorway as he comes up the stairs, stumbling like Mr. Speed, "putting his white forefinger to his red face" (492); after he has climbed the stairs, an act symbolizing coitus, and entered her room, she remembers "something like a longing for my brother to strike me" (493), but since he does not and therefore does not symbolically enter her, she presumably has failed to cope with her fears.

She also remembers the box, a female symbol,[6] containing the stillborn infant when it is buried, and she associates it in a rapid sequence of images with Mr. Speed, who apparently epitomizes maleness, with her last moments with her mother, and with her mother's death, which her "memory did not dwell upon" (486–7). When Mr. Speed finally enters the house, one assumes Betsy cannot help but react as she does. The maid Lucy, who could be but is not Betsy's surrogate mother, pleads with Betsy to climb the stairs, that is, to perform, in Freudian terms, a symbolic coital act. Instead, she reacts unconsciously, circling defensively behind Mr. Speed to telephone the police, thereby repressing her desire for the male "invasion." A few minutes later Mr. Speed's "limp body" (508) is taken away.

Betsy sees herself as having acted with a mixture of cruelty and courage, and instead of being fearful of or attracted to Mr. Speed, she both despises and pities the old man lying unconscious in the mud. In the last paragraph the narrator says, ". . . my hatred of what he had stood for in my eyes has never left me . . . not a week has passed but that he has been brought to my mind by one thing or another" (508). The child Betsy may appear to have been victorious, but in Freudian terms the adult Elizabeth is the regressing victim of the girl's failure to overcome her terror.

An Adlerian point of view leads to a different conclusion. According to Alfred Adler, the biological and environmental "givens"—for example, Betsy's plain looks, adolescent stirrings, and isolation in a discouraging male world—are re-created by a person with her "private logic" to attain "success": "Experiences, traumata, and sexual developmental mechanisms cannot yield an explanation, but the perspective in which they are regarded . . . which subordinates all life to the final goal, can do so."[7] In *Superiority and Social Interest*[8] Adler sees the neurotic as striving toward a goal of superiority in order to overcome past and current feelings of inferiority. Rather than reacting automatically to events which determine her to be a spinster, Betsy is actively carving out her niche in the world, a niche that in her eyes is inferior to none. Betsy's fear of heterosexual intimacy, for example, may express the direction she is taking to attain her goal of superiority over men.

From this point of view, the incidents from her puberty that the narrator recalls are important not in themselves but because she remembers them and because of the way the girl Betsy chooses to respond to them. In *Individual Psychology* Adler says, "There are no chance memories. Out of the incalculable number of impressions which meet an individual, he chooses to remember only those which he feels, however darkly, to have a bearing on his situation."[9] The narrator's selective *re*-collection of pubescent experiences mirrors her present biases and view of life, and, as the story's title suggests ("A Spinster's *Tale*"), her reconstruction of events does not necessarily correspond to the historical truth. The purposeful delving into the past has the power of repetitive rehearsals or of a self-fulfilling prophecy, expressing the narrator's intention of continuing with the symbolic, spinster-like life of her youth. These memories, Adler says, a person ". . . repeats to himself . . . to keep him concentrated on his goal, and to prepare him by means of past experiences, so that he will meet the future with an already tested style of action."[10]

When Betsy is frightened by Mr. Speed, her ultimate symbol of maleness, for example, she construes the image of her dead mother, whom she remembers as wan, smiling, gentle, and religious—the opposite of the stumbling drunk. By symbiotically escaping into this idealized memory, Betsy sidesteps a social problem—confrontation with the old man and thereby with males in general—thus avoiding possible defeat or humiliation in a relationship. In choosing "not to dwell upon" (487) the memory of her mother's death, Betsy thus denies it, as well as the challenges of adolescence, i.e. the stepping toward new freedom and adult responsibilities. Betsy calls her memories of her mother "sudden and inexplicable" (486), but they are neither: they manifest her preference for nonexistence, passivity, and social withdrawal. After seeing Mr. Speed the first time, Betsy stands "cold and silent" (486), a metaphorical and literal expression of her chosen life style.

Betsy recalls that her mother severely condemned drinking before her death, an attitude not shared by her brother or by her father, who has toddies with her uncles every Saturday afternoon. Her father calls "Old Speed" a "rascal" with "merry tolerance" (484), but simultaneously warns her brother of the consequences of drinking by using Mr. Speed as a bad example. Betsy cannot identify with her father's contradictory attitude and the well-defined masculine pattern he establishes in the house. She wonders whether he ever thinks of her mother, since he never mentions her. She seems to accuse him of indifference, saying ". . . in a year I had forgotten how he treated her when she had been alive" (499). Unable to establish satisfactory alliances with her brother or father, she replaces the human tendency for *gemeinschaftsgefühl* with an attitude of distrust and poor regard for her surviving family members and, ultimately, the world at large.

The development of this attitude appears clearly in the sibling rivalry between Betsy and her brother. Sober, he teases her mercilessly. Drunk, he tries to make her a conspirator by offering the passive, watchful girl candy, but she sees him as "giggling," "bouncing," and "silly" (484) and refuses to compromise the attitude about drinking that she has adopted from her mother. Rudolf Dreikurs, the popularizer of Adler in the United States, says such sibling differences indicate competition and the development of different personalities.[11] Betsy, feeling intellectually ignored by her father and class-valedictorian brother, sees her brother as the "boss" and herself as inadequate. To compete with her brother's ruling style, she chooses the feminine avoiding style, a typical example of familial confrontation between two Adlerian types. She requests, for example, her father and brother "not to talk about war, which seemed to [her father] a natural enough request for a young lady to make" (487). While father and son argue on a vast diversity of male-oriented topics, Betsy quietly observes her brother or slips away because she finds the contentious dialogue unbearable.

Dreikurs points out that where one sibling succeeds, a competing sibling gives up; and where the sibling fails (the brother's intemperance, for example), the competitor moves in, thus finding a place and significance in the family.[12] Betsy's behavior fits this pattern. Adler says a woman feels equal to a man she perceives as superior if she can experience herself in her "masculine protest" to be "equally superior" to him.[13] This striving for compensatory superiority reflects an exaggerated perception of male power and recognition such as Betsy sees in her small world on Church Street. Not being brave enough to confront them, Betsy resorts to what Adler calls "depreciation tendency" (the neurotic's tendency to enhance self-esteem by disparaging others)[14] in order to maneuver her brother and Mr. Speed, to sneak into power struggles with them, and to inflict sly revenge in their weak moments. Betsy's nearly incestuous encounter with her brother, for example, in which she appears uncharacteristically confident and well-rehearsed, may be an attempt to compromise him and thus gain a "victory" and revenge. Her desire for him to strike her could be seen as her search for confirmation of suspected male violence and cruelty.

Betsy has long been preparing for the "eventuality" (504) to settle completely with Mr. Speed. The narrator recalls, "And the sort of preparation that I had been able to make [was] the clearance of all restraints and inhibitions regarding Mr. Speed in my own mind and in my relationship with my world . . ." (504). The "restraints" and "inhibitions" that Betsy rids herself of are the foundations of Adler's *gemeinschaftsgefühl*. Instead of giving the drunk Mr. Speed shelter in her house from the rain, Betsy, in a tone of pretended innocence, calls the police. She is keenly aware that she deals with Mr. Speed, "however wrongly" (507), all by herself, that is, unsocially. Her father's curt remark, "I regret that the bluecoats were called" (508), underscores the disparity in father and daughter's life attitudes.

The passive-aggressive Betsy begins to find her place and power in her family by her success in hurting others through her one-upmanship games. She discovers a way to supervise her father's household staff by snooping around, springing out upon the unsuspecting servants, and intimidating them by threatening to call her father or the police. The narrator recalls, "In this way, from day to day, I began to take my place as mistress in our motherless household" (505).

Betsy's life-style is that of a cautious, contriving busybody. Even in her nightly dreams she allows no mysteries or loose ends and "pieces together" these dreams into a "form of logic" (497). The fearful Betsy grows into the controlling Betsy who says, "I would complete an unfinished dream and wouldn't know in the morning what part I dreamed and what part pieced together" (497). In one such dream a "big" Betsy, in control of everything, watches "little" Betsy "trembling and weeping" (497). Betsy then makes a "very considerable discovery" about herself—that instead of being fearful she can be feared. Betsy is not the victim of causality, but rather the pilot of her dreams and of the direction of her life as well. In her own terms, she has achieved "equal superiority" over Mr. Speed, her brother, and therefore all men. Just as the pubescent Betsy pieces together her dreams into patterns which suit her, the adult narrator continues to piece together her life in ways that, according to her private logic, reveal her to be superior and successful.

That "A Spinster's Tale" can sustain two such disparate interpretations of its protagonist demonstrates, we feel, the profundity of Taylor's characterization. We see in the story the dynamics of familial relationships, and little else, either shaping a girl and the woman to be or being used by the girl to shape the woman she chooses to be. The ambiguity in Taylor's fine story is satisfying, like truth.

Notes

1. Albert J. Griffith, *Peter Taylor* (New York: Twayne, 1970), p. 160.

2. First published in *Southern Review*, 6 (Autumn 1940), 270–92; collected in *A Long Fourth and Other Stories* (New York: Harcourt, 1948). The story is probably most accessible in *Short Story Masterpieces*, ed. Robert Penn Warren and Albert Erskine (New York: Dell, 1981), pp. 484–508. Subsequent references to "The Spinster's Tale" are to this edition, and page numbers appear parenthetically in the text.

3. In *The Basic Writings of Sigmund Freud*, trans. and ed. A. A. Brill (New York: Random House, 1938), pp. 179–549.

4. Freud, pp. 366–489.

5. Freud, p. 375.

6. Freud, p. 371.

7. *The Individual Psychology of Alfred Adler: A Systematic Presentation in Selections from His Writings*, ed. H. L. Ansbacher and R. R. Ansbacher (New York: Basic Books, 1956), p. 92.

8. Alfred Adler, *Superiority and Social Interest: A Collection of Later Writings*, ed. H. L. Ansbacher and R. R. Ansbacher (London: Routledge and Kegan Paul, 1965), p. 85.

9. Adler, p. 351.

10. *Individual Psychology*, p. 351.

11. Rudolf Dreikurs, *Psychodynamics, Psychotherapy, and Counseling* (Chicago: Alfred Adler Institute, 1967), p. 58.

12. Dreikurs, p. 59.

13. *Individual Psychology*, p. 250.

14. *Individual Psychology*, p. 268.

A Psychoanalytic Appreciation
of Peter Taylor's "A Spinster's Tale"

MAUREEN ANDREWS

Peter Taylor's short stories of the American south have been admired for decades, and in the last two years he has been given the PEN-Faulkner Award, the Pulitzer Prize for Fiction, and the Ritz-Paris Hemingway Award. Yet few critics have looked closely at his work. Although his early story "A Spinster's Tale" is one of his best known, partly from having been reprinted in at least two popular college anthologies, commentators are usually content to mention it just in passing as an example of the Southern Gothic or grotesque. I think it is worthwhile to examine the sources of this story's remarkable power: its images and processes arising from the unconscious, which psychoanalytic principles can most fully illuminate.

The main character in the story, Elizabeth, now grown up, narrates the events in her life from October to the following May of the year in which she turned 14 early in the twentieth century in Nashville. Her mother had died the previous spring from the complications of the birth of a stillborn child. The main actions of the story are Elizabeth's preparations for the day when Mr. Speed, the town drunk whom she first becomes aware of passing her house that October, should "come to her door" and what she does when he finally arrives. These actions are sparely framed by a scene with her mother just before her death and the last paragraph of the story from the point of view of the adult Elizabeth. The title, "A Spinster's Tale," also provides a context for the story.

When Elizabeth's mother dies, the girl is thirteen, "a maturing little girl" (76) on the brink of moving from childhood and assuming her adult identity as a woman. With her mother's death from childbirth, Elizabeth discovers that it is mortally dangerous to be a woman. One of her responses is to try to delay leaving her childhood. She continually refers to herself in her narrative as a little girl and, the most obvious sign to others in the story, she refuses to put up her hair. But she cannot stop her growth. She says "I tried lying down on the settee that went with the parlor set, but my legs had got too long this summer to stretch out straight on the settee. And my

Reprinted from *Journal of Evolutionary Psychology* 9 (August 1988): 309–16, by permission of Paul Neumarkt, editor.

feet looked long in their pumps against the wicker arm" (76). She tried to escape into another world as did "the wondrous Alice who walked through a looking glass." "I propped my hands on the borders of the narrow mirror and put my face close to watch my lips say. 'Away'. I would hardly open them for the 'a'; and then I would contort my face by the great opening I made for the 'way' " (76). Since she cannot get *away* she must instead find *a way* (she herself divides the word) to deal with the world she is caught in. She bursts into tears, turns from the mirror to the wide parlor window, and beholds the fearful Mr. Speed for the first time.

Certainly Mr. Speed in his name represents that passage of time which Elizabeth cannot slow down or avoid and which she so much fears, but he also represents the sexuality which her growth into adolescence demands that she face. Even on a surface level Mr. Speed is a frighteningly violent figure "walking like a cripple with one foot on the curb and one in the street" and "cursing the trees as he passed them, giving each a lick with his heavy walking cane" (76). Much of the imagery surrounding him is familiar from Freudian analysis, and it defines the particularly sexual quality of the fear he embodies. He uses the phallic cane as a weapon, not only to beat the trees but also to poke "into the soft sod along the sidewalk" (78). Freud identified landscape or earth as a dream symbol of female genitals, and the overcoat Mr. Speed carries as well as his hat as symbols of the male genitals (15: 155–6). Mr. Speed's hat blows off his head and over the lawn one day, a precursor of its owner's visit to the house. Later Elizabeth describes Mr. Speed to her brother as "like—a loose horse" (82), another male sexual symbol.

Elizabeth identifies Mr. Speed with her father and brother as well as with men in general. When her father "talked about the hundreds of men in the Union depot," thinking "of all those men there, that close together, was something like meeting Mr. Speed in the front hall" (77). At first she knew only that when the day should come when she must deal with Mr. Speed at close range "it must involve my father and my brother" (79), but later she "put into words the thought that in my brother and father I saw something of Mr. Speed" (84). There "was something in my brother's and in my father's natures that was fully in sympathy with the very brutality of his drunkenness" (87). But she knew, too, "that it was more than a taste for whiskey they had in common" (84). She also notices "the difference between the manner in which my father spoke before my uncles of Mr. Speed when he passed and that in which he spoke of him before my brother. To my brother it was the condemning, 'There goes Old Speed, again,' But to my uncle it was, 'There goes Old Speed,' with the sympathetic addition, 'the rascal' " (87).

The three men are first connected in Elizabeth's mind by their "taste for whiskey." Elizabeth's eighteen-year-old brother was in the habit of coming home drunk even before his mother's death, and her father, along with his two bachelor brothers, "had always had his toddy on Saturday afternoon. . . . But there was more than one round of toddies served in the parlor on Saturday now" since the death of Elizabeth's mother (83). Mr. Speed is also connected to her brother descriptively. Mr. Speed's face is "heavy, red, fierce like his body" (78). Brother's less frightening, but nonetheless "red face broke into a grin" and he "kept putting his white forefinger to his red face" on one of his drunken returns at night to urge her to be quiet (79). Mr. Speed "stumbles" after his hat (81), and brother "stumbles" up the stairs (79). Even the Benton boys, her brother's friends, the youngest not a year older than Elizabeth, share some of Mr. Speed's attributes in a somewhat milder form. Each "carried a cap in hand and a linen duster over his arm" (84). The occasion of their visit was to take her brother for a ride in that novelty of the time, a car. "I was frightened by the boys' impending adventure in a horseless carriage" (84). Calling the auto a horseless carriage points out that it is the modern successor of the horse in its symbolic value.

Certainly, a thirteen or fourteen-year-old girl named Elizabeth for her mother, who had just died in childbirth, might well be frightened by images of male sexuality impinging on her life, but for Elizabeth the enemy is within as well, and that is even more frightening. Her responses to Mr. Speed are ambivalent. Her "heart would beat hard" when she saw a figure coming up her street, and when it turned out to be someone else she "would sigh from relief and from regret" (76). When her father mentions her school at dinner one evening "[a]ll of those little girls safely in Belmont School . . . were a pitiable sight beside the beastly vision of Mr. Speed which even they *somehow* conjured" (my emphasis, 77). She believed that her brother knew what had happened to her by the window when she first saw Mr. Speed when he announced precipitously at dinner "I saw three horses running away out on Harding Road today! . . . They were running to beat hell and with little girls riding them!" (77). Freud connected the number three with male genitals for obvious reasons and the act of riding with sexual intercourse (15:154, 157). Mr. Speed is "like a loose horse" himself, but here the little girls are actively riding the horses who are running away, out of control.

Elizabeth's sexual desires are most active in the scene in which she invites her brother into her room upon his return to the house after an evening of drinking. When he awakened her accidentally on such occasions in the past, he appeased her by tossing her a piece of candy, a dream image of sexual enjoyment (15:156). This time when he offers the candy she is unsatisfied and beckons him to come into her room. She runs to get into bed so that he sits there beside her to talk. She throws her arms around his neck, sobs on his shoulder and smells "for the first time the fierce odor of his cheap whiskey" (80). "Fierce" has been a word reserved for Mr. Speed up to now, and the connection is furthered by her cheek on his overcoat, again a detail mentioned regularly in descriptions of Mr. Speed. She finds the odor of whiskey "not repugnant" to her "blended with the odor that [her brother] always had," and she thinks that he is going to strike her. He does not, but promises to spend more time with her in the afternoon to assuage her loneliness.

Later Elizabeth, as she says, "naturally repeated the whole scene" in her mind and found strange "something like a longing" for her brother to strike her. In a Freudian understanding of female sexuality, a certain degree of masochism is a "normal" characteristic. That is, the pains of defloration and childbirth are perceived as the necessary price to pay for sexual pleasure. But the price Elizabeth's mother paid is too high a price. In her meditation on the seduction scene she refuses to acknowledge fully her fear or her desire, and she makes a less threatening substitution: "I would not let myself reflect further on my feelings for my brother—my desire for him to strike me and my delight in his natural odor. I had got myself in the habit of postponing such elucidations until after I had completely settled with Mr. Speed. But, as after all such meetings with my brother, I reflected upon the posthumous punishments in store for him for his carousing and drinking, and remembered my mother's saying that she had rather see him in his grave" (80). She can accept the penalty her brother faces in death for being like Mr. Speed, but she fails to see the irony that it is her mother herself who is in the grave.

Elizabeth never satisfactorily "settle[s] with Mr. Speed," that is, with her own sexuality. The settlement she does make shapes her as an adult into a spinster whose sleep is still haunted by images of the drunken old man. A dream she recounts from the period between the bedroom scene with her brother and the day Mr. Speed comes to her door reveals the shape her sexuality will take:

> Once upon a time there was a little girl whose hands began to get very large. Grown men came for miles around to look at the giant hands and to shake them, but the little girl was ashamed of them and hid them under her skirt. It seemed that the little girl lived in the stable behind my grandmother's old house, and I watched her from the top of the loft ladder. Whenever there was the sound of footsteps, she trembled and wept; so I would beat on the floor above her and laugh uproariously at her fear. But presently I was the little girl listening to the noise. At first I trembled and called out for my father, but then I recollected that it was I who had made the noises and I felt that I had made a very considerable discovery for myself. (83)

Even though this is an artificial dream in a work of literature, it seems to be constructed according to the patterns discovered by Freud. The most obvious characteristic of Elizabeth's dream is displacement, that is, the substitution of a neutral element for a highly charged one. It is not a little girl's hands that grow large and attract the attention of men as she matures, but her breasts. The dream also represents the fulfillment of a wish. She has revealed her desire for sexual attention not only in her ambivalent attitude toward Mr. Speed, but also in luring her brother to her bedroom. In her dream "grown men came for miles around." Her ambivalence here shows in the girl's shame and attempt to hide the attention getting hands, but hiding them under her skirt effectively transfers male attention to the genital area. Although Elizabeth at first seems to be present in the dream as an observer, she is also the little girl from the beginning. We have seen the mixture of fear and desire in Elizabeth already.

Another characteristic of dreams is that they work through condensation; that is, any element can carry more than one meaning. Hiding her hands under her skirt suggests not only Elizabeth's ambivalence, but also masturbation. Children then were nearly always prevented from masturbating, often with threats of punishment and being told that they were "bad." Here the little girl lives in the stable behind her grandmother's old house, which was already identified in the story as being in a "formal" neighborhood. She is banished from living in the house to the stable in the dream rather appropriately since the stable is the proper abode for horses, the representatives of sexuality. The stable behind the house is an implicit recognition of the sexuality behind even the formal or proper sort of life of her grandmother. The idea of masturbation is repeated in the image of beating on the floor, which promotes anxiety in the dream child at whose fears Elizabeth the observer "laughs uproriously." The principle of reversal in dreams means that things are often expressed in terms of their opposites; here laughing probably stands for crying. The autoeroticism of infantile masturbation normally gives way to the desire for a love object outside the self, and calling out for her father in the dream represents that stage of development. A girl's attachment to her father functions as the bridge to her relationships with other men. But the final element of the dream shows her drawing back from that: "I recollected that it was I who made the noises," that is, caused her own sexual excitement, and "I felt that I had made a very considerable discovery for myself." She remains self-enclosed then and set on the course of spinsterhood.

Elizabeth's house functions in the story in the same way that Freud saw houses functioning often in dreams (15:159), and it, too, helps us to see her evolution. The lower regions of a house represent the lower part of the body and sexuality, the upper, mental and spiritual qualities. The parlor on the ground floor, described as dark, shadowy and cold, is the place where she must first face the world. She sees Mr. Speed through its wide window, and when he is too threatening she retreats upstairs either in her thoughts or physically. After her first frightening sight of Mr. Speed she has a "sudden inexplicable memory of [her] mother's cheek and a vision of her in her [upstairs] bedroom on a spring day." She spends the afternoons of the next week in her own upstairs room "arranging on the chaise lounge the dolls which at this age I never played with" (77). Returning to the dolls of her childhood is a regression; they are safer than facing Mr. Speed, or sexuality, and a real baby such as the one that killed her mother. As she inures herself gradually to the sight of Mr. Speed, she even "ventured into such forbidden spots as the servants' and the men's bathrooms. The filth of the former became a matter of interest in the study of servants' natures, instead of the object of ineffable disgust. The other became a fascinating place of wet shaving brushes and leather straps and red rubber bags" (86–7), the sexual imagery of the last items being unmistakable.

Perhaps the most powerful house image is that of Mr. Speed's coming to the door. Elizabeth "felt a sort of anxiety to know what would ever drive him into my own house" (78), and she felt his existence to be something "to be thoroughly prepared for when it came to my door" (81). Freud mentions that "opening closed doors" is "among the commonest sexual symbols" (5:397). When Elizabeth's brother left the house to help Mr. Speed chase his hat in the wind, Elizabeth "ran to the front door lest Brother be locked outside" (82), consonant with her luring him to her bedroom. The hallway to which he returned is described suggestively as Elizabeth sat there and looked "about the walls of the cavernous hallway at the expanse of oak paneling, at the inset canvas of the sixteenth-century Frenchman making love to his lady, at the hat rack and at the grandfather's clock in the darkest corner" (82). Freud noted that rooms and wood often represent women in dreams (15:156); the hatrack by its shape and function suggests male sexuality, and the gender of the grandfather's clock is inherent in its name as well as its form. When Mr. Speed finally arrives at the house, first Elizabeth heard "his cane beating on the boarding of the little porch before our door," and after the maid let him in thinking he was the brother, he "threw his stick on the hall floor" (88). The images of violent penetration force Elizabeth to act. One part of her was "vaguely longing to hide my face from this in my own mother's bosom," that is to regress to the earliest presexual state of oneness with the mother, "but there was another part which was making me deal with Mr. Speed, however wrongly, myself. Innocently I asked the voice [on the telephone] to send 'the Black Maria' to our house number on Church Street" (88). The term "Black Maria" for the police coach suggests the way the South managed to maintain its ideal of pure, white womanhood. As Elizabeth located "filth" in the servants' natures as well as their bathrooms, she turns sexuality over to black women. She lives in a world where her father insists she must "shut [her] eyes to some things. 'After all,' he said, '. . . you're a young lady now' " (86).

Denying Mr. Speed is denying a part of Elizabeth's self as well. We have seen that she knows her father and brother share his attributes, and here her own identity with him becomes clear too: "I saw myself as a little beast adding to the injury that what was bestial in man had already done him" (88). "Beast" and "bestial" link Elizabeth with Mr. Speed and with "man." She "despised and pitied him at the same time" and was "afraid to go minister" to him on the porch steps where he had slipped and fallen (88). It is safe to say that Elizabeth despised and pitied herself as well, and her fear, for her very existence, generates the cruelty she finds herself capable of here and elsewhere in the story. Whereas Elizabeth has been unable to stop time in the story, must eventually put up her hair and act the role of an adult, she remains fixed psychically at fourteen. "My hatred and fear of what [Mr. Speed] stood for in my eyes has never left me. . . . It was only the other night that I dreamed I was a little girl on Church Street again and that there was a drunk horse in our yard" (89).

The society in which Elizabeth defines her identity requires a girl to become a "lady" and "shut [her] eyes to some things" (86), sexual things, despite her obligation to bear children. The death of Elizabeth's mother is a shaping event in the girl's life, but it is also an emblem of the deadly effect of the role assigned to women in that world, a world which maims men as well.

We see the process of Elizabeth's becoming a spinster, but in fact the story is peopled almost entirely by spinsters and bachelors. Elizabeth's parents were the only married people, and now her mother is dead. Her school is run by Miss Hood and Miss Herron, and Mr. Speed's "old-maid sister" is "still with him" (85–6). Both Elizabeth's uncles are bachelors, her brother at eighteen is more attracted to alcohol than to young women, and there is no sign that any of the several servants is married. We first see Mr. Speed "stumbling like a cripple," and the other men in the story are also shown most characteristically drinking or drunk. Religion, which should be a culturally creative force, is relegated to women (Elizabeth's mother and the girl herself are the only ones who seem to subscribe to it despite the whole family's living in a house with stained glass windows on Church Street), and it is a religion which teaches Elizabeth her brother will burn in hell for his drinking. It seems to teach him nothing. Male intellectual life is parodied by the conversations between Elizabeth's father and brother. "Once . . . the discourse shifted in two minutes' time from the Kentucky Derby to the languages in which the Bible was first written" and again "in the course of a small dessert, from the comparative advantages of urban and agrarian life for boys between the ages of fifteen and twenty to the probable origin and age of the Icelandic parliament and then to the doctrines of the Campbellite Church" (78). Elizabeth defines her sexual identity not only in the context of a family life disturbed by the death of her mother, but also in her society, satisfactory for no one in the story.

I have focused here on the main images in "A Spinster's Tale," character-ized by Albert Griffith, who has commented on the story more fully than any other critic, as "grotesque symbols" by which Taylor "gravely endangers the psychological verisimilitude which is the hallmark of his most distin-guished work" (156). A knowledge of psychoanalytic principles provides a very different measure of these images. The power and appeal of "A Spinster's

Tale" arise from the reader's deep recognition that it embodies fears and needs usually expressed only in our own "grotesque" dreams.

Works Cited

Freud, Sigmund: *The Standard Edition of the Complete Works.* James Strachey, trans. 24 v. Hogarth and the Institute of Psycho-analysis, 1963–74.

Griffith, Albert J: *Peter Taylor.* New York: Twayne, 1970.

Taylor, Peter: "A Spinster's Tale" in *To Read Literature.* Donald Hall. Rev. printing. New York: Holt, 1983.

Peter Taylor's "Porte Cochère":
The Geometry of Generation

SIMONE VAUTHIER

There is something slightly baffling about the reception of Peter Taylor. As one critic put it, his place "in modern fiction is secure." His craftsmanship, in particular, is widely acknowledged but has received little critical attention. It is praised for its "purity," "quietness," "austerity," qualities that too often partake of the ineffable; in the words of Gene Baro, Peter Taylor "writes so simply and powerfully he seems scarcely to be exercising his craft."[1] Surely the ways in which the writer exercises his craft in order to create the illusion that he is not doing so deserve to be investigated. Peter Taylor himself, when speaking of his stories, stresses the element of deliberate construction that goes into their making. In one interview, he declared that he had "worked some stories out just the way you'd work out a theorem," and offered "Venus, Cupid, Folly and Time" as an example of his method.[2] Criticism ought to take the hint and attempt—at its own level and with its various tools—to "work out the stories systematically."[3] This paper is intended as a modest start to a reexamination of Peter Taylor's fiction which will depart from the usual thematic approaches.

Rather than "Venus, Cupid, Folly and Time," "Porte Cochère" will serve as my exemplum of what the author calls his "more schematic stories."[4] Though not so well known, this early story has the advantage of being shorter and easier to encompass within the scope of an essay. Even so, I make no claim to any sort of completeness in the present study. Here I investigate the story from the angle of spatial scheme and will not deal, for instance, with narrational processes except where they are relevant to the spatial approach.

At the threshold of the story, the title is an "Open Sesame," which enables us to enter the fictional world through a semantic code. Since like any door a porte cochère both delimits and links two areas, the phrase evokes the opposition outside/inside. In fact, better than any other door, it ties together a nexus of spatial relationships: insofar as it usually implies another entrance, and has to be located in relation to this, it brings in the opposition

From *Southern Literature and Literary Theory*, ed. Jefferson Humphries (Athens: University of Georgia Press, 1980), 318–38. © 1990 by The University of Georgia Press. Reprinted by permission.

left versus right (horizontality); insofar as it denotes a carriage entrance going through a building, it sets up a double polarity of up above and down under (verticality) and of front versus back (prospectivity).[5] As a door involves a passing through, the phrase "porte cochère" strongly implies the larger category of directionality, and it clues us not simply into the semantics but into the syntax of the story to come.

Furthermore, as a synecdoche, the porte cochère connotes a certain kind of house, large and substantial, and as a metonym, a certain kind of life. Thus to any reader already familiar with the work of Peter Taylor, the title immediately relates to the author's fictional world, in which the house is "the central, the prismatic symbol,"[6] so that we can guess that the "topic space" (Greimas), the space of transformations, will be the inside rather than the outside of the house that boasts a porte cochère. As a lexical item, porte cochère is also arresting. A French phrase, it has been adopted into English to the extent that it is listed in dictionaries; yet it is not wholly anglicized and still often flaunts its foreign grave accent. Thus the word, though unambiguous, is not so transparent (if indeed words ever are) as an English equivalent would be. The title therefore has a "defamiliarizing" impact: it does not simply convey information, it draws attention to itself and to its linguistic status. The effect is not counteracted but, rather, strengthened when we are told in the second paragraph of the story that "porte cochère" was Mrs. Brantley's expression, Ben Brantley, the protagonist, and his children preferring for their part the more vernacular "drive-under." Since two phrases are used to denote the same object, more must be in question in the text than their fictional referent. The translation emphasizes the link between the phrase and its speaker, its connotative value for a particular locutor; or, to look at the problem from another angle, the double nomination draws attention to the relativity implied in a subject's perception and/or construction of his or her environment.

The warning is all the more needed because the short story builds the fictional space largely through the focus of perception of Old Ben. To summarize it briefly, "Porte Cochère" explores an elderly man's state of mind as he waits out in his study the half-hour before his birthday dinner party, for which his children have gathered from various parts of the country. In this restricted time, Old Ben shifts from a complacent projection of himself as an undemanding liberal father to a realization of his devious possessiveness and tyranny and eventually to an acting-out of his inner rage against his children. The story is told by an undramatized narrator in external focalization.[7] But the narrator deprives himself of the freedom and scope which such a position normally entails by focalizing his narrative fairly strictly on Ben Brantley, and by choosing to see him from within. Thus he can present the narrated world as the focalized character turned focalizer perceives it. The spatial indications which we are given create the fictional character at the same time as they create the fictional world.

THE CONSTRUCTION OF SPACE

In fact, as gradually appears, Old Ben is involved in the construction of his space in more ways and on more levels than his present immobility and passivity would lead us to expect. Certainly, at first, he seems merely the point of reference around which the description of the various fictional loci can be organized: "Old Ben kept listening for Cliff's voice above the others. They were all down on the octagonal side porch, which, under its red tile roof, looked like a pagoda there on the side lawn. Old Ben was in his study" (7). The invisible observer, building a system of localizations ("down," "there") in relation to the place occupied by the old man, gives it a sort of self-evident quality, although the room itself is only named, as an afterthought, with the last word of the last paragraph. Then increasingly, as the narrator makes Ben the focus of perception, the character functions as a "discursive subject" through whose selective focalization a space is projected and produced.[8] Ben Brantley, "seventy-six and nearly blind" (388), might be considered an inadequate post of observation. Yet, if he cannot see through the walls and focuses only vaguely on those objects he can perceive, he is able at least to hear and interpret the noises that reach him and, perhaps more important, he *wants to know* what is going on in the house. "Old Ben could recognize Cliff's leave-taking and the teasing voices of the others, and then he heard Cliff's footsteps on the cement driveway, below the study— a hurried step. He heard Cliff in the side hall and then his footsteps at the bottom of the stairs" (389). The layout of the house—and the important fact that the study is above the driveway—becomes clearer to the reader, as do Ben's relation to his surroundings and his propensity to eavesdrop. The spatial indications provided are narratively motivated and authenticated because they enter into the cognitive program of the character which produces them (and is produced by them).

Given the choice of focalization, the extent of the area where the action takes place is of necessity very limited. With one exception no glimpse is afforded of the whole house. (The only view that is offered—introduced by the narrator-focalizer, though it could also contain a mental image emanating from the character—interestingly juxtaposes inside and outside, grounds and house: "he seemed to peer between the open draperies and through the pane of the upper sash, out into the twilight of the wide, shady park that stretched from his great yellow brick house to the Pike" [393]. The expanse of the park, the building material and its color, the Nashville location, all confirm what the reader and surmises: this is indeed a substantial house.) The study receives a good deal of attention but never in the form of a set description; the windows, the quality of light in the room when the draperies are drawn, the umbrella stand and the old-fashioned radio, such things are called up in the narration when they come under the notice of the character. Otherwise, the house exists only as a collection of loci, the side porch, the hall, the living room, the stairs. Rather than described, these are simply located in relation to one another: "the octagonal side porch which was beyond the porte cochère," "His study was above the porte cochère," "the cement drive-way below the study," and so on. It will be seen that a double system of reference is operating here, according roughly to whoever is the focus of perception, the narrator-focalizer or the character. Whether focalized by the narrator or Ben, these other parts of the house, after the first expository paragraphs, are mentioned only as the character is made aware of them.

But the protagonist, intent on his cognitive program, is also led to remember other places. The strange quality of light in his study affects him: "For one moment, he felt that his eyes or his glasses were playing him some new trick. Then he dropped his head on the chair back, for the strange quality now seemed strangely familiar, and now no longer strange—only familiar. It was like the light in that cellar where long ago, he used to go to fetch Mason jars for Aunt Nelson" (389). One space calls up another space and another time. But this is no nostalgic dwelling on the past. Ben remembers how his aunt used to send for him all across town and "made him whistle the whole time he was down in the cellar, to make certain he didn't drink her wine," though he was but ten or twelve. The memory of the cellar leads him back to the present through the evocation of yet another space: "Where Aunt Nelson's house had been, the Trust Company now stood—a near-skyscraper. Her cellar, he supposed, had been in the space now occupied by the basement barbershop—not quite so deep or so large as the shop, its area without boundaries now, suspended in the center of the barbershop, where the ceiling fan revolved" (389). In Ben's mind, the two spaces coexist but, let it be noted, not the two times, and Aunt Nelson's cellar is now a ghostly area. Later he will recollect not the lost cellar but the present shop: "Old Ben's eyes, behind the smoked lenses, were closed, and he was visualizing the ceiling fan in the barbershop" (393). That he does not grieve over the destroyed place is already suggested in the word "visualizing," which here implies *vouloir-voir*, some sort of voluntary action. The associative train of his ideas immediately confirms the suggestion. "Presently, opening his eyes"—incidentally, the closing and opening of his near-blind eyes is itself most suggestive—"he reflected, almost with a smile, that his aunt's cellar was not the only Nashville cellar that had disappeared. Many a cellar!" (393). One lost place calling up another, he now remembers his father's cellar, "round like a dungeon" because it "had been a cistern in the very earliest days" (393). The memories lodged within that remembered space are much more traumatic than those linked to Aunt Nelson:[9] a more expanded flashback shows that descending into the cistern on a ladder was frightening to the boy, as "his father's voice, directing him, would seem to go around and around the brick walls and then come back with a hollow sound, as though the cistern were still half full of water" (393). One day, "in his fright at the very thought of water," he drops the lantern, which goes "whirling and flaming to the brick floor, which Ben had never before seen" (393). Though the flames quickly die out, his incensed father beats him mercilessly. The incident is told with a wealth of details, many of them concerned with spatial objects—notably walls.

Thus Old Ben is made responsible for the projection of a double space, an actual, immediately observable space and a recollected, absent space, which is itself composed of various places, including the present barbershop. (This, of course, enlarges the potential volume of the fictional space.) Because of Ben's role as the discursive subject, the actual and the mental spaces share many common features even though they are intended to stand in contrast to one another. Neither the present nor the past houses are evoked as living wholes. They are synecdochally or metonymically represented. The aunt's house is reduced to its cellar, the father's to the cistern, the porch, the carriage house, the kitchen window, and the yard with its big shade trees. Ben's house is actualized in slightly more detail but remains a collection of discrete, albeit related, loci. The places which Ben is mostly aware of are not, with the exception of the study, living rooms in the etymological sense. The Brantley children talk animatedly on the porch, the final confrontation with their father takes place on the staircase just as Ben had to confront his father's angry face over the rim of the cistern. Such areas are in-between areas, partaking of both inside and outside qualities, setting up a problematics of inside versus outside. They are transit places in which one never stays for long, however deeply Ben's expeditions into the two cellars have stamped his personality. Since the remembered places are located underground, and the actual places are above it but at different levels, verticality also becomes a prominent feature which, however, qualifies as much the position of the actors in the family scenes as the places themselves.

It is precisely the position of the actors which makes for the main contrast between the two spatial systems and can be said to account for the thymic quality of each, as we shall see in a moment.[10] But the characters' placing is first indicated in the neutral terms of the spots they happen to occupy. Thus while the Brantley children are *down* on the side porch, their father sits in his study *above* the porte cochère: their position is inferior and lateral. Moreover, Ben's study "open(s) off the landing halfway up the stairs," and is "not part of the second floor" (388). So, clearly, it is not only in a superior location but it is *aside* from the main or communal part of the house. From the very beginning, the distribution of the different parts of the house and of the characters in the fictional space shows that father and children, on this family occasion, are not really reunited and that even if the study is the focal point where the protagonist sits and registers the sounds that tell him what his children are doing, it cannot be thought of as the center of the house. In fact, although the house exists as the virtual surrounding of the study, it is never presented as a concentric area; on the contrary, the off-center placement of the few other parts that are mentioned is constantly underlined. As a consequence, the focalized focalizer's centrality appears as a narrative strategy which emphasizes his egocentricity but raises questions as to his role in his family. Now this off-sidedness contrasts with a recurring feature associated with the remembered places. Not that they are presented as central but, being repositories of food and drink, they are, perhaps, more directly related to the ongoing life in the respective houses, and strikingly they both carry circular associations. The father's cellar is "round like a dungeon"—a comparison which, of course, introduces suggestions of medieval tyranny and a two-fold male-female symbolism—and it has "circular shelves" (393). The aunt's is more conventionally rectangular but, in its ghostly state, it is associated both with centrality and circularity, being now "suspended in the center of the barbershop, where the ceiling fan revolve(s)," drawing another invisible circle (389). As a child, Ben willy-nilly had to go down into these underground places, while adults, listening like the aunt or looking at him like the father, kept close watch over him from above. Now, in the present of reference of the story, the situation has been reversed, Old Ben, from a topographical position of superiority, keeps his children under surveillance.

With such remarks, we have already touched upon another function of Ben in the narrative, one indeed that imposes itself more readily perhaps on the reader's attention. Being the protagonist, he is naturally an "actant," to whose actions we tend to pay attention. As it happens, the narrative program in which he is engaged has much to do with space. Before we examine this aspect of the narrative, we may note how the fictional space envisaged as a set of attributes already appears as an elaborate development of the polarities encapsulated in the compound noun of the title. In addition, the deployment of spatial indications around and/or through the character, the juxtaposition of loci with a different ontological status, the oppositions and parallels created—all contribute to the construction, together with the fictional space, of a number of connected themes—the interdependence of space and consciousness, the reciprocal definition of related places, the possibility of spatial change and variable topology, the temporal dimension of space. And, of course, the emblematic virtualities of spatial placement.

THE ACTOR'S USE OF SPACE

In the present of the story, apart from taking possession of his surroundings through hearing, Old Ben is the subject of two narrative programs. In the past, he was similarly involved in two programs, which, though they are not granted the same narrative volume, nicely balance the present ones, all the more nicely, indeed, since the narration embeds the former into the latter. The first program starts fairly early when Ben hears Clifford, his favorite son, leave his brothers and sisters. Sitting apart from the family circle by his own choice (he needs a nap and also finds Laura Nell's "chatter" "particularly taxing and obnoxious" [388]), Ben is not content with his present isolation. He "longed to have Cliff come and talk to him about whatever he would" (390). The operative word here is "come," not talk. For "whatever Cliff was thinking about—his law, his golf, or *his wife and children*—would be of no real interest to Old Ben" (389–90, emphasis added). If he longs for his son's presence, he does so precisely at the moment when Clifford hurries up the stairs to go and write a letter to his wife. Ben's objective is to get his son into his study, thereby capturing his attention. Thus his first action, his calling out to Clifford, "almost despite himself," that the news will be on in a few minutes, is a matter of *proxemics*. It is not enough for Old Ben to know that his son is in the house: Clifford must be induced to come inside his own personal space. The development of the scene shows indeed that conversational exchange is not the desired end but rather the means to ensure that Clifford will first enter the study, then remain there. When Cliff claims he must go and write Sue Alice, "Old Ben felt that he didn't need good sight to detect his son's ill-concealed haste to be off and away" (390). So, enticement having failed, he tries aggressive baiting: "Cliff had, in fact, turned back to the stairs when Old Ben stopped him with a question, spoken without expression and almost under his breath. "Why did you come at all? Why did you even bother to come if you weren't going to bring Sue Alice and the children? Did you think I wanted to see you without them?' "(390). Then he resorts to taunts and even to a form of blackmail, declaring that he is "not going to the club or anywhere else for supper," as is the family tradition on his birthday (391). In the battle of wills between father and son, Ben's victories are marked by Clifford's replies; even when the latter loses some of his self-control and tells his father, "Don't be so damned childish" (391), Ben avails himself of the opportunity to pursue the conversation: "I'm getting childish, am I, Clifford?" Upon which Clifford indulges in a lengthy analysis of his father's character. But Ben's victories (and occasional defeats) are also marked by Cliff's physical moves: "He stopped at the doorway" (victory); "he turned back to the stairs" (defeat); "he stopped with one foot on the first step of the second flight," "Clifford took several steps towards his father," "Clifford came even closer" (victories); "Clifford was turning away again" (new threat of defeat); "During his long speech he had advanced all the way across the room until he was directly in front of his father" (etc., 390–93). Clifford bothering to reply is always a plus for Ben, who controls the exchange, but the young man's movements indicate his intentions and show more clearly that the battle is not easily won. On the whole, however, as Clifford advances into the study, he concedes more and more ground to his father. Ben, for his part, does not care to establish a real communication with his son. His only concern is to keep Clifford away from his room and writing table and to inveigle him into staying in the study. No matter how candid his son's part of the exchange becomes, Ben pays it only surface attention, as it were, because the only important thing is that their talk should not stop. When, provoked into saying a few home truths, Clifford asks a telling question, "What the hell do you want of us, Papa? I have thought about it a lot. Why haven't you ever asked for what it is you want? Or are we all blind and it's really obvious?" The old man does not trouble to answer and only enjoins him to go "write your spouse" (392). (Yet he will answer the question later, but when he makes his wishes known, his utterance, deprived of context, will not make sense to his children.) As a matter of fact, the deeper Clifford's emotional involvement in what he says to his father, the deeper his penetration of the study, and therefore the more satisfying the situation from the father's point of view. While Old Ben manipulates Clifford through words, verbal language is in fact simply an instrument the better to speak "the silent language" of proxemics.[11] And the message of this latent communication is, "I still am the Father, the master."

In the course of Clifford's expostulations, it appears that the silent language of proxemics has long been spoken between them, even if neither perhaps quite knows what it is all about. For the situation, Clifford notes, is a familiar one. When his father snaps that he is free to go, "You have all been free as the air, to come and go in this house," the son smiles: "Free to come and go, with you perched here on the landing registering every footstep on the stairs and every car that passed underneath. I used to turn off the ignition and coast through the drive-under, and then think how foolish it was, since there was no back stairway. No back stairway in a house this size! [. . .] And how like the old times this was, Papa—your listening in here in the dark when I came up!" (392). Although no reproach has been uttered, Clifford interprets the use which his father has made of their spatial environment, and the connotations of the drive-under come into full play in this passage.

In addition, the power play of the apparently helpless old man has a marked temporal dimension as well. Tactics are ever a question of space and timing. In this case, the whole episode starts with Ben's awareness of time: "It was almost time to begin getting ready for that expedition [to the club] now, and simultaneously with the thought of it and with the movement of his hand toward his watch pocket, he became aware that Clifford was taking his leave of the group on the side porch" (388–89). Throughout the meeting, he is conscious of time. "Old Ben held his watch in his hand, and he glanced down at it quickly" (391). "His fingers were folded over the face of the watch," he "slipped his watch back into his vest pocket nervously, then slipped it out again, constantly running his fingers over the gold case, as though it were a piece of money" (392). This byplay, however, stops when time ceases to matter because the interval which had to be bridged is now over. Old Ben interrupts Clifford in the midst of a tirade by moving in his turn: "Old Ben pushed himself up from the chair. He put his watch in the vest pocket and buttoned his suit coat with an air of satisfaction. 'I'm going along to the club for supper,' he said, 'since there's to be no-un here to serve me.' As he spoke, he heard the clock chiming the half hour downstairs" (392–93). His timing has been perfect. Because this revealing gesture and remark occur just as Clifford was attempting to express to his father and to himself the puzzling nature of their relationship, any doubt which a trusting reader might have entertained is dispelled: the father has engineered the confrontation so that he could while away the half-hour before supper time in an ego-gratifying manner. In order to kill time satisfactorily, he had to consume his son's time, and time, as the comparison between the gold watch and a coin reminds us, is money.

So far Old Ben's strategy has been successful. He has proved his competence in performing the program he had set himself—thus playing both Sender and Subject (Greimas). He has entrapped Clifford in a place and in a role—that of the Child of transactional analysis.[12] One is all the better reminded of Eric Berne's theories, since Clifford accuses his father of playing "sly games" with his children (392). In his part as Parent involved in a Crossed Transaction, instead of a transaction between Adults, Ben does not act the overbearing father, but in fact assumes the tolerant role of the benign father. He never gets indignant over Clifford's increasingly bitter accusations, he simply does not take them into consideration and can be said to sidestep the issue—and the relationship.

Before the narration comes to the second narrative program, which involves Ben in the present of reference, it introduces, by means of the two flashbacks, programs he had to engage in as a child. In both cases, the Sender is an adult dispatching the child on missions which require a change of space and are either boring or frightening. His recollections are of being ordered about. Aunt Nelson "would send for him all the way across town to fetch her Mason jars"; here, the distance between the two houses, the crossing of Nashville, are made to convey the unreasonableness of the aunt's demands. In his father's cellar, a similar chore exposes him to even greater ordeals, since the old cistern is intrinsically terrifying, the expedition more fraught with dangers, real and imaginary, and his callous authoritarian father ever ready to administer corporal punishment. The trials which the subject has to undergo in such places assign to them—and metonymically to the houses of which they are a part—a negative, dysphoric value. On the most fateful of his descents into the dungeonlike cellar, the memory of which still makes Old Ben draw back from the window "with a grimace" (393), the father's house appears as the locus of grievous power. When the lantern crashes to the floor, and sends up "yellow flames that momentarily lit the old cistern to its very top," the boy, looking upward, sees "the furious face of his father with the flames casting jagged shadows on the long, black beard and high, white forehead" (393). What with the contrast between yellow flames and shadows, black beard and white forehead, and the child's wish that "the flames might engulf him before he came within reach of those arms," the scene is reminiscent of hell. After the severe beating which he gets, Ben "remained for a long while standing with his face to the wall" then goes to the summerhouse—a place removed from the house. "There he had lain down on a bench, looked back at the house through the latticework, and said to himself that when he got to be a grown man, he would go away to another country, where there were no maple trees and no oak trees, no elms, not even sycamore and poplars; where there were no squirrels and no niggers, no houses that resembled this one; and most of all, where there were no children and no fathers" (394). The father as an individual has vanished from his son's thoughts but has been metonymically replaced by the house seen through latticework, which though denoting a typical building material may also connote something of the jail. The child has never found in the house *la coquille initiale*, the originary shell which offers those euphoric values of intimacy which Gaston Bachelard has so well analyzed.[13] Neither of the houses evoked in the flashbacks could have represented for the boy "le non-moi qui protège le moi," the non-I protecting the I. His childish desire, which makes him the Sender and the Subject of a fantasized program, is summed up in a double wish: to leave the familiar space in order to find another that would be different scenically, socially ("no niggers") and architecturally, *and* to be rid of family ties. The link between the two wishes is foregrounded in the juxtaposition of his simultaneous rejection of "houses that resembled this one" and of filial succession. Thus his fantasized program involves the transformation of space as a preliminary, if not a prerequisite, to the transformation of the world of generation.

Apparently, the adult has not left his region or even his hometown and he has got over his fear of family entanglements to the extent of fathering no less than five children. But the reader is made aware, even before the final recognition scene, that Ben has succeeded in transforming his immediate environment. The house is which he has raised his children and in which the present action unfolds is, in a sense, a counterhouse. Time could only destroy materially, indeed has destroyed, the hated environments of his childhood; his house does more than Time could insofar as it is a standing negation of the other places. As an actant, Sender, Subject, and—as we shall see—Receiver of his program, Ben has shaped a space in which he could be a different kind of father from his own father—which shows him to be a different kind of father. How different, however, is a matter of evaluation. As Ben boasts to Clifford, his children "have been as free as the air to come and go in this house" (392). In *his* view he has created a space of freedom.

The last narrative program in which he is involved results in a reevaluation of his space and his role. Now ready to go out to the club, Old Ben "stepped to the door" for the first time and "looked down the dark flight of steps at his four younger children" (394). Out of the shelter of his study, or almost out, he is in a new space which will prove the topic space of his new experience. For there he must confront his children: The four younger children "stood in a circle directly beneath the overhead light, which one of them had just switched on. Their faces were all turned upward in the direction of the open doorway where he was standing, yet he knew in reason that they could not see him there" (394–95). Though, looking down at them, he seems to be in his customary position of domination, his apartness and emotional isolation are indirectly shown in the contrast with his children's position. They stand "in a circle" "directly beneath the overhead light" so that the idea of the circle, a common metaphor for family life, is reinforced by the idea of the center that holds things together. While they stand in light, he is in darkness, looking at them through dark glasses. We are prepared for a change, moreover, because a link is established between Aunt Nelson's cellar and Ben's house through the iconic image of the circle defined by the overhead light. And though Ben is still in a position of domination, though he can dimly see them, he has to push away the idea that they can see him in their turn, which deprives him of his superiority as voyeur and eavesdropper and returns him to his childhood condition of being under surveillance. Though he can hardly distinguish their lowered voices, he is certain they are talking about him, certain that Clifford whom he can hear upstairs is thinking about him. This provokes an offended outburst: "Never once in his life had he punished or restrained them in any way. He had given them a freedom unknown to children in the land of his childhood, yet from the time they could utter a word they had despised him and denied his right to any affection or gratitude. Suddenly, stepping out onto the landing, he screamed down the stairs to them: 'I've a right to some gratitude!' " (395). Frustrated and feeling perhaps the need to make some connection, though it be only to claim his right rather than utter his desire, he shouts at the group what is in fact a belated answer to Clifford's earlier question, "What is it you want?" He wants, as he phrases it to himself, the affection and gratitude they have denied him, but characteristically he only demands gratitude, which must render his statement even more puzzling to his four younger children. Upon this, the children, at first stunned, start moving slowly toward the stairs while Clifford comes out into the upstairs hall. "The four children were advancing up the first flight, and Clifford was coming down from upstairs. Old Ben opened his mouth to call to them, 'I'm not afraid of you!' But his voice had left him" (395). Projecting his inner hostility against them he can only stand momentarily in fear of them. No longer the producer of spatial conditions, no longer the Subject of a program of which he is also the Sender and the Receiver, Old Ben perceives himself as the victim, the Object, of his children's aggression, expressed in their movement through the topic space.

The momentary fright triggers a flash of recognition: "in his fear that in their wrath his children would do him harm, he suddenly pitied them. He pitied them for all they had suffered at his hands. And while he stood there, afraid, he realized, or perhaps recalled, how he had tortured and plagued them in all the ways that his resentment of their good fortune had taught him to do" (395). In his self-awareness, he "even remember(s) the day when it had occurred to him to build his study above the drive-under and off the stairs, so that he could keep tabs on them. He had declared that he wanted his house to be as different from his father's house as a house could be, and so it was. And now he stood in the half darkness, afraid that he was a man about to be taken by his children and at the same time pitying them" (395). Ben realizes how he has used space and positions in space to torture his children mentally, though he has never abused them physically. He has manipulated space in order to gain some sort of power. The man Ben has enjoyed what the downtrodden child lacked, a location of superiority from which to control the members of his family. Thus he reproduces, by different means and without the physical harshness, the parental position as he symbolically remembers it, up above looking at, overseeing, the child down there. Until this moment of recognition, he has blinded himself to the role which he has ensured with his spatial arrangements. (Numerous references to his impaired vision and his dark glasses recur through the text.) Ben's preference for "drive-under" is not simply a liking for the more vernacular phrase; the expression really conveys what is the more or less hidden purpose of the drive-under, which is a means of domination and subordination.

Space, however, has betrayed him. The very layout that enabled him to spy upon his children now enables them to invest him from above and below. Just as his father's house was not safe for Ben the son, so now the house built to his own specifications is not safe for Ben the father.

Nor does the protagonist's flash of insight really lead to cathartic forgiveness, of self or of others. Significantly, the old man withdrew into his study, "closed the door and locked it," and then performed a belated acting out: "As the lock clicked, he heard Clifford say, 'Papa!' Then he heard them all talking at once, and while they talked he stumbled through the dark study to the umbrella stand. He pulled out the stick with his father's face carved on the head, and in the darkness, while he heard his children's voices, he stumbled about the room beating the upholstered chairs with the stick and calling the names of his children under his breath" (395). The foray into the area outside the study has failed to reunite him with his children for the family celebration of his birthday. But his retreat is not simply retrogression. Having regained the safe place where he has played voyeur for so many years, he resorts, on this occasion, to action. Having recognized in himself the unjust, oppressive father who exercises his authority over his children because they are his children, he now makes, vicariously, the paternal gesture of aggression, in a private ritual of repetition.

To sum up this part of my analysis, "Porte Cochère," for all that it deals with an almost motionless protagonist, is about changing space, and changing places, and also about the desire to change the world and the failure of this desire. Assuredly, no narrative can exist without reference to the spatial dimension, and fiction, as Ricardo Gullon has shown, is fundamentally a medium in which "absolute space is replaced by a context of changing space with precise functions."[14] Only in "Porte Cochère" this "context of changing space with precise functions" becomes the subject's narrative program. The hero's project has been to transform space, to shape it in order to position himself in it in such a way as to fulfill his inner needs. To this extent, spatialization can be said here to be an "intervention of the will" (Gullon), though this intervention is bound to the character's unconscious drives. Thus space appears to be the theme of the story as well as its shape. Or, rather, one of the story's themes. According to Greimas in *Sémiotique et sciences sociales*, we must regard "l'espace comme une forme susceptible de s'ériger en un langage spatial permettant de parler d'autre chose que de l'espace." [15] Even a thematics of space may, indeed, probably must, be the support of another thematics. One might, for instance, show that the many references to up versus down and to light versus darkness (features of the narrated loci that define the fictional space) support an axiology which indexes /up/ and /light/ positively, but since this does not depart from widely accepted valuations, it is not necessary to dwell on such an aspect of the narrative. One might more profitably demonstrate how the spatial language of the story enables the reader to construct an image of Ben which diverges from his early self-appraisal as a tolerant father who has treated his children as "equals" and approximates more closely his later self-image, without, however, coinciding with it entirely. On the one hand, the two topographical systems which establish the spatial lexicon of the narrative do not stand, as we have seen, in simple opposition. The present setting and the remembered places share some common features, in spite of their difference, so that Ben's world cannot be as unlike that of his father as he thinks. On the other hand, the spatial syntax of the story is deeply revealing of Ben's habitual strategy. In the course of the preceding developments, however, I have given enough examples of such functioning. It seems therefore more urgent to insist on what I shall call the geometry of the generational pattern.

THE GEOMETRY OF HUMAN RELATIONS

The theme of paternity is, needless to say, implemented through semantic clusters, figures, and narrative devices which are not always linked to space, but these, for one thing, do not function independently from the general context with its emphasis on space and placement. Furthermore, the temporal line of succession is itself spatialized. On the whole, therefore, the theme maybe considered to be largely carried through the use of spatial elements.

Take, for example, the religious isotopy. Throughout the text a number of isolated items build a configuration that discreetly confers upon the father certain godlike attributes. First the comparison established between the octagonal side porch and a pagoda amplifies the symbolism of the octagon which Christianity inherited from the Greek tradition and which associates this geometric form with resurrection. Here, the children, gathered to celebrate their father's birthday, sit in the pagoda, while Ben from his study listens, a *deus absconditus*, to their talking, "his watery eyes focussed vaguely on the peak" of the red tile roof (a color the obvious realism of which does not mask its imperial and liturgical associations). Here, of course, the religious suggestions emanate from the spatial environment and the use the characters make of it. Since the house was conceived, if not designed, by Old Ben, the templelike structure reflects back on him in a new way. Another instance of religious imagery is to be found when Ben Junior teases his brother, "No letter written?" and Clifford answers him with a "Nope, no letter this day of Our Lord" (393). The old-fashioned turn of phrase, which clashes with the informal "Nope," transforms an obsolete way of dating into a joke against their almighty father. In this case, the religious allusion is playful, which is no reason for discounting it. Such scattered notes further enter into resonance with the gold watch insofar as gold is the metal of the gods. The byplay with the gold watch in the confrontation between Old Ben and Clifford, while serving as a narrative time-marker and as an index to Ben's motivation, gives to an object that is in itself highly symbolic a prominence that is arresting. Old Ben, fingering his watch, and devouring his son's time, becomes a trivialized, watered-down version of Kronos/Saturn, the god who devoured his children and became conflated with Chronos. I do not mean to intrude a mythological interpretation upon a text of such restrained elegance as "Porte Cochère," simply to say that, for this reader at least, the old gods that have symbolized the father-son relationship in Western culture hover in the intertext of Peter Taylor's story. On a different cultural plane, the devilish connotations that surround Old Ben's father develop further the religious isotopy and endow the paternal figure with similar power. Rounding off the religious paradigm, however, a latent metaphor deeply modifies the father image. This is even less obtrusive than the allusions to Father Time. Look at the narrator's description of Ben: "he stood motionless, at the window, his huge, soft hands held tensely at his side, his long body erect, his almost freakishly large head at a slight angle" (393). The hugeness, the posture, the freakishness, as well as the choice of words (singularly, "erect") make one think of a bear. (We may have been prepared for such a reading by his name, Old Ben, which is that of the bear in a famous story of Faulkner's.) A sacred animal in many parts of the world, regarded in several mythologies as the ancestor of mankind, the bear used to be feared and worshiped.[16] Thus, implicit as it is, the metaphor enhances the religious paradigm deployed through the story. The particular note it sounds (especially clear if one remembers "The Bear") is a hint, insofar as the bear often plays *sacrificial* god, at the ambiguous nature and fate of the father-god. Old Ben at the end is afraid of being "taken"—like a city or a hunted beast. The religious imagery, therefore, suggests the dual aspect of fatherhood, destroying and destroyed.

In the story, a sort of doubling affects the image of the liberal, good father, which turns into the mask of the oppressive, bad father. However different their means, Ben and his father seek to control their children. Whereas, about to punish him, Ben's father shouts "the deafening command: 'Attention!' " Ben demands attention from his children, which is, in truth, no small demand. Similarly the filial and parental roles of Ben combine in a dual performance. On the linear, irreversible development that transforms the son into a father—a permutation of roles in the diegesis—the narration, through the two flashbacks, the process of spatialization and the use of imagery, emphasizes commutations. Old Ben, while acting as father, remembers his suffering as son, indeed remains a son. A minor instance of this occurs when, in the dimmed-out study, Ben reaches for one of the walking canes in the umbrella stand. "His hand lighting on the carved head of a certain oak stick, he felt the head with trembling fingers and quickly released it" (393). Although the narration reveals only later that this was the father's stick with his head carved on the knob, the stick which he used to beat young Ben with, the overreaction of the character strongly intimates to the reader aware of the disciplinary use of canes and of their phallic symbolism that something of the sort might indeed be the case, so that the vagueness of the reference, "a certain oak stick," reveals more of the character's continuing fear of his father than it hides of the facts. More important, Ben as father attempts to wipe out what John Irwin aptly calls "the affront of sonship, the affront of dependency," compounded here by the affront of violence.[17] Through his very attempt to reject his father's model of fatherhood, and his failure to do away with some form of domination, Ben still behaves like a son. For he is seeking for revenge against his father. He is unable to treat his children as equals, notwithstanding his claims to the contrary, but in his "resentment of their very good fortune" he unconsciously aligns himself with them, as though they were his siblings. And through his lifelong behavior to them, of which his treatment of Clifford in the present is but an epitome, he has been seeking revenge against his father, making them substitutes for his father.

That the children serve as substitutes for the father is particularly evident in the case of Clifford: this son, "the real man among the others," Ben identifies with himself at least once when he notes that his footsteps are "heavy footsteps like his own" (388, 389). But the narration also links Cliff in unobtrusive ways with his grandfather. Old Ben admires his son's athletic physique, is very much aware of his body, the way he moves, turns around on the ball of one foot, and so on.[18] So was he aware, in the past, of his father's body; even as he was about to be caned, he noticed that the old man's coattails were "somehow clinging close to his buttocks and thighs, so that his whole powerful form was outlined—his black figure against the white brick and the door" (394). Furthermore, the only detail given about Clifford's apparel is that he wears white shoes, which implies that he is in white: now white is, together with black, strongly associated with Ben's father, his face and his house. Finally footsteps signal in both cases the coming of the two men. Such conflations between grandfather and grandchildren have long been observed by psychoanalysts, from Sigmund Freud and Ernest Jones on.[19] The fantasmatic doubling of grandfather and son offers a clue to the impact on Old Ben of the final confrontation with his children to which I would like now to come back.

The old man's fantasy of being "taken" by his children is indeed striking. With it, there hangs dimly over the decorous, bourgeois Nashville home the shadow of collective parricide, of the Freudian myth of the murder of the primal father. But one may be a little more precise. If Ben is unable to bear that position in between Clifford and his other children, it is partly because he is caught between (a fantasmatic image of) the powerful Father and his own offspring. The scene on the staircase, or rather the positioning of the actors, is emblematic of his situation in life. Although we only see him engaged in dual relations, with his aunt or with his father on the one hand, and with Clifford or with his children as a group on the other, Ben's experience depends on his place in the chain of generations and is triangulated by three terms, Father-Ego-Son. As Ego he is normally led to fear both Father and Sons because of the aggressive desires he has felt toward them and now projects upon them. His childish wish was to live in a country where there would be no children and no fathers, where he could be an isolated Ego, self-engendered and without descent—an old fantasy of mankind, at least as old as Melchisedec and Sophocles' own Oedipus.[20] And though he built his house in order to position himself differently from his father, up above and aside from the family he has reared after all, he eventually finds out that there is no place where one can transcend the positioning, the conflict of generations. Like all human beings, he is caught in the chain of generations, caught in the guilt of violence. Choosing his father's cane to beat his children by proxy, he still affirms himself a son in the very assertion of his fatherhood, of his right to victimize his children, and in the symbolic killing of the father whose phallic weapon he now has assumed. Just as he fears and pities his children, so now the reader must fear and pity the fictional character—must fear and pity in him the representative of the human plight.

For, of course, to fear generation is not simply to fear involvement and sexuality, whatever part this particular fear may play. (Significantly, women are almost absent in the story.[21] Ben's mother is not even alluded to; his dead wife mentioned only in connection with the naming of the "porte cochère." Needless to say, it is important that *her* word for it should stand at the threshold of the narrative, thus making the father's word the contextually marked one. The title, therefore, subtly undermines the language and the law of the father.) The ultimate fear proceeds from the fact that the succession of generations is succession in death. The fantasy of being *causa sui* is linked to a dream of immortality. "Without descent, without genealogy; no more generations; the world of generation and death transcended"—thus Norman O. Brown.[22] It is no coincidence that the family reunion should take place on the birthday which, celebrating Ben's entrance (or fall) into the world of generation, brings him closer to death. When he seizes his dead father's cane, the protagonist uses this symbolic weapon to punish his children for being his and being his successors. But the carved face on the head of the cane functions, for the reader, almost like a skull, as a *memento mori* which in his fury Old Ben does not heed.

"Porte cochère" and "drive-under" become symbols of the ineluctable conditions under which all human beings enter and experience life. Space as the setting for a microdrama turns, in Peter Taylor's brilliantly understated treatment, into the emblematic arena where the geometry of family relations regulates our positions, into a symbol of our existence in the world.

Notes

1. Gene Baro, "A True Short-Story Artist," *New York Herald Tribune Book Review*, Dec. 6, 1959, 9, quoted by Barbara Schuler in "The House of Peter Taylor," *Critique* 9, no.3 (1967): 17.

2. Stephen Goodwin, "An Interview with Peter Taylor," *Shenandoah* 24 (Winter 1973): 9.

3. Ibid., 14.

4. "Porte Cochère" was first published in the *New Yorker*, July 16 and 21–24, 1949, then reprinted in *Fifty-Five Stories from "The New Yorker"* (New York: Simon and Schuster, 1949). It has been included in the last collection of Peter Taylor's stories to date, *The Old Forest and Other Stories* (Garden City, N.Y.: Doubleday, 1985). It is a more expanded version, slightly different from that of the *New Yorker*, and some of the changes (the aunt's name is different, the presence of the narrator is more clearly felt, etc.) would have been relevant to my interpretation. Unfortunately, this edition is marred by a few typographical errors and what is clearly the omission of one line (263) so that the text is not reliable enough for my purposes. Nor do I know whether this represents the author's latest version. Under the circumstances, I have preferred to use the Simon and Schuster version; all the page citations, indicated within parentheses in the text, will refer to this edition.

5. I have borrowed these and other terms from A. J. Greimas, *Sémiotique, dictionnaire raisonné de la théorie du langage* (Paris: Hachette, 1979), but as my reader will soon discover, this reading of "Porte Cochère" does not pretend to be a semiotic reading of Peter Taylor's story.

6. Schuler, "House of Peter Taylor," 7.

7. The distinction between focalization (who perceives) and narration (who tells) has been introduced by Gèrard Genette, *Figures III* (Paris: Seuil, 1972), and adopted with some modifications by Shlomith Rimmon-Kennan, whom I follow here (*Narrative Fiction: Contemporary Poetics* [London: Methuen, 1983]).

8. Again I borrow concepts, which I have found useful in my eclectic kind of analysis,

from a confirmed semiotician, Denis Bertrand, *L'espace et le sens, Germinal d'Emile Zola* (Paris: Hadès-Benjamin, 1985).

9. I might have added that these places share a feature which is not intrinsically spatial but which characterizes space, namely,/light/: the aunt's cellar has the same dim light as Ben's study, the father's cellar is dark. /Light/ is related to the major isotopy of /sight/or, rather, /impaired vision/, which I shall only glance at but which would deserve further investigation.

10. The thymic category is articulated into euphoria/dysphoria; see Greimas.

11. "Proxemics" is the term Edward Hall coined for the "interrelated observations and theories of man's use of space as a specialized elaboration of culture" (*The Hidden Dimension* [Garden City, N.Y.: Anchor Books, 1969]). According to Greimas, "la proxémique est une discipline—ou plutot un projet de discipline—sémiotique, qui vise à analyser les dispositions des sujets et des objets dans l'espace, et plus particulièrement, l'usage que les sujets font de l'espace aux fins de signification."

12. Eric Berne, *Games People Play: The Psychology of Human Relationships* (New York: Grove Press, 1964).

13. Gaston Bachelard, *La Poétique de l'espace* (Paris: Presses Universitaires de France, 1957), 24.

14. Ricardo Gullon, "On Space in the Narrative," *Critical Inquiry* (Autumn 1975): 112.

15. A. J. Greimas, *Sémiotique et sciences sociales* (Paris: Seuil, 1976), 130.

16. Jean Chevalier et al., *Dictionnaire des symboles* (Paris: Robert Laffont, 1969); Sir James Frazer, *The New Golden Bough*, abr. ed. (New York: New American Library, 1959), esp. 545–49, 551.

17. John Irwin. "The Dead Father in Faulkner," in Robert Con Davis, *The Fictional Father: Lacanian Readings of the Text* (Amherst: University of Massachusetts Press, 1981).

18. The motif of whirling or turning about is associated both with Clifford and Old Ben (390–91, 394).

19. The idea of the "identification" of grandfather and grandchild has received a more recent formulation in Alain de Mijolla, *Les visiteurs du moi* (Paris: Les Belles Lettres, 1981).

20. Cf. Heb. 7: 3; Norman O. Brown, *Love's Body* (New York: Vintage Books, 1956), 54–55; and Claude Simon, *Le sacre du printemps* (Paris: Calmann-Levy, 1954).

21. In the Doubleday edition, Aunt Nelson is named Aunt Nell Partee and one of Ben's daughters is Nell instead of Laura Nell; the naming thereby strengthens a female line in the family.

22. Brown, *Love's Body*, 54.

Engaging the Past:
Peter Taylor's "The Old Forest"

DAVID M. ROBINSON

Peter Taylor's achievement in fiction rests on his mastery of a retrospective narration with a dual purpose: detailed social observation that marks the best fiction of manners, and an accompanying depth of psychological revelation that transcends social forms. The paradigm of Taylor's best fiction is the recollection of an event deep in the past of the narrator or the community, which is reported with a consciousness of its personal significance or with an attempt to assess that significance. The past holds Taylor's characters powerfully, molding their identity while inhibiting their free development. The struggle for identity and the struggle with the past are, as Taylor portrays them, very much the same. The power of Taylor's narration comes in part from the almost hypnotic engagement of his narrator with the past, and the intensity of the attempt to understand it. It is not the past, however, but the act of remembering, of retelling, and of reinterpreting the past in the retelling that reminds us that the work of self-creation is still in progress. The events of the past continue to have resonance in the present because they are still being assimilated. Taylor distances his narrators from their earlier selves and exploits that distance to achieve his psychological portraits. But as the narrator moves toward self-analysis, the distance of the past becomes illusory, for the past comes to dictate even the terms by which he attempts to recreate it and to recreate himself.

In "The Old Forest," arguably the best of Taylor's stories, Nat Ramsey describes his own struggle for maturity in the midst of the demise of the upper-class Memphis of 1937. Nat's recollection begins with an explanation of why, when he "was already formally engaged," he "sometimes went out on the town with girls of a different sort" (3). Nat has much to say about that "sort" of girl in the course of the story, remembering that these women were "facetiously and somewhat arrogantly referred to as the Memphis demimonde." The casual social brutality of the phrase designated "a girl who was not in the Memphis debutante set" (31). Such labeling marked out those women who might lack the right social status for marriage but also suggested

Reprinted from the *Southern Literary Journal* 23 (Spring 1990): 63–77, © The University of North Carolina Press. Used by permission.

an air of the exotic in the otherwise absolutely predictable lives of Nat and his friends.

These women are interesting and stimulating companions, "bright girls certainly and some of them even highly intelligent," who "read books, . . . looked at pictures, and . . . were apt to attend any concert or play that came to Memphis," not "the innocent, untutored types that we generally took to dances at the Memphis Country Club and whom we eventually looked forward to marrying" (31–32). As we see Nat come into closer contact with these women, his sense of their strength and complexity grows. He discovers that in addition to a "physical beauty and a bookishness," qualities that we might associate with the traditionally feminine, they also had "a certain toughness of mind and a boldness of spirit" (59). They are modern women, who, though still restricted by the persisting division of sexual roles, were in the process of transforming those roles.

Curiously, Nat comes to identify the symbol of this transformation as the Old Forest, "a densely wooded area which is actually the last surviving bit of primeval forest that once grew right up to the bluffs above the Mississippi River" (38). A week before his marriage, Nat has driven near the forest with Lee Ann Deehart, one of the "demimondaines," when his car collides with a skidding truck on a frozen road. Nat is mildly injured in the accident, but before anyone can arrive to give assistance, Lee Ann walks away from the car and into the Old Forest, disappearing for four days. Lee Ann's disappearance raises the threat of scandal and endangers Nat's engagement to one of the Memphis Country Club girls, Caroline Braxley. In his attempt to find Lee Ann, he confronts her world and begins to learn the limitations of his own.

Lee Ann is associated with the Old Forest because it represents what is beyond the control of Nat's ordered life. "Here are giant oak and yellow poplar trees older than the memory of the earliest white settler" (38). Surrounded by the man-made city, the forest has not submitted to that power. In escaping into the forest, Lee Ann unwittingly proves how tenuous Nat's control of his life is. It is a lesson that experience continues to repeat for him. Almost casually dropped in the middle of his reminiscence is this stunning list of personal tragedies: the loss of two brothers in the Korean War, the death of his parents in a fire at his home, and the accidental deaths of two of his teenage children (42). It would seem that the incident with Lee Ann would pale to insignificance when weighed against those pains, but, in fact, these instances of loss and grief augment its importance. Here Nat began to learn his mortal limitations. As Nat remembers it, "life *was* different" (42) in the Memphis of 1937. It is not life that has changed, of course, but his perception of the boundary of the possible. "Our tranquil, upper-middle-class world of 1937 did not have the rest of the world crowding in on it so much" (43). But the remark tells us more about Nat's maturing consciousness of tragedy than about the degree to which persons of his class were insulated from experience. Lee Ann's walk into the forest proves how fragile Nat's world really was.

Nat's sense of vulnerability begins to grow after he realizes the gravity of his situation, and the forest looms in his mind, embodying the threatening forces that delimit his social world. "More than the density of the underbrush, more than its proximity to the Zoo, where certain unsavory characters often hung out, it was the great size and antiquity of the forest trees somehow and the old rumors that white settlers had once been ambushed there by Chickasaw Indians that made me feel that if anything had happened to the girl, it had happened there" (44). Nat is ironically right that "something" had happened to Lee Ann, though it was not the violence that he had feared. Her disappearance is an assertion of independence from the grips of Nat's world, which will attempt to exert a benevolent but nonetheless firm claim on her in the aftermath of the wreck.

Her disappearance, though we eventually find it to be considerably more complex, carries the resonance of women's resistance to paternalistic authority of which Nat finds himself a rather reluctant emissary. He recognizes the symbolic threat of the forest to the world made by his male ancestors, and he realizes with some discomfort that his own fear is similar to that of generations of men in Memphis, who "have feared and wanted to destroy [the forest] for a long time and whose destruction they are still working at even in this latter day." That destructive impulse is the push to modernization, the drive behind the steady development and conquest of the land. "It has only recently been saved by a narrow margin from a great highway that men wished to put through there—saved by groups of women determined to save this last bit of the old forest from the axes of modern men" (53).

As a persisting wilderness, the forest thus represents a counterforce to masculine control, and, in a larger sense, to all forms of social control. Nat's mediations on the symbolic connotations of the forest is punctuated by stories of "mad pioneer women, driven mad by their loneliness and isolation, who ran off into the forest" to be later "captured by Indians" (53–54). The Old Forest reminds Nat that "civilization" is male civilization, and he begins to discover how deeply implicated in that civilization he is. As the Memphis city fathers reach out in a show of concern for Lee Ann's welfare, they also enact their own insecurity in the viability of their social structure, and their guilt over its basis in oppression.

But Nat is worried about more than Lee Ann's fate. He wonders "if all this might actually lead to my beautiful, willowy Caroline Braxley's breaking off our engagement" (45). But the story's heightened tension about this point is at least superficially without basis. Nat had described Caroline early in the story as his wife of many years. Our knowledge that the incident did not end Nat's engagement emphasizes the particular burden of Taylor's retrospective narration. By minimizing the tension over the consequences of

Nat's accident, he has focused it instead on Nat's tone as he recalls those events. The question is not whether he will marry, but what the marriage will mean to him.

As Nat flounders in the exigencies of Lee Ann's disappearance, Caroline begins to demonstrate a capacity to meet the gravity of the situation. Her stature grows as the story progresses. When she eventually takes over the search, Nat docilely cooperates with her. So it seems that his life continues for most of the next forty years. Caroline's "good judgment in all matters relating to our marriage," Nat says, "has never failed her—or us" (36). But despite Nat's persuasive depiction of his concern that his engagement might be ruined, he undermines our faith in his absolute contentment in his relation with Caroline when he describes the customs of engagement and marriage in upper-class Memphis. Engagement "was in no sense so unalterably binding as it had been in our parents' day," he explains, adding that "it was not considered absolutely dishonorable for either party to break off the plans merely because he or she had had a change of heart" (45). Even more ominously, Nat admits that "the thought pleased me—that is, the ease with which an engagement might be ended" (46). Afraid on the one hand that he will not be able to marry Caroline, he is also afraid that he *will* marry her. While visiting with Caroline and her parents, he admits "indulging in a perverse fantasy, a fantasy in which Caroline had broken off our engagement and I was standing up pretty well, was even seeking consolation in the arms, so to speak, of a safely returned Lee Ann Deehart" (46). Nat's fantasy suggests his attraction to Lee Ann, but it tells us more about his vague sense of confinement in the world that he inhabits. If Caroline represents a secure place in that world, Lee Ann represents escape. His dreams of Lee Ann are indeed fantasy—she had earlier treated the possibility of their marriage with humorous contempt—but like all fantasies, they are revealing. They suggest Nat's stirring of resistance to the predictable course of his life. He never directs that resentment toward Caroline, for whom he has profound respect. He resists instead the sure movement of the machinery that will take him through a "good" marriage and into a predictable life in his father's business. One of the story's ironies is that the crisis transforms what might have seemed a marriage of convenience into a meaningful and durable relationship.

The accident sets in motion a process of maturing. This accounts for his returning in memory to it after so many years. When Nat finally tells Caroline that Lee Ann had been in the car with him, he is surprised to find that she already knows this. Her reaction convinces him to go ahead and tell an "uncensored version of the accident" (47). Caroline's capacity to take command of the situation impresses Nat, who is characteristically in a state of indecisiveness. " 'You do know, don't you,' she went on after a moment, 'that you are going to have to *find* Lee Ann? And you probably are going to need help' " (48). Caroline understands that Lee Ann's disappearance might force an end to her engagement. In recognizing her relative powerlessness in the situation, a fact that is only beginning to dawn on Nat, Caroline finds the source of a surprising strength. Nat's eventual comprehension of her complex and courageous reaction to the events is an essential aspect of the maturity that he achieves.

Caroline might have been expected to play an unsavory part in the story, a manipulative individual attempting to assert the requisites of privilege. But in Taylor's deft touch, she begins to capture our sympathy and seize the moral momentum of the story, supplying the drifting Nat with both a will and a purpose in finding Lee Ann. Her motives are not disinterested, but her courage in the face of the possible disaster contrasts favorably with Nat's fantasy-punctuated passivity. While Nat has begun to awaken to the ways that Memphis Country Club life insulates him from experience, Caroline is more keenly aware of those limits and of their concomitant restrictions to her capacity of choice. As Nat eventually comes to understand, Caroline's social position carries a burden with it, a knowledge of "what was going to be expected of [her] in making a marriage and bringing up a family there in Memphis" (48). Lee Ann represented a threat to those expectations, competing for the husbands that were the requirements for survival as it had been defined to Caroline. While it is the narrowness of the definition of success and not girls of a lower social standing that are the real threat to Caroline and her peers, Taylor builds a measure of sympathy for her. He depicts Caroline and Nat as people trapped in a value system as it crumbles. However we scorn those values, it is hard to blame them for the world into which they were born. Taylor has written a devastating indictment of the narrowness of the upper class but has treated the people of that class with fair-minded sympathy. While Caroline's quest seems superficially like the attempt to protect her privilege, it is much closer to an effort to overcome the vulnerability that Nat's accident has revealed to her—the restricted scope of her possibilities for self-definition. The story thus develops around the hunt for Lee Ann, but its actual fuel is this struggle for self-definition that the hunt initiates, not only in Nat, but also in Caroline.

Since the source of their insulation from experience is their social class, Nat and Caroline experience their search for self-definition in versions of humiliation, as the perspectives and protections of their upbringing are stripped away in their dealings with Lee Ann's friends. Lee Ann's circle has a good-natured scorn for Nat and his friends, and in order to communicate with them at all Nat and Caroline must repeatedly meet that scorn. It leaves their inherited view of the world, already shaky, impossible to sustain. As they surrender that view, their move toward self-understanding advances. Nat searches for Lee Ann in the company of Memphis police, making the rounds of her friends and inquiring of her whereabouts. Nat is thus immersed in the world of these women, and he finds himself fascinated by the comparative freedom of their lives. "At any rate, they were all freed from old restraints put on them by family and community, liberated in each case, so it seems to me, by sheer strength of character, liberated in many respects, but above all else—and I cannot say how it came about—liberated sexually. . . . They were not promiscuous—not most of them—but they slept with the men they were in love with and they did not conceal the fact" (63). The issue of Nat's possible sexual involvement with Lee Ann is always present to the police, who ask him at one point if she is pregnant. Even after he has told them she is not, he finds himself later asking one of her friends, Nancy Minnifee, the same question, thereby opening himself to the deepest humiliation of the search. "Nancy's mouth dropped open. Then she laughed aloud. Presently she said, 'Well, one thing's certain, Nat. It wouldn't be any concern of yours if she were' " (62). Nat's blunder reveals the kind of overbearing assumption that provides Lee Ann and her friends with fuel for their resentment and at least part of the motive for Lee Ann's defiant flight.

Nat's second day of searching is in the company of his father, the mayor, and the newspaper editor—representatives of the Memphis establishment who were the last generation "to grow up in a world where women were absolutely subjected and under the absolute protection of men" (67). Nat sees in retrospect, and perhaps begins to see during the time of the events, that they were protecting a patriarchy that they sensed was being threatened from within. "They thought of these girls as the daughters of men who had abdicated their authority and responsibility as fathers," and of themselves as "surrogate fathers," acting to hold the fabric of the society that they knew together. "It was a sort of communal fatherhood they were acting out" (67). While Nat has been formed by his father's world, and clings to it with part of himself, he is also stifled and finds in himself some resistance to it. But the very structure of authority that has molded him is beginning to change, making his ambivalence even more complex. As Nat recalls, "I actually heard my father saying, 'That's what the whole world is going to be like someday.' He meant like the life such girls as Lee Ann were making for themselves" (67–68). Lee Ann represents, to Nat, a future which is both attractive and frightening.

Nat's relations with Lee Ann and her friends have been one expression of his tentative reluctance to follow the expected course of life. Another small mode of resistance has been his persistence in studying Latin poetry, a subject in which his interest is less than passionate and his skill minimal. His continuing in the study baffles his family, and he himself professes not to understand his motivations fully. But it is precisely because it is extraneous, even an encumbrance, to the expected that he persists in it. When Caroline finds him at home after the accident, a copy of his Latin text nearby, her greeting is revealing. " 'I hope you see now what folly your pursuit of Latin poetry is' " (41). This petty defiance of the expected in his study of Latin was an attempt at self-possession, and, although he drops it, this mild nonconformity grows in more meaningful ways during the crisis.

This helps to explain Nat's fascination with Lee Ann, which grows in proportion to her defiance of the Memphis order. His dating of the "demimondaines" has been a flirting with the forbidden, a safe way to test the limits of the social restrictions. But as Nat begins to search for Lee Ann, the gravity of conflict in those relations becomes clear. Lee Ann's friends call to warn him to leave her alone. These only add to his curiosity to find her. Yet he is simultaneously pushed toward a closer intimacy with Caroline. After the day of searching with his father, Nat and Caroline "tell each other how much we loved each other and how we would let nothing on earth interfere with our getting married" (70). While the pledge reassures Nat somewhat, he is still plagued by the phone calls that he has kept secret and eventually tells Caroline of them. "And before I left that night she got me to tell her all I knew about 'that whole tribe of city girls.' " That Nat trusts Caroline deeply enough to be frank, and that she accepts his "confessions" with a non-judgmental determination to make good use of them, is an indication of the growing strength of their relationship. For Nat gives her not only "an account of my innocent friendship with Lee Ann Deehart" but also "an account of my earlier relations, which were not innocent, with a girl named Fern Morris" (72).

While Nat's relationship with Caroline grows deeper, so does his confusion about his feelings for Lee Ann. In their frank discussion, he had held one thing back from Caroline, a growing sense that in his search for her he was "discovering what my true feelings toward Lee Ann had been during the past two years." He had begun to feel, he admitted, "that [Lee Ann] was the girl I ought and wanted to be marrying" (72). The story's central question is whether this is escapist wish-projection. Is he attracted to Lee Ann because she is what he cannot have, or is he belatedly learning the truth of his own feelings? Even as he entertained them, he "realized the absolute folly of such thoughts and the utter impossibility of any such conclusion to present events" (72). While this at first seems like a confession of Nat's weak inability to resist the pressure of conformity, other evidence suggests that the impossibility of the fantasy, and thus its essential safety, is part of its appeal. It is not that he lacks the courage to act on his attraction for Lee Ann but that his attraction to her depends on his conviction that he will never be able to enact it.

One remark about his relationship with Lee Ann is particularly significant:

> I had never dared insist upon the occasional advances I had naturally made to her, because she had always seemed too delicate, too vulnerable, for me to think of suggesting a casual sexual relationship with her. She had seemed too clever and too intelligent for me to deceive her about my intentions or my worth as a person. And I imagined I relished the kind of restraint there was

between us because it was so altogether personal and not one placed upon us by any element or segment of society, or by an outside circumstances whatever. (72)

But of course the contours of their entire relationship had been determined by the class barriers that existed between them. Nat was destined to marry a woman from his social set, and he and Lee Ann understood this from the outset of their friendship. There would never have been such a friendship except for the distance that social structures had decreed between them. The impossibility of marriage had had the effect of freeing them from some aspects of sexual tension. But to consider that freedom as an indication that no "element or segment of society" had placed restraints on them is the kind of obtuseness that marks Nat as still seriously immature.

Caroline's emergence as a central figure in the story is the result of her capacity to replace Lee Ann as an embodiment of reality for Nat. In her presence, "my thoughts and fantasies of the day before seemed literally like something out of a dream that I might have had" (73). Nat grows toward a more mature self-knowledge through his rejection of immature fantasy.

Nat's explanation of his relations with the "city girls," and his sexual affair with Fern Morris, provide Caroline with the information to negotiate successfully the hostile territory of Lee Ann's network of friends. To act on the information, Caroline also must go through a certain humiliation, parading her vulnerability before these hostile women and openly struggling to regain what she once might have regarded hers by right—her coming marriage. Caroline's humiliation undermines the perspective from which she has hitherto seen the world and thus makes a fuller self-development possible. She must finally appeal to Nat's former lover, Fern Morris, who offers her a clue to Lee Ann's location. It is Lee Ann's possession of a snapshot of a woman whom Nat has known as the proprietor of a nightclub, Mrs. Power. She was a woman with "a huge goiter on her neck" who "was never known to smile" (66). This sinister figure is Lee Ann's grandmother, to whom she has returned a few days after the accident. But Lee Ann has tried to keep her connection with Mrs. Power a secret because of the social embarrassment that it might cause her. Her motive for hiding is not to avoid the scandal of having been caught with Nat, nor is it to make herself an obstacle to Nat's marriage. Caroline deduces the complex motivations behind Lee Ann's disappearance when Nat tells her what he knows of Lee Ann's past at a number of boarding schools away from Memphis. " 'They kept her away from home,' Caroline speculated. 'And so when she had finished school she wasn't prepared for the kind of 'family' she had. That's why she moved out on them and lived in a boarding house' " (79). Lee Ann's motives in disappearing thus turn out to be very different from those that Nat had surmised.

Her flight is less a defiance of the social order than an indication of her fear to be exposed to it. It is primarily to avoid social embarrassment that she tried to protect her past from discovery and publication.

Caroline's discovery of Lee Ann's whereabouts is the catalyst for the self-confrontations that form the climax of the story. When they find Lee Ann at the apartment above her grandmother's nightclub, Caroline tells Nat to stay in the car while she goes up to talk to Lee Ann. Although we may suspect that her gesture is in part motivated by a jealous insecurity, its operative motive is Caroline's recognition that Nat may inhibit her communication with Lee Ann. But Lee Ann's near presence prompts Nat to a painful moment of self-analysis. As he waits in the car, he imagines his separation from Lee Ann as a sign of his closure to experience. Should he accept that closure? To leave the car and enter her apartment, against Caroline's instructions, would be the culminating act in Nat's growing defiance of the course of his life. "I suddenly realized—at that early age—that there was experience to be had in life that I might never know anything about except through hearsay and through books. I felt that this was my last moment to reach out and understand something of the world that was other than my own narrow circumstances and my own narrow nature" (79–80). This interpretation of his course of development is an advance over his earlier misdirected feelings of love for Lee Ann. "The notion I had had yesterday that I was in love with her and wanted to marry her didn't really adequately express the emotions that her disappearance had stirred in me" (79). As Nat has come to understand something of Lee Ann's suffering, he has come to see her as a symbol of experience, an alternative to the sheltered life he has led. His decision to stay in the car, ending his pursuit of Lee Ann, thus becomes an important moment of self-definition. "It may be that the moment of my great failure was when I continued to sit there in the car and did not force my way into the house where the old woman with the goiter lived and where it now seemed Lee Ann had been hiding for four days" (80). While we may grant that Nat's feeling of crisis is genuine and that it locates an essential element of his personality, it is not hard to see that his impulse to burst into Lee Ann's house—an action that represented for him an active grasping of experience—would have been a ludicrous and tragic mistake. Whether from good judgment, loyalty to Caroline, or simple cowardice, Nat remains in the car. His inaction is an act of wisdom—or at least an avoidance of folly. What could he have said to Lee Ann that would have constructively addressed her situation? What could he have said that she would not have rightly rebuffed? His feeling that it is within his power to reestablish some connection with her, if that is what his impulse to enter her house means, is a sad overestimation of his capacity to exert control over experience. Nat's failure was not that he did not burst into Lee Ann's room, grasping for the experience of life that she represented to him. It was in labeling as a failure an act that was, under the circumstances, the only decent one that he could have taken.

While Nat does indeed grow in recognizing the narrowness of his own experience, he has not yet achieved a full and tragic acceptance of the limits from within which he must pursue experience. Nat's failure to act is appropriate. His real failure, and one which he seems to labor to understand as he recalls the incident, is not to recognize the appropriateness of the decision.

There is some evidence, although it is by no means conclusive, that Nat may have grown toward an acceptance of the limits of experience, and thus learned in a small way to meet it more constructively. He refers to it as his "extraordinary decision" to leave his career in business at age thirty-seven and "go back to the university and prepare myself to become a teacher" (80). The decision is a break in the pattern of life that had been established for him by his parents and that had been preserved in the final success of his four-day search to locate Lee Ann. Nat qualifies the impact of the decision with frank self-assessment: "But I knew then, at thirty-seven, that I was only going to try to comprehend intellectually the world about me and beyond me and that I had failed somehow at some time to reach out and grasp direct experience of a larger life which no amount of intellectualizing could compensate for" (80). While many of Taylor's readers may be loath to accept the pursuit of a teaching career as a signpost of personal growth, it is exactly that for Nat, despite his mild denigration of it. Nat is less a victim of his inability to act than of his tendency to romanticize some vague notion about the grasping of experience. There is something of a Proustian flourish in Nat's romantic sense of his failure to grasp experience and his retreat into the intellectual life to analyze that failure. Insofar as this bespeaks immaturity, the story charts an arrested self-development. But without exaggerating the significance of his change—it is a vocational change which occurs after his father dies, leaving him financially secure—Nat does eventually alter the course of his life in a delayed but seemingly genuine effort to understand. His accident with Lee Ann at least shook the foundations of his comfortable ignorance and accelerated a process in which his recognition of his narrow personal and social experience became a stimulus to self-improvement.

One strand of the story, however, works against this building indictment of the past—Nat's nostalgia for the lost world of Memphis. The story resists a linear reduction to any thematic certainty. Nat himself is no complete convert to modernity, but he continues to yearn with part of himself for the world that his accident shattered. "Our tranquil, upper-middle-class world of 1937 did not have the rest of the world crowding in on it so much," he recalls (42–43). Nat's desire for the past, despite the lessons of his experience, is itself problematic for any definitive thematic reading of the story, but it is augmented by the fact that Taylor creates a similar nostalgic reaction in his readers. "The Old Forest" evokes an attraction for the Memphis of the 1930s in its oblique glimpses of the lives of the upper class, despite the fact that the logic of the narrative condemns that world and shows it empty.

Consider Nat's account of his dinner with the Braxleys the day after the accident. During the evening, Nat is taken by one of the Braxley's black servants to receive a telephone call from his father. "As he preceded me the length of the living room and then gently guided me across the hall to the telephone in the library, I believe he would have put his hand under my elbow to help me—as if a real invalid—if I had allowed him to" (43). Obviously the suggestion of infantile dependency accurately reflects the weaker parts of Nat's character. But the social trappings of the Braxley house, particularly the brief image of the plantation South that Nat's dependence on the faithful servant evokes, cuts both ways in the story. It is precisely the kind of life that has damagingly restricted Nat and Caroline's vision of the world, against which they must struggle to attain a mature identity. But it is also a potentially seductive hook into the world of rare privilege. Nat is quite explicit about his attraction to this now extinct world when he recounts being driven home by the Braxley's servant, Robert. Nat falls asleep on the brief drive home and has to be awakened when they arrive.

> I remember how warmly I thanked him for bringing me home, even shaking his hand, which was a rather unusual thing to do in those days. I felt greatly refreshed and restored and personally grateful to Robert for it. There was not, in those days in Memphis, any time or occasion when one felt more secure and relaxed than when one had given oneself over completely to the care and protection of the black servants who surrounded us and who created and sustained for the most part the luxury which distinguished the lives we lived then from the lives we live now. (46–47)

That modern lives are indeed different is, at least in part, a lamentable fact for Nat, even though he goes on to admit the injustice of the arrangements that made his former luxury possible. "They [the servants] did so for us, whatever their motives and however degrading our demands and our acceptance of their attentions may have been to them" (47). There remains some part of Nat which has not been weaned from the comfortable and ultimately unjust innocence of his upper-class childhood. That has, of course, made the achievement of such maturity as he has all the more difficult. And it has made him a much more compelling subject for fiction. It behooves us to recognize that Nat's nostalgia is an oblique affirmation of the very world that his experience has proven to be both crippling and unsustainable. Insofar as his evocation of that nostalgia is an appealing part of the texture of the story, Nat's dilemma is the reader's as well, who must reject the lost world of Memphis even as he or she responds to its allure.

Although we know much less about it, Lee Ann's change after the accident is also significant. After her talk with Caroline, a profile emerges of a woman pushed by the circumstances of her past toward self-knowledge. As she hid in the Old Forest after the accident, Lee Ann realized that "she had no choice but to go back to the real world" (81). The forest had been for her a momentary shelter from the crisis of self-knowledge that the accident threatened. Her return to the "real world" meant the acceptance of her grandmother and, as that implies, an acceptance of herself. Her friendship with Nat, who lived in a social and economic world that was unattainable for her, is one of the things that she had to abandon in her return. Nat's search for her had thus been an insistent attempt to reconfirm a destructive connection that she wished to abandon. As he sits in the car to wait for Caroline, Nat still does not understand that he is a potential obstruction to Lee Ann's process of healing.

While Caroline has been the catalyst for these crises, Nat has been largely unaware of the stress that she feels. He begins to realize her pain only as they drive away from Lee Ann's house, having resolved her disappearance and insured that there will be no damaging publicity. In this moment of success, Caroline reveals for the first time the vulnerability which drove her. Caroline asks Nat to drive "as far and as fast" out of town as he could, a revealing gesture of escape from Memphis. As she tells him what she has learned of Lee Ann's past, she "burst into weeping that began with a kind of wailing and grinding of teeth that one ordinarily associates more with a very old person in great physical pain, a wailing that became mixed almost immediately with a sort of hollow laughter in which there was no mirth" (83). Caroline's wail is prompted in part by her sympathy for Lee Ann, but it is also self-directed, a recognition of the fundamental emptiness of the social forms that she has preserved in finding Lee Ann. Caroline confessed "her own feelings of jealousy and resentment of the girl—of *that* girl and of all those other girls, too," whom she had confronted as friends of Lee Ann. Her resentment transcends romantic jealousy, and is rooted in her sense of imprisonment within the social forms that she has striven to preserve. Caroline is disturbed "not with what [Lee Ann] might be to you but with her freedom to jump out of your car, her freedom *from* you, her freedom to run off into the woods . . ." (85). What follows this declaration of resentment is an important exchange that anchors the story firmly in the context of social commentary, even as it details the psychological development of its central characters. " '*You* would like to be able to do that?' I interrupted. It seemed so unlike her role as I understood it. '*Any*body would, wouldn't they?' she said, not looking at me but at the endless stretch of concrete that lay straight ahead. '*Men* have always been able to do it,' she said" (85). Nat has presented Lee Ann and her friends as modern women who have taken control of their lives in ways that were impossible to previous generations. The conflict over Lee Ann's disappearance is not merely one between Nat and Lee Ann but between Lee Ann's generation of women and the male power structure. In her assertion of survival, Caroline has been forced ironically to reaffirm that power structure, and her conversation with Lee Ann has brought that home to her. Like Nat, she sees Lee Ann perhaps for more than she is, a figure of freedom whose existence outside the Memphis upper class is a reminder of her own confinement within it. She describes Lee Ann and her friends as women "who have made their break with the past." "How I do admire and envy them! And how little you understand them, Nat" (85–86). Caroline understands her difference from women like Lee Ann, and the achievement of that knowledge, however painful, confirms her strength and intelligence.

Caroline has recognized the way her choice has been restricted by her sex and social position, and she resorts to the language of power to explain her motivation. "Don't you see, it was a question of how very much I had to lose and how little power I had to save myself. Because I had not set *my* self free the way those other girls have. One makes that choice at a much earlier age than this, I'm afraid" (88). Like Lee Ann, Caroline has recognized that an acceptance of even a restrictive past is necessary and can be a progressive and affirming step. Throughout his fiction, Taylor suggests that the past cannot be ignored, and that the attempt to do so is ultimately destructive.

Caroline has come to recognize that "Power, or strength, is what everybody must have some of if he—if she—is to survive in any kind of world." In preserving her own power through preserving her engagement, she is also helping Lee Ann to gain a new power in her restoration to her family on more open terms. Caroline has come to see that power may arise from the very circumstances that have made for weakness. "I know now what the only kind of power I can ever have must be," she tells Nat. "You mean the power of a woman in a man's world," Nat replies (88). Restricted as this power is, Caroline's capacity to exercise it with a knowledge of its limits is her source of strength. And her explanation of it forces Nat to a deeper understanding that his strength must also come from an exercise of power in a world in which his own situation is limited. Thus he concludes with a recognition of the "support and understanding" that she gave him "when I made the great break in my life in my late thirties" (89). These are not dramatic victories of self-assertion or the overcoming of adverse events. They are closer to forms of accommodation with experience, assertions of self within tragically limited spheres of action. Taylor's fiction revolves on his analysis of the tragedy of human limits, both psychological and social. But Nat tells a story in which the response to experience, not the negation of experience, bears the emphasis. Even in his telling, he continues to respond.

Works Cited

Taylor, Peter. *The Old Forest and Other Stories*. Garden City, N.Y.: Dial Press, 1985.

Telling Irony: Peter Taylor's Later Stories

David H. Lynn

One of the principal marks of greatness in Peter Taylor's later stories is his deliberate wrestling with the irony that mediates our every attempt to make sense of our lives. As he addresses it, a tension arises between lived experience and the act of creating a story, giving shape and therefore meaning to that experience. Stories such as "In the Miro District" and "The Old Forest" and the novel *A Summons to Memphis*, all published in the 1970's and 80's, are marked by a rich narrative irony unlike anything Taylor has used before. This particular form of irony represents the narrator's uncertainty about the significance of the story he is telling—a tale whose final shape and meaning he seeks precisely through the act of translating experience, and memory, into language. The irony, in other words, mediates the relation between the teller and the tale; it creates the tension that holds teller and tale, language and meaning, in juxtaposition.

Taylor further employs this narrative irony to set the reader at a critical distance from the events and characters, a distance that approximates the narrator's own. Rather than being caught up in the chronological sweep and suspense of events as in a traditional narrative, we are reminded time and again of the gap between story and meaning, and our role is parallel to the narrator's. We come to share in the odd detective game: not to discover *what* happened—something we know largely (through not entirely) from the start—but *why* it happened and with what significance. By comparing "In the Miro District" with the earlier "Dean of Men," a story rich with ironies but of a fundamentally different kind, we will gain a better perspective on Taylor's achievement.

The beginning of "In the Miro District," with its quiet and wistful tone, suggests the narrator's yearning to make sense of events long past: "What I most often think about when I am lying awake in the night, or when I am taking a long automobile trip alone, is my two parents and my maternal grandfather." ("In the Miro District," *In the Miro District and Other Stories*, Knopf, 1977).

This turning and returning in the narrator's mind of distant memories, characters, and scenes is mirrored in the structure he generates for the tale; he shuffles the chronological order of events throughout. Indeed, for the

Reprinted from *Virginia Quarterly Review* 67 (Summer 1991): 510–20, by permission.

reader there is precious little mystery to the events of the denouement. On the story's second page we are given our first glimpse: "What actually happened was that. . . ." During a distant summer, we are told, when the narrator was struggling to pass the threshold of adolescence into manhood— and rebelling against the figure of authority, his grandfather, who seemed to balk him at every gesture—that grandfather, Major Manley, discovered his grandson's "girl" hiding naked in a wardrobe.

Such jumping the gun in and of itself is not unusual to Taylor's later fiction, of course. As we shall see, he uses similar strategies in the earlier "Dean of Men." By anticipating events, by giving away what we expect to learn only in due course, he focuses attention, as I have already noted, not on what happened but on *why*. The chronological course of events is violated; we learn bits and pieces out of turn. Taylor, in other words, creates an unusually potent disjunction between what we can call "history"—the chronological track of events, the order in which thing happened—and "discourse"—the method and order in which the narrator shapes the story and presents those events to his audience.

In such later works as "In the Miro District," however, this characteristic technique achieves a new richness and even justification. For the interplay between "history" and "discourse" also reflects the action of the narrator's own imagination as he repeatedly, all but obsessively, scours the same memories, seeking to discover the meaning of an experience long past. For the *why* has eluded him as well. He may reveal early on Major Manley's discovery of the "nice" girl stashed in the wardrobe, and that this sundered the old man from his grandson, the narrator, forever. But what's at stake in the narrative is the recognition that *what* happened will not suffice, that the challenge is to discover the significance of events and why, rather than how, one has led so disastrously to another.

Inevitably, when the disjunction between "history" and "discourse" is this profound, a potent tension arises between them, reflecting the narrator's own uncertainty. That tension, therefore, is a reflection of the narrative irony that, to define it once more, mediates the relation of the teller to the tale. The tension and the irony are products of the narrator's anguish or bafflement, his "complications of feeling." In an important sense, the tale becomes ultimately successful only if this narrative irony collapses at the end, if the distinction between history and discourse disappears, and if the narrator and reader together have accomplished, at least partially, at least briefly, their task of understanding.

II

To make clearer the distinction between the narrative irony of Taylor's later stories and some of the many other forms of irony in his earlier fiction, it is helpful to examine "Dean of Men," first published in *The Virginia Quarterly Review* in 1969 and chosen as the opening work of *The Collected Stories*.

The narrator, dean at a small college, is writing a letter to his son, a long-haired young man of the sixties. The actual impulse behind the letter is mean-spirited, though we may not recognize that at once. The dean wants to demonstrate the folly of his son's idealistic hopes for the future: "I must try to warn you that I don't think even your wonderful generation will succeed in going very far along the road you are on." ("Dean of Men," in *The Collected Stories of Peter Taylor*, Farrar, Straus and Giroux, 1969). For were the son and his generation to succeed, they would perforce escape from the past and capture a freedom of action and possibility. This thought the dean cannot bear because of his own past failures. And so, as a weapon against his son, he recounts a family tale, juxtaposing and anticipating events outside of a strictly historical pattern (Taylor again deliberately interweaving history and discourse), revealing not simply the profound bonds between generations but a pattern of behavior or, as the dean all but imagines it, a curse along the male line of his family.

The dean's grandfather, father, and he himself all once led lives of promise and early achievement in the public worlds of politics, business, or the academy. Yet each of these men, made vulnerable by (apparent) idealism and love (and we come to suspect, by a yearning for stasis and even martyrdom), has succumbed to manipulation and betrayal by male friends.

Grandfather, a politician of "beautiful oratory" rather than the daring and substance of his own forebears, is betrayed by younger political scoundrels and withdraws to the feminine bosom of his family, an embittered and quarrelsome old man. In reaction, the "guiding principle" of his son, the narrator's father, is "that he must at all costs avoid the terrible pitfall of politics." Yet as a successful businessman he too eventually falls prey to the wiles of a man, Lewis Barksdale, whose friendship he trusted. (Another version of this latter story is central to Taylor's novel *A Summons to Memphis*.)

And the narrator of "Dean of Men," himself shunning both politics and business, has withdrawn almost before the fact to the petty stage of a college campus where he repeats the disaster, egged on by the machinations of young colleagues, erstwhile friends. "With their bright, intelligent eyes, with their pipes and tweed jackets, and with a neatly trimmed mustache or two among them, they gave one a feeling that here were men one would gladly and proudly be associated with. . . ." Of course, driven by their own fears, timidity, regrets, these men betray him in the paltry politics of who on the faculty totem pole is to receive a particular house on the campus. For this apparent trifle the narrator resigns and begins a more profound and telling flight away from the human responsibilities of marriage and fatherhood. His deanship, at another college, becomes his impregnable bastion of self-deceit and self-righteousness.

By the end of the tale the narrator has revealed himself to be a distorted creature worthy of a Browning monologue, unwilling to be loved, supported, or consoled, insisting on acting out his trivial tragedy with an absurd willfulness. Yet, with serene blindness, he claims in this letter to his son that his has been a "happy, active life." Of course, he admits, "one sacrifices something." But the trade, the sacrifice has been worth it. Of this he is *certain*. And that certainty is crucial.

Not until the lull following his own betrayal by colleagues on the faculty have the pieces of the intergenerational puzzle first fallen together in the Dean's mind. His father's behavior, his grandfather's, his own, "suddenly now became very easy for me to understand." This sense of understanding is unshakable. It bears the heavy mark of fate and self-justification, and it seems to drive him toward the self-immolation of smug burlesque.

What emerges, as we discover that progression from sensitive writer and teacher to curmudgeonly self-righteous dean, then, is not a quicksilver narrative irony, representing a search for answers in the shaping of a story, as in "In the Miro District," but what we may recognize as a form of a more stable *dramatic* irony. Again, as in a Browning monologue, the attentive reader comes to perceive more than the narrator who is so sure of his story, who senses no detachment from the truth he intends to impart. In "Dean of Men" it is the reader's responsibility to judge the judge and to see him for what he is.

III

In an important sense, "In the Miro District" has *two* narrators: the boy, now grown, and his grandfather, Major Manley, who moves from telling stories of his escape from nightriders to becoming, not unlike the narrator of "Dean of Men," something of a caricature of himself, dressed in a black suit and string tie, reciting stories of valor from the War between the States.

Despite the crucial differences between them, these two narrators engage in very much the same task. They struggle to make sense of their experiences through the shaping power of story. For Major Manley this takes on a ritual quality. For decades he reveals his personal testimony to men sitting late at night in a hunting lodge and after strong drink. The act is far more than entertainment; Major Manley is something of an Ancient Mariner, forced by his own nature to repeat tales that both reveal and reinforce the way he makes sense of the world.

Years before—yet long after the war—Major Manley, a prominent lawyer, was kidnapped from his bed at gun-point. Witness to the torture and murder of his best friend, refugee in a primeval swamp where he wandered and hid for ten days, he glimpsed a potent vision of reality around which he has structured a code of living. "And I myself [says his grandson] heard him speak of those hallucinations . . . as though they were real events he had experienced and heard him say that his visions of the earthquake were like a glimpse into the eternal chaos we live in, a glimpse no man should be permitted, and that after that, all of his war experiences seemed small and insignificant matters. . . ."

The traditional codes of social behavior, how one behaves as a proper Southern gentleman, for example, assume a vital new quality for Major Manley: more than merely a matter of appearance and good manners, they provide a framework for keeping that "eternal chaos" hidden and in check, making civilized life possible.

The underlying question of all action for Major Manley—and we may say for Peter Taylor throughout his work—is what will suffice to hold the social world together. Alan Williamson, in *Shenandoah*, [30, No. 1 (1978), 71–84], has argued that Eros is the binding force in Taylor's stories, "In the Miro District" a particular case in point. Jane Barnes Casey, in *The Virginia Quarterly Review*, [54 (1978), 213–30], rather along the same lines we spy in Major Manley, suggests that what holds the world together in Taylor's stories is reason: characters become aware of threatening chaos within themselves and without, and of how necessary custom is to provide shape and shelter, arbitrary though custom may be.

But what quite literally holds the world together for Major Manley (a world already largely consigned to the past by others), is the act of telling his stories. They shape, they renew, they endure when all about him has been reduced to the quotidian norms of latter-day Nashville. The story of his experience with the nightriders, therefore, represents a personal history, a claim to identity. This sets him apart from the more conventional Civil War tales of other men his age, a conventionality his children—the parents of the narrator—most desire. His insistent cling to the story he chooses is a testament not to past valor so much as to his own continuing immersion in life.

As a boy, the narrator of "In the Miro District" believed that what separated him from his grandfather was a radical chasm between generations, of time and belief as much as of sensibility: "Perhaps I felt that day that it was my parents, somehow, who would forever be a wall between us, and that once any people turned away from what he was, as they had done, then that—whatever it was he was—was lost to them and to their children's children forever."

Of course, we grow increasingly aware of the many bonds and parallels between the man and boy, that they are engaged in much the same struggle to define themselves, that this is, in fact, a story about two comings of age: the boy from dependence into maturity even as his grandfather desperately resists the slide from mature defiant independence into the dependence of old age. Yet what may be the clearest mark that the two do indeed belong to different worlds is the nature of the stories they tell, one marked by a profound narrative irony—radical doubt about the story he tells—the other not.

Major Manley, like the dean of men, is *certain* of both his story and its meaning. He is certain even of the truth that hallucinations in the swamp have revealed about the nature of the world. In an important sense, the old man is an absolutely reliable narrator. Whether or not his tales present an objective historical truth that an audience can accept without reservation, no distance or self-consciousness—no narrative irony—separates him from his story, at least as far as we can tell. Its truth lies in his unwavering belief, and is the foundation to his character.

Small wonder, then, that one of the most significant ways in which the boy should seek to demarcate the boundaries between them is to throw the same stories back in the old man's face: "I had the sensation of retching or of actually vomiting, not the whiskey I had in my stomach but all the words about the nightriders I had ever had from him and had not known how to digest—words I had not ever wanted to hear. . . . I knew only that this was the beginning of my freedom from him." In order to create himself, his own story, he tugs free of his grandfather's tales that have weighed on him like parables of his own inadequacy.

The distance he stakes out brings with it a new self-consciousness. This maturity is not an end in itself, however. The narrator, for better or worse a creature of the modern world, isn't certain of the tale he tells. He must establish a distance from it, just as he has from his grandfather, in order to make sense. *Pulling back in order to understand is the tension at the heart of the narrative irony in this story.*

And of course the reader is engaged in a similar task: pulling back from the narrative in order to understand. We must disentangle history from discourse in hopes of resolving the narrative irony so that we may have some sense of what happened, of why, and of the haunting significance for the narrator.

Typically, the boy's "vomiting" up of the old man's tales results in a failure of understanding between them. He intends this as a desperate, almost uncontrollable mockery; his grandfather senses only a test of wills and, with a laugh, wins that test. "[W]hat his wicked smile and the light in his eyes spoke of was a victory he was reveling in at that present moment."

Hearing his grandson spew up the tales is a reminder to the old man of a larger victory; that by insisting on the primacy of the stories of the nightriders rather than of the Civil War, Major Manley has maintained his independence. But for the boy, chanting his grandfather's stories, even in mockery, is testament to his own inability to stand free of those stories as yet.

A second confrontation has much the same culmination: a victory for Major Manley. Again he arrives "unheralded and unannounced," and discovers that his grandson has brought two male friends and three girls home while his parents are away. Major Manley, moving from room to room, lands several ceremonial whacks of his cane to usher the guests on their way. But once the girls appear from their rooms, Major Manley assumes a different tone, one less condescending perhaps than that of the boys they have slept with. And the girls recognize this at once. They call goodbye to the old man rather than to the narrator, who concedes that: "when he spoke with such composure and assurance to those girls in my parents' living room, I felt that there was nothing in the world he didn't know and hadn't been through."

The third incident that same summer is more telling. As we have been forewarned, Major Manley discovers the narrator's girlfriend, a "nice" girl, stashed away in a wardrobe. Our anticipation doesn't mute the drama of the moment, but we, like the narrator as he gazes back on the scene, have achieved a certain critical detachment; we too are struggling to understand the significance of the action, to make sense of the old man's reaction.

The resonance of the scene surely is oedipal. For by this point we can acknowledge that Major Manley is more a father to the boy than is the pale, nameless creature of an intervening generation whose greatest trial is a prostate problem. If all boys feel it difficult to live up to the standard of their fathers, how much more so of a father with the courage, the glory, the stories of Biblical certainty and apocalyptic echo of a Major Manley. The challenge to the boy is suffocating; his individuality depends not on measuring up to this father—something he cannot do—but on toppling him. "But I knew that there was yet something I could do that would show him how different we were and that until I had made him grasp that, I would not begin to discover what, since I wasn't and couldn't be like him, I *was* like. Or if, merely as a result of being born when I was and where I was, at the very tail end of something, I was like nothing else at all, only incomparably without a character of my own."

The action is flagrant: taking a "forbidden" girl into the room Major Manley uses when he visits the city (and thoroughly despoiling the bed with food, books, and other detritus); hiding her naked in the wardrobe where Major Manley, disbelieving the boy's declaration of innocence, discovers her. Stunned, the old man leaves the house and gives up the fight, within hours appearing before his own children and their conventional friends at a summer oasis as that Colonel Sanders-like caricature. The boy has broken free; he has experienced love and freedom; he has won.

But victory, naturally enough, is problematic. Questions remain, and these will haunt the boy. Why did the symbolic "killing" of the grandfather extend so far into the real world? If by the struggle the boy established his own identity, why did it spell such ignominious defeat for the old man? Soon Major Manley, having abandoned the stories of the nightriders, costumed appropriately as he recites tales from the Civil War, will fail even to recognize his grandson sitting among other young people of a new, alien age.

The questions are never fully answered for the narrator or for the reader, who has come to share in the detective work. Certainly, those enduring questions are given shape and, therefore, meaning by the tale—and that is much. But the narrator's efforts can never be entirely fulfilled. The irony separating him from the tale, from his grandfather, from certainty, never completely collapses. Even the mystery of why this boyhood experience should remain so deeply troubling decades later is never fully answered. Just as Major Manley once felt compelled like an Ancient Mariner to repeat the tale of the nightriders, the narrator, when he is "lying awake in the night" or "taking a long automobile trip alone," returns to this story and seeks, through the telling, to become as reliable as the old man.

The Expenses of Silence in
A Summons to Memphis

CHRISTOPHER METRESS

At the end of Peter Taylor's first published short story, "The Party" (1937), Albert Winston stands at the front gate of his newly purchased country estate and wishes the last of his evening guests a safe ride back to the city. Albert and his wife Susan have recently left their city home of many years in order to resettle into the rural life of their youth. In the aftermath of the party, Albert fears that his wife bitterly regrets their decision. As she waits for him in the library, Albert "was sorry that he had invited [the guests] down. But he could not have stood her silence of the last month any longer. He had to know what she was thinking."[1] As Susan sits at the piano looking at her "short, clean, shapely and natural" nails that she knows "could never dig in the black earth," Albert asks her if life in the country will "be easier or harder after to-night?" (7), believing that "she would learn to love him and to read his books and to care for his farm" (7). Anticipating that "At last, his quiet wife was going to speak her mind," Albert repeats the question: "Will it be easier or harder, after to-night?" (8). But again he receives no answer:

> She must not have heard him for the wind was blowing that shutter against the house—
>
> Susan stood up. "Good-night," she said. "I'm glad I told little Tom to shut the baby chickens up to-night. I believe it's going to rain to-night."
>
> Albert climbed into bed ten minutes after Susan did, but she was already asleep. He listened to the frogs singing by the ponds, and [the] dog howling over at the Johnson's house and the eleven strokes of the courthouse clock upon the quiet air of the town (8).

Against our expectations, Albert's question remains unanswered. Instead, we hear only the singing of frogs, the howling of dogs, the ringing of distant clocks. These noises heard against the "quiet air of the town" serve to highlight in full the human silence which has come to dominate the Winstons' neo-agrarian existence.

This essay was written for this volume.

The ending of this story marks an important moment in Taylor's fiction. The silence that comes between Albert and Susan Winston, a silence informed by uncertainty and despair, is the first in a long line of similar moments in Taylor's oeuvre. Even the most cursory reading of Taylor's fiction reveals an impressive array of personal, familial, and social confrontations marked by the unarticulated or unarticulatable. At the end of "A Long Fourth" (1946), Harriet Wilson and her servant Mattie face "each other in uncommunicative silence for an indefinite time. Finally Harriet moved to the door again, but she looked back once more and she saw that besides the grief and hostility in Mattie's eyes there was an unspeakable loneliness for which she could offer no consolation."[2] In "A Wife of Nashville" (1949), Helen Ruth Lovell, because she is unable to tell her family "about the 'so much else' that had been missing from her life and that she had not been able to name," must embrace without articulation "her loneliness, the loneliness from which everybody, knowingly or unknowingly, suffered."[3] Like so many of Taylor's characters, Edmund Harper of "Guests" (1959) finds "a part of himself always reaching out and wanting to communicate with [others] and another part forever holding back, as though afraid of what *would* be communicated."[4] In "The Elect" (1968), Judge Larwell, awakening to "the silence, the unspeakable, intolerable silence of [his] private house" the morning after his gubernatorial victory, discovers that "Somehow, he felt he couldn't bear it, could never bear silence of that sort again."[5] The narrator of Taylor's late masterpiece "In the Miro District" (1977), recalling his childhood conversations with his grandfather, concludes that beneath their forced exchanges "We had nothing to say to each other—nothing we *could* say."[6] These and other similar moments give credence to James Curry Robison's recent claim that Taylor's fiction is concerned "with powerful expectations, with manners, with crucial things unsaid. Frequently in his scenes, the unspoken words are the most important ones."[7]

It is not surprising, then, that Taylor should offer his most sustained exploration of "crucial things unsaid" in his most extended fiction, *A Summons to Memphis* (1986). Despite the fact that Jonathan Yardley has called *A Summons to Memphis* "a work that manages to summarize and embody its author's entire career," critics are sharply divided as to exactly what it is that Taylor's novel summarizes and embodies.[8] David Robinson is right to assert that "Our judgment of [the narrator] ultimately rests on our sense of the degree of his self-comprehension," but, as Robinson himself notes, Taylor is "masterfully ambiguous" on this point.[9] John F. Desmond, however, makes a strong case in favor of Phillip Carver's self-comprehension, arguing that Taylor's protagonist "achieves a new, more compassionate understanding" of his world and of his father.[10] Another reviewer claims that "Through a final, wrenching irony, Phillip eventually comes to understand the wellsprings of his father's character, and he is able to achieve empathy and forgiveness."[11] For Paul Gray, however, Phillip's "only visible passion is his self-absorption."[12] Ann Hulbert concurs, claiming that "the happy ending that Taylor stages in the last frigidly lyrical paragraph of these notebooks in heavily ironic . . . This narrator is numbly suspended between the past and the future, between the power to will and the power to feel."[13] The competing interpretations of A Summons to Memphis are perhaps best explained by Robinson, who notes that "Taylor deftly balances the novel between a depiction of Phillip's gradual and positive coming to terms with the causes of the 'ruin' of his life and the exposure of the narrator as a weak and passionless phantom. . . . On the one hand, the novel is a positive portrayal of the cultivation of an understanding through memory, but on the other hand, it is an almost merciless exposure of a life of cowardly failure."[14]

Examining the demands for and consequences of silence in A Summons to Memphis will allow us to comprehend more fully the extent of Phillip's ambiguous self-comprehension and to evaluate more effectively the degree of "cultivation" or "cowardice" implicit in the final pages of his notebooks. Beneath what Douglass Paschall has called "a delusively calm and inviting surface," A Summons to Memphis is a dark tragedy of crucial things unsaid, a troubling drama of two generations sterilized by a history of self-imposed demands for silence.[15] Certainly, there are a few moments of genuine triumph and comprehension in Phillip's tragic narrative. These moments, it must be noted, exist because some character—or set of characters—is willing, if albeit briefly, to penetrate the challenging terrain of the unspoken, to speak the crucial things that have remained suppressed. For the most part, however, Phillip and his family are unable to move beyond the confines of their self-imposed silences because they are unwilling to violate the unspoken spaces they have spent so much of their lives maintaining. Ultimately, this commitment to preserving silence exacts a great price from the Carvers, especially Phillip. Having for so many years deferred confrontation by retreating into silence, Phillip, by his own admittance, finally can not engage in meaningful communication. Because he has led a life in which the most important tensions, the most crucial confrontations, were suppressed, he can no longer, when he chooses to communicate, speak of anything truly important.

The ultimate cost of Phillip's experience is clear: a life of silence, a life in which the most meaningful events and most passionate epiphanies are evaded, can lead only to "nonsense," meaningless and dispassionate communication. Phillip seems to understand this as he closes his notebooks for the final time, and this recognition may encourage us to see his narrative as a "positive portrayal of the cultivation of an understanding." But his passive and "serene" acceptance, his willing surrender to the "inconclusive nonsense" of his life, marks his narrative as "an almost merciless exposure of a life of cowardly failure." It is, moreover, because we know that Phillip can see the nonsensical life which lies before him that we can judge his final surrender as such a cowardly and effete response to the challenges of history, family, and memory.

Appropriately, Phillip Carver's narrative commences with a suggestive juxtaposition of the spoken and the unspoken. As he begins his tale of family intrigue, Phillip reflects upon the garrulous Memphis of the 1930s, where "one was always hearing of some old widower or other whose watchful, middle-aged children had set out to save him from an ill-considered second marriage."[16] But, as Phillip tells us, to his family so recently come to Memphis from Nashville, "this seemed a vulgar and utterly ridiculous situation. We were not accustomed to people's airing their personal problems so publicly" (4). Phillip's observation suggests that when personal problems are aired it is best that such airing go on in the security of the home. And yet the public silence that the Carvers insist upon seems to have penetrated their own household, creating private, self-imposed family silences: "There was nothing Deep South about our family—an important distinction in our minds. Father made no public denunciation of the man who betrayed him and who had made the move from Nashville to Memphis necessary. Instead, that man's name simply became a name that was not allowed to be spoken aloud in our new Memphis household" (4–5).

As Phillip begins to probe his family's history, we learn of the profound silences of his youth. He recalls how, as the family was preparing for its move from Nashville to Memphis, his mother told the children "that we must not, above all, allow Father to feel that we were grieving about leaving Nashville or brooding about the changes to come in our lives" (19). His mother's demand for suppression as they leave Nashville foreshadows the world of silence that awaits them in Memphis. Tellingly, Phillip remembers that soon after arriving in Memphis his mother "no longer quoted her mother to us. She no longer said the things she and we thought were expected of her" (24–25). His mother's decline in health soon follows this fall into quiescence. She becomes a victim of silences which, though self-imposed, are ultimately beyond self-remedy.

But she is not the first victim. Within six weeks of the Memphis arrival, Betsy loses her Nashville fiance Wyant Brawley. Soon after the move, the young man comes for visits and is met coldly on each occasion by the Carver patriarch: "Father could hardly be brought to speak to him," Phillip notes. "And he did not speak to Betsy for several days following each visit" (37). When Wyant returns several months later and challenges George's silence, he is told that George "had come to realize that Wyant could not be trusted" (38). Seeking out the reason for this mistrust, Wyant is turned away without an answer. The engagement is thus broken, the brief confrontation between Wyant and George giving way to "a calm that turned into a terrible silence on Father's part, one which was beyond our endurance" (38).

The destructive power of these terrible silences is not reserved for only one sister. Not long after Wyant Brawley is banished, Josephine's suitor suffers the same fate. At dinner one night after having consumed an extra highball with George Carver, young Clarkson Manning mentions in passing his mother's kinship to Lewis Shackleford. Phillip describes the reaction to Manning's fatal mistake: "[He] undoubtedly observed the changed look on our faces. His account stopped then and there. I thought the silence that followed would go on forever" (43). Within a few days, Phillip tells us, Josephine and Clarkson Manning end their romance.

Living in a house of such devastating silences, it is no wonder that much of Phillip's narrative is a remembrance of things unspoken. For Phillip, for instance, the striking characteristic of the curiously intimate relationship between his father and Phillip's own friend Alex Mercer is the fact that George Carver would reveal to this family outsider "episodes of his early life that he never bothered to tell his own children about—or at least not his sons" (75). Even the event that Phillip recalls as the "great love affair of my youth" is dominated by destructive and conspiratorial silences. While stationed at Fort Oglethorpe during the Second War World, Phillip falls in love with Clara Price. George Carver once again seeks to wield his fatherly power over his children. In an effort to end the romance between Clara and Phillip, George considers his options, but first he must ask Alex's opinion as to "whether or not he thought it would be dishonorable for him, as my father, to go to Chattanooga and talk with Clara Price's father about Clara and me without first telling *me* he was going to do so" (85). Despite Alex's objection, George goes to Chattanooga. Before this conversation with George Carver, however, Alex has been receiving long-distance telephone calls from Phillip, calls, Phillip remembers, "in the course of which I had declared I could see no reason to go on living if I did not have the love of Clara Price" (85). Having heard things from George and Phillip which the two have not heard from each other, Alex is in a sense trapped by the Carver family's habit of silence. He fails, however, to challenge that habit and expose the hidden passions and destructive conspiracies. Instead, he tells neither George nor Phillip what the other said. Alex's opting for silence effectively ends Phillip's first romance as love gives way to further repression: "I was in Europe for more than two years," Phillip tells us, "and never once had occasion to speak Clara Price's name or to hear it spoken. I returned to Memphis after the War and remained there for another two years without once hearing Clara's name mentioned" (101).

Decades later, however, as he considers answering his summons to Memphis, Phillip decides to break the established Carver pattern of silence. His sisters want to stop their now eighty-year-old father from remarrying, and their scheme demands that Phillip sees his father as "utterly pathetic and altogether vulnerable in his ignorance of how his two daughters at that very moment were preparing to proceed against him and were on the telephone with me, inviting me to conspire with them against him" (130).

Despite the fact that his father's history is one of silent conspiracy against his own children, Phillip feels that he has a "mission to perform" (132) in service to his father and his sisters. In order to perform this mission, Phillip must first acknowledge the devastating implications of his silent, unvoiced past:

> The fault I found with myself that night and next morning, in my present mature view of human nature, my fault was that I had at that tender age of thirteen, and always afterward in dealing with my father, repressed my feelings about my father's conduct. I had found no voice within me to protest. (But I knew I ought to have found the voice and having spoken out at the proper time ought by now to have forgotten all seeming injustice. Probably his own conflicts with *his* father he *had* protested and forgotten. That was the essence of maturity in a son.). . . . I ought as a young man to have asserted my feelings of resentment, to have protested what I thought was parental injustice, and then to have forgotten the whole business. But now, since I had not, it was the part of maturity to forget those old conflicts. (133–34)

Phillip's mission involves spreading his "doctrine of forgetting" (134). As he sits on the plane, he devises a plan of spoken confrontation that will correct the unspoken mistakes of the past: "I knew that after first protecting my Father from my sisters, I must then convert the two middle-aged women to my own views on forgetting wrongs done them by their parents. 'Forget, forget,' I kept insisting silently, as if further to convince myself before confronting Betsy and Josephine. I resolved that my sisters must be made to accept my doctrine of forgetting. It was too late to forgive, of course" (134). Finally, it seems, the powerful hold of silence upon the Carver family is about to be challenged.

When Phillip lands in Memphis, however, his evangelical resolve disappears. When his father greets him and begins to tell him of his marriage at high noon, Phillip admits that he himself "said nothing" (143). This lack of response sets the tone for Phillip's brief visit to Memphis. While his father chatters away about the wonderful coincidence of Phillip's arrival on the day of the wedding, Phillip sits in the back seat of Alex's Chevy recalling to himself his "recently articulated theme of forgetfulness" (145). The irony here, of course, is that Phillip's theme of forgetfulness has never truly been articulated. Phillip's call to "Forget, forget" was something that he insisted "silently" to himself. Now Phillip sits silently beside his father thinking of the "profound generalization and truth" of his doctrine of "forgetting the injustices and seeming injustices which one suffered from one's parents during childhood" (146).

Musing on the "certain oblivion . . . we must undergo in order to become adults," Phillip feels that he has reached a "wonderful kind of epiphany." Again, he intends to voice his discoveries: "I congratulated myself that now there could be no interference [with his father's marriage] and promised myself that immediately after the ceremony I would go to my sisters and make what I had done right with them" (146). But intention does not execution make. When George Carver learns that his bride-to-be has changed her mind, Phillip knows that his sisters' conspiracy against their father has succeeded. He, however, says nothing. When George tells Phillip, " 'I want to get home and see what else the girls have prepared for me' " (148), this is the only acknowledgement of the conspiracy that is afoot. Phillip seems to have forgotten his mission to break the family silence, for as the car pulls away from the church, silence has returned and Phillip notices his father "in some kind of dialogue with himself" (149).

When the two arrive at the Carver house and discover a moving van outside, George Carver realizes that his two daughters have decided, as they put it, to " 'come home to roost' " (152). He enters the house, greets his daughters, and then goes off toward his bedroom, and Phillip now stands alone with his two sisters. Instead of confronting them with his earlier epiphany, his "recently articulated" ruminations on forgetting, he remains silent yet again. Ironically, his very first flight from Memphis over thirty years ago was a secret flight *away* from the oppressive, unspoken conspiracies of his father. Now his current leave-taking can be seen as a flight back into silence, for the language of the following passage, which concludes the events surrounding his father's foiled remarriage, suggests that for all of his doctrines and promises Phillip still seeks shelter in a world of silence: "I couldn't bear to spend the one night in the house with them. *I couldn't bear to think of the unreal conversations that would take place there that night and in all the future.* Fortunately when I telephoned the airport to make reservations I was able to get a five o'clock plane back to La Guardia" (152–53, emphasis added).

But the Carver family saga remains unfinished. The compelling event which forces Phillip to "reopen" (154) his notebooks is the unlikely reunion of George Carver and the man who betrayed him, Lewis Shackleford. In the final four chapters of the novel, Phillip must engage in an even deeper confrontation with the family silences he has both accepted and perpetuated for most of his life. After more than thirty years without speaking, when George Carver and Lewis Shackleford begin "talking as if their old flow of conversation had never been interrupted" (191), the family's embraced heritage of silence is called seriously into question. With such an important part of the family's unspoken past now being voiced, Phillip must reposition himself in relation to his father. The relationship he establishes will, of course, depend on his ability, or inability, to react generously to his father's violation of the old demand for silence.

At the beginning of his postscript, Phillip speaks of his own surprise reunion with Holly Kaplan, his long-time lover. Just a few weeks before the summons to Memphis, Phillip and Holly had agreed to a trial separation.

But shortly after his return, Holly contacts Phillip. Reunited, they talk "of almost nothing but our two families and of the problems of looking after old people" (156). Since the separation, Holly's mother has died and Holly has been involved in her own personal struggle to understand her family past (which, like Phillip, she feels angered by and alienated from). In a way, Phillip and Holly are themselves overcoming an imposed silence which exists in their own relationship, for, as Phillip notes, the topic of family "had until now been taboo between the two of us for a number of years" (155). Instead of the silent world of Memphis, we are now given a picture of a kind of openness and communication.

At Holly's urging, Phillip begins revising his doctrine of forgetting. Accordingly, he achieves yet another epiphany. This time, however, he reaches his epiphany not through silent musings aboard an airplane but through voicing his unspoken past: "[Holly] began teaching me at this point to seek a still clearer understanding of my own father. She wished me to do more than forget the old wrongs. She wished me to try to see him in a light that would not require either forgetting or forgiving. She frequently urged me to talk about him, as she certainly had not urged me to do in years, and to try to give her a whole picture of what his life had actually been and to try to imagine how it must have always seemed to him" (159). Because Holly urges him to break his silence, Phillip can recover a more honest narrative about his father's past. Throughout the entire novel, we have watched Phillip complain about the catastrophic ramifications of his father's betrayal and his subsequent decision to uproot the family from Nashville. Now, nearly two-thirds of the way into his narrative, Phillip finally recounts in full this event. Talking now to Holly rather than musing silently to himself, Phillip slowly moves to a more empathic understanding of his father and the unspoken betrayal that forever altered the lives of both father and son: "Instead of forgetting, I soon discovered that I was now able to imagine more about Father's life than I had in the past ever had any conception of—not of his professional or his business affairs, though I felt I understood more of all that than I had previously realized, and not his family life even, but his inner life, his inmost, profoundest feelings about the world he was born into and in which he was destined to pass his youth and most of his adult years" (159).

Such reflections lead Phillip to see his father in a more admirable light and, finally, to reinterpret his father's friendship with Lewis Shackleford. Phillip's remembrance of that friendship is startling, for until now we have known only of the silence erected between the two men. Before the falling out, however, George Carver and Lewis Shackleford could be found "always talking, talking" (168). Rather than the silence he had discovered when remembering his own youth in Memphis, Phillip recalls the time when he stumbled upon the two friends sitting together in the men's locker room "talking, talking, talking" (168). For Phillip, this scene seems to epitomize the friendship: "While they talked on, I came up even closer to them since my own clothes were in a locker just behind the bench on which they were sitting. They went on talking, unaware of their own nakedness and of my standing there before them rather impatiently. That is how I often think of them when remembering the intimacy of their friendship" (168). Of course, this world of intimate exchange dissolves with Shackleford's betrayal of George Carver and George's demand that he "never hear any of [his children] mentioning Lewis Shackleford's name again" (179).

When Phillip joins his father and sisters on Owl Mountain the summer following the summons to Memphis, this edict of silence is finally broken by George Carver himself. Dining one afternoon at the Owl Mountain Inn, the four encounter two important figures from their family past: Clara Price and Lewis Shackleford. Phillip's response to his old lover and George Carver's response to his old friend are markedly different. When Phillip first spies Clara sitting in the restaurant with her husband and five children, the dilemma facing him is once again a choice between silence or articulation: "It was a question really of whether it would be more awkward to confess to my father and sisters who it was over there and to go over and be introduced all round or more awkward to say nothing and to keep my eyes averted throughout the dinner hour" (187–89). Despite the satisfaction he has achieved by breaking imposed silences in his dialogues with Holly, Phillip chooses to avoid confession and confrontation. When Betsy sees Clara and points her out to Phillip, his hopes for avoidance are shattered. Hearing Clara's name spoken, however, Phillip is struck by "a terrible thought" (188). That Betsy should recognize Clara Price, whom she has supposedly never met, leads him to conclude that his father was not the only one to visit Chattanooga during that summer of romance nearly thirty years ago. Whatever the two sisters did in Chattanooga, and whether or not their advances had as much to do with Clara's leaving Phillip as George Carver's visit did, Phillip reaches "an inescapable truth about the meddling interference of my old-maid sisters . . . and a new insight as to the lengths they had been willing to go to revenge themselves upon their father, to wound him most deeply, to divide him forever from his two sons" (188).

Before Phillip can confront his sisters with this inescapable truth buried beneath years of silence, Josephine proclaims "Clara Price is nothing" (189). Pointing across the restaurant, she says, " 'It's Mr. Lewis Shackleford!' . . . with precisely the horror of someone suddenly identifying a ghost" (189). When George Carver then rises from the table to embrace Lewis Shackleford, Phillip is almost moved to tears, until he glances at his sisters and remembers "the ugly significance the moment held for all three of us" (190). George turns to his family in order to reintroduce Lewis Shackleford, but his family, rather than rejoicing at the reunion, offers in return only a petty, childish silence: "We acknowledged his exclamation only with solemn nods of our heads and at last with the lowering of our eyes to the despoiled remnants of food on our dinner plates" (190).

While George and Lewis go off together, Phillip again achieves one of his now frequent, but always tenuous, epiphanies:

> All I cared about now was how I had been treated by my family in the long-ago affair of Clara Price. . . . I could think only that indirectly at least it was this Lewis Shackleford who had affected my life so that I would become a man who would find it so difficult to fall in love with a woman that it could happen only once in my life. I felt my narrowness and cowardice about love was all due, inadvertently or otherwise, to my father's treatment of me and Lewis's treatment of my father. I hated the skinny old man walking there beside Father. I felt the impulse to shake my two stout, behatted sisters off my arms and dash forward and push the two old fellows apart. What right had they to such satisfaction as this reunion apparently gave them? (192)

Of course, Phillip "said nothing to Betsy and Josephine about this impulse" (192). Instead, the three of them decide to leave without finishing their meal. When they see their father and Lewis on the front veranda, they choose to leave "silently" (192) by a side door. An hour later, while they are seated together on the front porch of their cottage, their father rejoins them. "We all four sat on the porch and talked for another hour before I got into my rented car to drive to the Knoxville airport," Phillip recalls. "But while we sat there none of us made any mention of the people we had seen in the dining room. It was as though the whole episode had been an unhappy dream, and it was indeed so much like the bad dreams one has that when I was alone in the rented car and later in my seat on the plane I could almost doubt its reality" (192).

The "unreality" of the dinner at Owl Mountain Inn is twofold. First, the great family silence that has covered the unspeakable betrayal by the man with the unspeakable name, no longer exists. With a warm embrace and affectionate talk, George Carver and Lewis Shackleford wipe away thirty years of imposed silence. This is the "unreality" that Phillip perceives. We, on the other hand, see a different unreality about the events at the Inn. While George and Lewis do indeed break down one barrier of silence during this episode, we witness Phillip and his sisters doing what the Carvers do best: they answer the challenges of life by erecting silences. First, Phillip refuses to speak to or of Clara Price. Second, Phillip withholds yet another epiphany from his sisters. Third, in response to their father's embrace of Lewis Shackleford, the Carver children offer only the disrespect of silence. And, finally, as they sit together "talking" on the front porch, not one of the Carvers, not even George, speaks of the episode in the dining room. Despite the fact that the most unspeakable name is now finally spoken, the Carvers choose once again to retreat into silence, revealing how deeply rooted is their desire to leave crucial things unsaid. George's warm response to Lewis might lead us to believe that the self-imposed silences in the novel will soon begin to dissolve, for, if the great family silence dissolves, should not the lesser silences follow? Holly and Phillip's happy reunion at the beginning of Phillip's postscript also tempts us to a similar faith. Unfortunately, the remainder of Phillip's narrative becomes a devastating record of either ruinous and irreversible silences, or, finally, communication that is only nonsense.

Six weeks after the dinner at Owl Mountain, Phillip receives a second summons to Memphis. This time Phillip's mission involves undermining yet another union: he is now called upon to stop his father from visiting Lewis Shackleford in Nashville. Since their reunion six weeks ago, George and Lewis have been holding "rambling exchanges over the telephone" that prove a "source of mounting irritation to both sisters" (193). Meanwhile, as his father speaks freely with the man whose name he would not utter for thirty years, back in Manhattan Phillip extends the silence he has chosen on Owl Mountain: "I had not told Holly Kaplan of the impulse I had had in the dining room of the Inn—that is, the impulse to use violence in separating the two old men" (194).

Having answered the second summons, as Phillip enters his father's house in Memphis he is greeted by the one thing which seems to have filled so much his life: "Inside, there was silence. Or at any rate in the front rooms during the first moments there was silence" (196). This presence is so strong that Phillip feels that "Somehow it was the silence that kept me from pushing on into the back part of the house where the bedrooms were" (196). With Alex by his side, Phillip has arrived just as his father is preparing to leave for Nashville. When George sees his son and questions his presence in Memphis, Phillip's silence becomes all the answer his father needs. What talk the Carvers do engage in is banal and commonplace: "We exchanged a few sentences about the weather then, the four of us did. It was beautiful, bright fall weather, we said, perfect for travel. It was beyond belief, I added. Father threw back his head and laughed at that reflection. Then he looked at me very seriously and said: 'It really is, you know' " (197). George Carver understands at this moment what so many of Peter Taylor's characters fail to understand—that is, that so much of what we say to each other is hollow and evasive, merely a means of maintaining a useful silence about something much more meaningful. The Carvers' history has become so enmeshed in unspoken conspiracies and betrayals that either silence or nonsense is inevitable. No one, it seems, can say anything of significance. The demand for silence has become so ritualized, so necessary, that what actually gets articulated is of little or no consequence. Shortly after George Carver's ironic remark, the telephone rings, and Betsy receives the news that Lewis Shackleford has died the previous night, and of course there is nothing meaningful to be said.

It is no wonder then that when Phillip arrives back in New York he feels "empty of thoughts and words" (204). As Holly waits for Phillip to speak, he "couldn't say anything." Finally he tells her about Lewis Shackleford's death, but he remarks to us, "I did not tell her that had I not arrived when I did, Father would certainly have got away, that he might at least have been able to attend Lewis's funeral." What Phillip does reveal to Holly leads her to console him. " 'I know what suffering it must have caused you,' " she says. " 'But you did what you could. It's the most any of us can do.' " Phillip sees this consolation for what it truly is when he concludes that "Now *she* was talking nonsense too." Holly's consolation brings Phillip's final epiphany, for the "nonsense" she speaks leads him to realize that "This is how it is to be from now on. And I found it did not displease me to think so" (205). "Nonsense" rather than intimate communication will be the condition of his life from here on out. The wages of silence, it now seems, must finally be paid in full.

The manner in which Phillip offers Holly his mother's gold clover-leaf pendant symbolizes how intimacy is all but gone from his world. The pendant, which Phillip received from his mother while he was still courting Clara Price, was given to his mother by someone she loved before she met George Carver. " 'I suppose I have always kept this little pendant out of sentiment for a good many years, though I have none about it now' " she tells Phillip. " 'I have always kept it hidden from your father . . . But I have no sentiment about it now. I am afraid I have no sentiment about anything any more. You will do me a favor and take it off my hands. Your friend is just the person I would have liked to give it to' " (97). Phillip never does give the pendant to Clara, but now, more than thirty years later, he offers it to Holly. He does so, however, "With equal sadness and almost without thought of what I was doing" (205). Holly takes the pendant, hinting that she has seen it before among Phillip's things. Phillip withholds the history of the pendant, telling her merely that " 'it's supposed to bring you good luck' " (205). He seems to be offering her the pendant for the same reason that his mother offered it to him so long ago—because he, like his mother, has no sentiment about anything anymore. In place of sentiment, emotional attachment to objects or people, there now exists only nonsense and the absence of shared meanings: "Presently Holly slipped the pendant into the pocket of her dress and took up her drink. And we sat there in the twilight and sipped our drinks while we talked our own combined nonsense together, each his or her own brand of inconclusive nonsense about the reconciliation of fathers and children, talked on and on until total darkness fell . . ." (206). Phillip and Holly's doctrines of forgiving and forgetting, in which they have placed so much emotional investment, fade into "inconclusive nonsense."

In the twilight of this "combined nonsense" with Holly, Phillip is still allowed some final moments of genuine communication, moments that in the end only highlight even more the quiet surrender that will mark the remainder of his life: "Our conclusions and resolutions were all nonsense, of course," Phillip tells us. "But one sensible thing I did manage. Two days after I returned to New York I telephoned Father" (206). At first, father and son can communicate only "vapid exchanges" (206), but soon they begin to discuss the formative events of the family past. For the first time in the entire novel, Phillip and his father share the unspoken, break the silences: "finally we got into talk about those distant times when I trailed after him and Lewis Shackleford when they were fox hunting in the Radnor Hills or swimming at Franklin. It gave me special satisfaction to use Lewis Shackleford's name casually in conversation with Father" (206). "We talked about Mother," Phillip continues, "and her sense of humor and history. From that time on I called him every week. . . . On the long-distance telephone we were able to speak of things we had never been able to talk about face to face" (207).

When his father dies the following spring, Phillip's foray into the unspoken past ends, and the "special satisfaction" of breaking silences is markedly juxtaposed to the "combined nonsense" of Phillip's life in New York. Phillip and Holly have inherited enough money to move out of their cramped apartment, but the two stay put, agreeing "that it hardly seemed worth all the trouble, hardly worth all the upheaval of our paper and books" (208). During his telephone conversations with his father, Phillip shared a history that was for a brief moment sensible and satisfying. But now both Phillip and Holly have turned away from the past and given themselves over to a cultivated disengagement: "As for Holly and me, I don't know what the end is to be of two people like us. We have our serenity of course and we have put Memphis and Cleveland out of our lives. Those places mean nothing to us nowadays" (208). Phillip and Holly may have secured their "serenity," but they have lost the energy for even the sort of engagement displayed at the beginning of the postscript when they made a serious attempt to confront something of importance by talking of the two families. Now, however, they indulge in nothing but nonsense, which, we must remember, does not "displease" Phillip.

He ends his narrative with a "fantasy" of the future:

I have a fantasy that when we get too old to continue in the magazine and book trade the two of us, white-haired and with trembly hands, will go on puttering amongst our papers and books until when the sun shines in the next morning there will be simply no trace of us. We shall not be dead, I fantasize. For who can imagine he will ever die? But we won't for a long time have been "alive enough to have the strength to die." Our serenity will merely have been translated into a serenity in another realm of being. How else, I ask myself, can one think of the end of two such serenely free spirits as Holly Kaplan and I? (208–09)

That Phillip believes he and Holly will simply disappear, leaving "no trace," is stunningly appropriate. In a novel so inundated with silences, so full of unspoken spaces which seek to erase conflict and tension, we should have foreseen such inevitable self-erasure. The Carver's long history of imposed silences has proven finally too enervating. Lacking the energy and will to speak of the very things that could help him make sense of the world, Phillip can do nothing but embrace the nonsense of his twilight years and wait for total darkness to fall.[17]

Of his intent in *A Summons to Memphis*, Taylor has remarked, "how successful are we ever in understanding what has happened to us? That's what I want to suggest in the novel."[18] Phillip Carver has certainly gained insight into his family past, understanding what has happened to his family and why. This cannot be denied. But his insight is both limited and brief. Early in the novel, during one of the phone calls constituting Phillip's first summons to Memphis, Betsy warns her brother, "These silences are expensive, Phillip" (12). As we finish Taylor's novel, the resonant irony of these words is not lost upon us. The Carver history of silence has been indeed expensive. It has not only cost Phillip, for all but a few months, a genuine and honest relationship with his father, but it has also cost him his future. With little but silence behind him, an intentionally evasive condition he helped to create and to perpetuate, Phillip is unable to imagine for himself a future of meaningful engagement with the world. Phillip's life has been one long retreat into silence, and now, even after having witnessed the final wages of that silence—a fractured and sterile family at war with itself—he is sadly without the means and the desire to reverse this retreat. Phillip Carver may want us to believe that he is a man "serenely free." But we know better. If Phillip is "serene," then it is a cowardly serenity attained only by refusing to be displeased by the inconclusive and self-erasing nonsense that will mark the remainder of his life. All of us, I imagine, could be as "serenely free" as Phillip Carver. All we need do is disengage ourselves from our pasts and our families and our memories, and retreat into the nonsense that we, through our evasions and silences, have made of our lives. Few of us, however, would be as willing as Phillip Carver is to pay so great a cost for such serenity, for such freedom.

Notes

1. Peter Taylor, "The Party," *River* 1 (March 1937): 7; hereafter cited in the text.
2. Peter Taylor, "A Long Fourth," in *The Old Forest and Other Stories* (Garden City, NY: The Dial Press, 1985), 235–36.
3. Peter Taylor, "A Wife of Nashville," in *The Collected Stories of Peter Taylor* (New York: Farrar, Straus and Giroux, 1969), 280.
4. Peter Taylor, "Guests," in *The Collected Stories of Peter Taylor*, 410.
5. Peter Taylor, "The Elect," in *The Collected Stories of Peter Taylor*, 393.

6. Peter Taylor, "In the Miro District," in *In the Miro District and Other Stories* (New York: Carroll and Graf, 1983), 172.

7. James Curry Robison, *Peter Taylor: A Study of the Short Fiction* (Boston: Twyane, 1988), 12.

8. Jonathan Yardley, "Peter Taylor's Novel of Fathers and Sons," *Book World— Washington Post*, 14 September 1986, 3.

9. David Robinson, "A Summons from the Past," *Southern Review* 23 (Summer 1987): 758.

10. John F. Desmond, Review of *A Summons to Memphis*, *World Literature Today* 62 (Spring 1988): 282.

11. Anonymous, Review of *A Summons to Memphis, Publisher's Weekly*, 1 August 1986, 68.

12. Paul Gray, "Civil War in the Upper South," *Time*, 29 September 1986, 71.

13. Ann Hulbert, "Back to the Future," *New Republic*, 24 November 1986, 38.

14. Robinson, "A Summons from the Past," 754.

15. Douglas Paschall, "Tennessee: And the Trembles There," *American Book Review* 11 (March–April 1989): 1.

16. Peter Taylor, *A Summons to Memphis* (New York: Knopf, 1986), 4; hereafter cited in the text.

17. The alienation created by this history of silence is further highlighted by Phillip's allusion to Hardy's "Neutral Tones," a poem which emphasizes the failure of communication and, perhaps more important to Taylor's purposes, the devastating bitterness beneath apparent serenity.

18. Hubert H. McAlexander, "A Composite Conversation with Peter Taylor," in *Conversations with Peter Taylor* (Jackson: University Press of Mississippi, 1987), 127.

Digression and Meaning:
A Reading of "In the Miro District"

RON BALTHAZOR

Peter Taylor has said, "If you have the right instinct, you will find the thing you want to write."[1] Taylor has the right instinct. His masterful stories demand as much as they offer, inviting the reader to enter the text, expecting the reader to look closely. "In the Miro District" is one of the richest and most demanding of Taylor's texts, raising difficult questions of structure and meaning. A story of memory, it is structured like memory: a series of digressions and reflections. Taylor is a good storyteller; his digressions are carefully placed. We read the turnings of a mind, encountering the complexity of a great mind at play, as we follow the narrative. And yet for the reader, meaning may remain elusive, elusive as a memory. Reminiscences as story mean something, or should. Yet reminiscence implies loss. Taylor's story, a graceful rambling memory, tells of great loss and the need for stories to fill the loss.

The opening lines of "In the Miro District" create an atmosphere of solitary reflection: "What I most often think about when I am lying awake in the night, or when I am taking a long automobile trip alone, is my two parents and my maternal grandfather."[2] For this unnamed narrator, moments of solitude introduce a memory, a memory which is this story. The stillness of the night "when . . . lying awake" and the ramblings of a journey, "a long automobile trip alone," present the movement of this memory. In a way, these lines present a metaphor for the presentation of memory itself, a kind of rambling journey which ever circles back to a still point, even if it is only the place where memory begins and ends. The still point, the center of Taylor's story, is the storyteller, the unnamed first-person narrator.[3] Or, to be precise, the still point of "In the Miro District" is the story he tells, the words on the page. Moreover, teller and tale present a fitful memory, never fully there, never completely gone. The telling of this story is memory-like, circling about that which remains hidden, telling and retelling, focusing here or there, fitful, like a dream.

This memory-like story, like many of Taylor's stories, wrestles with family relationships. Although the narrator thinks "most often" about his

This essay was written specially for this volume.

parents, he presents them, at best, obliquely. He never names them. He sees them primarily as unseeing; at least, he does not know what they see. In his eyes, they know nothing of their father or their son: "Because I realize that living their busy, genteel, contented life together in the 1920s they didn't have the slightest concept of what that old man my grandfather was like. Or of what that boy, their son, was like either. (Of what the one's past life had been or of what the other's would be like in the future.) They weren't people to speculate about what other people and other times were 'like.' They knew only that what they did was what everybody else still did about grandfathers and grandsons" (149). In the memory of the "I," the narrator, these parents know only "what everybody else still did about grandfathers and grandsons." They seem an empty and unseeing repetition of those "like" them. Nameless and faceless, they are in between grandfather and grandson, a kind of empty center. They are a nearly blank background upon which our narrator must write himself.

Yet these parents, conspicuously absent throughout the story and conspicuously blind to the effect they have on father and son (at least in the eyes of the narrator), the narrator names as the motivation of the conflict: "They had put a grandfather and a grandson in so false a position with each other that the boy and the old man would one day have to have it out between them" (150). What could be "so false" about the relationship of a grandfather and grandson? These parents, the narrator suggests, have erased free will and left their son to a brutal fate. What memory chooses to forget cannot be told; what it chooses to blame is the subject of storytelling. The narrator, recalling his emotions, begins to collect the events of the story: "It [the as yet unnamed crisis of the story] left me with complications of feeling that nothing else had ever done. For my grandfather, of course, whose story this is meant to be—more than mine—it did something considerably worse than leave him with complications of feeling" (150). This "it" is the first of many anticipations ("beggars" if you will) that structure the narrative. Like a flicker of memory, this hint of emotion and event begins the unravelling of the narrator's story.

The insight of the narrator, his memory, draws the reader into the conflicts of a boy, and possibly an age, seeking to discover identity. The story tells the memory of the narrator, a kind of creation of the past, and also reflects his identity, the still point from which the story is told. The place of seeking is the Miro District. The narrator describes the site of his story: "The world I am speaking of isn't the hard-bitten, monkey trial world of East Tennessee that everybody knows about, but a gentler world in Middle Tennessee and more particularly the little region around Nashville which was known fifty years ago as the Nashville Basin and which in still earlier times, to the first settlers—our ancestors—was known somewhat romantically perhaps, and ironically, and incorrectly even, as the Miro District" (151). This digression denotes more than geography. Here, apparently, the narrator rehearses the quality of all naming, of all memory: romantic, ironic, even incorrect. "World" suggests not only a location but a way of seeing. Simply put, the Miro District is the world of this memory. The narrator confesses, albeit obliquely, the significance of the Miro District: "it has something or other to do with this story" (152). Even in memories, digressions cannot come at the beginning or end but must be somewhere in the middle, like parents between grandfathers and grandsons, like the present between the past and the future. The Miro District is in Middle Tennessee; it is not the larger world "that everybody knows about." Whether he is romantic, ironic or incorrect, the narrator knows that this is the world of his "ancestors," the world mirrored in his memory. As the narrator rambles, the words create a world, a way of seeing and a place from which to see his grandfather and himself: "He used often to say to me, all irony about grandeur aside, that knowing such odd pieces of history about the place where one lived made the life one lived there seem less boring. He didn't couch it quite that way . . . But there is no doubt that's what he meant" (152). Whatever the grandfather meant, "boring" is the narrator's word and describes his present, a present so mundane that he fills it with ghosts. His digression on "the Miro District" repeats the emptiness of all things in between (another still point) and leads to another rambling memory, his memory of his grandfather, Major Basil Manley.

The relationship of the narrator and his grandfather finds contrast with the romantic relationships of other grandfathers and grandsons in Nashville, or rather with the narrator's adoption of his parent's perception of such. Their perception, he reports, was myopic; "they saw everything in terms of Acklen Park . . . in the first quarter of the twentieth century" (155). Again they knew neither future nor past and expected their father and their son to participate in the homogeneous world of suburban Nashville: "When you saw one of those other grandfathers out walking with a little grandson along West End Avenue, it was apparent at once that the two of them were made of the same clay or at least that their mutual aim in life was to make it appear to the world that they were" (155). Whether real or feigned, the homogeneity of genteel Nashville in the 1920s, the narrator rejects: "It was as though we [grandfather and grandson] faced each other across the distasteful present, across a queer, quaint world that neither of us felt himself a part of" (154). In resistance to this "queer, quaint world," the grandfather, though a major in the Confederate Army, refuses to submit to the illusion of the genteel Southern gentleman, the Civil War veteran who happily rehearses the glory of the fallen Confederacy. Such is a false history, a lie of myopic memory. In a sense, the grandfather prevents the grandson from adopting a romantic version of the past by refusing to masquerade as a relic of that past. The mothers and fathers of Acklen Park, too busy to be parents to their children or children to their parents, dressed their old men up to act like grandfathers until they reached "extreme old age [when] either they became absurd martinets, ordering the younger men and boys in their families about in their quavery old voices" or they became "thoroughly domesticated as any old woman," distorted images of their own children (156). The imposition of a romantic past upon the grandfathers generates absurd parody. Grandfather Manley refuses: "He did not turn into an old woman and he did not try to play the martinet" (157).

The narrator clearly sees how his grandfather is different from the other grandfathers of Nashville. The boy's identity is less sure. He begins to define himself (how is he different from the other Nashville grandsons?) by remembering his relationship with his grandfather. The memory of the narrator gently circles back to hint at the crisis, the break in their relationship. But then he digresses: "It will be useful at this point to explain that before that day when I hid my girl in the wardrobe, there actually had been two other serious and quite similar face-offs between my grandfather and me, and useful that I give some account of those earlier confrontations" (158). The first of these episodes is an almost archetypal first drinking binge of the narrator: he gathers with friends at his house, his parents conveniently absent (at the hospital for his father's prostate operation), and the boys get drunk. Grandfather Manley's appearance, "unheralded and unannounced," quickly sobers the boys. The narrator's memory of the moment generates metaphor: "I faced him across the gold pocket watch that he was now holding out in his open palm like a piece of incriminating evidence" (160). The illusion of continuity between grandfather and grandson (did not all good Southern men have this first binge, especially in private, among men), is dispelled by the truth of time, the "incriminating evidence." The old man comes from a different age. Still the moment is more complex, for Grandfather Manley rejects the "time," that is, the present generation of Nashville grandsons ("It's a fine sort of company you are keeping nowadays here in Nashville" [161]). But he will not reject, will not even scold his grandson.

The whiskey and the awkward nature of their relationship generates an absurd conversation, if it can be so called, a conversation that begins with silence. The boy expects but does not receive chastisement from the grandfather; the narrator reflects on that which is not said: "It was just as it had always been before. We had nothing to say to each other—nothing we *could* say. And thinking about all the times we had been left together like this when I was a little boy, it seemed to me that I had always been somewhat drunk whenever he and I had had to talk, and had always been unable to make any sense at all" (163). To cover the silence ("We had nothing to say to each other"), the boy mocks the grandfather and babbles away: " 'Tell me what it was like,' I suddenly began now in a too loud voice. 'Tell me what it was like to be kidnapped by those nightriders . . . out in Lake County' " (163). This is the story the grandson has always heard. Despite the insistence of the parents and the encouragement of the grandson, the old man has refused to recount the stories of the War. In their stead, he retells the "nightrider trouble." Here the boy "giv[es] it all back." He recalls, "I had the sensation of retching or of actually vomiting, not the whiskey I had in my stomach but all the words about the nightriders I had ever had from him and had not known how to digest—words I had not ever wanted to hear" (166). The grandson holds the mirror to him. In his drunken babble, in what seems an empty parody of the grandfather, the narrator sees what the grandfather will not reveal: "Only now and then a vague thought or an image took shape for me—of him as the young soldier on horseback or of the War itself that he would not reveal to us, that he always substituted talk about the nightriders for" (166). The moment explores the nature of storytelling. To cover the powerful silence of the grandfather (the grandson desires chastisement; he wants to be told what to do, who to be), the boy adopts the story of his grandfather. He has no stories of his own; he has, at best, a tenuous identity. Yet in the boy's drunken parody, he comes to epiphany. As the boy babbles, he understands, vaguely, mysteriously, something of his grandfather. The parody becomes a kind of ritual: the retelling of stories that mysteriously hold meaning.

The boy's bourbon and bravado eventually wear off, though, and he submits to the silence and "sardonic laughter" of the grandfather: "Finally I was silenced by his silence" (169). For a moment, the boy enters into the silence of his grandfather, sees him, and knows: "And to him, I somehow understood in a flash of insight, it [the account of the nightrider trouble] meant above all else what was perhaps dearest to his soul of all things during those years. It meant how many times he had successfully avoided reminiscing about the War" (169). The grandson sees how central to his grandfather's identity this story is. As the episode concludes, the narrator notes the grandfather's understanding of the boy as well: "And at the end, when he dismissed me from his room, it occurred to me that seeing an eighteen-year-old boy drunk was nothing new to a man of his experience in the rough sort of world he came along in and that my pilfering my father's whiskey while he was in the hospital seemed to him almost a natural and inevitable mistake for a boy my age to have made" (170).

As the first episode circles in toward the Grandfather's silence about the War, so the second episode circles out from this same center. As preface, the narrator tells of Major Manley's rejection of Decoration Day (for Decoration Day is the day of the second episode). The occasion offers this insight into the silence: "For more than a dozen years now he had insisted that it would not be possible for him to pass in through the Fairground gates on any Decoration Day without being sure to come out with the rank of colonel. He could not countenance that. And he could not countenance that gathering of men each year to repeat and enlarge upon reminiscences of something that he was beginning to doubt had ever had any reality" (171). The rejection of Decoration Day represents the old man's rejection of the romantic glorification of the Civil War. The making of foot soldiers into colonels promotes a distorted history. No memory is involved; indeed, Major Manley "could not countenance that." The reminiscences of the veterans have lost their point of reference, the "something" Manley "was beginning to doubt had ever had any reality." They are more the product of Acklen Park residents, of the children of Civil War veterans, than of the veterans themselves. In the space left by the rejection of this illusion of tradition, Manley tells the story of Reelfoot Lake and his hallucinations. Similarly, the narrator, following his own remarks on Decoration Day, digresses again "to say a few things about those hallucinations he had" (173).

The narrator retells the hallucinations of his grandfather as a memory of his own early childhood when he, only three or four years old, had gone to Reelfoot Lake on a hunting trip with his father and grandfather: "During those hours on the screened porch I would think about the tales I had heard the men tell the night before when they were gathered around the iron stove and when I was going off to sleep on my cot in a far corner of the room" (174). "Reelfoot" plays on the metaphoric significance of the place: close to "real foot," a true foundation, a kind of definitive standing place which leaves a mark or track (is this not history?).[4] "Reel" might suggest rotating, spinning and the thread which is spun, or dancing. The narrator's story spins or dances around a truth which is never fully told; we never read the real. The authority of memory and history, the realness of it, seems remarkably tenuous, as thin as a thread; this story is a dreamy recollection of a three-year-old boy. Yet the narrator retells without hesitation or doubt the story of his grandfather's hallucinations, "hallucinations about the hooded men mounted on strange animals charging toward him like the horsemen of the apocalypse" (174). Similarly, in what seems an infinite regression, the narrator tells of his grandfather's telling of "the accounts he had heard or read of the earthquake that made the lake" (175).

> Among the hallucinations that my grandfather had while wandering in the low ground after his escape was that that earthquake of a hundred years before—almost to the day of the month—had recurred or commenced again, or that he was living in that earlier time when the whole earth seemed to be convulsed and its surface appeared as it must have in primordial times. And he imagined that he was there on that frontier in company with the ragged little bands of Frenchmen and Spaniards and newly arrived American settlers, all of whose settlements had vanished into the earth, all of them in flight, like so many Adams and Eves, before the wrath of their Maker. (176)

The regress of story here pushes back to the first storytelling and the first need for story. The creation myth and the Fall tell the first separation, the separation of God and man, the first loss, the first lie, the first history, and the first flight from place. The very nature of language seems tied to loss. The hubris of man's desire to be autonomous, the quest for self-naming (the illusion of autonomous self-creation), generates the need for telling stories. The denial of that which has gone before creates a vacuum that history endlessly seeks to fill. Taylor spirals in toward this first story to represent a similar loss. Grandfather Manley has tried to live in hallucinations that seem real, in a kind of history of his own (his-story). He seeks to pass it on (for history must be passed on) to his grandson. Yet Manley's story as well is subject to the pride of self-naming. He wishes to maintain his honor and identity, to somehow maintain the moral order of his age, and to see himself in his grandson.

It may seem a paradox to suggest that the center of identity for Major Basil Manley is hallucination. Yet in contrast with the false reminiscences of Civil War veterans, the narrator tells, in yet another digression, of how he heard his grandfather "speak of them [the hallucinations] as though they were real events he had experienced and heard him say that his visions of the earthquake were like a glimpse into the eternal chaos we live in" (176). The syntax here is telling, for the "eternal chaos" is, present tense, that which "we live in." The hallucinations seem real for they speak of how things "really" are. This story, as an escape from a banal present, pushes back to the first judgement, the Fall ("like so many Adams and Eves . . ."), and pushes forward to the final judgment of apocalypse. The chaotic and indeterminate desire judgment, the blessing and curse of being named. His truth is in hallucination. Or rather, his truth, his way of making the world meaningful, is in the ritual telling of these hallucinations. [5]

With the rather long digressions on Decoration Day and Basil Manley's hallucinations completed, the narrator begins to tell the second of the three "face-offs" with his grandfather. But he begins with still another digression. This digression loosely conjoins his story and identity with sexuality: "With one's real girl, in those days, a girl who attended Ward Belmont school and who was enrolled in Miss Amy Lowe's dancing classes, one might neck in the back seat of a car. The girl might often respond too warmly and want to throw caution to the wind. But it was one's own manliness that made one overcome one's impulse to possess her and, most of all, overcome her impulse to let herself be possessed before taking the marriage vow" (178). At stake for Basil Manley, and for his progeny, is "manliness." Taylor's play on the name is all too apparent. [6] Here the narrator expresses his sense of traditional Southern sexuality: to overstate only slightly, women are whores or mothers (virgins until they are mothers) and men are responsible for the maintenance of the sexual order. [7] Like the narrator's "first drunk," the boy's frolic with girls of the "other sort" in his parent's house does not separate grandfather and grandson. Rather the grandfather's knowing way with the girls creates a moment of complicity between the two. Still in the moment, the boy desires separation: "I knew that one day there was something he would have to know about me that he couldn't forgive" (181). Here the narrator employs a foreboding, almost Biblical rhetoric to foreshadow the impending break, a break that points not to his own autonomy, but to the actions of his nameless, faceless parents: "Perhaps I felt that day that it was my parents, somehow, who would forever be a wall between us, and that once any people turned away from what he was, as they had done, then that—what ever it was he was—was lost to them and to their children and their children's children forever" (181). Every step the boy makes toward self-naming, every attempt at independence, is somehow frustrated by his parents.

As a kind of preface to the final episode of the story, the unnamed narrator wrestles with his identity: "But I knew there was yet something I could do that would show him how different we were and that until I had made him grasp that, I would not begin to discover what, since I wasn't and couldn't be like him, I *was* like. Or if, merely as a result of being born when I was and where I was, at the very tail end of something, I was like nothing else at all, only incomparably without a character of my own" (182). The first person narration seems at once personal and distant, for although he has revealed much of himself, as this passage demonstrates, he remains "incomparably without a character of [his] own." At least the storyteller is a careful discloser. The "something I could do" hints of premeditation and of desire, but "as a result of being born when I was and where I was" denies free will and draws close to fatalism. The problem of self-presencing ("I was . . . incomparably without a character of my own"), the "I" sees as both indeterminate and determined. His character or his lack thereof appears both a product of "the very tail end of something" and a self-generated discovery. Like memory, like his own memory, the "I" is both discovering and discovered, both fixed and moving, very much present and absent. The absence of identity creates the need for narrative, the need for telling; the telling flickers with meaning.

The identity of the narrator is defined by how he is different from his grandfather. He remains, at best, a reflection of the old man, at worst, without his own identity, as blank as his parents. Now the focus shifts to the grandson and his rite of passage, the passage of an age as well as an individual. Here the narrator breaks the essential thread of traditional Southern "manliness," the protection of female virginity until marriage (that is, of the "good girl"). The heralded and much delayed love affair, every boy's realization of "true love," is interrupted by the grandfather. His entrance resonates with the myth of the Fall: "Already I had heard Grandfather Manley calling my name out in the front hall. It was something I think he had never done before when arriving at the house" (187).[8] In a story of persistent digression, this long delayed event marks a turn in the structure of the narrative. Grandfather, for the first time, announces himself. And Taylor subtly notes the separation which the grandson experiences, not as a moment of self-naming, but as a moment of loss: "When I closed the big bureau drawer I looked at myself in the wide mirror above it, and I was almost unrecognizable even to myself" (187–88).[9]

The break from the traditional Southern sexual order completes for the grandfather the passing of an age. It is that which he cannot endure; it is that which the old South cannot endure. The grandfather's judgment is complete, though silent: "Anyway, he turned on me a look so cold and fierce and so articulate that I imagined I could hear the words his look expressed: 'So this is how bad you really are?' " (191). The narrator tries to fill the silence with imagined words, words that trivialize the moment, words that explain it. The boy needs more. The old man's stories never had an explanation, not one that he would tell. The expression of the grandfather's silence, "his look," fills the space no words can fill; the judgment, the loss, the final separation can only be expressed in a kind of absence, a kind of death of the grandfather and a loss of the grandfather's identity.[10]

Like the grandfather's story, the narrator's story has no explanation. The naked girl in the closet holds no hidden truth: "eros" is not the answer.[11] Rather she is a carefully placed prop, as significant as the blanket that covers her. She too is never named and passes in the narrator's memory as just a motivation for this story: "Since this is not the story of our romance, it will suffice to say that though our romance did not endure for long after that time, these events were not necessarily the cause for its failure" (184). And he becomes for her (as he imagines) as anonymous as she is in this story: just "a boy I went with in Nashville."

The denouement of "In the Miro District" is, metaphorically, a funeral. Major Manley dresses in black, abandons his stubborn and eccentric ways, comes to live with his children, becomes the Civil War veteran they had always hoped for, and is promoted to the rank of colonel. The narrator reminds the reader of the falseness of this show: "In those days in Nashville, having a Confederate veteran around the place was comparable to having a peacock on the lawn or, if not that, at least comparable to having one's children in the right schools" (194). Indeed, our narrator went to the University of the South at Sewanee. In the mild tone of the closing paragraphs, the narrator states the greatest loss of the story, the loss of his grandfather: "He seemed quite as strange and interesting an old character to me as he did to them [the narrator's college friends]. . . . and at those times I would have the uneasy feeling that he wasn't quite certain whether it was I or one of the others who was his grandson, whether I was not perhaps merely one of the boys visiting, with the others, from Sewanee" (197). The story told is of the loss of a grandfather; here the storyteller has an "uneasy feeling."

Just what the narrator knows or does not know of himself and his relationship with his grandfather at the end of "In the Miro District" is unclear, at least elusive. Clearly, it is elusive to him. The crisis of the story, the great break between grandfather and grandson, produces a loss of identity.[12] The last pages of the story present grandfather and grandson as indistinguishable from other grandfathers, the storytelling Civil War veterans, and other grandsons, boys who go to the "right schools." The last line remains puzzling and disturbing, for the narrator sees himself as faceless; he was, in the eyes of his grandfather, "perhaps merely one of the boys visiting, with the others, from Sewanee." The still point of the story, the center from which the story is told, disappears, leaving only the story, the words on the page. The "meaning" of the narrator's story seems to him now rather empty: "And what I understood for certain . . . was that it had, after all, been their battle all along, his and theirs [his parents], not his and mine. I, after all, had only been the pawn of that gentle-seeming couple who were his daughter and son-in-law and who were my parents" (192–93). In a sense, the "I" loses his story; at least he misses the meaning.

The complexity of Taylor's "In the Miro District" denies a conclusive or comprehensive reading. The characters seem to lose all distinctiveness; the storyteller seems to lose his story. Like a dream that sticks in your mind, these digressions (are they not really all digressions?), these scraps of stories, like Grandfather Manley's hallucinations, are simply an attempt to make sense of the chaos of self-identity, identity that has no center, no author, no god. These stories that tell stories of a center make a life of their own, taking in the play of tropes, refiguring the first stories. Like Manley's hallucinations, the stories within "In the Miro District" become that which is most real. The reading then, like the writing, becomes a matter of "the right instinct."

Notes

1. From an interview with James Curry Robison, *Peter Taylor: A Study of the Short Fiction* (Boston: Twayne Publishers, 1988), 137.

2. Peter Taylor, "In the Miro District," *In the Miro District and Other Stories* (New York: Knopf, 1977), 149; hereafter cited in the text.

3. In some ways, the narrator of this story is like the digressive and reflective first-person narrator of Taylor's "The Old Forest." But the narrator here never has a palpable identity; unlike Nat Ramsey, he is never named.

4. Reelfoot Lake, of course, is a real place.

5. David H. Lynn correctly notes the purpose of Manley's stories and makes an apt analogy: "Major Manley is something of an Ancient Mariner, forced by his own nature to repeat tales that both reveal and reinforce the way he makes sense of the world" ("Telling Irony: Peter Taylor's Later Stories," *The Virginia Quarterly Review* 67 [1991]: 515).

6. The play on the name marks Taylor's own ability to see the metaphor, the fictive, in the real. His great-grandfather's name was Basil Manley Taylor; see *Conversations with Peter Taylor*, ed. Hubert H. McAlexander (Jackson: University Press of Mississippi, 1987), 88. Of course, as the old man is the boy's maternal grandfather, "Manley" is a name our narrator never receives.

7. The Southern sexual order is inextricably tied to Christianity. In a sense, as the story moves toward the climax, Taylor subtly conjoins the loss of the old moral order with a loss of faith. The death of "manliness" is the death of God, the loss of a controlling center. Again, this loss generates the need for narrative.

8.   "And they heard the sound of the Lord God walking in the garden in the cool of the day, and the man and his wife hid themselves from the presence of the Lord God among the trees of the garden. But the Lord God called to the man and said to him, 'Where are you?' " Genesis 3:8–9

9.   Lynn writes of this episode: "The boy has broken free; he has experienced love and freedom; he has won" ("Telling Irony," 520). The critic does concede that this victory is "problematic." I would argue that it is no victory at all. Love and freedom for the boy are fleeting if not empty. He recognizes that the victory is not his, but his parents'. In this episode, he only loses. Lynn's discussion, although often insightful, fails to note the relationship of loss and story.

10.   Jane Barnes Casey writes that "this is not entirely a story of defeat." She argues that "if one world has clearly passed away, another has come in its place" ("A View of Peter Taylor's Stories," *The Virginia Quarterly Review* 54 [1978]: 226). The poignancy of the ending, the power of the loss of the grandfather, denies the sense of "renewal" that Casey suggests. The character of the grandson remains rather vacuous, a shadow of the character about which he speaks; he emerges only as narrator and distant from his own story.

11.   Alan Williamson writes, " 'In the Miro District' might be seen as Mr. Taylor's own unresolved debate between a traditionalist point of view, in which the battle lies between institutions and chaos, and a late-civilized one, in which imposed rules and divisions are rendered superfluous by the free community of love" ("Identity and the Wider Eros: A Reading of Peter Taylor's Stories," *Shenandoah* 30 [1978]: 72).

12.   Simone Vauthier reaches a similar conclusion about the end of Taylor's "First Heat" ("Trying to Ride the Tiger, A Reading of 'First Heat,' " *Journal of the Short Story in English* 9 [1987]: 73–90).

Facing Outward, Yet Twirling Inward: Mannerist Devices in "Venus, Cupid, Folly and Time"

SIMONE VAUTHIER

By indirections find directions out.
Hamlet, II, i, 63

Whether as a chronicler of Southern—or rather Tennesseean—mores and their changes, or as an explorer of family relationships, Peter Taylor is generally praised for his "truth to life." In an essay which represents a trend in Taylor criticism and is significantly entitled "Life Studies," Stephen Goodwin writes that "the best of Taylor's stories . . . exposes us to life as only the greatest novels do. If questions of art occur to us as we read (they don't always; our first concern is that we are learning something of life) we are usually tempted to defer them."[1] I always wonder about such statements, even when properly qualified with various modalizers as here. Though to "learn something of life" should be our basic concern, can we really "defer" questions of art? "Venus, Cupid, Folly and Time" is a narrative to which access is from the outset mediated through art. Of course, it is sometimes regarded as atypical: Albert J. Griffith, for example, while concluding that it is "a worthy contribution to the modern Southern literature of the grotesque," goes as far as to claim that it is "a little bit untrue to Peter Taylor's own unique vision."[2] But then why is it so often selected as one of the author's best stories? To look closely at "Venus, Cupid, Folly and Time" throws light not simply on a wonderfully complex story but on the flexibility of Peter Taylor's craft and on his "unique vision." To some extent, I must admit, my method goes counter to much of Taylor criticism, which, following the example fondly reported in various memoirs of Taylor the teacher of creative writing, tries to reimagine the stories rather than to analyze them, because "to try to understand them critically [is] to depart from the source."[3] I feel that Peter Taylor's stories should more often be examined critically. Nor do I consider that such an approach gets us away from the "source," although I do not, naturally, pretend that it can account for the mystery of

This essay was written specifically for this volume.

creation. Pedantic as my dissection of "Venus, Cupid, Folly and Time" may be, its dryness should not mask, I hope, my enjoyment of, and reverence for, the flesh of the text.

"Venus, Cupid, Folly and Time" confronts us with a Janus-like title: looking forward it names the narrative to come but simultaneously, looking backward to the writer/reader's "encyclopedia,"[4] it designates a famous painting which itself is one more version/translation of mythological motifs. The pictorial reference immediately orients the reading pact towards some sort of parallelism or interweaving between the fictional representation and the painterly one. But at the same time, the Bronzino painting is not merely conjured up but incorporated by the narrative which having appropriated its title also transforms the picture into a fictional object. The Dorsets, whose house is the setting for the action, make the Bronzino an important and subversive element of their decor, even though in an ironically degraded reproduction: "On the landing of the stairway . . . was the only picture that one was likely to learn the title of at the time. It was simply tacked on the wall, and it had obviously been torn—rather carelessly, perhaps hurriedly— from a book or magazine. The title and the name of the painter were printed in the white margin underneath."[5] Thus the reader is caught in a tourniquet: s/he must read the story through what s/he knows of the painting, which is never described, but s/he must also see the painting as a textual object with its fictional uses. I will, however, concentrate on the first of these two phases, at the risk of some distortion. And to tell the truth, because the author proceeds by omission and indirection, the presence of the painting in the text is largely a remanence of the title and of our memories of the work. My contention, nevertheless, is that if we follow the signpost of the title, we are invited to set the narrative not so much within an out-referential framework but within an artistic one. Needless to say, I do not mean that the story has no connections with the world out there: the author has said, "I suppose I could probably mention somebody as the original of every character in that story,"[6] but that was as an afterthought to the interesting statement that he had "worked out" the theme of it as you would a theorem. Granted that there are other avenues of investigation which could be as promising, [7] an approach through the painting yet seems to me to be particularly enlightening and it is, if not justified, at least comforted by the biographical fact that Peter Taylor wanted to be a painter. "My only serious early training was as a painter," he says in the interview with Stephen Goodwin.[8] I propose therefore to read "Venus, Cupid, Folly and Time," certainly not as a transposition of Bronzino's painting, but as a palimpsestic bringing together, for the reader's benefit, of two heterogeneous spaces. Obviously, however, such reading is rendered difficult, perhaps perilous, by the fundamental incommensurability between the verbal and the painterly codes. "The relation of language to painting is an infinite relation. Not that speech is imperfect and showing a deficit which it tries to make up when faced with the visible.

They are irreducible one to the other."[9] To compound the difficulty, the mannerist style, which the Bronzino exemplifies, is itself hard to define because it is a style in which "each painting, statue, façade, each poem and play is a special case, a personal manipulation of design, material, situation, language, response."[10] I will look at the narrative through a projection of mannerism which is admittedly debatable, and I can only plead that the ambiguity at the root of my essay is related both to the methodological problems of using similar codes to interpret literature and art and to the particular flexibility of Mannerism. Although the paradigm on which my reading relies is that pointed to by the story's title, Italian Mannerism of the late Renaissance—rather than, say, Dutch Mannerism—I think that we can legitimately step across centuries and continents, because Mannerism, like Baroque, being a need of, and search for, deviation from the "classical norm," is a recurring trend in the history of art and letters.[11] I should perhaps add that I align myself with those recent art critics who employ the word neutrally without any of the pejorative connotations it has often acquired.

THE TITLE(S)

In one respect, however, the two spaces, pictorial and verbal, overlap, as it were, since the pictorial space is introduced by words, according to tradition, and the short story's title seems to coincide with the painting's. But wait . . . First, this is the title in English of an Italian work which is called in French "l'Allégorie de l'Amour." Indeed, the Bronzino is also subtitled in English "An Allegory"; therefore, seen as a quotation, the phrase is incomplete even though it suffices to designate the work. But the subtitle, if we happen to remember it, alerts us from the start to the possibility of an allegorical reading. Consequently, the title functions both as reference and as allusion, paradoxically delimiting then laying open a relation between the pictorial and the verbal. Apart from that, the sequence "Venus, Cupid, Folly and Time" posits a cast of actors, two mythological *stricto sensu* (in the strict sense), two more abstract. Though it names them, it fails to indicate the relationships between the figures, relying on the viewer/readers' encyclopedia for their placing. In both cases, though perhaps less naturally in that of the picture, the sequence creates expectations of a narrative which will somehow link the four characters. "Venus, Cupid, Folly and Time" might have set up a similar expectation, but the appearance of Time, that indispensable requirement for narrative to exist, of course, increases the odds that something has happened or is about to, and announces a different thematics. Critics, however, have disagreed about the action of Time in the painting: is his powerful arm unveiling the pains of love while the inner frame depicts its pleasures, or is he drawing a veil over the scene? According to some art historians, "Forgetfulness and time, contrary to the gesture which has hitherto been attributed to them, do not reveal the scene, with its murmurings and hints, but instead cover it up again, thereby completely reversing the sense of the composition."[12] Likewise in the story, though the part of Time and its impact is clearer, as we shall see, what actually happens remains somewhat mysterious.

Even without the help of the subtitle, of course, we are ready to read analogically; for, if we do not anticipate that Greek Gods and Goddesses will put in direct appearance in a Peter Taylor story, we do expect that the reference to the four pictorial figures will have some bearing on the fictional characters. By the end of the short story, we know that the subject matter of the narrative—love and incest, the pleasures and pains of Eros, the passing of time—is related to the subject of the painting. At the same time, we have been made aware of an element of parody in the story's title, for instead of Bronzino's handsome pair, the pearly-fleshed Venus, the dashing Cupid, we have the grotesque couple of an elderly brother and sister—while Folly and Time play a more conspicuous, albeit not more important, role in the narrative. The elegant eroticism for which the painting is famous has been translated into the muted tragicomedy of the "wider Eros"[13] so that retrospectively, one word in the title sequence becomes foregrounded in its now usual sense of foolishness, without using its polysemy, thus introducing associations of lewdness and of madness.[14]

Moreover, I submit that the two works share what Walter Pater would call the "spirit" of the "handling."[15] In spite of the tremendous gap in time between them, analogies may be observed between the mannerism which Bronzino's painting brilliantly embodies and some features of the narrative. In other words, overarching the two heterogeneous spaces, there is, I contend, a "mannerist aesthetics," which I summarily define as an art of deviance, of tensions and disjunctions, extremity and ambiguity, conspicuous quotation (art refers to earlier art) and uncertain address.[16]

THE NARRATED UNIVERSE: THE DRAMATIC ARTIFICE

THE DORSETS' MISE EN SCÈNE   The sole members left in Chatham of a rich and distinguished family, the Dorsets, have become impoverished and have taken the extreme measure, in violation of the zoning laws of their wealthy neighborhood, of having the third story of their mansion "torn away," and "the south wing pulled down," sealing the scars with "a speckled stucco that looked raw and naked" and leaving the house "curiously mutilated" (294). As a result, the house itself has mannerist overtones. ("Mannerism," Wylie Sypher writes, "is experiment with many techniques of disproportion and disturbed balance.")[17] Though considered "a foolish pair of old people," the Dorsets have, according to the I-narrator, become "social arbiters of a kind in our city" (295). The first ambiguity is that their age, financial circumstances, and foolishness would seem to make them outsiders, while their role is precisely to define who is inside or outside the elite group of Chatham citizens: their annual dancing party is a must for young people of the upper class for it is a stamp of social status, a "way of letting people know from the outset who you were" (296). Nothing very exceptional? Yes, but at these parties "peculiar things went on, unsettling things," so that they fill the children with "dread" (299). The *unheimlich* (uncanny) atmosphere is never dissipated and will remain a source of wonder to the I-narrator.

Significantly, the Dorsets stage their party as a performance in which life and art intersect. First they turn their house into an ambiguous stage setting; there is a pervasive "awful fragrance," "like a mixture of spicy incense and sweet attar of roses," connoting at once religion and oriental sensuality; and there is "the profusion of paper flowers" which Louisa Dorset makes and sells to the children's parents, after the event. "The flowers were every-where—on every cabinet and console, every inlaid table and carved chest, on every high, marble mantlepiece, on the bookshelves. . . ." While their "overpowering masses" have a sort of mannerist excess and energy, their colors stress that they are artifacts: "they were fuschia, they were chartreuse, they were coral, aquamarine, brown, they were even black" (298). This is art triumphing over mere life which it does not so much imitate as improve upon—only one word in the list is semantically linked to a flower (fuschia)— not to mention the association, frequent in mannerist pictures, of a purplish with a yellowish green color. One element of the decor, however, is more than any other reminiscent of an effect often sought after by the mannerist painters: "Everywhere in the Dorsets' house too were certain *curious illumina-tions* and *lighting effects*. The source of the light was usually *hidden* and its purpose was *never obvious* at once. The lighting was a subtler element than either the perfume or the paper flowers and ultimately it was more discon-certing. A shaft of *lavender light* would catch a young visitor's eye and lead it, *seemingly without purpose*, in among the flowers. Then *just beyond the point where the strength of the light would begin to diminish*, the eye would discover *something*" (298, emphasis added). What with the hidden source, the apparent purposelessness of the ray of light, and the discovery deferred until the very moment when the light begins to fade, the result is that the Dorsets use lighting effects in a mannerist way. The disconcerting light is a snare in which the viewer is caught, just as "the mannerist painting sets at play imaginary capture."[18] What is the visitor trapped into looking at? "In a small aperture in the mass of flowers, or sometimes in a larger grotto-like opening there would be a piece of sculpture. . . . Or just above the flowers would be hung a picture, usually a black and white print but sometimes a reproduction in color" (298–99). Thus artifice is used to enhance artifacts. Three of the works of art thus hidden/displayed are mentioned: a plaster replica of Rodin's "The Kiss," "an antique plaque of Leda and the Swan," and, of course, the print of Bronzino's "Venus, Cupid, Folly and Time." Erotic pieces all, they play upon what Mauries calls "the rhetoric of bodies."[19] Only "The Kiss" presents a "natural" relation, while the Bronzino and the Leda are doubly linked by the hint of "unnatural" relations and by the mythological heightening created by ascribing such relations to Gods and Goddesses.

The eroticism of art is, in fact, an integral part of the experience in which the Dorsets want to immerse their young guests: "moments would come when she or he would reach out and touch the other's elbow and indicate, with a nod or just the trace of a smile, some guest whose glance had strayed among the flowers" (299). In the process of initiation through art, the paper flowers are a metonymic trap for the innocent. "About those works of art most of us had been warned by older boys and girls; and we stood in painful dread of that moment when Miss Dorset or her brother might catch us staring at any one of their pictures or sculptures" (299).

It would seem that the Dorsets envisage the whole party as a rite of initiation in which they play the role of initiators and not simply, as even "sensible parents" believe, that of social arbiters. But the initiation fails, in a sense, partly because the party fails for the children: the Dorsets are obsessively indulging in a rite the ultimate purpose of which is to celebrate their love. The young people are reduced to passive observers, just as the party "was more of a grand tour of the house than a real party," a tour during which they are entertained by "a continuous dialogue" between their hosts. The Dorsets rehearse their own story: they tell how much they "had given up for each other's sake," how their "wicked in-laws" (i.e. relatives)[20] "had tried to separate them" and "marry them off to just anyone"; they speak of their past splendor and of their knowing "from [their] upbringing what things to give up" (305). Important as speech and theatrics are in the ceremony, they do not make it more understandable to the audience since rhetoric and gesture emphasize the double level of the actors' utterances: "Both of them spoke in a fine declamatory style, but they frequently interrupted themselves with a sad little laugh which expressed something quite different from what they were saying and which seemed to serve them as an aside not meant for our ears" (306). The hearers are sensitive to the dissociation between an overt, public and a latent, private discourse but cannot interpret this second level of discourse. In another phase of the ritual, the guests are "taken down to the ballroom—purportedly for dancing." But "it was only Miss Louisa and Mr. Alfred who danced." Far from being ridiculous as expected, "they danced with such grace and there was such perfect harmony in all their movements that the guests stood about in stunned silence, as if hypnotized" (307). Then the tour and the dialogue are resumed, although with a change of tone. Reminiscences are accompanied with exhortations: "and then, exhorting us to be happy and gay before the world came crowding in on us with its ugly demands, the Dorsets would recall the happiness they had known when they were young. This was their pièce de résistance." They remind each other of "his or her naughty behavior in some old-fashioned parlor-game, or of certain silly flirtations" (308). Normally the ceremony culminates when, barring the door to the dining room where lemonade and English biscuits are awaiting the young guests, the Dorsets issue one more series of injunctions in a stichomythic dialogue whose theatrical and ritualistic quality is enhanced by a narrational shift to the present tense: " 'Tonight you must be gay and carefree,' Mr. Dorset enjoins.

'Because in this house we are all friends,' Miss Dorset says. 'We are all young, we all love one another.'

'And love can make us all young forever,' her brother says.

'Remember!'

'Remember this evening always, sweet young people!'

'Remember.'

'Remember what our life is like here' " (308). The call-and-response ends on Miss Dorset's remark: "This is what it is like to be young forever" (309). Then Alfred can make his invitation, however clichéd, to some sort of final and pagan communion: "Now, my young friends," he says, "let us eat, drink and be merry!" In short, the Dorsets have transformed a collective rite of initiation into a rite of celebration of their own love—a displacement or distortion which is in keeping with the mannerist spirit.

Further tension is created by their self-absorbed blindness. They believe that they provide an example to be remembered, that they have a message to transmit, indeed a double message: the snobbish message that money cannot take the place of "living with your own kind" or of "being well-born" (306, 307); the larger message that love can overcome time ("we are all young") and create a community of love ("we all love one another") (306). To the reader, though, belief and rite are but delusions of the characters. The Dorsets may unexpectedly dance with grace but after the dance they are grotesquely dishevelled, Alfred with "the strand of gray hair which normally covered his bald spot on top" now hanging "like a fringe about his ear," Louisa even more disarrayed so that her statement, "This is what it is like to be young forever!" is pathetically ludicrous (307). Similarly all their behavior toward the young guests denies the community of love which they extol. The extreme contrast per se is reminiscent of mannerism. Likewise, their inversion of the rite of initiation strikes a mannerist note. For while a coming out party is a mild form of initiation into a social group, here the young people, who are not even introduced to one another, are in fact subjected to a sort of counterinitiation, inasmuch as the junction with the loved one which the Dorsets celebrate means disjunction from society. (Significantly, they do not allow grown-ups into their house; they do not socialize except on two occasions when Louisa goes selling her paper flowers and Alfred his figs.) Were they to follow the Dorsets' lesson, the young people would remain outside society, whereas initiation is meant to bring about a new societal integration. Nevertheless, by another contradiction, may we not say that some form of dark initiation is achieved since the experience is unforgettable and untellable, although endlessly talked about by the participants? The evening, says the narrator, "cast a shadow over the whole of our childhood" (299). It is, as it were, an incomplete initiation into an unknown world of sensuality and mystery, of a world of whirling and conflicting signs which they cannot decipher.

THE MERIWETHER CHILDREN'S MASQUERADE   The ritual of the party which has gone on for years is destroyed when Ned and Emily Meriwether, "because they dreaded" the event, decide "to play a trick on everyone concerned" and to smuggle in an uninvited guest from beyond the pale, the neighborhood's paper boy (300). They have Tom Bascomb play the part of Ned, while the latter slips in unobserved. The Dorsets who never make any effort to "distinguish which of their guests was which" and who pride themselves on being able to tell "one of us," are taken in by Tom but come to suspect Ned of being an interloper because he behaves differently (309). The double impersonation is the first level of the masquerade.

The prank, moreover, requires the plotters to be active participants in the ritual: according to plan, Tom kisses Emily when the Dorsets' back is turned, raising giggles and laughter among the other children, but Ned is "not quite able to join in the fun" and increasingly isolates himself from the rest. There comes a point when seeing "Tom and Emily half hidden in a bower of paper flowers and caught directly in a ray of mauve light," he can no longer accept the consequences of the trick, which leads to one more mimicry: "the two had squeezed themselves into a little niche there and stood squarely in front of the Rodin statuary." A tableau vivant, as it were, has taken the place of the statue, with Tom "kissing [Emily] lightly first on the lobe of one ear and then on the tip of her nose" and Emily standing "as rigid and pale as the plaster sculpture behind her and with just the faintest smile on her lips" (313). Again life imitates art, and Emily is transformed into the "reified body" of mannerism. As Mauries observes, "This reified body is often affected by the small commentary which an art object obliquely makes about it: a statuette discretely placed in a corner or handled by a connoisseur, either a work of Classical Antiquity or a copy."[21] Although here the body imitates the object of art, this supplementary twist does not detract from the general effect: "The figurine," Mauries goes on, "generally adds to the irony of the situation; it offers a supplementary case to the thousands of variations of life and death at work in the mannerist painting."[22]

While the spectacle adds to the dismay of Ned, it contributes to the delight of the Dorsets, whose voyeuristic expectations are thereby fulfilled. Unlike their young guests, who "dread" the moment when the hosts might catch them "staring at any one of their pictures or sculptures," the Dorsets openly enjoy their voyeur's role: Ned "found Miss Louisa and Mr. Alfred gazing quite openly at Tom and Emily and frankly grinning at the spectacle" (299, 313–14). Apparently, the approval of the Dorsets is the last straw for Ned. " 'Don't you *know*?' he wailed, as if in great physical pain. 'Can't you *tell*? Can't you see who they *are*? They're *brother* and *sister*!' " (314) In this comedy of errors, his accusation manages to be both true and false: it is true on the level of appearances—the spectacle given to the deceived Dorsets who are being rebuked for allowing it; it is false on the level of reality—the kissing couple's relationship is not that of siblings. At any rate, by one more inversion, because of Ned and Emily's prank, the pseudoinitiation designed by the Dorsets becomes more clearly an initiation: whereas the Dorsets proceeded by indirections, Emily and Tom publicly enact, in their adolescent way, the eroticism they are intended to observe in the works of art, offering in a sense a parody of it. Moreover, Ned and Emily certainly become aware of themselves as sexual beings, the boy negatively, through his feeling of jealousy, the girl positively: in the words of Williamson, "for one person, it would seem, the Dorsets' contrivances have succeeded, as a genuine myth of the half-narcissistic, unfocused beauty of the moment of sexual awakening."[23] Originally the prank was conceived of by children but Ned does not watch the execution of the plan as a mere child, thus spoiling things, while, with all the turmoil of the chase around her, Emily withdraws into a new world: she remains standing in the niche, looking "very solemn and pale still . . . but her mind didn't seem to be on any of the present excitement" (316). There would be much more to say on the episode but I simply want to draw attention to the dramatic artifice of the scene, which is the prelude to both farce and pathos.

For Ned's outcry is mistaken by the other guests to be "the cream of the jest" and gives rise to guffaws and a "cacophony" of "shrieks and trills." For several moments, the Dorsets continue "wearing their grins like masks," yet Miss Louisa soon turns "all the queer colors of her paper flowers" (note that the comparison again draws attention to life imitating art); then "every bit of color went out of her face. She took a step backward. . . . Her brother didn't look at her, but his own grin had vanished just as hers did, and his face, all drawn and wrinkled, momentarily turned a dull copperish green" (314–15). Only exterior signs—described largely in terms of color—are given. White with anger, Mr. Dorset accuses Ned of being an intruder "among these nice children" and wants to know who he is. Ned then claims his assumed identity: "I am Tom Bascomb, your paper boy," and flees up the stairs with Mr. Dorset soon in pursuit (315). There follows a series of frenzied chases until the Meriwether parents, called up by Tom, arrive on the scene; the comedy of errors goes on for a while, for the Dorsets cannot believe they would make "a mistake of that kind. People are different" (319). Finally they are convinced—and shattered. Alfred disappears into one of the rooms upstairs and his sister leaves her guests to join him "with the slow, steady gait of a somnambulist." Meanwhile the Meriwethers alert the other parents, who since it was "the first time in many years that any adult had set foot inside the Dorset house," make the most of the opportunity and linger "much longer than was necessary" (320). By more reversal, the Dorsets' attempt to expel the lower-class intruder results in their privacy being violated by the cream of their society and, ultimately, their being dislodged from their position as social arbiters. Though the old couple live on for nearly ten years, they "gave up selling their figs and paper flowers and of course they never entertained young people again" (321); in the end they are almost recluses: the demonic has become the *pharmakos* (both remedy and poison) and been sacrificed.

But the story of that last party continues to be told in Chatham and is now being related to an extradiegetic narratee by a middle-aged male I-narrator, who belonged to the elite invited to the Dorsets' entertainments but was too old for the most famous one of all.

THE REPRESENTATIONAL PROCESS: THE NARRATOR'S INVOLVEMENT

The narrator tries to reconstruct the story of the last party from his own and other people's memories of earlier ones, since not only was the pattern the same but even those other evenings were enigmatic: the participants keep talking about the experience: "it seemed we were half a lifetime learning what really took place, during our one evening under the Dorsets' roof . . . the one evening when you were actually there never seemed quite so real as the glimpses and snatches which you got from those people before and after you—the second-hand impression of the Dorsets' behavior, of things they said, of looks that passed between them" (297). In short, story-telling makes things more real. For the fateful soirée the narrator also uses the very unclear accounts the children were able to give, completed with what Tom divulged and what the Meriwether parents reported. He evaluates the accuracy of the reports he got; for instance, Tom's is "a very truthful and accurate one," but the account he gives of Emily is presented with diffidence: "And I believe the account which I have given of Emily's impressions and her delicate little sensations while on the way to the party has a *ring* of truth about it, though actually the account was supplied by girls who *knew her only slightly*, who were *not at the party*, who could not possibly have seen her afterward. It may, after all, represent only what other girls imagined she would have felt" (314, 311, emphasis added). Thus the truth is but the truth of an image. The narrator is nothing if not honest, yet not only was he not present but his understanding is somewhat limited. Griffith speculates that "it is perhaps as a result of Peter Taylor's own distrust of this unfamiliar material that he chooses to keep the narrator distant from the main action."[24] It seems to me, on the contrary, that the narrator embodies the trust Taylor has in his material insofar as he is part and parcel of the mannerist technique which informs the narrative.

THE NARRATOR AS MANNERIST "SPRECHER" (SPEAKER)   In the words of Sypher, "one of the most dramatic devices of mannerist painting is using the 'Sprecher' [the speaker] . . . a sharply accented foreground figure who faces outward toward the spectator, yet twirls inward, gesturing or glancing toward the action behind him. The Sprecher is a mannerist mode of direct address corresponding to the intimate soliloquy of Jacobean drama, a form of brusque communication between actor and audience that tends to violate dramatic distance."[25]

In "Venus, Cupid, Folly and Time," though he remains nameless, the I-narrator is a foreground figure who from the first involves his narratee in the act of narration. Already in the opening sentence, "Their house alone would not have made you think there was anything so awfully wrong with Mr. Dorset or his old-maid sister," he resorts to the dialogic "you" rather than to the nondialogic "one," thereby implicitly including an exterior addressee and assuming that s/he shares his values (291). He frequently draws his narratee into the world he presents, for instance, with an inclusive, generalizing "you": "In a busy modern city like Chatham you cannot afford to let people forget who you are—not for a moment, not at any age" (296). Or with an exclusive one which yet insists on resemblance between narrator and narratee: "their house was one that *you or I* would have been ashamed to live in" (295, emphasis added). But conversely, as he scatters overjustifications—modalizers ("probably," "it seems," "must," "I believe," "I imagine") and metacomments ("a clear picture of the whole evening wasn't to be had . . . accounts from the other children were contradictory and vague" [311–12]), he signals to his audience the interactive and relative nature of story sharing, thereby underscoring the narrative act. Thus he both faces outward and twirls inward. Nor do his contradictions stop there: he is both distant from the narrated action, in the sense that he was not a direct observer, but close to it insofar as years later the image of Emily standing among the paper flowers still "tantalizes" him and makes him "wish that [he] had been there," and he keeps discussing the incident with Ned's wife (316). Similarly, he is close to the narratee with whom he establishes a relationship of confidence and trust, yet he is distant from the reader. Or rather, although the reader normally associates him/herself with extra-diegetic narratees and can therefore imagine that s/he is in immediate contact with the world presented, in this case, notwithstanding the narrator's good-will and desire for truth, it soon becomes obvious that we ought to be somewhat wary, since we cannot coincide with the addressee that his narration conjures. When one reads the first paragraph, one may accept the opening statement that the Dorset house alone would not make us think there was anything "so awfully wrong" with the owners. But one may tend to feel that the response of West Vesey Place and of the narrator to the slovenliness of the Dorsets is somewhat overdone. By implication, wearing one's bedroom slippers in town becomes something "awfully wrong," an evaluation which we may consider exaggerated to say the least. Conversely, later, the description of the house, "mutilated" and scarred, "raw and naked" on its *southern* side, seems much more impressive and becomes for the reader accustomed to the metonymic and metaphoric use of the Southern mansion a hint at the owners' decadence, which counts for more than a pajama cuff showing from underneath everyday clothes. What may seem "wrong" to the reader is the narrator's sense of priorities.[26] As a result, while we are constantly tugged, along with the narratee, into the fictional universe, we are also reminded of the act of narration and of our participation in it; deciphering the blanks of the text, extrapolating from image to meaning, we are fiction-makers. Henceforth we weave back and forth between the world of life and the world of art, across that unbridgeable gap between the two to which mannerist painting often alerts the spectator.

Naively, it would seem, the narrator (not to be confused with the author) conveys the attitudes of a milieu in which the code of manners is all powerful. Some things just are not done. For the first three pages, the narrator is concerned with the Dorsets' clothing. Because these matters do not at first glance seem relevant to the main situation, the narrator may appear to be garrulously belaboring a point; yet such deflection of attention from the center to the margins is also a frequent mannerist feature. "An art of the *lapsus* (unconscious slip), mannerism ceaselessly substitutes a minor element for a major one . . . as has been seen, it accumulates supplements at the expense of the essential."[27] Retrospectively, however, such supplementary information on the Dorsets' state of dress or undress can be reintegrated into a larger vision of the narrated world. Mauries, observing this recuperability of what he calls the *lapsus*, gives as his example Bronzino's "Venus, Cupid, Folly and Time" with its many snares and ambiguities. To him this is the very *modus significandi* (manner of signifying) of the mannerist picture which lures the reader into fragmentary, incomplete interpretations, into a reading that s/he will be likely later to reject so that a "naive immediate reading" of a mannerist painting is always impossible. In Peter Taylor's story, what is likely to be deferred, among other things, is the realization that the opening pages are not so much about clothing and propriety as about the body and nakedness, not simply about complying with one's neighbors' very rigid code of manners[28] but about the emergence of the Repressed whether in "the hem of a hitched-up nightgown" under a coat or hair hanging undone "like the hair of an Indian squaw" (291, 293). The way Alfred has "his sweater stuffed inside his trousers" is "extremely distasteful to the women in West Vesey Place," because it made them feel as though he "had just come from the bathroom." Even more offensive are the "*skin-tight* coveralls" which he wears to wash his own car and in full view of the whole neighborhood, "skin-tight coveralls" (the phrase is repeated) which are "faded almost to *flesh* color" (292, emphasis added). Instead of properly hiding the body, clothes are reminders of bodily functions. As for Miss Louisa, she comes "out on her front terrace at midday clad in a faded flannel bathrobe." And, *horresco referens*, (horror of horrors) she cleans her house "without a stitch of clothes, on," as a young Peeping Tom, Tom Bascomb as a matter of fact, has occasion to observe; "when she finally got hot and tired she dropped down in an easy chair and crossed her spindly blue-veined, old legs, and sat there completely naked, with her legs crossed and shaking one scrawny little foot" (293). When one reads the opening pages against the luminous nudity of Venus, Cupid and the putto in Bronzino's painting, one is aware of the displacement of the mannerist insistence on the body to external apparel which as it hides yet signifies the body; one is alert to the sudden appearance of a naked body[29]—and to the contrast between the goddess's firm rosy flesh and the woman's "spindly, blue-veined, old legs" so that the whole appears as a parodic transformation, with the Bronzino Venus's elongated feet reduced to a scrawny little foot. And yet the scene does not lack eroticism of a kind, enhanced by the voyeur's presence. In short, the Dorsets' and their neighbors' excessive attitudes towards clothing, which bespeak either the irreverence toward the taboos that are obviously related to sexuality or an inordinate inhibition, contribute to the development of the theme of desire and its contradictions, to the elaboration of the allegory of love, and to a degree of metaphorisation of the Unconscious.

Other instances of the narrator's displacement of the center abound. They may be a narrative swerve from the topic at hand: after relating Ned's outcry, the narrator first interposes an eight-line metacomment: "None of the guests present that night could—or would—give a satisfactory account of what happened next" except perhaps Tom Bascomb (304). Now the narrator, more knowledgeable than Bascomb, has an interpretation for this: "We could have told him what it was, I think. But we didn't. It would have been hard to say to him that at one time or another all of us had had our Tom Bascombs. Tom lived with his parents in an apartment house on a wide thoroughfare known as *Division* Boulevard and his only real connection with West Vesey Place was that that street was included in his paper route . . . He was *well thought of as a paper boy*" (304, emphasis added). Snobbishly and somewhat ingenuously, the narrator sets the problem within a social frame, certainly an important one which I wish I had time to explore, but he entirely disregards the psychological dimension of the rivalry, which is more likely to tantalize the reader. But then I am myself substituting a psychological interpretation to what may be also regarded as a concern with surfaces and manners in keeping with the "style" of the narrative.

Indeed, throughout, the limitations of the narrator, voluntary or involuntary, confront the reader with enigmas—some perceived (and unsolved) by the "I," such as "the matter of what did happen" that evening, or the mystery of Emily's attitude; some never articulated by him, such as the relation between the Dorsets, so that we have to formulate them—only to leave them unsolved as well. Although the language and the rhetoric of the story could not be more different, one is reminded of Hemingway's stories or rather of his iceberg theory whereby the narrative depends for its strength on the submerged part. It is this *unsaid* which ensnares the reader into tentative interpretations. The narrator's hesitations, omissions and indirections can be regarded as part of the mannerist technique of deferred meaning and ambiguity, which both invites and blocks deciphering. At the same time as he says too little, the narrator also occasionally says too much, or rather he uses phrases and words, like "awfully wrong," "offensive," "disgrace," "dread" that seem exaggerated, the whole effect of which is to demonize the Dorsets, who are not simply "this foolish pair of old people" but, it is suggested, a force of subtle evil. However, not only is this never stated but we do not know where exactly to lay the responsibility for the demonizing, if demonizing there is. For when he presents the Dorsets, the narrator pretends to be a spokesman for West Vesey Place (and pronominal traces of this community of view abound in the "we," "us," "ours"). So one more question is added: Who needs the demonic Dorsets and what for?

Furthermore, if at first it might seem that West Vesey Place and the "I" are at one on this point, the narrator's attitude turns out to be more ambiguous than supposed. For he makes an unexpected volte-face in the middle of the narrative, an inversion which is in keeping with the manneristic paradigm. After presenting the Dorsets as ludicrous and judging them according to the standards of a rather narrow-minded group, he has a moment of compassion: "[The Meriwethers] tried to spare their children and they tried to spare Tom, but *unfortunately* it did not occur to them to try to spare the *poor old* Dorsets" (317, emphasis added). This time it is the Meriwethers, the, if anything, liberal representatives of West Vesey Place, who are mildly rebuked. The change of heart may be perceived as a lack of logic on the part of the narrator, all the more since from then on the tone tends to nostalgia, and, towards the end, the point of view is less that of a community than that of an observer with a personal, albeit never clearly motivated, interest in the affair. But again this works towards a specific effect; as in mannerist art, the illogical shift of perspective, the "variable accent,"[30] creates a tension inasmuch as laughter and pathos are not reconciled but enhanced by their continued coexistence; and it reinforces, without imposing, the idea of the interdependence of deviance and conformity. Another deviation concerns the handling of time: the narrator interweaves an iterative account of the Dorsets' party, summing up several events which were similar, with a singulative one which purports to relate something that happened only once, a merging which is largely responsible for the slight sense of unreality which, notwithstanding the specification of detail, pervades the narrative. Certainly, such temporal manipulation is not exclusive to mannerism; however, in my eyes, it does promote the *maniera* (manneristic) mood inasmuch as the narrator's logic does not operate by chronological, sequential relations but relies on a pattern of similarities and differences.

Needless to say, the narrator is not conscious of being a mannerist: for him his story is an attempt to account for something in the past which he still fails to understand; for him "Venus, Cupid, Folly and Time" is but one of the Dorsets' works of art, one of the puzzling notes of their decor. For the author, on the contrary, it is the title of a painting and that of a story which he "constructed deliberately," working it out "just as you'd work out a theorem."[31] Though he probably had no conscious intention of writing in a mannerist mode either; nevertheless he chose to set up complex relations between Bronzino's picture and his own tale.

THE NARRATIVE AS GEOMETRY   The short story's mathematical deliberateness is not per se manneristic but it includes effects that are. Among these, one may note the contrast and torsion between a narrator's discourse which develops often by association and digression, and the calculatedness of the construction of the narrative. The systematic use of connections and parallels builds up a fictional space which is highly reticulated. The connections may work at various levels. To give but one example, the Dorsets' efforts to supplement their income involves not only repetition (Louisa selling paper flowers and Alfred figs), but the creation of a complex semantic network of similarities and differences, and the crisscrossing of contradictory connotations. Since Louisa's flowers look "like sprays of tinted potato chips," while Alfred's figs are *"dried up* little things without much taste," an isotopy of dryness and tastelessness unites the two products, though they are opposed inasmuch as one is an artifact and the other real fruit (295). At the same time, both motifs evoke and invert well-known symbols. Flowers are in themselves antithetical, suggesting spring and beauty but also the transitoriness of life, the inevitability of death and decay—an antithetical quality with which the narrative subtly plays; for Miss Louisa, it is to be presumed, the paper flowers stand for beauty, youth, and art and they are emblematic of the Dorsets' attempts to deny transience; yet paper flowers too will fade, if not die, and in the overall textual system they symbolize not life but barrenness. Similarly, while figs and fig trees are very generally symbols of abundance and fertility and often associated with sexual organs (as in the fig leaf), these are "dried-up," connoting a blockage of fecundity, and death. (Interestingly, the fig bushes are "very productive," but the fruit are such that "nobody could really have wanted" them [295]). The dessicated world of two elderly people is a declension of the green world. At the same time, the flowers and figs also enter into relation with other indications of the text: though without a perfume of their own the paper flowers belong to a nexus including the incense and the attar of roses which combine a liturgical association and a connotation of fecundity.[32] Even taken in isolation, the flowers and figs are not entirely negative: after all, they function as offerings of the Dorsets to the neighbors they consider worthy, for though they sell them, they "charged next to nothing for them" (295)—hence, flowers and figs are a sign of minimal exchange, a token of social life going on. In short, even the accessory motif of the figs and flowers is at the intersection of the most important themes of the short story.

Whereas one can only figure out the semantic and semiotic possibilities of such details, gradually, by going backward and forward through the text, the pattern of echoes and doublings will strike the most unwary reader. Mauries has remarked on a particularity, "accidental or apparent," of mannerist art, "which consists of repeating, in the interior of a single text, of a single pictorial surface, identical faces, poses and gestures, filling the canvas with similarities. . . . a play of abstract identities, a pattern of likenesses which, artificially linking the parts of the canvas, finally undermines its unity."[33] In "Venus, Cupid, Folly and Time," this corresponds to a series of mirroring effects which is highly contrived, albeit easily accepted, and richly problematic. Everything comes in twos from the play with Ned's and Tom's hats and coats to the duplication of Mr. and Mrs. Meriwether's attitudes: on their children's leaving the house, each parent sees but refuses to believe and admit to the other that their daughter's escort is not their son, Ned, self-deception following upon deception. Their twin concern is itself echoed by the later and converse mistake of both Dorsets who "see" Ned when they should recognize Tom. Ned-as-Tom is twice chased upstairs, first by Mr. Dorset then by Miss Louisa. Sometimes obvious reversals occur: thus the failure of the Dorset family to send young Alfred and Louisa to boarding school is paralleled by the Meriwethers' successfully packing off their children after the party. Life not only repeats itself but, as I have shown, it imitates art, and the kissing children to some degree reproduce the situation in the works of art displayed in the house.

Structurally and thematically, the major and most pregnant instance of this patterning, of course, concerns the mirroring of the elderly pair by the youthful pair of Emily and Ned/Tom: it is on this doubling that the story hinges since, apparently, the older couple take Ned's remarks as being intended for them and since thereby the theme of the incest taboo can be briefly articulated. This doubling is enhanced in many ways, not the least of which is the contrast between youth and age. In both cases a revelation is made which depends on the disturbing presence of a third person, who himself acts as a double—Tom of Ned and Ned of Tom. In both cases, the third person is eliminated but things can never be again as they were before the revelation; the Dorsets are cut off from Chatham, and so are Ned and Emily, sent off to boarding schools, and furthermore forever alienated from one another to the point of "animosity" (322). Before the crisis occurs, however, the Meriwether children themselves can be seen as doubles of one another in their rivalry over Tom. Thematically, the most complicated in-

incest, Bertrand d'Astorg calls the love between brother and sister "the
lphic mystery."[38] It is this mystery which the mannerism of "Venus,
pid, Folly and Time" serves so well.

ELABORATE THEMATICS   Taylor's "Venus, Cupid, Folly and
ne" both stimulates the reader's active search for meaning and not only
cks it, as I have said, but also suspends it in moments of what, for lack
nother word, I will call contemplation. The last, of course, defeats analysis
l all I can do is give an example of this "freeze frame" effect which the
t can induce in the reader—an experience which, I think, underlies Alan
illiamson's comment that "the story leaves us with one curiously radiant
age: that of Emily withdrawing contemplatively, during the chase, into
 niche where she and the interloper have previously substituted themselves
 Rodin's 'The Kiss.' "[39] For me, too, the image of Emily entranced has a
ange attraction which I cannot entirely account for. But in my eyes, this
n is a companion piece to, works together with, another image, which
s an even more mysterious radiance of its own, so that again and again I
urn in my mind to old Miss Louisa sitting in her easy chair, completely
ked after her household chores, and "shaking one scrawny little foot." It
Peter Taylor's magic gift, in his best stories, to create with perfectly clear
gnettes a sense of the luminous opacity of the world.

On the other hand, seduced by the text into producing more and
ore readings, I can, from the starting-point of the overlapping between
onzino's painting and Taylor's story, develop a whole series of interpreta-
ns. To speak in the most general terms, painting and short story are
llegories of Love." In his interview with Goodwin, Taylor has remarked
 this quality of his story: " 'Venus, Cupid, Folly and Time' and 'Miss
onora' are for me complete allegories, although they may not be for the
st of the world."[40] The pictorial and verbal spaces both emblematize the
easures and the pains of Eros, its "folly" and its submission to Time, even
 in its treatment, the narrative departs from the allegorical pattern set by
e picture. Among other things, it doubles the loving couple, assigning
em very different ages; fiction being "an art of incarnation," it distributes
easures and pains and obstacles among the characters of the little drama,
stead of having Jealousy or Fraud or the merry putto hovering in the wings.
hus for all that they talk of the sacrifices they have made for each other,
e Dorsets seem to embody the pleasures of love, until confronted with a
aud that betrays the self-deception in which they live, while Ned and
mily, embodying trickery and deception, discover the ambiguities of desire,
elphic or otherwise. Furthermore, their roles are split. To Ned is reserved
e anguish of Jealousy—an important figure in the painting—and to Emily
e gratification of sensual awakening. (As a result, too, the short story works
it its allegorical effects more in metonymico-metaphoric ways than in
mbolic ones.)

stance of doubling involves Ned himself who is split
roles: he acts as both rival and "lover" of his sister; he
ego becomes jealous of him or possibly about him; pran
in his place, he ends by putting himself in the other
ambivalence, the situation recalls the triangle formed b
Sutpen and Charles Bon in *Absalom, Absalom!*, with its
and undertones of homoeroticism.[34] Unlike Henry Sutp
cannot accept even the vicarious satisfaction of his own
and denounces the guilty shadow self—under his own
mirror play. Moreover, while in Faulkner's novel the inces
referred to in some of the narrators' discourses and eve
Compson's,[35] in Peter Taylor's story, the taboo is only
in Ned's outcry, "They're *brother* and *sister*!" Even then o
of the syllogism, the fact of the blood relationship, is s
major premise of it, the sexual interdiction, and its cor
injunction, remain unuttered, however easily suppliable

THE NARRATIVE AS PUZZLE   Because so mu
the construction of the short story's thematics, as we have
much on the reader's willingness to bridge gaps. But excep
such gaps cannot be satisfactorily filled.

To stay with the incest motif, for the reader Ne
rhetorical questions, "Don't you *know*? . . . Can't you
become unanswerable queries: were the Dorsets "grinning
an incestuous couple or merely pleased at a manifestatio
sexuality which they seek to awaken? Later when they
outburst, are they outraged at the breach of propriety
accusations, his open rejection of their ceremony? Do the
they take for "an intended exposure of their own guilt
implies that they are not innocent? Or do they respond
realization of the way their relation may appear to the wor
tion which their delayed reaction seems to support and w
probably innocent. Or are they struck by a revelation abo
their relationship, in which case they are truly innocent?
the story leaves the choice open with, in fact, possibil
such as slightly perverse and mostly foolish, mostly demo
foolish. "The mannerist directions are truly, as Pevsner o
reich—'rich in problems.' "[37] When all is said, the doul
their love is platonic or not, while it powerfully heightens
the text, does not profoundly matter to the thematics of t
it. For though it represents a different stage, the relationsl
and Emily remains something of a puzzle as well—and
most enigmatic character in the story? Founding his study
incest on Claude Lévi-Strauss's concept of the correlation bet

But before coming to differences, one can push further the comparison between the two renderings of the theme. Assuredly, at first glance, it seems ridiculous to identify the Dorset siblings with Venus and Cupid. Neither can one see in their relation simply a comic lowering of the mythological theme. In any case, the Bronzino, it must be noted, is already a light treatment of a dread and awe-inspiring transgression and it expresses what Julia Kristeva, speaking of the beginning of the Renaissance, calls "the joyous serenity of incest with the mother."[41] Except for, and in spite of, the crisis which shakes their world, the Dorsets exemplify the humdrum tranquility of adelphic love. Beyond this, there is a striking analogy between picture and narrative. In the mythological painting, Venus and Cupid behave as they do because they are divinities, outside the law which regulates human action, and divinities of love, at that. In Peter Taylor's short story, the main characters attempt through their behavior to reach such a god-like condition. To this degree, they are typical since in Pierre Legendre's word, "incest is finally aimed at the gods," as it calls into question the limit that separates men and gods.[42] What the Dorset ritual celebrates is their having withdrawn from the conflicts and stresses of society in an effort to recover a primordial world of innocence and unity and happiness, where the Law does not obtain. Thus in their ceremony, a necessary stage is to recall their former "naughty behavior" and "silly flirtations" when as adolescents they mistakenly looked beyond the family circle for (provisional) partners: these breaches of their rules are, in fact, a transposition of the true transgression, a way of heightening "how much [they] had given up for each other's sake" in order to achieve their present involvement and happiness (305). Incest understood as the refusal to engage in exchange with the other is the very basis of their life, which has enabled them to establish, as it were, a green island of love in which "we are all young, we all love one another" (308). In short, theirs is the age-old drama of Paradise, "a sweetness eternally denied social man, of a world where people can live among themselves," a dream which Catherine Clément, quoting this remark of Claude Lévi-Strauss, compares to the youth of the world, as described by Rousseau.[43] Having managed to "live among themselves" in a Golden Age of their own, the Dorsets have retained their youth, or so they would like to believe: "This is what it is like to be young forever," affirms Miss Louisa, innocently (or perversely) claiming for herself an attribute of the gods (309). And to some extent, the narration hints that while youth has escaped brother and sister long since, in some ways they have remained children. When Louisa says, " 'All the children are mischievous tonight,' . . . it was quite as though she had said, 'all we children' "; and later the narrator states that "she sounded like a little girl about to burst into tears" (318, 319). When Alfred finally follows Mr. Meriwether, he does so with "quick little steps—steps like that of a small boy trying to keep up with a man" (319).[44] Of course, immaturity is not eternal youth; it indicates, on the contrary, the failure of the Dorsets to live outside Time.

In any case, if the Gods are immortal, one of the points which Bronzino's "Venus, Cupid, Folly and Time" makes beyond discussion is that they are not immune to the influences of Time. However one interprets Father Time's gesture, his arm is very much in evidence, at least to the viewer, though not to the loving pair. Similarly, whatever the characters may believe, signs of the effects of time abound in the narrative. There is the "dilapidated" house which, ironically, was "mutilated" so that the owners could avoid change; there is the antiquated car and the old people themselves, grotesquely unaware of the marks of time. Because they have refused exchange and change, the Dorsets are shown to lead self-contained, barren lives and after the fiasco of their last party, they are deprived of the one link with Chatham which publicly testified to the meaning of their life. Because the reader is made so much aware of Time, the elderly couple must appear at once as ludicrous and pathetic in their delusions, as both foolish and slightly crazy. Their narcissistic enclosure may seem like the isolation of shared madness, of folie à deux.

And so we are led back to the third figure in the title(s), Folly in all its polysemy. In the painting, Folly has also been identified as Fraud, a creature with a lovely face and a dragon's tail, offering a honeycomb with her left hand and holding a scorpion in her right. In the narrative, Folly is not a separate figure but a component of the action and the characterization and, as such, of paramount importance. One may easily see the plot of the short story as depending on folly as a "piece of unwise conduct" leading to "mischief" and involving "fraud" (in the sense of an instance of deception, with the irony that "the nice children" set up a destructive prank); one may also read analogically the "folly" of the title as referring at once to the seductive beauty of the Dorsets' age-old dream and to its being a dangerous delusion, indeed a form of madness.

If, in deciphering the allegory, we consider that the Meriwether children's prank and their parents' intervention represent change, Time exposes the folly of the Dorsets and implicitly that of the Meriwethers. The Meriwethers accept the lesson and "bundle" Ned and Emily off to boarding schools. Separating them, the parents assume their role, which is to preclude the shift from infantile complicity in play between siblings to sexual attraction. As for Ned and Emily, the party marks "the end of their childhood intimacy, and the beginning of a shyness, a reserve, an animosity between them that was destined to be a sorrow forever" to their parents (322). The ambivalence of this animosity is what exercises Ned's wife, who "after a few drinks [likes] to talk about Ned and Emily and Tom Bascomb and the Dorsets" (322). Time, far from effacing the night at the Dorsets, has rather made it more obscure and tantalizing; thus it works as ambiguously in the story as in the painting. One major difference between the narrative and the picture, however, is again in the former, Time is no abstraction; it is embodied in the characters and their setting which includes much more than I could examine here.

BEYOND MANNERISM AND MYTHOLOGY: THE REFERENTIAL FRAMES   When the narrator tries to tell Ned's wife about the Dorsets, he puts them back within a double frame: in the first place the history of Chatham, "one of the first English-speaking settlements West of the Alleghenies" "named after the Earl of Chatham," now a "border city" regarded by some as "geographically Northern and culturally Southern," and in the second place the history of the Dorsets, who settled in Chatham in those earliest times not as pioneers from Virginia or Pennsylvania, but as "an obscure mercantile family" straight from England (323, 322, 323, 324). Nor did they strike roots in Chatham, although within two generations they had become wealthy and were "looked upon as our first family." They could leave the town "except for one old bachelor and the one maid" without regret, for Chatham was simply "an investment which had paid off" (324). Meanwhile the remaining Dorsets are left to play the role of social arbiters and if "it was only by a sort of chance. . . . no one questioned their divine right to do so"—a divine right which is all the more ironical in view of the "obscure mercantile" origins of the family and of Chatham's fine sense of social distinctions (324). The citizens of Chatham—and West Vesey Place in particular[45]—still differentiate between the first settlers, among whom one may distinguish two "categories," the families "with a good Southern name" and those which had their origins in New England, on the one hand, and the later immigrants, the Irish, the Germans, the Italians, on the other: "If the distinction was false, it mattered all the more and it was all the more necessary to make it" (323). (What with their paradoxes and contradictions, their sense of protocol and manners, cannot the good people of Chatham be called mannerists, too?)

By placing Mr. Alfred and Miss Louisa in a general context, the narrator can all the better mark their difference from the successful members of their family, now scattered from Santa Barbara to Newport. For, seeing the move of the other Dorsets as embodying the American spirit ("They were city people, and they were Americans" [324]), he identifies his own group with them even if he does so reluctantly, because it means denying another difference which West Vesey Place holds dear: "And the truth which it was so hard for the rest of us to admit was that, despite our families of Massachusetts and Virginia, we were more like the Dorsets—those Dorsets who left Chatham—than we were *un*like them. Their spirit was just a little closer to the very essence of Chatham than ours was. The obvious difference was that we had to stay on here and pretend that our life had a meaning which it did not" (325). The narrator seems once more to go off at a tangent although the digression leads him to conclude on the Chatham Dorsets' "divine right" to be social arbiters of the town. Yet as the narrative has shown, the old Dorset brother and sister represent an attitude, which by implication is nonChatham, nonAmerican, insofar as they have refused the changes of modern life, have stayed put. Money, as they are fond of repeating, is not everything, and they "tore away [their] in-laws because [they] could not *afford* them" (306, emphasis added). All they have is the social status which the family acquired through wealth, and they cling to that, while happily ignoring the codes that obtain at West Vesey Place, the zoning laws of the city and perhaps a much older law, which the narrator, for his part, never mentions. Thus the Chatham frame, while explaining certain things, does not really account for the main events.

Indeed, the analysis in which the narrator indulges may seem, to some extent, a side-stepping of the real issues, a defensive way of putting the Dorset couple at a safe distance. For one might say that if the other Dorsets represent the American way of success, the Chatham Dorsets represent a deeper temptation: the attraction of endogamy—which society forbids in some extreme forms (but allows in other cases, and, significantly, Alfred and Louisa's parents were themselves both Dorsets). In the plot, the temptation is incarnated anew in Emily and Ned who might have turned into Dorsets, had not their prank happened to reveal something about the old couple which West Vesey Place still fails to acknowledge, preferring, like the narrator, to think of the Dorsets' "folly" as foolishness. Only the Meriwether parents' reaction implies a realization of what is at stake. Yet, though Ned and Emily have escaped the old people's fate, and both marry spouses from outside Chatham, they still have the scars of the tearing away.

Furthermore, the temptation is renewed with each telling of the enigmatic story. For it is the narrator's unavowed desire which keeps him compulsively returning to the scene of the crime, as it were. Telling about the party may well be an attempt to locate himself in the place of incestuous sibling, a manifestation of that *recherche de la fièvre* (feverish quest for passion), which is for Georges Bataille the essence of mannerism. The narrator's beginning and ending on general considerations is a way of framing the core of his narration all the better to encyst it. But his fascination is with "what did happen," with the forbidden. As a consequence, while his discourse states one similarity—thus reversing the difference formerly established—it also inverts into the implication of yet another similarity where we had been shown difference. The explicit lesson is: "we" are not unlike those Dorsets who left, knowing that "what they had in Chatham they could buy more of in other places" (324). But the reader operates another reversal which the narrator cannot envisage, namely, that he and his fellow citizens are not unlike the Chatham Dorsets, whose manners they may resent but who stand for psychic possibilities that are attractive: indeed with all their eccentricity they represent what Andrew Lytle discussing incest in his work calls "an habitual impulse, the refusal to engage in the cooperating opposites that make life."[46] This incest is in Freud's view the primordial wish of the child; Freud has taught us that the boy's "first object selection" is "directed to the forbidden objects, the mother and the sister," and although the mature individual frees himself from the child-like conditions of psychosexuality, "incestuous fixations of the libido still play . . . the main role in the [neurotic's] unconscious psychic life."[47] Since we are told nothing about the narrator's family, apart from their social rank, the narration precludes further speculation on his own incestuous feelings, once again blocking interpretation. The unsaid remains unsayable and incest an enigma.

On the other hand, the narration invites a comparison between the Dorsets snobbishness, their closeness, their sense of belonging to an elite, their role-playing which gives a meaning to their life, and the exclusiveness, the self-centerdness of West Vesey Place with its sharp but shifting divisions between "us" and "them," its pretending that its "life [has] a meaning." This last parallel leads Jan Pinkerton to assert that "the conclusion is unmistakable: all the 'meaning' of the old order is pretense, an elaborate defensiveness on the part of those who are non-enterprising and defeatist."[48] As far as I am concerned, the conclusion is less "unmistakable" and is more multilevelled than such a statement suggests. Leaving aside the issue of role-playing, and sticking to my subject, I would say that the network of oppositions reversing into similarities—which is one more mannerist feature—orchestrates the theme of incest without resolving its dissonances. To put it briefly, when the attraction of the same for the same is so much developed, [49] endogamy becomes an ideal, and incest, the rejection of difference, becomes any asymptotic, however impossible, pole. The "allegory of love" therefore does not restrict incest to a family or a group but makes it a metaphor for a basic feature of human behavior: since incest always goes beyond the genealogical nucleus, as Pierre Legendre has remarked, it is a question that underlies society as a whole, "the principal characteristic of the problematic of incest is that of being the bearer of unconscious wagers among humanity."[50] It is this problematics which both Bronzino's and Taylor's "Venus, Cupid, Folly and Time" gives us a glimpse of.

In this larger sense, the narrator as observer can be regarded as "incestuous" insofar as he identifies so closely with his community that an ideal of, and desire for, sameness underlies his evaluations. But telling the story to an outside narratee, however like-minded, marks a departure from the customs of the country, away from ingrownness and incest. Is the narrator qua narrator, if not qua actor, innocent then? Not really, if we follow some theoreticians influenced by psychoanalysis who consider that to narrate is to place oneself in the place of the incestuous son.[51]

Be that as it may, someone else, of course, stands unequivocally accused: the reader who has been led to attribute incestuous wishes to the characters. And what of the critic, who trying to entangle the threads of the story's problematics, counts on the complicity of her reader, and thereby relies at once on the identifying power of a shared critical language and on the assimilation of a word—"mannerist"—smuggled from another area in the face of all difference?

In conclusion, a mannerist text makes a mannerist reader, or is it the other way around: has the mannerist reader turned a "traditional" story into a mannerist text? It is enough, I believe, that the experience should be possible, whatever it may, like all interpretations, either leave out or let in. Mannerism, after all, is in Sypher's definition "experimental response."[52] Moreover, is "Venus, Cupid, Folly and Time" really so apart in Peter Taylor's production? Of another story, Jane Barnes Casey wrote: "the story, like so many of Mr. Taylor's stories—is a tissue in which the parts of the subject become so enmeshed that we finally feel there is no difference between things that seemed opposite at the start. It is not that opposites become indistinguishable but rather that they become equivalents."[53] Such a remark would in my view argue in favour of a mannerist trend in such narratives. Without claiming that the mannerist label is more than a heuristic metaphor or that it applies to the whole work of the author, perhaps, it would be worthwhile investigating its further use: Peter Taylor's "life studies" are definitely art studies.

Notes

1. Stephen Goodwin, "Life Studies," *Shenandoah* 21 (Winter 1970): 100.
2. Albert J. Griffith, *Peter Taylor* (New York: Twayne, 1970), 128, 125.
3. Stephen Goodwin, "Like Nothing Else in Tennessee," *Shenandoah* 28 (Winter 1977): 56.
4. Umberto Eco, *The Limits of Interpretation*: "Two semantic models are today competing to explain how human beings produce and understand texts: the dictionary model and the encyclopedia model. . . . The encyclopedia model is based on the assumption that every item of a language must be interpreted by every other possible linguistic item which, according to some previous cultural conventions, can be associated with it. Every sign can be interpreted by another sign that functions as its interpretant" (Bloomington: Indiana University Press, 1990), 143.
5. Peter Taylor, *The Collected Stories of Peter Taylor* (New York: Farrar, Straus and Giroux, 1969), 299. Hereafter cited parenthetically in the text.
6. Stephen Goodwin, "An Interview with Peter Taylor," *Shenandoah* 24 (Winter 1973): 4.
7. In fact it might be interesting to study the story in the light of American, and singularly Southern, myths of origins.
8. Goodwin, "An Interview," 4.
9. Michel Foucault, *Les mots et les choses* (The order of things) (Paris: Gallimard, 1966), 25. This and all subsequent passages from the French have been translated by Professor Ronald Bogue of the Department of Comparative Literature, University of Georgia.
10. Wylie Sypher, *Four Stages of Renaissance Style* (Garden City, New York: Doubleday, 1955), 120.
11. Wylie Sypher has studied the analogies between painting, poetry and drama in an attempt to link "the changing configurations of the worlds revealed" and the "styles" he

analyzes, so that his rapprochements are justified by the historical frame selected. My enterprise has, I grant, no such legitimacy.

12. Patrick Mauries, *Manièristes* (The Mannerists) (Paris: Editions du Regard, 1983), 172. For a review of the various interpretations of the Bronzino painting see Mauries. For one of the best-known readings, see Panofsky's *Studies in Iconology: Humanistic Themes in the Art of the Renaissance* (New York: Harper and Row, 1962).

13. Alan Williamson, "Identity and the Wider Eros: A Reading of Peter Taylor's Stories," *Shenandoah* 30 (Fall 1978): 71–72.

14. The *OED* defines the current sense of "folly" as "the state of being foolish, want of good sense . . . ; also unwise conduct" and gives as now obsolete meanings "wickedness, evils, mischief, harm," "lewdness, wantonness" and "madness, mania."

15. John Dixon Hunt, "A Moment's Monument: Reflections on Pre-Raphaelite Vision in Poetry and Painting," in James Sambrook, ed., *Pre-Raphaelitism, A Collection of Critical Essays* (Chicago: University of Chicago Press, 1974).

16. Art historians have been revising their analysis and appraisal of mannerism. My laywoman's understanding, such as it is, of "mannerism" is largely derived from Mauries's brief but richly informative study of Italian Mannerists, which reconsiders previous approaches and itself holds a very positive view of the style.

17. Sypher, 116.

18. Mauries, 34.

19. At least the reader may presume that the anonymous plaque also plays on "the rhetoric of bodies" in view of the Leda motif: perhaps one of the best-known illustrations of this is another mannerist painting, Tintoretto's "Leda and the Swan," an exemplar called up, in any case, by the presence of the Bronzino in the same paragraph.

20. They speak of "their father's kin as Mama's in-laws" and vice-versa (294)—a detail which shows how they identify with the parental pair and therefore see themselves as a couple. This ties in with conceptions of incest as irradiating the whole family system and transforming it into a "magma." "The unconscious logic of incest, because it is handled within language, constructs its significations in such a way that the signifier provided with a very precise social signified (mother, father, sister, brother) can be led astray in a totally different direction and become unrecognizable" (Pierre Legendre, *L'Inestimable objet de la transmission* (The Inestimable Object of Transmission) [Paris: Fayard, 1985], 37).

21. Mauries, 247.

22. Ibid., 247.

23. Williamson, 80.

24. Griffith, 127.

25. Sypher, 144.

26. Griffith remarks that readers familiar with Southern fiction cannot fail to associate the decadent house with the characters' decadence but he concludes that, after the description of the mutilated house, "the reader should be convinced that something is 'awfully wrong' with Peter Taylor's usual style" (127). This interpretation, which I strongly disagree with, is premised on a confusion between narrator and author.

27. Mauries, 33.

28. Miss Dorset seems "quite beyond the pale" to her male neighbors because of her coming out on her terrace "clad in a faded flannel bathrobe." "To us whose wives and mothers did not even come downstairs in their negligees, this was very unsettling" (293).

29. Sypher writes, "mannerism discovered the more insidious pleasures of nakedness— which is self-conscious nudity; and it used nakedness insolently, provokingly, with intent to shock or to mock" (110). Here Miss Louisa is not provoking but the tale Tom and the others spread about her is intended to shock, while the short story itself may be intended to mock.

30. Sypher.

31. Goodwin, "An Interview," 9.

32. Rhodes, the island of roses, was the island of mysteries. Rose-trees were consecrated to Aphrodite in a symbolism of regeneration.

33. Mauries, 39.

34. Williamson comparing "Venus, Cupid, Folly and Time" to "Dean of Men" said that in the former "we have to do not with mild homoerotic overtones, but with a primordial threat, incest" (78). But part of the complexity of the story comes precisely from its blending mild homoeroticism and the "primordial threat" of incest.

35. See for instance Mr. Compson's suggestion that Henry identifying with Bon can vicariously satisfy his own desire for Judith and his comment that ". . . perhaps this is the pure and perfect incest; the brother realizing that the sister's virginity must be destroyed in order to have existed at all, taking that virginity in the person of the brother-in-law, the man he would be if he could become, metamorphose into the lover," etc. (William Faulkner, *Absalom, Absalom!* [New York: Random House, 1964], 96). On the association of doubling and incest see John Irwin's fascinating study (*Doubling and Incest/Repetition and Revenge* [Baltimore: The Johns Hopkins University Press, 1975]). By using both an elderly pair and children, Taylor, of course, locates differently the springs of the action and leaves aside the virginity motif so powerful in Faulkner.

36. Williamson, 80.

37. Sypher, 140.

38. Bertrand d'Astorg, *Variations sur l'interdit majeur, littérature et inceste en occident* (Variations on the Primary Taboo: Literature and Incest in the West) (Paris: Gallimard, 1990), 35. Pierre Legendre insists that the incest taboo is a "phenomenon of language," "tied to the reproduction of our species' life insofar as it is reproduced in speech. Not being biogenetic, the interdiction presents itself as an enigma" (75).

39. Williamson, 80.

40. Goodwin, "An Interview," 10.

41. Julia Kristeva, *Desire in Language, A Semiotic Approach to Literature and Art*, ed. by Leon S. Roudiez (New York: Columbia University Press, 1980), 156.

42. Legendre, 77.

43. Catherine Clément and Hélène Cixous, *La Jeune Née* (The Newly Born Woman) (Paris: Union Générale d'Editions, 1975), 54–55.

44. Their immaturity is also conveyed in the way they tell their own story and for instance at times turn it into a sort of fairy-tale with the machinations of "wicked in-laws" and the victory of the "young" heroes.

45. It is ironical that the best neighborhood in Chatham, Pitt County, should be called West Vesey Place: the toponymical system opposes to the English, with all their historico-political associations, a local note, no less political, Denmark Vesey being the leader of a famous slave rebellion.

46. Andrew Lytle, *The Hero with the Private Parts* (Baton Rouge: Louisiana State University Press, 1966), 184.

47. Sigmund Freud, *Totem and Taboo* (Harmondsworth: Penguin, 1942), 28. See also *The Interpretation of Dreams*, ch. V.

48. Jan Pinkerton, "The Non-Regionalism of Peter Taylor: An Essay-Review," *Georgia Review* 24 (Winter 1970): 439.

49. Jean Libis remarked that the theme of incest is often associated with that of androgyny and "virtually contains that of gemellity" (Jean Libis, *Le mythe de l'Androgyne* (The Myth of Androgyny) [Paris: Berg International, 1980], 206). At one point, the Dorsets are described in terms that remind one of twins: "Ned saw their faces change and grow solemn when their eyes—their identical, tiny, dull, amber-colored eyes—focused upon himself" (Taylor, 313).

50. Legendre, 72.

51. See, for instance, Phillipe Sollers, *Logiques* (Logics) (Paris: Seuil, 1968), 161: "perhaps the fact of *narrating* automatically puts one in the position of the incestuous son."

52. Sypher, 120.

53. Jane Barnes Casey, "A View of Peter Taylor's Stories," *Virginia Quarterly Review* 54 (Spring 1978): 227.

The Mastery of Peter Taylor

Madison Smartt Bell

When I was in college, I was part of a fiction class in which George Garrett suggested to us all that one of the problems of conventional undergraduate education for writers is that one is fed an unvarying diet of masterpieces. Nothing wrong with that if one wants to become a good consumer and appreciator and no more. But for someone who wants to be a writer as well as a reader, the problem with masterpieces is that the seams don't show. It's hard to tell where the screws went in; you can't see how the thing was done. Technique is not apparent. Therefore, George suggested to the gang, it would be a good idea for us all to spice up our reading with a little junk and genre fiction from time to time—whose technical apparatus is apt to lie a good deal closer to the surface.

One of the aspects of literary mastery is to be inimitable, certainly, and another is not to *be* an imitator. In the former category, the mastery of Peter Taylor is supported, somewhat unfortunately, by default; not only are there next to no younger writers who have imitated him with any degree of success but also there seem to be nearly none who have even made the attempt. The seamlessness of his work is such that it certainly would be difficult for any apprentice writer to figure out where to get a purchase on his methods. I can think of only one writer of a younger generation, Richard Bausch, who has in his latest collection, *The Fireman's Wife*, written one graceful and artful homage to Taylor's dramatic monologues, and has discovered ways to adapt many of Taylor's methods to his own purposes.

It's regrettable that by and large and with no more exceptions than to prove the rule the special skills and techniques of Taylor's fiction are apparently not being transmitted. Still in many ways it is an enviable thing to be inimitable. If a younger writer cannot pass through your shadow and survive the experience, you are strong indeed.

As for Taylor's own relationships with writers of earlier days, he has been most often compared to Chekhov and to James. Both comparisons sound flattering, are somewhat misleading, and at this point in Taylor's career, are unnecessary. It's easiest to separate Taylor from Chekhov; indeed there are more dissimilarities than resemblances there. Chekhov's stories are open, or

This essay was written specifically for this volume.

at least appear to be open, in a way that Taylor's deliberately are not. In Chekhov one finds a deceptive apparent simplicity, while in Taylor there is a deceptive apparent forthrightness, which is not at all the same thing. A Chekhov narrative is controlled by plot; a Taylor story is controlled by voice. And while almost every Taylor story rambles discursively over a long period of time, almost every Chekhov story is compact and immediate, bound so tightly to real time and present action as to be capable of being staged theatrically with only minor revision. These distinctions are clear and evident.

I think it likely that the readers and critics who have thought to compare Taylor to Chekhov have done so mainly as a measure of Taylor's importance, a not unreasonable strategy. And there is one very significant point of resemblance between these two writers, who are almost altogether different otherwise—although it comes about through an accident of history, really. Chekhov's vision and art range freely all through the Russian society of his day, so that his contemporary audience would presumably have been about as familiar with his milieu as he was himself. But for modern readers such is no longer the case, and the background of Chekhov's fiction now is as foreign to us as . . . the delicately nuanced and elaborately mannered social patterns of Taylor's Nashville and Memphis as they were some forty or fifty years ago. For Taylor, of course, that has always been so; he would have known from the beginning that only a tiny and dwindling number of people could understand from personal experience exactly what he was talking about. That is one reason that Taylor's stories carry an infinitely heavier load of exposition than Chekhov's do. And yet somehow the total effect is very much the same, in reading Chekhov or in reading Taylor: the distance seems to drop away, and we perceive that they who inhabit the foreign and remote place and time are men and women much like us, and that their behavior can do much to educate us about our own. Through intense and accurate concentration on the precise details and circumstances of life in his own time, both of these writers succeed in bringing something of universal human nature to the page. This quality of permanent relevance is a large element of Peter Taylor's mastery.

In expository matters, Taylor tends to explain where Chekhov would assume. The long opening explanations of his stories may appear to be overdetermined, though one must be aware that, in a Jamesian fashion, they usually reveal rather more than the speaker intends. They are necessary, in any case, to educate the reader in the manners of the society in which the characters exist, manners which give the subtle turns in their behavior their meanings. Again by accident of history, some of the social patterns of Taylor's milieu now appear (to some people) to be merely quaint, while others seem politically backward. At a time when political rectitude has been elevated, even in the most effete and decadent critical circles, to the position of highest aesthetic good, that can create a sort of bogus problem for a portion of Taylor's readership.

For instance there is the *New York Times* reviewer who wasted much of his review of *The Old Forest* apologizing for Taylor's incorrect (as he construed it) attitude toward relations between the races. It is possible too, and even trendy, to distort the stories so as to show that they are primarily about the disenfranchisement and oppression of women. Well, intellectual fashion will change, we may hope, and none of that will matter very much. Meanwhile, bear in mind that the only thing Taylor has really been guilty of is flawless and comprehensive accuracy—showing the life of a certain place and a certain time just as it was, in all its detail. He has only told the truth as he saw it. Of course in other countries they do hang you for that. The experiment of battering reality into the mold of one's political preconceptions has been tried with great fervor and conspicuous lack of success by such aestheticians as Stalin and Pol Pot. Let it be said once, though probably not for all, that the truth, and only the truth, can set us free.

To prove this point one need only reread a single story—"A Wife of Nashville." Peter Taylor would still be a master if he had written no other story than this. It is a remarkable story for several reasons. It manages to make a record of twenty years of perfectly ordinary domestic life interesting and compelling in its own right; there are no extraordinary events, not even a climax in the conventional sense. It is the story of an upper middle class white woman, Helen Ruth, and how she learns to get along with her black maids. Along the way much is also revealed about her marriage, how it almost fails, but metamorphosizes to survive and finally even prosper.

The whole business of "managing servants" will call up a cluster of unpleasant associations in the minds of many readers nowadays, obscuring the main point: the role of the black maids is to provide Helen Ruth with her moral education. The black women are the mirror in which she sees herself and as she learns to accommodate herself to them she becomes a wiser and better person in all the other departments of her life. Indeed the husband and sons are almost ciphers in the story, and Helen Ruth's greatest intimacy is with her servants, especially Jess McGehee, the last of them.

Jess is the only servant to stay very long, to live on the property, to become "one of the family." Her mission, like Helen Ruth's, is to minister to the men in the family, especially the two growing sons. When the boys are grown, Jess becomes almost superfluous. A movie buff, she makes a secret plan to move out to Hollywood with a friend who works for another family. Helen Ruth knows of this scheme but keeps it to herself. When Jess comes to her with a concocted story of a family illness that requires her departure, Helen Ruth accepts the tale at face value. The two women embrace tearfully and bid each other goodbye. Afterward, when Helen Ruth reveals what she knows, her husband and sons are appalled and cannot comprehend why she went along with the trick. Also they have no idea why Jess would have felt it necessary to practice such a deception in the first place. This is the moment where we discover that they are shallow where she is deep, the moment toward which the whole story has been tending. All of Helen Ruth's married life rushes forward to fill it:

Helen Ruth put her hands on the handlebar of the teacart. She pushed the cart a little way over the tile floor but stopped when he repeated his question. It wasn't to answer his question that she stopped, however. "Oh, my dears!" she said, addressing her whole family. Then it was a long time before she said anything more. John R. and the three boys remained seated at the table, and while Helen Ruth gazed past them and toward the front window of the sun parlor, they sat silent and still, as though they were in a picture. What could she say to them, she kept asking herself. And each time she asked the question, she received for answer some different memory of seemingly unrelated things out of the past twenty years of her life. These things presented themselves as answers to her question, and each of them seemed satisfactory to her. But how little sense it would make to her husband and her grown sons, she reflected, if she should suddenly begin telling them about the long hours she had spent waiting in that apartment at the Vaux Hall while John R. was on the road for the Standard Candy Company, and in the same breath should tell them about how plainly she used to talk to Jane Blakemore and how Jane pretended the baby made her nervous and went back to Thornton. Or suppose she should abruptly remind John R. of how ill at ease the wives of his hunting friends used to make her feel and how she had later driven Sarah's worthless husband out of the yard, threatening to call a bluecoat. What if she should suddenly say that because a woman's husband hunts, there is no reason for *her* to hunt, any more than because a man's wife sews, there is reason for him to sew. She felt that she would be willing to say anything at all, no matter how cruel or absurd it was, if it would make them understand that everything that happened in life only demonstrated in some way the lonesomeness that people felt. She was ready to tell them about sitting in the old nursery at Thornton and waiting for Carrie and Jane Blakemore to come out of the cabin in the yard. If it would make them see what she had been so long in learning to see, she would even talk about the "so much else" that had been missing from her life and that she had not been able to name, and about the foolish mysteries she had so nobly accepted upon her reconciliation with John R. To her, these things were all one now; they were her loneliness, the loneliness from which everybody, knowingly or unknowingly, suffered. But she knew that her husband and her sons did not recognize her loneliness or Jess McGehee's or their own. She turned her eyes from the window to look at their faces around the table, and it was strange to see that they were still thinking in the most personal and particular terms of how they had been deceived by a servant, the ignorant granddaughter of an ignorant slave, a Negro woman from Brownsville who was crazy about the movies and who would soon be riding a bus, mile after mile, on her way to Hollywood, where she might find the friendly faces of the real Neil Hamilton and the real Irene Rich. It was with an effort that Helen Ruth thought again of Jess McGehee's departure and the problem of offering an explanation to her family. At last, she said patiently, "My dears, don't you see how it was for Jess? How else can they tell us anything when there is such a gulf?"[1]

The point of Helen Ruth's single, seemingly noncommittal statement is that it cuts both ways. Both the black woman and the white are caught in a social spiderweb which neither can control or escape. As in all Peter Taylor's stories, the men are stuck to the spiderweb too, but in this instance, Helen Ruth perceives it where they do not. Jess's stratagem is tacitly a joint project with Helen Ruth, whose purpose is to allow the two women to exit their determined roles for a moment, show their real feeling for each other openly, and really say goodbye.

Of course there are some really nasty prejudiced people in Taylor's story, whose wickedness is personal as much as political. The sour side of the domestic dynamic comes out in "Cookie." The destructive potential of the complicated class hierarchy of Taylor's world is disclosed by stories like "The Hand of Emmagene."

For modern readers, accustomed by one circumstance or another to apprehending all narratives one-dimensionally, the tactics of a story like "The Hand of Emmagene" can be a little hard to understand. It matters very much in this area what Taylor really did learn from James about the uses of unreliable narrators. First-person narration is Taylor's favorite mode and the one at which he is most adept. It confuses things that all his narrators are tonally rather similar, but they are by no means all the same person, or even very much alike in character. Although there is always a moral unease, a sort of itch, a failure or problem which causes the story to need telling in the first place, sometimes (as in "The Old Forest" or "Guests") Taylor's narrator is genuinely ingenuous, with a reasonably complete understanding of events which he can finally convey to the reader. On other occasions, "The Hand of Emmagene" in particular, the narrator is deliberately disingenuous; despite that familiar tone of apparent forthrightness he understands the meaning of his own story very poorly and every word he says is aimed at distorting it.

This technique permits a kind of doubling of the narrative that Taylor has used over and over again. In "The Hand of Emmagene," despite the syrupy overlay of the first-person narration, Emmagene's very different voice is struggling most powerfully to get through. And in the end she has her say—though she has to resort to sign language.

In this way, Taylor has adapted some of James's techniques for his own purposes, much as Richard Bausch, on down the line, has adapted some of Taylor's for his. There is a real Jamesian influence operating, though in a considerably modified state, in Taylor's work. Also there is an oft-remarked similarity of subject matter, though this latter resemblance is not so strong as it has sometimes been made to appear.

In certain passages of "The Old Forest," Taylor comes as close as he ever has to putting a sort of ars poetica right into the text of the story. Most of the time, the narrating character, Nat, is in control (if we want to call it that, for he is utterly helpless to influence his own destiny, limited by the strictures of his social position and his drastically incomplete perception, first jeopardized and then rescued by the women in the story). But occasionally the author seems to speak through him, outright.

He defines two kinds of characters he has often written about, one by assertion, the other by default:

> Even in Memphis the great majority of people might say, Why is the little band of spoiled rich girls who lived here forty years ago so important as to deserve our attention? In fact, during the very period I am writing about it is likely that the majority of people in Memphis felt that way. I think the significant point is that those girls took themselves seriously—girls like Caroline—and took seriously the forms of the life they lived. They imagined they knew quite well who they were and they imagined that that was important. They were what, at any rate, those girls like Lee Ann were not. Or they claimed to be what those girls like Lee Ann didn't claim to be and what very few people nowadays claim to be. They considered themselves the heirs to something, though most likely they couldn't have said what: something their forebears had brought to Memphis with them from somewhere else— from the country around Memphis and from other places, from the country towns of West Tennessee, from Middle Tennessee and East Tennessee, from the Valley of Virginia, from the Piedmont, even from the Tidewater. Girls like Caroline thought they were the heirs to something. . . . [2]

Over against this imagination of identity there stands the old forest itself, "that immemorial grove of snow-laden oaks and yellow poplars and hickory trees. It is a grove, I believe, that men in Memphis have feared and wanted to destroy for a long time."[3] Without the tension between these two drastically different atmospheres Peter Taylor's work would not exist.

The whole point of the social order in Taylor's stories is its extreme fragility. Thus his subject is utterly different from James's rendering of the ancient social traditions of Europe. It's true that James's Americans threaten to destabilize these traditions, but because they are so much older and stronger it is a very different order of threat. James's Europe is centuries old and his is in so many ways a European sensibility. Taylor by contrast is all American. A century before the time of his stories, his cities had barely ceased to be frontier towns. Two centuries before, they were wilderness. The people in them form their community by joining hands and wishing it into existence. Were any one of them to break out of the circle, the whole bubble would burst.

That is why apostasy, the very possibility of social apostasy, is so important in Taylor's stories, why indeed it is his central subject. The revolutionaries and apostates in Chekhov are no more significant or dangerous than fleas in the fur of a hibernating bear. In James, apostasy is virtually impossible to consummate. In the environment of Taylor's stories, however, the most casual heedless gesture of an apostate might be sufficient to destroy the whole order of the world.

When Lee Ann Deehart runs away from the accident into the old forest, she steps momentarily outside of the unspoken social contract that governs the life of the town. Caroline Bagley perceives that very quickly, whereas it appears to take Nat several decades to understand it. But in exiting the social contract, Lee Ann makes herself dangerous and powerful, though it is not precisely the sort of empowerment beloved of feminist theory. Her power depends on the understanding of others that if a single card should be removed the whole card house may fall. It is a power to destroy that she possesses, as she passes through the old forest, where no rules apply, into her period of hiding. When she chooses not to exercise this destructive power, she shows a more personal strength, something that comes from within. She runs up to the brink of apostasy and at the last moment turns back, as people in Taylor's stories usually do.

In reality, however, our society as a whole has not turned back, and so one may well ask the question that Taylor openly asks within the story: that is, what possible difference does it make to the way we live now, "in a world where acts of terror are, so to speak, all around us—everyday occurrences,"[4] whether the people in this odd little bubble inflated into such a precarious existence half a century back were able to conform to the social standards they set for themselves or not? For Taylor and for his readership, this question is by no means rhetorical.

The answer is indicated, I think, outside the body of Taylor's work. There are maybe four or five truly important American short story writers still living. One is Peter Taylor; another is Paul Bowles. They are approximately of the same generation but otherwise it is almost impossible to think of two more dissimilar writers. Bowles has lived for most of his career as an expatriate in North Africa, and has written little about life in America. His work has to do with the experience of Americans and Europeans in contact with the alien cultures of what we are now pleased to call the "third world." With a sensitivity and comprehension which it would be welcome to discover somewhere, anywhere, in this nation's foreign policy, he has shown that these other cultures are so radically different from our own (and from each other, for that matter) as to produce radically different sorts of people. Not better or worse, just different, totally different, in their ways of understanding each other, the world and their place in it. A part of Bowles's vision is that individual identity is itself a cultural product. As he shows in works like *The Sheltering Sky* and "A Distant Episode," when the cardhouse cultures begin to collapse, individual identity also collapses. If all the structure of manners and mores that supports individual personality is completely removed the personality is seen, in Bowles's work, to decay until the soul is left vacant, a blank, zero, tabula rasa on which anything may be written.

Paul Bowles is a terrorist then, philosophically speaking, and his work is a terrifying vision. The same terror that openly declares itself in Bowles's work underlies everything in Taylor's. Bowles's characters usually go over the edge into the void, whereas Taylor's characters are forever skirting it. But for both writers the edge is really the same. Its presence is responsible for the sense of importance, of dread, even, that suffuses Taylor's stories. His characters know the edge is there, they sense what is beyond it, and they instinctively understand that the most intricate and finicking requirements of their social behavior are ultimately intended to restrain them from tumbling over. What is at risk is not merely their situation in society, but their very sense of self, the sense of being a self, at all. This, of course, is a subject that can never be outdated, one that presses on us now more urgently and immediately than ever before.

Peter Taylor has handled this subject masterfully, and in ways that are uniquely his own. Whatever may remain to be said about his education, his influences, he stands sufficiently alone now; he resembles no one but himself. It makes less sense at this point to compare him to other writers than to compare other writers to him. But in my generation at least there don't seem to be many writers who could hope to hold up under such a comparison. Taylor is the sort of writer to whom one would do well to apprentice oneself, as he apprenticed himself, after his fashion, to James. But it would be a long demanding apprenticeship, for his technical skills (apart from his vision) are so great, so various, and on the present literary scene so very rare. I can say right now, with perfect certainty, that Peter Taylor is one of the great masters of the American short story. I can also predict, with a little less certainty and a lot less enthusiasm, that his like will not be seen again.

Notes

1. Peter Taylor, *The Collected Stories* (New York: Penguin, 1986), 280.
2. Taylor, *The Old Forest* (Garden City: Doubleday, 1985), 49.
3. *The Old Forest*, 53.
4. *The Old Forest*, 42.

Index

♦

Adler, Alfred: Adlerian interpretation of Taylor, 19, 148, 150–53; *Individual Psychology*, 150, 152; *Superiority and Social Interest*, 150

African-Americans, 4, 10, 36, 38, 39, 44, 51–52, 64–65, 74, 83–85, 124, 133, 190, 256–58; *See also* race; race relations

Agrarian criticism, 5, 17

agrarian values, 6, 17, 100, 101, 103

agrarian *vs.* urban values, 37, 85, 87, 90, 92, 101–03, 160, 201

Albee, Edward: *The American Dream*, 120

allegory, 229, 239, 244, 246, 249

Allen, Walter: *The Short Story in English*, 11

ambiguity, 32, 59, 153, 203, 230–31, 240, 243, 244, 246

"Ancient Mariner, The" (Coleridge), 196, 200, 225n5

Andrews, Maureen, 19–20

animal condition, 10, 13, 127, 128, 129, 130, 134, 147; *See also* violence

authority, 55, 57–58, 169, 170, 173, 185, 194; *see also* power

Bachelard, Gaston, 171

Balthazor, Ron, 20, 216–26

Baro, Gene, 6, 8, 22n36, 38–39

Bataille, Georges, 248

Bausch, Richard, 254, 258; *The Fireman's Wife*, 254

Beattie, Ann, 15

Beaver, Harold, 13

Bell, Madison Smartt, 1, 21, 254–61

Bellow, Saul, 4, 8

Berne, Eric, 170

Bertrand, Denis, 179n8

betrayal, 63–64, 139–40, 146, 195–96, 208, 209, 210

Binding, Paul: *Separate Country: A Literary Journal through the American South*, 14

Blackman, Ruth, 6

Blum, Morgan, 7

body, the, 238–39

Bogue, Ronald, 250n9

Booth, Wayne, 99

Borges, Jorge Luis: "A New Refutation of Time," 50

Bowles, Paul, 260–61; "A Distant Episode," 260; *The Sheltering Sky*, 260–61

Brace, Marjorie, 3, 29–30

Bradbury, John M.: *Renaissance in the South: A Critical History of the Literature, 1920–1960*, 22n32

Brookner, Anita, 18

Brooks, Jeremy, 96

Brown, Norman G., 178

Browning, Robert, 196

Broyard, Anatole, 12, 13

Caldwell, Erskine, 2

Calisher, Hortense, 7

Capote, Truman, 4, 10

Carver, Raymond, 15

Casey, Jane Barnes, 13, 14, 20, 124–35, 137, 144–45, 197, 226n10, 250

Casey, John, 12

Cassill, R. V., 9, 43–44